While America Watches

While America Watches
Televising the Holocaust

Jeffrey Shandler

New York   Oxford
Oxford University Press
1999

Oxford University Press

Oxford New York
Athens Auckland Bangkok Bogotá
Buenos Aires Calcutta Cape Town Chennai Dar es Salaam
Delhi Florence Hong Kong Istanbul Karachi
Kuala Lumpur Madrid Melbourne
Mexico City Mumbai Nairobi Paris São Paulo Singapore
Taipei Tokyo Toronto Warsaw

and associated companies in
Berlin Ibadan

Published by Oxford University Press, Inc.
198 Madison Avenue, New York, New York 10016

Oxford is a registered trademark of Oxford University Press, Inc.

Library of Congress Cataloging-in-Publication Data
Shandler, Jeffrey.
While America Watches : televising the Holocaust /
Jeffrey Shandler.
p. cm.
ISBN 0-19-511935-5
1. Holocaust, Jewish (1939–1945), in television—United States.
I. Title
PN1992.8.H63S53   1999
791.45'658—dc21   98-4377

The author gratefully acknowledges permission for use of the
following:

Chapter 1 is a revised version of material presented at a Yeshiva
University conference in 1995, which will appear as an essay in
the forthcoming volume *Journalism and the Holocaust,* edited
by Robert Moses Shapiro, Yeshiva University Press.

Chapter 2 is a revised version of an article originally published
in *The Journal of Narrative and Life History* 4, nos. 1–2 (1994).

Parts of Chapters 4 and 5 appear in an essay in *The Americanization
of the Holocaust,* edited by Hilene Flanzbaum, © The Johns Hopkins University Press.

1 3 5 7 9 8 6 4 2

Printed in the United States of America
on recycled acid-free paper

contents

Acknowledgments

Writing this book proved a long and often surprising intellectual adventure. Among the most satisfying discoveries were that this project not only demanded long hours of work in solitude but also provided an unexpected wealth of opportunities to meet and learn from a great many people. It is a true pleasure to have this opportunity to express my thanks for their thoughtfulness, generosity, and kindness.

Several institutions provided much-appreciated support for this project. The research and writing of the doctoral dissertation on which this book is based were made possible thanks to grants from the Max Weinreich Center for Advanced Jewish Studies of the YIVO Institute for Jewish Research, the National Foundation for Jewish Culture, and the Center for Israel and Jewish Studies at Columbia University. I am also very grateful to the Koret Jewish Studies Publications Program and to the Lucius N. Littauer Foundation for their generous grants toward the research and production of this book.

I owe an inestimable debt to my teachers and mentors, both in the Yiddish studies program at Columbia University and at the YIVO Institute's Max Weinreich Center, particularly Adrienne Cooper, Marvin Herzog, and Jack Kugelmass. The training that I received at these institutions provided the foundation of my approach to the topic at hand. Yiddish dialectology, poems by Moyshe-Leyb Halpern, and folktales collected in East European *shtetlekh* may seem far removed from episodes of *The Twilight Zone* and nightly news telecasts. But the distinctive interdisciplinary approach to understanding Yiddish language, literature, and folkways as revealing artifacts of a diaspora community's portable, vernacular culture, situated in a complex multicultural environment, has informed my analysis of America's Holocaust television. This expansive approach to the principles of my training has been inspired by my work with Barbara Kirshenblatt-Gimblett, who supervised the writing of my dissertation, and to whom I offer especially heartfelt thanks. I consider myself most fortunate to have benefited from her exceptional intellectual vivacity and rigor, as well as from her unflagging commitment to my work, both during the dissertation process and beyond.

American Holocaust television is situated at a busy intersection of intellectual interests and approaches—media studies, popular culture studies, and American studies, as well as the study of modern Jewish culture and memory culture. My work draws on the critical thinking of anthropologists, literary scholars, historians, sociologists, art historians, and linguists, as well as work in Holocaust studies, Jewish studies, communications, and culture studies. Throughout this interdisciplinary study I have had the good fortune to encounter a diverse group of scholars and professionals who generously offered their insights.

In the initial stages of planning my research, Herbert Gans, Larry Gross, and Annette Insdorf provided thoughtful advice. Deborah Dash Moore's early guidance as well as her continued interest and support have been invaluable. During the years of research and writing the dissertation, I profited greatly from the assistance and suggestions of Raye Farr, Aryeh Goren, Iwona Irwin-Zarecka, Jenna Weissman Joselit, Elihu Katz, Marilyn Koolik, Edward Linenthal, Yosefa Loshitzky, Robert MacNeil, Peter Novick, John Osburn, Lucia Ruedenberg, James Shenton, Susan Slyomovics, Manfred Stanley, Aviva Weintraub, Liliane Weissberg, Brian Winston, Marjorie Wyler, and Barbie Zelizer. Thanks to Hanno Loewy of the Fritz Bauer Institut in Frankfurt am Main, I have been able to present my work to German audiences and discuss Holocaust remembrance with Cilly Kugelmann, Ronny Loewy, Thomas Mitscherlich, and Rainer Rother. I am grateful, too, to Hilene Flanzbaum, Tamara Liebes, and Robert Moses Shapiro for inviting me to publish portions of this work in volumes that they edited. At the conclusion of the dissertation process, Jeffrey Olick, Abraham Rosman, Michael Stanislawski, and James Young offered extremely helpful critiques and commentary as readers. Professor Young's work on Holocaust literature, film, and memorials has been a particularly valuable inspiration, and I am most grateful for his suggestions and encouragement.

The transformation of the dissertation into a book was enhanced by advice and assistance from Gulie Arad, Omer Bartov, Robert Berger, Pamela Brumberg, Lucjan Dobroszycki, Laurence Douglas, Judith Keilbach, Alvin Rosenfeld, and Stuart Svonkin. I owe a special debt to Sara Bershtel for her invaluable and generously offered insights into reshaping the manuscript and honing its prose. During postdoctoral fellowships at the Annenberg School for Communication and the Center for Judaic Studies, both at the University of Pennsylvania, I benefited greatly from the special opportunities that these institutions provided for further research and reflection, as well as from the insights of fellows, colleagues, and students. As a Dorot Junior Teaching Fellow of the Skirball Department of Hebrew and Judaic Studies, New York University, I was able to complete the final stages of realizing this book. At Oxford University Press I have greatly enjoyed the commitment and insights of Andrew Albanese, Laura Brown, Susan Day, and Brandon Trissler. I am especially thankful to Susan for the enthusiasm, diligence, and thoughtfulness that she brought to the task.

This study would not have been feasible without the generous assistance given by archivists and other staff members of the following institutions: Wanda Bershen, Kim Bistrong, Alessandro Cavadini, Andrew Ingall, and Michael Paley (National Jewish Archive of Broadcasting of the Jewish Museum, New York); Gary Stern (Motion Picture, Sound, and Video Branch of the National Archives, Washington, D.C.); Toby Blum-Dobkin and Bonnie Gurewitsch (Museum of Jewish Heritage: A Living Memorial to the Holocaust, New York); Roberta Newman, Jenny Romaine, Henry Sapoznik, Eve Sicular, and Marek Web (YIVO Archives, New York); and Tim Hanson and Julie Miller (Ratner Center, Jewish Theological Seminary, New York). I am also grateful to the assistance provided by staff members of the Museum of Television and Radio, New York; the Media Center of the Board of Jewish Education of Greater New York; the Motion Picture, Broadcasting, and Recorded Sound Division of the Library of Congress, Washington, D.C.; and the University of California Los Angeles Film and Television Archive.

Gathering the illustrations for this volume proved to be an extensive undertaking and would have been impossible without the efforts of Bridget Bower (Ithaca College), Roberta Carswell (Museum of Television and Radio), Phyllis Collazo (*New York Times*), Krysia Fisher (YIVO), Leah Oppenheim (Museum of Television and Radio), James Pollock (Ralph Edwards Productions), Bruce Pomerantz (CBS), Terry Rubin (NewsHour), Joanne Rudof (Fortunoff Archive for Holocaust Video Testimonies), James Ryan (A&E), and Leslie Swift (United States Holocaust Memorial Museum).

In addition, I owe much thanks to friends, family and colleagues, for all of their efforts on my behalf: Ilana Abramovitch, Frédéric Brenner, Mary Byrd and John Fisher, Tsafrir Cohen, John DeNatale, Shulamis Dion, Vivian Ducat and Ray Segal, Leonore Gordon and Amina Rachman, Morton and Annette Levitt, Barbara Reiser, the Schear family, Edythia Selman, Nina Warnke, Beth Wenger, and Debra Zane. From the suddenly inspired, offhand remark to assistance in tracking down obscure material, they have all helped me complete this study. I am particularly indebted to Robin White for urging me, one day in 1991, to have a look at a videotape in the National Jewish Archive of Broadcasting of a 1953 telecast of *This Is Your Life,* paying tribute to a Holocaust survivor, which, she insisted, had to be seen. It was this suggestion that sparked my interest in the subject of Holocaust television and eventually formed the basis of one of the first chapters of the book.

Above all, I have benefited from the loving support of my family. Although my mother passed away several months before this project was initiated, I have often felt that her boundless intellectual curiosity and rigorous work ethic were guiding my efforts. I am likewise indebted to my father for his patience, concern, and inspiration; he not only initiated my interest in Jewish studies when I was very young, but also was the first to teach me how to look at television critically. I am very grateful to my brother, Rick, for his unfailing moral support throughout the process and for having the thoughtfulness never to ask when it would be finished. Finally, I owe an inestimable debt to Stuart Schear; besides offering all the encouragement and reassurance that one could ever wish for from one's partner in life, Stuart has been an invaluable source of information and insight and a tireless enthusiast for this project.

Introduction

Television has become the privileged medium through which
moral relations between strangers are mediated in the modern
world.

—Michael Ignatieff, *The Warrior's Honor:
Ethnic War and the Modern Conscience*

The Holocaust has become a fixture of American culture. The subject of
best-selling books, major museums, and award-winning films, it is regularly invoked in speeches by national leaders and on the editorial pages of
major newspapers. It also comes up in the course of ordinary small talk and
can even be part of a chance encounter during the routine search for something to watch on television.

The powerful place that the Holocaust has achieved in contemporary
American life is more than the result of an ongoing fascination with the fate
of the Jews and other persecuted peoples during the Nazi era. This interest
extends to concerns for the political and cultural consequences of the Holocaust, its "lessons," its proprietary rights, and its ontological implications,
as well as to the nature of its representation. Above all, the Holocaust is
valued as an ethical touchstone, demanding moral accounting not only for
the atrocity that bears its name, but also for other atrocities.

This is a remarkable, perhaps singular phenomenon. For, unlike other
events of modern history that have achieved iconic status in American culture—the dropping of atomic bombs on Hiroshima and Nagasaki, the civil
rights movement, the assassination of President Kennedy, America's military
intervention in Vietnam and the antiwar movement, the Watergate scandal—the Holocaust touched only a small number of Americans directly; it
did not take place in the United States, nor was it engendered by national
policies. And yet the Holocaust looms large in the American moral landscape, where it has become commonplace to articulate the high magnitude

of a social wrong by deeming it "another Holocaust." Besides serving as a byword for more recent instances of genocide—the Iraqi persecution of Kurds, "ethnic cleansing" operations in Bosnia, and intertribal warfare in Rwanda, among others—the words "another Holocaust" now signal the gravity of an array of modern social ills, including the consequences of the nuclear arms race, Arab-Israeli conflicts in the Mideast, race relations in America, the abortion rights debate, the AIDS pandemic, and world hunger.

Indeed, over the course of the last half century, the symbolic value of the Holocaust in the United States has increased as this chapter of history has been elevated to the status of a nonpareil among human tragedies. More than a metaphor, the Holocaust has become a master moral paradigm, peerless both as a measure of enormity and in the catholicity of its application. Consequently, it has also become workaday. These days millions of Americans encounter frequent invocations of the Holocaust, often in the course of an evening of television watching. Consider, for example, these instances from 1995, fifty years after the end of World War II:

- *2 April 1995:* "Tales from the Dirty War," a report on the CBS newsmagazine *60 Minutes,* presents an interview with Adolfo Scilingo, a former Argentine naval officer, the first official to declare in public his role in the nation's persecution of thousands of dissidents during the 1970s. Scilingo describes participating in "death flights," in which political prisoners were drugged, stripped, and loaded onto airplanes; as they flew over the ocean, his crew tossed out the bodies. "Once they were all naked," he explains, "it was—have you seen photos of the Jews during the Second World War?" "The Holocaust," interviewer Mike Wallace interjects. "It was that," Scilingo replies.[1]

- *27 July 1995:* Frequent comparisons have been drawn between current interethnic warfare in the Balkans and the Holocaust since August 1992, when television news programs first aired reports of Serbian-run detention camps in Bosnia, showing scenes that many viewers found alarmingly similar to images of Nazi concentration camps. A thirty-second appeal by the Los Angeles–based Muslim Public Affairs Council, which is aired on CNN before the start of its main evening news report, juxtaposes vintage footage of victims of Nazi persecutions during the 1930s and 1940s with recently televised images from the war-torn Balkans. At the conclusion of the spot, a title reads: "President Clinton, you have allowed the Holocaust to happen again."[2]

- *28 September 1995:* In his closing argument in the trial of former football player O. J. Simpson for the murder of his ex-wife Nicole

Brown Simpson and her friend Ronald Goldman, defense attorney
Johnnie Cochran likens a key prosecution witness, Los Angeles
police detective Mark Fuhrman, to Adolf Hitler, describing
Fuhrman's attitude toward African-Americans as that of a "genocidal racist." Cochran's remark provokes angry denunciations, not
only from Goldman's father, but also, following the trial, from fellow Simpson attorney Robert Shapiro. This evening on *ABC News
Nightline,* commentator Leslie Abramson, a defense lawyer,
observes that "to use a Hitler analogy in a case with a Jewish murder victim is, in my Jewish opinion, very poor taste." Fellow commentator and former district attorney Robert Philibosian concurs,
adding, "I share much the same heritage, because the Armenians
suffered their own genocide at the hands of the Turks."[3]

- *23 October 1995:* The *New York Times* reports that, "with
increasing frequency, candidates from both political parties around
the country have used comparisons to Nazis, Nazi behavior and
the Holocaust to call attention to some perceived political horror."
Of particular note is Ken Barnett's campaign for sheriff of Henry
County, Virginia, against incumbent Frank Cassell. The *Times*
describes a television commercial for Barnett that juxtaposes portraits of Cassell and Adolf Hitler, characterizes Cassell's deputies as
"goose-stepping Gestapo," and includes a scene from the feature
film *Schindler's List* "in which the commander of a concentration
camp shoots an inmate in the back of the head for no reason." The
article notes that this is one of three instances in Virginia alone in
which candidates use "Nazi themes" to attack their opponents.[4]

While some observers find this "domestication" of the Holocaust cause
for concern, others champion the value of the Holocaust as a moral paradigm in American culture. The creators of the U.S. Holocaust Memorial
Museum in Washington, D.C., consider what they have termed the "Americanization" of the Holocaust to be fundamental to their mission. Michael
Berenbaum, director of the museum's research institute, has asserted that
the virtue of this "American institution" is that it presents a chapter of history that "cuts against the grain of the American ethos" and is "a violation
of every essential American value."[5] But critics of the museum's agenda,
such as Holocaust scholar Alvin H. Rosenfeld, have questioned whether
mingling such "very different historical experiences" transforms the Holocaust into an "empty and all but meaningless abstraction."[6]

The discomfort created by the "Americanization" of the Holocaust is
epitomized by its ready presence on television. What, many have asked, is
this awesome subject — so widely regarded as being situated at the limits of

human experience—doing here, vying for public attention along with situation comedies, rock videos, twenty-four-hour news channels, and ubiquitous advertising? How can the Holocaust be properly presented in this of all venues, so often thought of as appealing to the "lowest common denominator"? And what role has television played over the past half century in enabling millions of Americans to feel on such intimate terms with this profoundly disturbing chapter of history, from which they are removed by the distance of culture, space, and, increasingly, time?

Despite frequent questions as to whether poets, historians, or anyone else is capable of representing the Holocaust, the subject has engendered responses of great extent and variety since the end of World War II. Taken together, these histories, essays, and memoirs, works of fiction, drama, and poetry, films and broadcasts, rituals, monuments, and museums comprise one of the richest examples of memory culture—that is, the range of practices a community uses to recall its past. Much of Holocaust memory culture is produced by individuals with a personal connection to this period of history—its victims, persecutors, and witnesses, and their descendants—or is the work of scholars and artists. Even so, the American familiarity with the Holocaust extends well beyond the confines of elite or parochial circles. The United States is now home to several dozen Holocaust museums and study centers, including the Oregon Holocaust Resource Center (in Portland), the El Paso (Texas) Holocaust Museum and Study Center, and the Holocaust Memorial Center of West Bloomfield, Michigan, which claims to be the first such institution built in the United States (opened in 1984).[7] Washington, D.C.'s Holocaust museum, the largest of these, announced that it had some 750,000 visitors during the first seven months after opening its doors in April 1993. In a public statement unprecedented in the annals of American cultural institutions, the museum asked prospective visitors in the fall of 1993 to "stay away, at least for a while"; museum personnel and the building were "feeling the strain" of the "enormous" crowds.[8]

This would seem to suggest that Washington's Holocaust museum has managed to fulfill Berenbaum's agenda to present this subject "in such a way that it would resonate not only with the survivor in New York and his children in San Francisco, but with a black leader from Atlanta, a Midwestern farmer, or a Northeastern industrialist."[9] And there is certainly evidence that America's Holocaust memory culture has inspired citizens to recognize and to resist a number of instances of human intolerance.

In his *Preserving Memory: The Struggle to Create America's Holocaust Museum*, historian Edward Linenthal described events that occurred hundreds of miles from the museum on the Washington Mall. During the winter of 1993–1994, Billings, Montana, was the site of racist assaults against blacks and Jews, including the smashing of windows of Jewish homes in which Hanukkah menorahs were displayed. Led by the clergy of several churches and the local press, hundreds of citizens of Billings protested these attacks by placing menorahs or pictures of menorahs in the windows of their homes and cars. The incidents of anti-Semitic vandalism increased at first, then eventually abated. "Memory of the Holocaust motivated some members of the Christian community in Billings to counter the violence," Linenthal noted. "Margaret MacDonald, executive director of the Montana Association of Churches, said that memory of the Holocaust was 'absolutely present' in the response of many in the community . . . [It] 'offered us an example of where this kind of hatred ultimately leads.' " Linenthal concluded that the citizens of Billings "spoke with . . . the kind of courageous and compassionate voice that will need to be raised again and again if Holocaust memory is to serve us well."[10]

But how did the memory of the Holocaust become "absolutely present" in Billings? And what prompted James Cameron of Milwaukee to establish, in 1988, a museum documenting over three centuries of African-American oppression and resistance and to name it America's Black Holocaust Museum?[11] Or what does one make of a bumper sticker, sighted in the autumn of 1993 at a reenactment of the 1864 Battle of Cedar Creek in Winchester, Virginia, which read, "The Civil War—America's Holocaust"?[12]

The Holocaust's singular place in the moral vocabulary of so many Americans is largely a product of the distinctive nature of Holocaust memory culture in this country. In Europe, the former Soviet Union, and Israel, Holocaust remembrance has been realized as powerfully, if not more so, through the presence of survivors of World War II or geographical landmarks. But in America this subject has almost always been mediated through newspapers, magazines, books, theaters, exhibition galleries, concert halls, or radio and television broadcasting.

And yet, the most obvious and ubiquitous form of Holocaust memory culture in America—its presentations on television—is also the most overlooked. During the past half century this medium has provided more Americans with more opportunities for a greater diversity of encounters with the Holocaust than has any other forum. This is a striking phenomenon with extraordinary implications, most notably of scale. Following the premiere broadcast of the miniseries *Holocaust* on NBC in 1978—which was subsequently viewed by hundreds of millions around the world— Holocaust activist Simon Wiesenthal told a Los Angeles audience that these four evenings of television drama "reached more people than I could in a lifetime."[13]

The absence of television in any discussion of memory culture has much to do with a widespread contempt for the medium. Indeed, many regard television in general as a destructive presence that diminishes or distorts the quality of modern life—diluting cultural literacy, warping notions of geography and atomizing history, shortening attention spans, promoting conformity of behavior and thought, denying alternative viewpoints a public voice, desensitizing viewers to violence, and so on. From such perspectives—which assume television to be culture's nemesis, rather than a creator of culture—the medium seems inimical to the very notion of memory.

Not surprisingly, then, both scholars and the general public tend to hold Holocaust television in lower esteem than most other genres of Holocaust memory culture. Even when acknowledging what they grudgingly consider to be its achievements, critics generally assume the presentation of the Holocaust on American television to be essentially flawed. Thus, film scholar Ilan Avisar writes that despite an "inherent incapacity when it comes to dealing with a subject of the magnitude of the Holocaust," the 1978 miniseries demonstrated that the medium's "formidable power . . . can be instrumental in enlightening ignorant people about the course and nature of the Nazi evil."[14]

But Holocaust television is not merely an overlooked genre of Holocaust memory culture whose time for scrutiny has come. Television has been instrumental in situating the Holocaust in the prominent position that it now occupies in American public culture. In addition to offering numerous and diverse presentations of this subject to vast audiences, the distinctive nature of television watching has fostered a special relationship between American audiences and the Holocaust that other venues do not, indeed cannot, provide. The small scale of the medium—its place in the privacy of the home, its part in the daily routine—offers audiences an especially intimate acquaintanceship with the Holocaust. And, unlike the self-consciously elevated character of most other forms of its memory culture, television does not situate the Holocaust at what historian Saul Friedlander has called the "limits of representation," challenging "our traditional conceptual and representational categories."[15] Instead, television pulls the Holocaust, along with everything else that the medium presents, into its ceaseless, multichannel flow of programming, providing viewers with routinized as well as chance encounters with this remote and extreme chapter of history. Beyond any other medium or forum, television has brought the Holocaust into the thoughts, feelings, words, and actions of millions of Americans. If we want to understand what the Holocaust means for them, we must tune in to television.

To some extent, this study of Holocaust television resembles analyses of Holocaust literature, historiography, memoirs, drama, film, art, music, monuments, and museums. It, too, addresses certain general issues about Holocaust memory culture: the challenge of mediating a subject widely regarded as defying adequate representation, the dynamics of responses to the Holocaust over the course of the postwar decades, the responsiveness of works of Holocaust memory culture to particular national or ideological contexts, and so on. In addition, the nature of television in general and of Holocaust television in particular calls for an especially open approach.

The nature of television broadcasting—the way it readily absorbs other media, the steady flow of its programming—calls for a broad examination, which attends to individual broadcasts as well as to the contexts in which they appear: the commercials aired during breaks in a program; the positioning of broadcasts within the protocols of weekly or annual scheduling, or vis-à-vis other public events; the promotional material preceding and published responses following a broadcast; the work of archivists, critics, teachers, and others who identify, collect, and disseminate works of Holocaust television, and so on.

In keeping with this approach, I set aside the popular assumption that in Holocaust television there is an inherent incompatibility between medium and subject—a notion that did not gain wide currency until decades after the genre's earliest examples were aired. The Holocaust as a concept has developed since the middle of the twentieth century in a dynamic and complex process, which has produced an extensive public debate over what may be considered a legitimate work of Holocaust memory culture, whether on television or in any other form. While many studies of Holocaust memory culture are, in essence, exercises in moral connoisseurship, distinguishing "responsible" or "proper" representations of the Holocaust from works deemed "trivializing" or "distorted," this one is not driven by the need to evaluate the ethical or aesthetic worth of Holocaust television. Rather, I focus on the genre's value as a cultural phenomenon, so as to examine the emergence of the Holocaust as a moral paradigm in American culture and, more generally, the impact of a mass medium on memory in public culture.

Indeed, Holocaust television serves as an exemplary case study of the relation between a historical event and the memory culture it generates. Other forms of Holocaust representation—histories, novels, memoirs, documentary or feature films, paintings, dramas—already had established aesthetic boundaries, protocols, and conventions by World War II. But when television first dealt with the Holocaust, the medium was itself new. Thus, television and Holocaust memory culture have, in some ways, a shared history. During the same years that television was transformed from a technological curiosity into the dominant means for disseminating information and entertainment to the American public, the Holocaust began to emerge from the larger history of the Nazi era and World War II as a distinct and exceptional phenomenon. As a result, the earliest works of Holocaust television themselves have an openness, with regard to both form and content, that offers special insight into memory culture at its most inchoate.

Moreover, both American television and Holocaust memory culture reached thresholds in their respective developments at similar times. During 1961, for example, the war crimes trial of Adolf Eichmann was convened in Jerusalem. As the first major public recounting of the events of the Holocaust since the immediate postwar years, the trial is frequently cited as a landmark in public awareness of the Holocaust both in the United States and elsewhere. The year 1961 is also regarded as a watershed in the annals of American television broadcasting. This is the year that John F. Kennedy, widely hailed as the nation's first "television president," took office, as well as the year that FCC chairman Newton Minow pronounced American commercial television a "vast wasteland." Telecasts of the Eichmann trial—the first international broadcasts of the actual proceedings of a major court case—played a strategic role in shaping public response to the case and its presentation of the Holocaust. These broadcasts also reflect signal changes in the American television industry's coverage of world news events.

Similarly, the premiere telecasts of the *Holocaust* miniseries in the late 1970s, which engendered the first extended discussion of Holocaust television, coincide with a generational shift both in Holocaust memory culture—marked by the aging of Holocaust survivors and the coming of age of their children—and among American television producers and viewers, as the generation that "grew up on television" began to enter middle age. Most recently, the fiftieth anniversary of the end of World War II was also concomitant with sea changes both in the television industry, which has been in the midst of unprecedented expansion and diversification, and in Holocaust memory culture, which has focused increasing attention on the aging and eventual passing of the generation of Holocaust survivors.

More than an inventory of broadcasts, Holocaust television embodies an important cultural dynamic in American life during the past half century. Television has risen to the stature of master medium, influencing the form and content of other media while fostering cultural sensibilities of its own. At the same time, the Holocaust has become—thanks, in large measure, to television—a powerful and daunting presence in the nation's cultural landscape, achieving the status of a master moral paradigm.

The generation that grew up during the war, those who experienced the Holocaust or witnessed it at some distance, are now our elders, and the time approaches when connections to the Holocaust will rely exclusively on its memory culture. The close of the twentieth century also marks the aging of a generation of Americans who can remember what life was like without television. Television and the Holocaust may seem strange partners, but their half century of shared history has shaped how Americans now understand and respond to moral crises of modern life.

While America Watches

part one 1945–1960
Creating the Viewer

Holocaust remembrance is a dynamic phenomenon, shaped by the unfolding relationship between the rememberers and the object of recall. The establishment of the Holocaust as a widely known event in American public culture resulted from extensive efforts over several decades. As historian Hans Kellner has noted, "Creating a reader for the Holocaust has been the work of writers, artists, filmmakers, poets, and historians since the end of the war." Conceptualizing the Holocaust is closely bound up with "creating the reader"—and, one might add, the viewer—"who will recognize the event."[1] Since its earliest years, television has played a formative role in establishing the Holocaust as a recognizable event for American audiences.

And yet the late 1940s and 1950s are often characterized as a period of "omission" and "avoidance" of the Holocaust in mainstream American culture. Scholars argue that then the subject "was barely on the . . . communal or theological agenda" even among the nation's Jews.[2] During these years some members of the American Jewish community did begin to document, analyze, and commemorate the events that have since come to be known as the Holocaust. Most of this activity took place only among those who were closest to the Nazi persecutions, but efforts were also made to present this then-unnamed subject to the general American public. These include several dozen documentaries, news reports, dramas, and other kinds of programming aired on television.

From the vantage point of the late twentieth century, when the Holocaust is so prominent in American culture, these early telecasts are easily overlooked. And when examples are noted, critics tend to find them overly restrained and abstracted, improperly "universalized," bereft of "Jewish particularity," or lacking "the artistic will—or courage" not to mitigate the subject's horror.[3] Yet these broadcasts merit attention, not merely because they are among the first American responses to the Holocaust.

As with all works of Holocaust memory, these telecasts are shaped by the historical moment and the cultural environment in which they are produced, the people involved in their creation and reception, and the medium in which they are realized. They offer special insight into Americans' first efforts to understand the Nazi persecution of European Jewry during the years immediately following World War II, a watershed period for the United States in general and for the nation's Jews in particular. Early American telecasts that deal with the Holocaust mark larger shifts in American Jewry's sense of self and in the nation's understanding of minority identities.

Moreover, these broadcasts call attention to the impact that the advent of television had on public remembrance in postwar America. Indeed, America's early Holocaust television offers an unusual opportunity to consider how memory is shaped by the presentation of an emerging concept in a nascent medium. These first television broadcasts are key to understanding the dynamics of memory culture when mediations play a prominent role in the public's encounters with the subject at hand. Because television emerged as a national broadcasting medium after the end of the war, it has always relied on other mediations to create its own presentations of the Holocaust. Vintage photographs and film footage, radio reports and other sound recordings, historical accounts, oral testimonies, and works of art have all left their imprint on Holocaust television, which has been shaped not merely by their content, but by their conventions and sensibilities.

Of the various means of representing the Holocaust, two have been of particular importance for American Holocaust television from the start: vintage photographic images, especially footage of concentration camps filmed shortly after their liberation by Allied forces during the spring of 1945, and the testimony of those who directly experienced or witnessed the events of the Holocaust. Beginning in the late 1940s, these sources figure repeatedly in documentaries, news reports, public affairs programs, and other examples of Holocaust television. Moreover, they have attained a privileged status as representations of unimpeachable authority. (Consider, for example, the prominent placement of video displays of liberation footage and survivor testimonies in the Holocaust museums in Washington, D.C., Los Angeles, and New York.) From the final days of World War II to the present, these images and testimonies have played leading roles in establishing the Holocaust as a moral paradigm for a nation that has almost no direct experience of these events.

And yet, despite the compelling nature of vintage footage and survivor narratives, American television did not make its most powerful statements about the Holocaust in documentaries or other actuality-based genres during the early postwar years. Instead, the medium first explored this subject most extensively and memorably in dramas, which aired on live prime-time anthology series and ecumenical programs broadcast during the daytime on Sundays. These first television plays helped popularize drama as a vehicle for responding to the Holocaust. Indeed, the works of American Holocaust memory culture that have had the widest impact, both here and abroad, are all dramas: the stage play *The Diary of Anne Frank* (1955), the television miniseries *Holocaust: The Story of the Family Weiss* (1978), and the feature film *Schindler's List* (1993).

The early primacy of dramas has had lasting implications for television's other representations of this subject, extending to documentaries, news programming, and other broadcasts. In particular, the dramatic mode has helped establish the Holocaust as an accessible, engaging, and morally galvanizing subject for general audiences in the United States, regardless of their personal ties to this chapter of history. Even as the concept itself was being defined, these first dramas, documentaries, and other broadcasts of America's emerging television industry forged a national viewership for the Holocaust.

one

The Image as Witness

During the final weeks of the war in Europe, most Americans learned about the events now known as the Holocaust from newspapers, radio broadcasts, and newsreels shown in movie theaters. Television, however, was not an early source of information on this subject. The nation's fledgling television broadcasting industry of the late 1930s had been all but completely shut down once the United States entered the war and was not reestablished until after the war's end. The Holocaust is part of the prehistory of television as a national broadcasting medium.

Now mostly consigned to libraries and archives, the first mediations of the Holocaust had a formative influence on television's many presentations of the subject. The centerpiece of Americans' initial encounter with the subject was film footage recorded by the United States Army Signal Corps, documenting the Allied liberation of Nazi concentration camps. The initial presentation of these images established their viewing as an exceptional, morally galvanizing experience. American television has since perpetuated and expanded the significance of this footage. Besides transforming some of these images into widely and swiftly recognized icons of the Nazi era, television has reaffirmed their value as virtual witnesses of the Holocaust.

Shortly before Germany's surrender in the spring of 1945, movie theaters across the United States showed millions of its citizens graphic evidence of what were then referred to as "Nazi atrocities": sites of large-scale torture and killing of European civilians and Allied prisoners of war, emaciated and feeble victims of abuse, piles of corpses, and mass graves. These images, recorded only days earlier, document a moment that is now widely regarded, in historian Robert Abzug's words, as "a turning point in Western consciousness." Although the actual missions of liberating these camps during the final weeks of the war in Europe were not of strategic importance from a military standpoint, Abzug noted that they proved to be of great symbolic significance. He considered the direct encounters of Allied soldiers, journalists, governmental representatives, and others with the camps as critical to the enduring recognition of the Holocaust. Had this not occurred, Abzug argued, the Holocaust might well have been "reported and put out of mind, known and dismissed, prey to every denial and charge of political manipulation."[1]

General Dwight D. Eisenhower, commander of the Allied forces in Europe, played a leading role in arranging these encounters. Moreover, he was at the forefront of establishing the act of witnessing the conditions of recently liberated camps as a morally transformative experience. Within days of his first visits to liberated Nazi concentration camps at Ohrdruf (12 April 1945) and Buchenwald (13 April), Eisenhower began making arrangements for American soldiers stationed in the area to be brought to the camps, as well as for visits by an official congressional delegation and a group of editors of leading American newspapers. Allied occupying forces also compelled local German civilians to witness the conditions inside the camps and, in some cases, to participate in the burial of corpses or the care of surviving inmates.

In his initial communications to other military leaders, Eisenhower commented both on the enormity of what he had seen and on the importance of serving as an eyewitness to scenes that "beggar description."[2] Later, he reiterated these sentiments in *Crusade in Europe,* his memoir of World War II:

> I have never felt able to describe my emotional reactions when I first came face to face with indisputable evidence of Nazi brutality and ruthless disregard of every shred of decency. . . . I visited every nook and cranny of the camp [at Ohrdruf] because I felt it my duty to be in a position from then on to testify at first hand about these things in case there ever grew up at home the belief or assumption that "the stories of Nazi brutality were just propaganda." . . . I felt that the evidence should be immediately placed before the American and British publics in a fashion that would leave no room for cynical doubt.[3]

Eisenhower characterized the face-to-face encounter with "indisputable evidence" as a defining moment not only for himself but also for the Allied nations. Previous evidence — including military intelligence reports and civilian eyewitness testimony — had, Eisenhower implied, failed to convince the Allies that reports of Nazi atrocities were anything beyond mere "propaganda." But Allied liberators were, in his view, uniquely situated to verify the truth of what would otherwise leave room for "cynical doubt." Moreover, Eisenhower asserted that with this privilege the liberator bore a special obligation thereafter to offer testimony "at first hand."

Eisenhower's command also oversaw the filming of liberated concentration camps by members of the U.S. Army Signal Corps and cameramen working for commercial newsreel production companies. The making of

A U.S. Army Signal Corps cameraman films evidence of Nazi atrocities at Kaufering IV, a concentration camp in Hurlach, Germany, on 29 April 1945. (Hoover Institution Archives.)

these films was not simply a part of the liberation process. Cameramen documenting liberation became professional witnesses, as communications scholar Barbie Zelizer has observed, "standing in for the witnessing activity of the general public."[4] Liberation footage came to be seen as extending this uniquely privileged moment of witnessing and testifying "at first hand."

The political, emotional, and moral investment in the power of liberation footage exemplifies the motion picture camera's profound impact on the aesthetics of representation, or mimesis, in the twentieth century. Critic Walter Benjamin's seminal essay "The Work of Art in the Age of Mechanical Reproduction," published in 1936, offered telling insights into the mimetic power of film. Informed, perhaps, by how the medium figured in the promotion of Nazism, Benjamin's analysis presaged the strategic role that film would play in the defeat of the Axis powers. Arguing that the medium has revolutionized human perception by creating an optical "unconscious," Benjamin suggested that film possesses the potential to transform how people perceive and, consequently, how they respond to the world around them, facilitating "an immense and unexpected field of action."[5]

The transformative impact of viewing liberation footage relies on a valuation of the films as authentic copies and as replications of actual encounters with the victims of Nazi persecution. These properties of "imitation" and "contact" are essential to the mimetic experience in any form, according to anthropologist Michael Taussig, as is a distinctive "flash of recognition," a shock that "alters the very percept of recognizing, entailing transformation of the recognizing self."[6] There is, moreover, a particular onus in photography's mimesis, critic Luc Sante has argued, when it constitutes a virtual encounter with death. Sante has suggested that photographed images of the dead offer viewers "an excruciatingly intimate sight" along with "the burden of this intimacy. . . . The terrible gift that the dead make to the living is that of sight, which is to say foreknowledge; in return, they demand memory, which is to say acknowledgment."[7] Just as liberation footage became a virtual witness of mass death, the act of witnessing served as an organizing principle of the first presentations of these films to the American public and continues to be integrally linked to the images themselves.

"Don't Turn Away—Look!": American Newsreels

For some individuals, the first public encounter in 1945 with the photographic record of liberated Nazi concentration camps endured as a threshold event in their personal development, and they linked their own loss of innocence with this historic moment of revelation. Literary critic Alfred Kazin concluded his coming-of-age memoir, *Starting Out in the Thirties,* with an unsettling description of watching these images in a newsreel theater in London, where he was stationed with the U.S. Army:

> On the screen, sticks in black-and-white prison garb leaned on a wire, staring dreamily at the camera; other sticks shuffled about, or sat vaguely on the ground, next to an enormous pile of bodies, piled up like cordwood, from which protruded legs, arms, heads. A few guards were collected sullenly in a corner, and for a moment a British Army bulldozer was shown digging an enormous hole in the ground. Then the sticks would come back on the screen, hanging on the wire, looking at us. It was unbearable. People coughed in embarrassment, and in embarrassment many laughed.[8]

Perhaps the most oft-cited example is Susan Sontag's recollection of seeing, in the summer of 1945, still photographs of conditions in recently liberated concentration camps, which she described as "the prototypically modern revelation: a negative epiphany . . . Nothing I have seen—in photographs or in real life—ever cut me as sharply, deeply, instantaneously. Indeed, it seems plausible to divide my life into two parts, before I saw those photographs (I was twelve) and after, though it was several years before I understood fully what they were about."[9]

Such profound claims for the significance of Holocaust photography are not uncommon; its evidentiary importance and, moreover, its moral value have been invoked extensively in war crimes trials, public exhibitions, news reports, propaganda, and documentary films. This unwavering investment in the fundamental significance of these images is, however, at odds with much modern scholarship about the openness of a photograph's meaning. Challenging the simple equation of images recorded by cameras with actuality, scholars have long argued that the meaning of a photographed image is as much a product of the sensibilities of the modern age as of the technology of photography itself. As with any other cultural artifact, the photograph's significance is constructed and is, therefore, both open and mutable, dependent on context for completion. Indeed, Sontag herself wrote, earlier in the same essay cited above, that a "photograph that brings news of some unsuspected zone of misery cannot make a dent in public opinion unless there is an appropriate context of feeling and attitude. . . . Photographs cannot create a moral position, but they can reinforce one—and can help build a nascent one."[10] But from its first public presentations, Holocaust photography has been identified as a limiting case with regard not only to its graphic content, but also to its enduring significance.

Still photographs documenting liberated Nazi concentration camps appeared in the United States during the spring of 1945 in a wide range of newspapers, magazines, and public displays. In contrast, American civilians first encountered motion picture footage of liberation in only one venue—commercially produced newsreels screened in the nation's movie theaters. During the first days of May 1945 all five of the nation's major newsreels devoted most of their reports to the exposure of "Nazi atrocities."[11] In many ways this was an unprecedented phenomenon, and, though short-lived, it has proved to have a lasting impact on American remembrance of the Holocaust.

The newsreel might well seem an unlikely venue for presenting these images. First appearing in the 1910s, newsreels became a staple of the American movie-going experience with the advent of sound. By the 1930s, five different American companies—Fox Movietone News, MGM News of the Day, Universal Newsreel, Paramount News, and RKO Pathe News—regularly produced newsreels for national distribution. The work of motion picture studios rather than journalistic institutions, American newsreels were regarded by producers, exhibitors, and viewers alike as a minor component of the program of popular entertainment offered by the movie industry, as "nothing more than a convenient house-clearing device to be inserted between feature attractions."[12]

Producers had quickly developed a conventional format for the news-reels: They were released twice weekly and ran for eight to ten minutes, with each installment offering a series of some half-dozen short, unrelated reports linked by narration and an orchestral score. With their focus on subjects that were often more spectacular than substantial—natural disasters, state ceremonies, demonstrations of technology, athletic competitions, celebrity appearances, fashion shows—newsreels were considered a frivolous news source compared to print journalism. They were also held in low esteem by pioneers of documentary film, such as British filmmaker John Grierson, who dismissed the genre as offering only "the evanescent and the unreal, reflecting hardly anything worth preserving of the times they recorded."[13] Indeed, American newsreels steadfastly avoided controversy. For example, an industry-wide policy eschewed images of Adolf Hitler or of Nazi Germany during the 1930s, and newsreel producers refused to show pictures of dead bodies.

World War II wrought profound changes in the newsreels' content and significance. With the entry of the United States into combat in December 1941, newsreels quickly became an important source of war-related information and propaganda, and their content was closely monitored by the newly created Office of War Information. During 1943 and 1944 newsreels devoted nearly two thirds of their content to the war effort.[14] While they were never directly censored by the United States government or military, their producers voluntarily complied with federal restrictions and expectations as to the newsreels' form and content. All footage of combat and other military activity was filmed by a pool of government-approved commercial newsreel cameramen and by Signal Corps photographers, many of whom had been trained by newsreel production companies. The images they recorded were reviewed and selected by military intelligence before being provided to commercial newsreel producers.[15]

The newsreel installments reporting on liberated Nazi concentration camps were still considered extraordinary, primarily because of the graphic images of human devastation that they presented. Indeed, the screening of the footage became a newsworthy event itself, above and beyond the events depicted therein. Newspapers heralded the military's release of "Nazi prison cruelty film" and reported on audience responses to its exhibition. *The Film Daily* announced record-breaking audiences for newsreels and noted that in New York City, Signal Corps cameramen filmed audience reactions as patrons were leaving the Embassy newsreel house on Broadway. In an unprecedented move, the RKO Pathe newsreel containing this footage was screened for both houses of the U.S. Congress on 30 April and 1 May. *Variety* reported that some theater owners "were a bit skeptical of patron reaction to the more gruesome material but were willing to try the exhibition, particularly in view of General Eisenhower's expressed desire to have all the public see with its own eyes the treatment of Nazi victims." Radio City Music Hall was the only theater said to have refused to screen the "atrocity newsreels" because of its "considerable percentage of both feminine and juvenile patrons." Other exhibitors, however, "did a bit of editing on the reels themselves, pruning the more horrifying footage."[16]

Newsreel producers anticipated and encouraged the special attention paid to the presentation of this footage. In advance publicity distributed to theater owners, Universal Newsreel announced that these films contained "real-life horror pictures revealing the unbelievable atrocities."[17] The significance of the viewers' encounter with these images is also embedded within the construction of these installments, beginning with their opening moments. Following the title card "Nazi Murder Mills!" the Universal newsreel shown during the first days of May 1945 proclaims, on a second title card, that the audience is about to see the "first actual newsreel pictures of atrocities in Nazi murder camps. Helpless prisoners tortured to death by a bestial enemy . . . HERE IS THE TRUTH!"[18] Ed Herlihy, the narrator of "Nazi Murder Mills," later notes that "these newsreel and Signal Corps films were officially recorded for posterity." In language similar to that of Eisenhower's memoir, Herlihy explains at the segment's conclusion that "for the first time, Americans can believe what they thought was impossible propaganda. Here is documentary evidence of sheer mass murder — murder that will blacken the name of Germany for the rest of recorded history."

Similarly, the 2 May 1945 installment of Paramount News begins with the title "History's Most Shocking Record!" followed by a close-up image of a crematorium oven door, filmed in Buchenwald, which opens to reveal the charred remains of a human skeleton. The segment then presents the following text over a smoky background and accompanied by churning music, similar to the more lurid moments of a film noir score: "AN AROUSED AMERICA HAS AWAITED THESE FILMS. They are official Army Signal Corps pictures that will be shown throughout Germany — to *all* Germans. HERE, AMERICA, IS THE SHOCKING TRUTH."[19]

These presentations follow the aesthetic conventions of the newsreel genre in their use of heavily punctuated title cards, narration intoned in a sonorous baritone, and a running symphonic score to link discrete segments of film into a narrative continuum. At the same time, they also offer their subject, and its cinematic presentation, as exceptional. Like "Nazi Murder Mills," Paramount's "History's Most Shocking Record" speaks of the films' lasting importance as well as of their immediate value, articulating the necessity of seeing the footage, who should see it, and to what end. Toward the end of the segment the unnamed narrator intones, "It is not yet known whether these films . . . will be shown to [German] prisoners of war safe here in America. But to future generations it must be told—once man did this to his brothers."

The selection of liberation footage shown in the newsreels focuses both on the objects of witnessing and on the act of witnessing itself. Chosen from the many thousands of feet of film recorded at liberated camps, two kinds of images predominate in the newsreels: In addition to shots of the camps' former inmates, both the living and the dead, are scenes that document local Germans being forced to witness the camps' conditions and the fate of their victims. The latter include footage of Allied soldiers compelling German civilians and military prisoners to behold piles of corpses or to look at souvenirs of the camps fashioned by guards from human remains. There are also scenes of Germans' compulsory participation in burying or reburying the dead and washing or otherwise tending to the needs of surviving inmates. Narrators relate the ordeal of this enforced witnessing with cool *Schadenfreude*. In "Nazi Murder Mills," Herlihy states: "Germans are conducted to a murder shed [in Ohrdruf], where thousands [of prisoners] too ill to be herded to the rear by Nazis were slain in cold blood. The thought of the horror awaiting them is almost too much for the Germans themselves. But brutality is fought with stern measures."

At the same time, the newsreels make a moral distinction between the act of witnessing by Allied victors and that done by the vanquished enemy. As footage of U.S. Army commanders inspecting the concentration camp at Ohrdruf appears in "Nazi Murder Mills," Herlihy describes General Eisenhower as "a man hardened by the blood and shock of war," who "seems appalled at these unbelievable sights"; General Patton is similarly characterized as "hard-boiled, yet visibly moved." Thus, the structure of the newsreels—the choice of images and their montage, as well as narration, musical scoring, titles, and promotional information—codifies the act of witnessing for American audiences as unpleasant, shocking, repulsive, yet arousing, compelling, necessary, and ultimately redemptive.

Indeed, the newsreels both caution viewers that the footage may test their endurance of graphic images of horror and exhort the audience to confront this ordeal of witnessing. The introductory title card of Fox Movietone's newsreel shown during the first days of May 1945 warns, "These scenes of horror are an awesome indictment of Nazi bestiality. To the civilized mind such inhuman cruelty is incredible. We show these films as documentary evidence and warn you not to look at the screen if you are susceptible to gruesome sights."[20] Yet Paramount's newsreel of 28 April opens its screening of "Atrocity Evidence" with the printed caveat, "Grim and ugly . . . GI's at the front *had* to face it. We at home *must* see it to believe and understand."[21] And in Universal's "Nazi Murder Mills" a shot of

Universal Newsreel's "Nazi Murder Mills": As the charred remains of a human skeleton inside one of the crematorium ovens at Buchenwald appears on the screen, the narrator beckons to the audience, "Don't turn away—look! . . . Horror unbelievable—yet true." (National Archives and Records Administration.)

one of the crematorium oven doors at Buchenwald being opened to reveal burnt human remains within (the same image that opens Paramount's "History's Most Shocking Record") appears on the screen as Herlihy beckons to the audience, "Don't turn away—look! Burned alive. Horror unbelievable—yet true."

Allied soldiers echoed the newsreels' admonitions to their audience. An item in *Variety* reported that American troops liberated from prisoner-of-war camps were "unanimous in stating that 'people at home must be shown the atrocity films.'" In England soldiers confronted civilians who had left movie theaters because they found the newsreels unbearable and insisted that it was their duty "to return and see what other people had endured."[22]

Both the newsreels themselves and the publicity surrounding them promote the act of witnessing liberation footage as a distinctively transformative moment. The films are presented as a validation of the Allies' victory over the Axis countries on fundamental moral grounds ("man did this to his brothers") that transcend the particulars of their military conflict. This is, however, a moment composed of contradictory impulses. On the one hand, the newsreels' narrations identify these images as breakthrough evidence that proves conclusively the veracity of previous reports of Nazi atrocities. On the other hand, these images are offered as testing the limits of credulity; they are "unbelievable — yet true." At the same time that the newsreels situate the footage at the threshold of viewers' tolerance for horror, warning them that they might wish to avert their eyes, the newsreels also insist on the necessity of subjecting the viewer to the experience of watching, unpleasant though it may be.

Indeed, calling attention to the exceptional horror portrayed in these reports is essential to their transformative impact. A similar caveat was heard earlier in CBS war correspondent Edward R. Murrow's radio broadcast of 15 April 1945 on the liberation of Buchenwald. Murrow began his report by alerting listeners that it would "not be pleasant listening" and concluded by saying that if the audience was offended by his account, he was "not the least sorry."[23] Such warnings have since been sounded regularly in presentations of images or descriptions of concentration and extermination camps. For example, the promotional literature on a documentary containing liberation footage, which is offered for purchase from the National Archives in Washington, D.C., cautions potential customers that "because of the shocking nature of many of the scenes contained in this film, it is not recommended for viewing by young or impressionable audiences."[24]

In addition to articulating this tension between the repulsion and the compulsion of viewing liberation footage in the printed texts and narrations that accompany these images, the newsreels structure the montage of discrete pieces of footage, recorded at different times and places, into a unified narrative of escalating horror. "Nazi Murder Mills" proceeds from footage filmed in a prisoner-of-war camp in Grasleben showing "wounded and emaciated Yanks, captured in von Runstedt's bulge attack of last winter, [being] fed and given medical care by the Yank armies of liberation" to mass graves at a "converted insane asylum" in Hadamar, where "35,000 political prisoners [had] been slain." This is followed by the more graphic horrors of Buchenwald ("21,000 prisoners living in utter filth stumble around with their broken skulls. Agonized corpses lie everywhere with large tattooed numbers on their sunken stomachs.") and Nordhausen ("Starved corpses strew the ground. Creeping, jabbering, breathing skeletons are loaded into ambulances for possible treatment.").[25]

This sequence breaks with the newsreel's generic convention of proceeding, like a newspaper, from the most important stories to the most trivial. Instead, "Nazi Murder Mills" resembles the structure of fictional horror films, which create an anticipatory dread of horror to heighten the climactic impact of its eventual appearance. Like many fictional examples of the horror genre, these newsreels also balance scenes of horror with some kind of redemption or restoration of order.[26] Thus, installments of all five news-reels reporting the liberation of Nazi concentration camps during the first week of May 1945 either precede or follow these segments with a separate report on the United Nations conference in San Francisco.[27]

Excerpts from liberation footage appeared occasionally in later newsreel installments on the aftermath of the war, such as reports on the destruction of former concentration camps and on war crimes trials. Often these news-reels invoked the morally charged act of witnessing that the vintage images have come to embody. Of particular note is a Paramount newsreel of 26 February 1947, which reports the discovery of a cache of films made by and for Hitler's mistress, Eva Braun.[28] Scenes of her "cavorting" with Hitler and other Nazi leaders in Berchtesgaden are intercut with footage of London ablaze during the blitz and of piles of corpses in a Nazi concentra-tion camp. Both editing and narration implicitly polarize these cinematic documents of the war. The Eva Braun footage is marked as the height of decadence and frivolity by virtue of its juxtaposition against images docu-menting acts of destruction for which the frolickers were responsible; by then, newsreel audiences were expected to recognize these images as icons of the Nazis' thorough indifference to human suffering.

The presentation of liberation footage in commercial newsreels did not meet with universal approval. Terry Ramsaye, editor of the *Motion Picture Herald,* an American film industry weekly, dismissed the first newsreel reports on liberated concentration camps as "a fact of war, not of theatre. It should stand for what it is, desperate medicine in a world desperately beset. It is not a precedent for the screen as the screen. It opens no gates." Two weeks later, after the newsreels screened footage of Mussolini's hang-ing, Ramsaye insisted that, despite efforts to turn the newsreel into a "Chamber of Horrors, . . . the news obligation of the newsreel is happily trivial. . . . No one goes to the theater to get the news."[29] (A generation later, critics echoed Ramsaye's sentiments in their denunciations of the Holocaust's presentation on television, a medium similarly regarded as inherently trivial and therefore ill-suited to the enormity of the subject.)

Film critic James Agee was particularly outspoken about the newsreels' use of footage showing the graphic violence of war. After seeing newsreel reports on the invasion of Iwo Jima in March 1945, he wrote in his column for *The Nation* that "we have no business seeing this sort of experience except through our presence and participation." Likening watching these scenes to the debasing act of looking at pornography, he continued:

If at an incurable distance from participation, hopelessly incapable of reac-tions adequate to the event, we watch men killing each other, we may be quite as profoundly degrading ourselves and, in the process, betraying and separating ourselves the farther from those we are trying to identify ourselves with; none the less because we tell ourselves sincerely that we sit in comfort and watch carnage in order to nurture our patriotism, our conscience, our understanding, and our sympathies.[30]

Following the release of the newsreels reporting on liberated concentration camps, Agee described them in his column as "only part of what is rather clearly an ordered and successful effort to condition the people of this country against interfering with, or even questioning, an extremely hard peace against the people of Germany." Again, he saw a larger problem inherent in the presentation of these images: "The passion for vengeance is a terrifyingly strong one, very easily and probably inevitably wrought up by such evidence, even at our distance. . . . We cannot bear to face our knowledge that the satisfaction of our desire for justice, which we confuse with our desire for vengeance, is impossible." Significantly, Agee sidestepped the newsreels' moral imperative of witnessing liberation footage, noting that he did not feel it "necessary to see the films themselves" before making his judgment.[31]

These newsreels were part of the extensive domestic wartime propaganda produced by Hollywood studios, which also included feature films, animated shorts, and documentaries. Scenes of liberated POW and concentration camps thus provided powerful cinematic validation of both the Allies' war and Hollywood's home-front campaign against Nazi Germany. American newsreel producers underscored this by encouraging their audience to analogize its own viewing of liberation footage with the virtuous witnessing by Allied soldiers and to contrast its experience with the culpable witnessing by Germans. At the same time, these presentations made little effort to articulate connections between American viewers and the victims of the horror depicted in liberation footage as fellow human beings. The narrations accompanying these images in the newsreels repeatedly describe former inmates of Nazi concentration camps in terms that render them anonymous and less than human (e.g., bodies of the dead at Ohrdruf are stacked "like common cordwood"), and the distinction between the living and the dead is obscured (e.g., at Nordhausen lie "side by side with the dead—the living, or rather, the living dead. . . . Emaciated caricatures of men, they are more dead than alive").[32]

This portrait of camp survivors as "the living dead" is as much the result of the selection of images for inclusion in newsreels as it is a product of their narration. The first newsreels presenting this footage feature only a few minutes of the many hours of film recorded at camps liberated by the U.S. Army. The Signal Corps provided a selection of 2,500 feet of liberation images to newsreel producers, who used no more than about one fourth of this material.[33] Moreover, the Signal Corps filmed considerably more liberation footage than that made available to the newsreels. According to archival records, several hours were shot at Buchenwald alone, one of over twenty such sites. Among the inventory of footage recorded at Buchenwald are descriptions of images that never appear in the newsreels: "Survivors cooking a meal"; "Children (some singing), cooking and eating around a fire, older prisoners praying"; "Survivors showing the hanging rope and the club used for bashing out brains"; "A survivor being interrogated by an American soldier"; "Survivor speaking to French officer"; "Picture of Joseph Stalin on camp building"; "Memorial ceremony for the dead, with survivors marching in review with French, Polish and Russian flags. Survivors placing wreath at foot of monument to victims of the Nazis"; "Effigy of Hitler hanging in front of camp building."[34] The absence of such scenes in the newsreels denied the public any images of concentration camp survivors as striving to resume active lives, caring for themselves, expressing religious, political, and national identities, assisting in the documentation of the atrocities committed by their former persecutors, or paying homage to fellow inmates who did not survive.

The images selected for the newsreels from the full stock of liberation footage reflect an agenda to depict Nazi atrocities at their most thorough, extensive, and graphic. Absent, therefore, are images suggesting less than complete devastation, less than totally heinous and dehumanizing results, on less than an unprecedented vastness of scale. While entirely appropriate to the demands of wartime propaganda, this selection also erases the individuated humanity of the Third Reich's victims and ignores the tenacity of those who did not succumb to persecution.

Beginning with the commercial newsreels of April and May 1945, a highly limited canon of iconic images, culled from the dozens of hours of film recorded in liberated Nazi concentration camps, has been established through repeated selection and public presentation over the past five decades. Having largely excluded images of survivors in action, this canon mutes their ability to perform on their own behalf. The linking of the silent, passive, anonymous living with the dead in these earliest presentations of liberation footage portrays survivors as ghosts, creatures beyond the resumption of normal life routines. Along with the notion that most Jewish victims of Nazism responded passively to their persecutors, this spectral image of Holocaust survivors has persisted, informing many portrayals of them in American popular culture, especially during the first postwar decades.

The canon of iconic images inaugurated by the newsreels also excludes encounters between the photographers and the photographed, a defining feature of the creation of liberation footage. The Signal Corps's agenda for filming the conditions of newly liberated concentration camps centered on providing the military with a documentary record of the war, gathering evidence for war crimes trials, and confirming for the American public wartime rumors of Nazi atrocities against occupied civilian populations. Most of the images filmed by the Signal Corps focus on the Nazis' victims, both living and dead, and on the environment of the camps. Allied military personnel do appear in some of the images with former camp inmates, usually in auxiliary roles: helping to bury the dead, lifting ailing survivors onto stretchers, or assisting them, in the manner of stagehands, in reenactments of the techniques of torture or the display of their wounds. In contrast, the newsreels prominently feature encounters between members of the Allied forces and local German civilians, and scenes of the liberation of Nazi-run prisoner-of-war camps include shots of buoyant camaraderie between liberators and former POWs. Both of these types of scenes no doubt had special propaganda value as images of the triumphant conclusion of the war in Europe. In contrast, the near absence of footage of interactions between liberators and survivors in the canon reflects the sense of disbelief and dislocation reported by soldiers and the journalists who documented the liberations.

"Films Beget Films": United States Government Documentaries

Public screenings of the first newsreels reporting Nazi atrocities lasted for only a few days, but the selection of liberation footage presented in these films has loomed over subsequent presentations of the Holocaust. While most of the extensive film documentation of Nazi concentration camps liberated by the Allies has reposed, unseen, on archival shelves for decades, some of the images selected for the newsreels of April and May 1945 have become among the most widely seen photographic images of the twentieth century.[35] Since the early postwar years, this footage has been repeatedly reused and reconfigured in a process, as described by cinema scholar Jay Leyda, wherein "films beget films."[36] In addition to replicating much of the newsreels' choice of images and invoking the meaning originally attached to them, subsequent films elaborate the significance of liberation footage as material for postwar propaganda and as courtroom evidence. The selection and uses of these images in the earliest of these postwar films, which were made by the United States government immediately after the war, have had an enduring impact on the value ascribed to liberation footage in later presentations of the Holocaust in American film and on television.

The government's productions include staff reports and newsreels for American military personnel, as well as films used to educate the postwar German population about its culpability in war crimes. Propaganda films also targeted Allied civilian audiences; among these are Frank Capra's *Here*

German prisoners of war in Halloran General Hospital, New York, view U.S. Army film footage of conditions in recently liberated Nazi concentration camps. The caption to this International News photograph, taken in June 1945, testifies to the early interest in observing the moral impact of viewing liberation footage: "Many of the prisoners covered their eyes as they watched the horrible scenes, while others still smiled in arrogant indifference." (UPI/Corbis-Bettmann.)

Is Germany, Henri Cartier-Bresson and Richard Banks's *Le Retour* (also titled *Reunion*), and Garson Kanin and Carol Reed's *The True Glory,* all produced in 1945. These films were part of an extensive international use of documentary images in cinematic assessments of World War II, which constitute, in Leyda's words, a "trial by document" of Nazi war crimes.[37]

The United States government greatly enhanced the value of liberation footage as a virtual witness by screening it during early Nazi war crimes trials. In November 1945 the Allies began the most celebrated of these trials in Nuremberg. Twenty-two defendants—both leading figures of the Nazi regime and prominent German citizens whose activities in publishing, industry, and finance were linked to charges of war crimes—were tried before a tribunal of American, British, French, and Russian justices. During the preceding summer, American military personnel working for the U.S.

Counsel for the Prosecution of Axis Criminality produced two films to be screened as evidence at the trial.

The first of these, an hour-long compilation titled *Nazi Concentration Camps,* consists of liberation footage filmed by American and British military camera crews. Besides sites shown in the commercial newsreels, *Nazi Concentration Camps* presents footage of eight additional concentration camps, including Dachau and Bergen-Belsen (the latter, liberated by British forces, was filmed by the British Ministry of Information). All footage is black and white; most of it is silent.[38] A single voice reads the narration, which was "taken directly from the reports of the military photographers who filmed the camps."[39]

At the beginning of the film a series of typewritten affidavits, signed and witnessed by U.S. military personnel, appear on the screen as the narrator reads them aloud. The testimony avers that the compilation film constitutes a "true representation of the individuals and scenes photographed," and that it is also an authentic replication of the original film record, which has "not been retouched, distorted, or otherwise altered in any respect."[40] Moreover, *Nazi Concentration Camps* is sworn to be faithful to the full, original film record. Both the accompanying narration and the choice of which footage to include in the film ("six thousand feet of film, selected from eighty thousand feet") are characterized as in no way compromising the veracity of the original unedited footage.

While the commercial newsreels used much of the same footage, *Nazi Concentration Camps* reflects the Allied prosecutors' particular agenda of presenting the film as courtroom evidence. As the voice-over identifies locations and persons, it places them within the narrative framework of the war of aggression waged by the Axis powers, to which the liberation documented by the Allies' footage is, in effect, an epilogue. For example, as the image of former concentration camp inmates recuperating in a hospital appears, the narrator comments that they "are smiling for the first time in years," identifying the scene as the resolution of the survivors' wartime suffering. Unlike the newsreels, *Nazi Concentration Camps* also includes interviews with two former camp inmates. One of these is an American prisoner of war who, during the course of describing the ordeals of being in a POW camp, quips, "This is the first time I've ever been in the movies."

Other scenes in *Nazi Concentration Camps* demonstrate the camp survivors' awareness that they are participating in a performance that retells their wartime ordeals. In Breendonck inmates reenact how they were beaten by camp guards and demonstrate how torture devices, such as thumbscrews, were used on them. Elsewhere, former inmates display for the camera deformities and scars from diseases, punitive burnings, and beatings that they experienced in the camps. This reflects the leading role that former prisoners took, according to Robert Abzug, in the documentation of their wartime ordeals: "In virtually every camp, prisoner guides eagerly showed the highlights to arriving troops, dignitaries, and press persons" and offered "endless personal stories of sacrifice and heroism."[41]

Nazi Concentration Camps also reenacts wartime activities through its selection and editing of liberation footage. A notable example of this occurs in the section on Dachau, in which a series of close-up shots—the sign "*Brausebad*" (showers) over a doorway; showerheads in a ceiling; a can labeled "*Giftgas*" (poison gas) lying on the ground; a network of ducts, valves, and pressure gauges (which the narrator describes as leading from a control room into an unseen gas chamber); a gloved hand (whose?) turning a winch—are spliced together and identified, through the narration, as the operational procedure of gassing to death groups of camp inmates.

The claims put forth in the U.S. military's affidavits equate *Nazi Concentration Camps* with the full storehouse of the Allies' footage of liberation and, moreover, with the actual events that they depict. Nevertheless, there is a fundamental difference between the film and what it is called upon to signify. The prosecution's compilation film, the raw footage, and the actual events depicted are three distinct phenomena. Moreover, they are all presentations made (whether performed, filmed, or edited) at a temporal and narrative distance from the acts of atrocity that they are intended to evince. In the absence of depicting actual crimes, *Nazi Concentration Camps* retells and reenacts them and displays their traces and consequences. Although this footage is largely a record of encounters between Allied liberators and camp survivors, its ultimate value as evidence centers on the missing party—the Nazis who ran the camps and their collaborators. In this regard, the film record of liberated camps resembles what Luc Sante has observed about all photographs of crime scenes. These images are distinguished not by what they present, but by what (and who) is absent from the image: "If photographs are supposed to freeze time, these crystallize what is already frozen, the aftermath of violence." Such images "have no reason to be except to show that which cannot be shown."[42]

The contribution *Nazi Concentration Camps* made to the case against the defendants at the first Nuremberg war crimes trial is questionable, but the reactions to the film are telling, foreshadowing future responses to these images when shown to the public in films and on television. As legal scholar Lawrence Douglas has observed, the prosecution's ambition of introducing filmed images as witnesses that would simply "speak for themselves" produced "less than straightforward results." Douglas has argued that the composition of the film was "anything but an unambiguous document and its use by the prosecution exemplifies how imperfectly evidence of Nazi genocide was presented and digested at Nuremberg."[43] The film was screened in the courtroom on 29 November 1945, at the start of the second week of the proceedings. Telford Taylor, then a member of the American prosecution staff, wrote in his memoir of the trials that the decision to screen the footage at that time was "dictated not by logic but by felt necessity." With this emphasis on the affective value of liberation footage, the screening of *Nazi Concentration Camps* at the trial resembled the presentation of these images as wartime propaganda in commercial newsreels, although the prosecution's film incorporates none of their sensationalizing features.

The emotional impact of seeing these images in the courtroom proved powerful, yet the consequences of this act of witnessing were unclear. Taylor recalled that the responses provoked in the defendants by the film ranged from indignation at the association with running concentration camps to appearing shamed, depressed, "shattered." He concluded that while the screening of *Nazi Concentration Camps* during the trial "certainly hardened sentiment against the defendants generally, . . . it contributed little to the determination of their individual guilt."[44]

Although *Nazi Concentration Camps* was produced only for use at the Nuremberg trials, the United States government subsequently made it available to show to American audiences. Some of its sequences, such as the demonstration of the gas chambers in Dachau and the bulldozing of a mound of corpses into a mass grave in Bergen-Belsen, have appeared in numerous documentaries. *Nazi Concentration Camps* also found its way onto American television in the late 1950s as an important element in the docudrama *Judgment at Nuremberg*. When the cable channel Court TV marked the fiftieth anniversary of the Nuremberg trials in November 1995, the film was resituated in the context of its original screening.

As with previous presentations of *Nazi Concentration Camps,* Court TV offers repeated caveats to viewers of this telecast that the footage, while important as evidence, is "graphic," "upsetting," "distressing." Between segments of the film, contemporary legal authorities and veterans of the original trial recall initial reactions to *Nazi Concentration Camps,* debate its value as evidence, and consider the implications of its use as an effort to turn the proceedings at Nuremberg into a "show trial." These remarks suggest that assessing the value of liberation footage—even with regard to its emotional impact—remains an unresolved issue. Several of the commentators, including renowned attorney Floyd Abrams, champion the continued showing of *Nazi Concentration Camps* as a defense against the claims of Holocaust deniers. Ben Ferencz authenticates the veracity of the film, based on his own visits to camps after the war as a member of the United States prosecution team. Yet he also remarks that the film is "unable to convey . . . the real trauma of the scene—the smell, the excitement, the drama . . . , the despair, the joy at being liberated. . . . None of this is comprehensible, really, by just viewing a few cold pictures."[45]

A Crime "as Old as Man":
Early Television Documentaries

Given the frequent telecasts of Holocaust documentaries in the United States during the 1980s and 1990s, the apparent lack of such presentations during the early postwar years might suggest indifference, reluctance, or some other "failure" to engage with the subject at the time. Only with such works as *In Dark Places: Remembering the Holocaust* (1978) and *Holocaust: The Children* (1981) did American television begin to present documentaries distinguished not merely by their use of the term *Holocaust,* but by their presentation of the subject as a distinctive historical entity, centered around the Nazi-led persecution of European Jewry.

Beginning in the late 1940s American television did air a number of documentaries dealing with what has come to be known as the Holocaust. The nature of its presentation in these early broadcasts evinces the inchoate status of the Holocaust as a historical concept during the first postwar years. What would later be distinguished as a separate "war against the Jews" was not yet codified as a discrete unit of human experience with its own authoritative sources, narrative boundaries, vocabulary, historiography, and scholarly apparatus.[46] Jews were not singled out as the quintessential victims of Nazi persecution, nor were Jewish responses regarded as central to the postwar understanding of this chapter of history. Moreover, the Holocaust had not yet been distinguished as an event of ultimate or paradigmatic stature, against which other moral issues might be measured.

Indeed, an American conceptualization of the Holocaust had yet to emerge from the nation's formative understanding of World War II. The recently ended war still dominated American life. As the United States adjusted to the profound political, social, and economic changes that came with peace, national attention was also taken up with the war's aftermath abroad, in which the United States assumed a leading activist role. Television soon became an important venue for presenting Americans with a master narrative of the war, often drawing on the extensive footage filmed by the Signal Corps to do so. Two major documentary series chronicled America's military role in the war: *Crusade in Europe,* based on Eisenhower's memoir tracing the Allies' military campaign in the European Theater of Operations, aired on ABC in 1949; *Victory at Sea,* a chronicle of American naval campaigns during the war, was broadcast on NBC in 1952–1953. Individual documentaries also examined the years of combat and the period leading up to the outbreak of war, especially in Nazi Germany. These retrospective broadcasts also reflected emerging postwar American perspectives, especially with regard to the future course of a rapidly changing world order.

The early broadcasts present places and events now associated with the Holocaust as they were understood during the war and its immediate aftermath. Several early television documentaries briefly mention Nazi concentration and extermination camps and incorporate images from liberation footage; among these are Episode 22 (of 26) of *Crusade in Europe* and the final segment of *Victory at Sea*.[47] Both series, organized around military campaigns and drawing primarily on Signal Corps footage, present the Third Reich's mass murder of Jews and other civilians only when it was encountered by Allied forces at the end of the fighting in Europe.

These atrocities are also an oblique presence in documentaries devoted to the history of the Third Reich, such as *The Twisted Cross,* a 1956 presentation of the NBC series *Project Twenty* that traces the rise and fall of Nazism, and *Trial at Nuremberg,* aired in 1958 on CBS's *The Twentieth Century*.[48] The latter series, which ran from 1957 through 1967, broadcast numerous documentaries on individuals (Mussolini, Churchill, Rommel, Patton) and events (the D-Day invasion, the liberation of Paris, the Battle of Stalingrad, the bombing of Hiroshima) that were part of the combat narrative of World War II. None of these programs, however, dealt exclusively, or even primarily, with sites, actions, or persons associated with the Holocaust. *Trial at Nuremberg* focuses on the personalities of the Nazi leaders who were on trial, rather than dwelling on the war crimes themselves or on their victims.

The use of liberation footage in these early documentaries recalls the commercial newsreels shown in the spring of 1945 and *Nazi Concentration Camps*. Victims of Nazi persecutions — their prewar backgrounds, their wartime experiences, their postwar lives — are not treated as a subject of interest in themselves. Rather, these documentaries present the victims of Nazism as confirmation of the Axis powers' maleficence, which is the films' focus. Nor are concentration and extermination camps presented as the ultimate measure of wartime atrocities. A sequence in the final segment of *Victory at Sea,* covering the war's last days, parallels images of the skeletal former inmates in Nazi concentration camps with footage of emaciated Allied soldiers in Japanese prisoner-of-war camps, each sequence testifying to the brutality of the vanquished enemies. *The Twisted Cross* does not distinguish the victimization of Jews as central or egregious among Nazi persecutions, nor are the historical and ideological particulars of Nazi anti-Semitism examined. The documentary introduces Jews as "a convenient and defenseless scapegoat" for Nazism; then the film's narration proceeds to Nazi attacks on Christian churches, noting that "when one faith is persecuted, no faith is safe."

Even a documentary that focuses on Nazi crimes against humanity approaches the subject differently than do later works of Holocaust memory culture. *Genocide Convention,* a 1949 installment of the CBS public affairs series *UN Casebook,* discusses the events of the Holocaust in the context of telling "the story of the greatest of all possible crimes."[49] (The term *Holocaust* is not mentioned in this telecast; the word *genocide* was itself of recent vintage then, having been coined, the broadcast explains, by Yale University law professor Raphael Lempkin and was first used at the Nuremberg war crimes trials in 1946.) Whereas the Holocaust is now often characterized as an event without parallel in human history, *Genocide Convention* identifies the Nazi persecutions as "the most recent and by far most efficient" of a series of analogous crimes, which are "as old as man and his recorded history." These date back to Herod's Massacre of the Innocents and include the Spanish conquistadors' persecution of the Carib Indians in the sixteenth century, the slaughter of French Huguenots on the Night of St. Bartholomew in 1572, and the persecution of Quakers in colonial Boston, as well as more recent attacks on Serbians, Macedonians, and Armenians. Nor does *Genocide Convention* distinguish the Nazi effort to annihilate Jews, "the ancient scapegoat," as more egregious or ideologically central than its persecution of other civilian populations—Gypsies, Poles, Russians—during World War II. The documentary includes footage of emaciated survivors sitting or standing in groups behind barbed wire, but rather than describing the camps they were in as the sites of a unique *univers concentrationnaire,* the accompanying narration is glib, even playfully ironic:

> This is a concentration camp—a nice name for a bad place. The fences kept the campers home, and the high-tension wiring kept the fences effective. . . . After a while—a short while, usually, because of the accommodations and the service and the cuisine—the fences were academic. There was nowhere to go, no desire left to go, no strength with which to go. There was just one sad fact, and you could camp around and concentrate on it: You were still alive.

Despite the different tone of its narration, *Genocide Convention* resembles the newsreels that reported the liberation of concentration camps by making explicit the moral charge incumbent on its audience as vicarious witnesses of this crime. Following a call for the ratification of the Genocide Convention by the UN's member nations, the broadcast concludes by exhorting viewers, "You are a member of the United Nations—you can help wipe out genocide."

At the same time that early postwar newsreels, films, and television programs established the power of watching liberation footage as a morally galvanizing act, they also demonstrated the limits of these images. Despite their graphic power, these images demand completion, in the form of compilation, narration, and other cinematic devices, in order to fulfill their transformative function. Indeed, the many appearances of liberation footage over the decades not only testify to its lasting iconic value, but also demonstrate how malleable is its meaning.

Over the past half century, American television has broadcast dozens of documentaries and countless news reports featuring vintage images first shown in the newsreels of April and May 1945. American audiences have also encountered some of this footage while watching television and film dramas, such as *Judgment at Nuremberg,* first presented on CBS's *Playhouse 90* in 1959, and later released by United Artists as a feature film in 1961; the 1981 film version of Chaim Potok's novel *The Chosen;* and CBS's 1985 television movie *Kojak: The Belarus File.*[50] The presence of these vintage images also hovers more obliquely around other dramas, including Ernest Kinoy's teleplay *Walk Down the Hill,* aired on CBS's *Studio One* in 1957, and the 1993 feature film *Schindler's List.*

Presentations of liberation footage in documentary films of the late 1970s, 1980s, and 1990s implicitly invoke the first, shocking experience of its witnessing as well as the moral response that its early public presentations demanded. The shock that these images once induced may have abated over the years, in the wake of their frequent reuse and the appearance over the years of other, more recent graphic images of horror. At the same time, the symbolic value invested in watching liberation footage has increased, and it endures as a mainstay of Holocaust memory culture.

This is exemplified by a public service announcement (PSA) aired on MTV and other cable television channels in the fall of 1992, one of a series of PSAs designed to encourage young Americans to participate in the national election that took place the following month. The PSA opens with a montage of overlapping clips of vintage black-and-white footage; prominent among them are images of Nazis burning books and beating people in the street. A voice-over comments: "We'd like to take this opportunity to remind you of why so many of us came to this country in the first place." Liberation footage appears on the screen, showing groups of gaunt figures in striped uniforms, some standing behind barbed wire, as the voice-over continues: "Vote—for all the people who didn't make it." Then the sentence "There is no excuse not to vote" appears in white letters against a black screen; the spot is over.[51]

No caption or narration identifies the footage used in this thirty-second sequence. Instead, its producers assumed that the young adult audience the PSA targeted could quickly recognize these vintage scenes as icons of the Holocaust. Moreover, the PSA's creators expected that its viewers could take its decidedly American reading of these images and the historical moment they represent—a reading that presumptuously identifies victims of Nazi persecution as "people who didn't make it" to the United States—and link this with reasons for participating in the upcoming election. While this is among the more unusual uses of liberation footage to appear on American television, it typifies the images' complex and powerful status in American culture at the end of the twentieth century. Awe-inspiring yet accessible, they are icons of an essentialized morality whose meaning is nonetheless open to ever-new possibilities of completion.

two

"This Is Your Life"

If one other form of Holocaust representation has achieved the same privileged status of liberation footage, it is the testimony of those who directly experienced or were eyewitnesses to Nazi persecution. These accounts complement the documentary evidence of liberation footage. Whereas scenes of mass persecution predominate in the film images, testimonies focus on the experience of the individual. In contrast to the emphasis on the dead (or "living dead") in vintage footage, the stories of survivors center attention on the living. In the films, most of which are silent, the visual dimension is primary, and they are fixed at the time of the war's end. In contrast, narrative is central to the testimonies of eyewitnesses and survivors, even when these are photographed, and they are shaped by the temporal distance between the Holocaust era and when it is recalled—years, sometimes decades later.

Just as the conceptualization of the Holocaust coalesced over time, so did the notion of Holocaust survivors. During the immediate postwar period, they were variously referred to as refugees, Europe's homeless, Displaced Persons (DPs), or, within much of the Jewish community, as *sheyres hapleyte* (Yiddish for "the saving remnant"), all terms that connote a liminal status. The early postwar existence of Holocaust survivors was understood as a transitional state, in which they were to resolve the disparity between their experiences of the recent past and their aspirations for the future. Survivors' wartime experiences were, at first, largely regarded as something they should overcome and put behind themselves. Only decades later would there be repeated public calls for survivors to recall their lives during the Holocaust, and their stories would be vaunted as a uniquely privileged source of insight into this historical epoch.

Thus, the earliest appearances of Holocaust survivors on American radio and television usually focused on their postwar existence rather than their wartime experiences. For example, Richard C. Hottelet briefly interviews two survivors of Nazi death camps living in Berlin as part of a 1953 report

27

on life in the former German capital for the news series *See It Now* (CBS, 1951–1958).[1] The two interviewees—a man identified as "half Jewish" and a woman, described as a "full Jewess," who survived the war because of her marriage to an "Aryan"—are asked nothing about their life during the prewar era or the war years, but only about their current existence as Jews in postwar Germany.

These early broadcasts paid particular attention to the relocation and rehabilitation of DPs. During the postwar years there was extensive international debate over the proper resettlement of the many thousands of men, women, and children, both Jews and non-Jews, temporarily housed in DP camps in Germany, Italy, and Austria. In the United States, Jewish organizations campaigned both to admit DPs to America and to enable their safe and legal emigration to Palestine. As part of these efforts, DPs appeared on a variety of American radio programs sponsored by the United Service for New Americans and aired on New York's municipal station, WNYC. *Reunion,* a radio series aired by New York station WOR in the late 1940s, featured actual reunions of Jewish families that had been scattered during the war. Jewish DPs were also the subject of radio dramas on episodes of the religious series *The Eternal Light,* produced by the Jewish Theological Seminary in conjunction with NBC.[2]

Television soon followed with occasional presentations of DPs' wartime ordeals and postwar struggles on news reports, public affairs programs, and prime-time dramas. These include *Hunger Takes No Holiday,* a 1945 installment of CBS's *The World We Live In* about the challenges of feeding postwar Europe; *Placing the Displaced,* a 1948 docudrama made by the Hebrew Immigrant Aid Society, and the appearance of two DPs on a "Bill of Rights Day" program aired on NBC in 1951. The question of admitting DPs to the United States was debated on public affairs programs in 1948 and 1950. New York independent station WPIX featured reports on DPs in a number of local newscasts between 1948 and 1952. Among the early television dramas in which DPs or refugees figured as characters are *Homeward Borne* (*Playhouse 90,* CBS, 1957) and *Thirty Pieces of Silver* (*Alcoa/Goodyear Theater,* NBC, 1959). Jewish installments of Sunday ecumenical television series also occasionally dealt with DPs during the 1940s and 1950s. The earliest of these is a 1948 broadcast of CBS's *Lamp Unto My Feet,* which included an appearance by "two recently arrived D.P. children, among the first to come under the new quota, who spoke in Yiddish of the happiness of their first Thanksgiving in America."[3]

Even the earliest broadcasts evince the distinctive impact that television can have on the presentation of a Holocaust survivor's testimony. One of the first American telecasts devoted to telling an individual's story of surviving Nazi persecution is an exemplary case—an episode of the series *This*

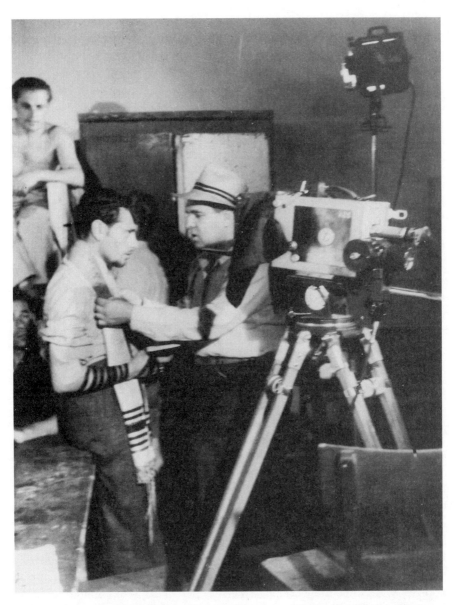

Filming the Hebrew Immigrant Aid Society's docudrama *Placing the Displaced* on location at Funk Kaserne, then the largest emigration assembly center in the U.S. Zone in Germany, 1947. In addition to being televised by CBS in 1948, this film about Europe's Displaced Persons was shown in theaters and distributed to American Jewish community organizations. (YIVO Institute for Jewish Research.)

Is Your Life aired on NBC on 27 May 1953.[4] This half-hour telecast presented survivor testimony as part of one of the most popular entertainment programs of the 1950s, which has come to be recognized as a quintessential example of America's early television culture. A close reading of this broadcast demonstrates how television—a collaborative, corporate medium—can shape the telling of an individual's life story. The broadcast also reveals the extent to which a Holocaust survivor's story was understood during the early postwar years as emblematic of a larger chapter of history regarded as somehow singular.

"This Is Your Life, Hanna Bloch Kohner"

As the series name appears amid dancing spotlights and the offstage orchestra plays a fanfare, an announcer introduces *This Is Your Life* as "television's most talked-about program," sponsored by Hazel Bishop No-Smear Lipstick. The program's theme music plays as host Ralph Edwards strolls down the aisle of the El Capitan Theater in Hollywood, California. He stops to ask the name of a young woman in the front row; she is Hanna Kohner, the wife of talent agent Walter Kohner. Edwards asks her to identify the young man next to her; he is actor Jeffrey Hunter. Edwards asks Hunter what is written on the cover of the large album that he carries. "*This Is Your Life*—Hanna Bloch Kohner," Hunter reads aloud. Hanna's smile drops and she buries her face in her hands, shouting, "Oh, no! Oh, my God!" But soon she is smiling again and laughing as Edwards teases her about the ruse—her family led her to believe that the program would be a salute to Hunter.

Edwards escorts Hanna to the "Hazel Bishop stage" to sit in the "chair of honor." The set consists of an upholstered sofa, drapes, floral arrangements placed on pedestals, and a coffee table—evoking a posh living room; in the back a large sign bears the sponsor's name. Once seated, Hanna asks Edwards if he has an extra handkerchief, and she expresses astonishment at how her family conspired in this surprise. Edwards assures Hanna that she deserves this honor and begins his presentation, remarking that she hardly appears to be someone who has already experienced a "lifetime of fear, terror, and tragedy"; she seems like a "young American girl just out of college, not at all like a survivor of Hitler's cruel purge of German Jews." Edwards promises to "relive" with Hanna both this and "happier" episodes of her life. But because her story is "so intense," the series' sponsor "wants to devote full time to it without interruption." The program cuts away to a commercial for Hazel Bishop No-Smear Lipstick.

This Is Your Life returns with the fanfare from Beethoven's Fifth Symphony as Edwards begins to recount Hanna's life story. He describes her hometown of Teplitz-Schönau, Czechoslovakia, where Hanna was born in 1919 near the old castle. Edwards invokes the presence of Beethoven, Goethe, and Wagner in Teplitz—a "rich heritage" for Hanna and her brother, Gottfried—as the camera cuts to pictures of the city and portraits of their parents.

A voice offstage announces that he was a schoolmate of Hanna. Edwards asks Hanna if she knows who it is—someone she hasn't seen in over fifteen years. It turns out to be Frank Lieben, a childhood friend who is now a research engineer in Manitoba, the first of five people from her past with whom Hanna is reunited during the program. Lieben enters through a curtained archway, accompanied by a glissando on a harp and audience applause. He and Hanna embrace and reminisce briefly about teachers and school holidays. She giggles as he recounts how she fell in love with Walter Kohner at a school dance. Strings playing a waltz accompany his narrative, and a photograph of Hanna in her teens appears. When Lieben finishes, Edwards directs him off camera, to sit in "Hanna's past."

Edwards asks Hanna what happened to her and Walter, whom she planned to marry, when the war began. As the musical accompaniment switches to a minor mode, Edwards recounts the Anschluss and invasion of the Sudetenland as vintage film footage of German soldiers marching through a city appears and brass instruments play the anti-Semitic Nazi marching song "Horst Wessel." A slow cross-fade back to Hanna superimposes her face on the footage. A bass drum beats heavily as Edwards mentions the Nazis' torching the local synagogue. The music abruptly changes to the plaintive strains of Kol Nidrei, played on strings, and a photograph of a ruined synagogue appears. Edwards asks Hanna if she saw the troops enter Teplitz-Schönau. "No. It must have been very awful," she replies.

Accompanied by strings and harp, Edwards relates how Walter got a visa for the United States and tried to send for Hanna, but she was unable to follow him due to American immigration quotas. Hanna sought refuge in Amsterdam, finding work as a servant. In May 1940 the Nazis invaded the Netherlands, "putting a merciless end to your dream." The camera cuts to a map of Europe, showing Germany in black, and the blackness spreads into Belgium, Luxembourg, and the Netherlands. Hanna reappears on the screen, blotting her tears with a handkerchief. The theme of Kol Nidrei returns as Edwards describes Hanna as "alone, friendless, and hunted as a non-Aryan in Hitler's world."

Edwards continues: In Amsterdam Hanna met and married Carl Benjamin, a young German Jewish refugee. They were arrested by Gestapo agents in the winter of 1943 and sent to the detention camp at Westerbork. A new offstage voice states that she and Hanna first met there. Hanna recognizes Eva Herzberg (now Mrs. Werner Florscheim), also a resident of

Hollywood. The two women, Edwards explains, remained friends throughout their imprisonment in four concentration camps. Eva enters, embraces Hanna, and, in response to a question from Edwards, continues the narrative, explaining how they were transported to the camp at Theresienstadt in cattle cars. Edwards comments that on this journey Hanna passed through Teplitz-Schönau. "It wasn't a nice homecoming," Hanna responds.

Eva explains that they were soon sent to Auschwitz. Edwards interjects that each woman was "sent to the so-called 'showers.' . . . Some showers had regular water, some had liquid gas, and you never knew which one you were sent to." Among the less fortunate were Hanna's husband, father, and mother, who all died at Auschwitz. Hanna then learned that her brother was in the camp and sent a message to him on his birthday via the camp underground. Today, Edwards notes, Gottfried is a doctor, living in Israel. Eva recounts that she and Hanna were sent to Mauthausen in the winter of 1944, and Edwards reminds Hanna that there she was assigned to shovel coal, that she became frail and ill, "and then on May seventh, 1945—"

A photograph of liberated concentration camp prisoners appears as the fanfare from Beethoven's Fifth Symphony is heard. "V for victory," Edwards proclaims, and he tells of Mauthausen's liberation by American troops, which prompts the introduction of the next guest: Harold Shuckart, one of three Jewish GIs who took part in liberating Mauthausen and befriended Hanna in the early postwar days. Shuckart also wrote to Walter Kohner to inform him that Hanna, now widowed, had survived the war. (Walter, Edwards explains, had last heard from Hanna when she informed him of her marriage.)

In July 1945, Edwards continues, Hanna returned to the Netherlands, and another person from her past appears: Irene Sachs, a fellow refugee, who lived in the same house as Hanna in postwar Amsterdam. Irene explains how one day an American sergeant came to the door to see Hanna; it was Walter Kohner. Walter himself enters at this cue, embracing his wife and sitting beside her on the sofa. He recalls that he had been stationed in Luxembourg when he received Shuckart's letter and then learned that she might be in Amsterdam. Edwards asks Walter if he proposed to Hanna straightaway. "No, I waited till the next day," Walter replies, and the audience laughs. Edwards relates that they were married on 24 October 1945 in three separate ceremonies (European and American civil ceremonies, as well as a Jewish ritual); their "dreams come true at last," as they sail to America the following July.

"This is your life," Edwards sums up. Now that Hanna is "safe" in her adopted homeland, he says, she has "but one prayer"—to make a trip to see her brother in Israel. "Hanna, Hazel Bishop has moved that far-off day into the present. The last time you were in touch with him was in a Nazi

Series host Ralph Edwards reunites Holocaust survivor Hanna Bloch Kohner with figures from her past on *This Is Your Life,* aired in May 1953. From left to right: Edwards, Hanna's childhood friend Frank Lieben, fellow survivor Irene Sachs, brother Gottfried Bloch, Hanna, fellow survivor Eva Herzberg Florscheim, husband Walter Kohner. Standing behind Gottfried Bloch is Harold Shuckart, a U.S. soldier who befriended Hanna after her liberation from Mauthausen. (National Jewish Archive of Broadcasting, theJewish Museum, New York. Reproduced with permission of Ralph Edwards Productions.)

concentration camp, nearly ten years ago. Now, here he is!" Gottfried Bloch enters and embraces his sister. "This is my happiest day in all my life," he says. Edwards responds, "It's a happy day for all of us," as all the participants assemble on stage. "Out of darkness, of terror and despair, a new life has been born in a new world for you, Hanna Kohner." Edwards promises that Hazel Bishop will address the question of her future, after another message from the sponsor.

Following the commercial, Edwards, Hanna, and all the guests reappear. On behalf of Hazel Bishop he presents Hanna with a 16-millimeter film copy of the evening's program and a projector from the Spiegel catalogue, so that she and her family "can relive this memorable night," and a fourteen-karat-gold charm bracelet designed by Marchal Jewelers of Fifth Avenue in New York for Hanna, each charm symbolizing an important episode in her life. Finally, Hazel Bishop presents her with a lipstick in a jeweled case. (All of these are standard gifts presented to the program's honorees.)

Edwards explains that while Hanna's unforgettable, tragic experiences have been "tempered by the happiness" she has found in her new home, there remain throughout the world "countless thousands of others like you, who are still in desperate need of the barest living essentials." In Hanna's honor, "Hazel Bishop turns to our viewers of all creeds and races" and appeals to them to make a donation to the United Jewish Appeal (UJA). Edwards recites the UJA's address as it appears on the screen and announces that the sponsor will initiate the campaign with a $1,000 contribution.

"This is your life, Hanna Bloch Kohner. To you in your darkest hour, America held out a friendly hand. Your gratitude is reflected in your unwavering devotion and loyalty to the land of your adoption." Walter thanks Edwards, his staff, and Hazel Bishop for "making the impossible possible." Edwards reminds viewers to tune in the following week for another show and then bids them good night as the program's theme music swells and the credits roll.

The "Hanna Kohner" episode of *This Is Your Life* reveals how, even in the early postwar years, television could shape the telling of a Holocaust survivor's life story. The broadcast demonstrates television's facility for ingesting other media—notably, the use of vintage photographs and footage—and creating hybrid performances, here drawing on conventions of genres ranging from documentary and newsreel to melodrama and game shows. The series also exploits the medium's small scale and the intimacy of television viewing by making extensive use of close-ups, especially of Hanna's face.

In many ways this telecast is typical of *This Is Your Life,* in which Edwards evolved a unique approach to presenting the story of someone's life. Most works of life history—including written memoirs, oral histories, and nonverbal examples in the form of paintings, musical compositions, crafts, and so on—are essentially either autobiographical or biographical. In addition, there are various collaborative efforts, ranging from interviews and surveys to such group projects as theater pieces, quilts, and murals. In these works, the conventional boundaries between biographer and subject are often obscured or otherwise transformed. *This Is Your Life* is a kind of collaborative life history, given the many participants involved. However, it is distinguished by the fact that, even though the subject appears and is involved in the actual performance of his or her life story, the enterprise is undertaken without the subject's prior consent or cooperation.[5]

Like Hanna Kohner, honorees on *This Is Your Life* were, with rare exceptions, completely unaware of having been selected by Edwards and his production team. Extensive research on the honorees' personal histories was undertaken behind their backs, usually with the assistance of family members, friends, and colleagues, who were sworn to secrecy. This ensured the honoree's unrehearsed responses during the broadcast, which were considered essential to the series' appeal. Edwards himself described its agenda as being centered around provoking emotional response rather than being concerned solely, or perhaps even primarily, with paying tribute to honorees' achievements. A 1956 *Saturday Evening Post* feature on the series, which dubbed *This Is Your Life* the "weepiest show on television," explained that its producer "will not hang the garland on any subject whose tear ducts are gummed up. The researchers establish beyond a reasonable doubt that the principal will sob, choke, flutter or even cry out."[6]

The "Hanna Kohner" episode fulfilled the series' demand for emotion as it conformed to its ritualized structure. Once she was identified, her story was presented, largely in chronological order, through a combination of narration delivered by Edwards, questions that he asked her, photographs and other documentary images, and—most important—through a series of reunions between the subject and people from her past.

The bursts of emotion that these reunions precipitate punctuated what was essentially a tightly scored production (literally so, as much of the program was performed, like nineteenth-century melodrama, to orchestral accompaniment). The producers of *This Is Your Life* considered careful scripting and rehearsal to be essential, in order to ensure that the program would provide viewers with demonstrations of genuine emotion—even instructing participants "how to kiss or hug the subject on cue."[7] Such close control of the proceedings did not deprive the program of its emotional impact. Rather, limiting the scope of spontaneity created tension between the highly structured ritual of *This Is Your Life* and the expression of unrehearsed emotion. The breaks in the carefully orchestrated protocols of *This Is Your Life*, however slight, signify the emotional power of these moments.

The affective drama of this episode of *This Is Your Life* depended as much on the human embodiments of Hanna's past as on the honoree herself. Their serial appearance constituted a pageant that enacted Hanna's life in a continuous dramatic present, much like medieval paintings that depict on a single panel a sequence of scenes forming a narrative continuum. At the same time, their reunions with Hanna were very much a modern phenomenon—miracle plays of the jet age, in which the program's sponsor figured as deus ex machina, using broadcast technology and commercial air travel to restore family relationships and friendships that had been fractured and scattered around the world by the ordeals of the twentieth century.

Each reunion between Hanna and her "past" itself constituted the climax of a brief drama, in addition to being an element of the entire episode's narrative, which the reunion reflected in miniature. This episode of *This Is Your Life* was thus a series of dramatic climaxes that came rapidly one after another over the course of a half hour, thereby sustaining the program's affective power. Like the presentation of Hanna's life story, the reunions themselves posed a series of trials: Would she remember the person who is speaking offstage? Would their reunion be joyous? tearful? surprising? Would this reunion be the one that causes her to break down completely? Ultimately, a happy resolution followed, with the reward of a celebration in the embrace of devoted companions and loved ones.

Edwards employed this narrative structure to transform Hanna's experiences of rupture, loss, and displacement into a cohesive narrative of triumph over adversity. Most notably, the deaths of Hanna's parents and her first husband at Auschwitz were given the briefest mention, as they were subsumed by a narrative shaped by the course of her romance with Walter. Thus, *This Is Your Life* presented Hanna's life simultaneously as an exceptional tale of personal victory over genocidal evil and a conventional girl-meets-boy-girl-loses-boy-girl-gets-boy story.

While the "Hanna Kohner" episode largely conformed to the ritualized format of *This Is Your Life*, it occasionally demonstrated that its producers regarded Hanna's story as being somehow singular. But it was not the only episode of the series to end with similar appeals for contributions to charities. Nor was it the only episode to call attention to a tragic world event. The 11 May 1955 episode of *This Is Your Life* honored Reverend Kiyoshi Tanimoto, a survivor of the atomic bomb dropped on Hiroshima at the end of World War II. Reverend Tanimoto was in the United States to raise funds that would enable the "Hiroshima Maidens," a group of twenty-five young women disfigured by the bomb blast, to receive plastic surgery.[8]

And yet, Edwards's mention of the exceptional "intensity" of Hanna's story and of the decision not to interrupt its telling with commercials signaled a special sensitivity to the subject. This gesture resembled the warnings to audiences that were sounded before the earliest presentations of the Holocaust in American newsreels. Moreover, the decision to move the sponsor's advertisements from their usual place in the structure of *This Is Your Life* for the "Hanna Kohner" episode foreshadowed future controversies over the "intrusion" of commercials into Holocaust dramas on television. Debates over the validity of Holocaust television have often focused on the presence of advertisements during these programs, and this is frequently invoked as epitomizing the incompatability between medium and message. On the occasion of the broadcast premiere of *Schindler's List* in 1997, NBC responded similarly to the question of advertising by airing the three-and-a-half-hour-long film without interruption; instead, it was framed by commercials for the broadcast's sponsor, Ford Motor Company.[9]

The "Hanna Kohner" episode of *This Is Your Life* is also a cultural artifact responsive to its time, especially to anxieties about cultural and political difference prevalent in cold war America. Although the program presented Hanna's story as one of special significance for Jews, its universal nature was emphasized in Edwards's appeal to viewers of "all creeds and races," for funds to aid Jewish refugees. Moreover, *This Is Your Life* repeatedly conceptualized Hanna's life as an American story. Edwards praised her as looking more like an American coed than a European Jewish victim of Nazi persecution, and he celebrated her story as the triumph of an American spirit, which "held out a friendly hand" to the heroine in "her darkest hour"—this despite the fact that Hanna was unable to follow Walter to the United States in the 1930s because of the nation's restrictive immigration policies. The solicitation of funds for the United Jewish Appeal, initiated by a contribution from Hazel Bishop, simultaneously validated American Jewry's corporate philanthropy and the power of American business to do good.[10]

In light of the UJA's participation, the "Hanna Kohner" episode can also be considered part of the extensive public relations efforts made during the early postwar years by a variety of agencies to promote the acceptance of DPs as American citizens. Many of these efforts stressed the parallel between the DPs' recent experiences and America's long history as a refuge for immigrants—some going so far as to describe DPs as "Delayed Pilgrims."[11] In addition, this was a time when Hollywood and the broadcast industry were under intense scrutiny by anti-Communist activists in both the federal government and the private sector. Therefore, praising Hanna's "loyalty and devotion to the land of [her] adoption" might be read in the spring of 1953—less than one month before the execution of "atom spies" Ethel and Julius Rosenberg—as an oblique defense of the patriotism of American Jews, including those who worked in the nation's entertainment industry, such as Hanna's husband and the program's producers, Axel Gruenberg and Alfred Paschall.[12]

At the same time, *This Is Your Life* manifests the preoccupation during the early cold war years with espionage. Indeed, the series depends on conspiracy and covert intelligence gathering for its realization. (More than once Hanna responded in astonishment to biographical details that Edwards imparted, exclaiming, "You know everything about me!") This is not a unique instance in early American television; the popular series *Candid Camera* (which aired, at one time or another, on ABC, CBS, and NBC from 1948 to 1953) also used television to expose private experience to the public. Despite his program's popularity—or, perhaps, precisely because of it—Edwards was frequently criticized for being insensitive to the individual's right of privacy. Even Edwards's friend Dwight Newton, media columnist for the *San Francisco Examiner,* excoriated *This Is Your Life* in print, writing that "it becomes cruelty when all the country is permitted to peer and peek into the private emotions of a private life."[13] Although the program was presented as a tribute to her, Hanna often appeared to be more its victim, the camera fixing on her face in extended close-ups throughout the broadcast. Edwards only nominally involved Hanna as an active participant in the proceedings, asking her occasional rhetorical questions to which she could give only the briefest of answers.

As media scholar Lynn Spigel has observed, the notion of television as an agent of surveillance appeared frequently in discussions of the medium during the postwar years.[14] In the mid-1950s sociologist Murray Hausknecht wrote that, while it does not constitute the first assault on privacy in the modern age, "the magic of television makes *voyeurs* of us all." Commenting on *Person to Person* (CBS, 1953–1961), an interview program in which host Edward Murrow visited from his television studio with celebrities in their homes via remote television cameras, Hausknecht observed that "within the context of the persistent cliché that television brings the world into our living room . . . , Mr. Murrow has hit upon the most intriguing variation of this theme: he brings other living rooms into ours." The same could be said of *This Is Your Life,* with its stage-set parlor and its changing casts of families and friends. Indeed, describing *Person to Person* as "merely the sugar-coated end of a continuum at the other end of which is *This Is Your Life* and [1950s quiz show] *Strike It Rich,*" Hausknecht wrote that on these programs "the boundaries between the public and the private sphere have disappeared," and he expressed concern that this invasion of privacy is linked to the increased pressure on individuals to conform to social disciplines.[15] By invading our own private worlds with the private worlds of others, he argued, television makes it harder to resist the internalization of social discipline. Thus, at the same time that it purported to celebrate the individual, Hausknecht would argue, *This Is Your Life* robbed its honorees of their privacy and undermined the notion of the private individual in general.

The idea that television's attempts to tell the story of ordinary individuals are perverted by the very nature of the medium was also explored at this time in Gerald Green's 1956 novel *The Last Angry Man.*[16] In this look behind the scenes of the production of a fictional television series, *Americans, U.S.A.* (which bears some resemblance to *This Is Your Life*), Green suggests that relating someone's genuine life history is beyond the powers of commercial television. (Green acquired his cynicism about the medium, presumably, as an industry insider; he worked as a producer for NBC's *Today* show in the 1950s. His subsequent credits include writing the script for the 1978 *Holocaust* miniseries, which, ironically, was attacked by critics for some of the problems Green had attributed to television in *The Last Angry Man*.)

But such reservations about the medium were not universally shared. The decision to honor Hanna Kohner on *This Is Your Life* evidently had the support of her family and friends, as well as the endorsement of a major American Jewish philanthropic organization. Nor did the program's producers or sponsor consider the subject of the Nazi persecution of European Jewry incompatible with the ritualistic, entertaining format of *This Is Your Life*. Indeed, the "Hanna Kohner" episode was evidently enough of a success for Edwards and his staff to produce at least five other broadcasts in which the series honored other Jewish survivors of Nazism, Jewish refugees, and individuals who rescued Jews from Nazi persecution.[17]

Moreover, the experience seems to have had a lasting impact on both Hanna and her husband, who years later presented their life histories in a book entitled *Hanna and Walter: A Love Story*.[18] Like the *This Is Your Life* broadcast, the book focuses on the period beginning with their first meeting in prewar Czechoslovakia and ending with their reunion in postwar Amsterdam. *Hanna and Walter* provides a considerable amount of information not mentioned on *This Is Your Life*. In addition to offering an extended account of Walter's life, there is more about Hanna, including the fact that she underwent an abortion while at Auschwitz. Nevertheless, the Kohners' memoir bears some resemblance to the presentation of their story as offered by Edwards on the television program.

In addition to structuring its overall narrative around their "love story," *Hanna and Walter* has a number of details in common with the telecast; this suggests something of how the exchange between the Kohners' family lore and the editorial selectivity of Edwards and his production staff shaped both the televised and written accounts. For example, in an early chapter of their memoir, the Kohners make references to Teplitz-Schönau's castle and its being the place where Wagner and Beethoven once composed some of their works, similar to the narration of the *This Is Your Life* broadcast. A later chapter of the book includes a description, similar to the one offered on television by Edwards, of Hanna seeing the countryside near her hometown from the train en route to Theresienstadt.

During the last decades of the twentieth century the advent of popular interest in the Holocaust, both as a subject in itself and as a moral paradigm, has transformed the status of Holocaust survivors. From objects of occasional curiosity during the early postwar period, they have since become much sought after as the bearers of memory, as witnesses to history, and as sources of insight into the historical experiences that they and other victims of Nazi persecution endured. In the 1980s and 1990s, American television has presented the stories of numerous Holocaust survivors in documentaries, dramas, news reports, and other types of programming. These broadcasts generally situate the survivor at the active center of the telling of his or her story and privilege the survivor's observations as unparalleled insights into the Holocaust.

In contrast, Hanna Kohner played a role in the televised telling of her personal history that was essentially passive, epitomized by Edwards repeatedly telling her, "This is your life." In more recent examples of Holocaust television, not only have survivors' words been accorded greater attention; each survivor has also been called upon to bear the onus of memorializing the millions of Holocaust victims through his or her individual recollections and insights. Instead, the presentation of Hanna Kohner's story on *This Is Your Life* was, true to the program's name, emphatically about living. The broadcast celebrated her endurance and that of her friends and family in a presentation unhaunted by anger, grief, or guilt over the millions of dead. American television's "most talked-about program" in 1953 offered Hanna's life as an extraordinary, moving tale of one Jewish woman's endurance of Nazi persecution. It was not, however, presented as a story of the Holocaust—a term, and a conceptualization of history, that did not yet exist in American public discourse.

three
The Theater of Our Century

Among television programs aired in the United States during the 1940s and 1950s, those that have most influenced how Americans understand the Holocaust are, arguably, dramas. These include original plays by such pioneering television playwrights as Paddy Chayefsky, Reginald Rose, and Rod Serling, and they feature performances by John Cassavetes, Charles Laughton, Robert Redford, and Maximilian Schell, among other renowned actors. These productions offered to American audiences some of the first portrayals of the Warsaw Ghetto uprising, Anne Frank's diary, and life and death in concentration camps.

These early television plays are now largely forgotten. Nevertheless, they remain formative landmarks of Holocaust drama, which has been an ongoing presence on American television more consistently than it has on the nation's stage or in film. For example, playwright Serling, actor Schell, and producer Herbert Brodkin first dealt with the Holocaust in their television work during the early postwar years and revisited the subject repeatedly over the course of their professional lives. Beyond leaving an imprint on individual careers, these dramas have had a pervasive impact on Americans' public remembrance of the Holocaust, familiarizing millions with a repertory of events, sites, characters, themes, and images. The dramatic mode of representing the Holocaust has informed other genres of media, and its influence extends to other forms of Holocaust commemoration, such as public ceremonies and museum installations.

The breadth of this influence rests on the powerful role that television has played in establishing what Raymond Williams termed the "dramatised society." Engendered by motion pictures and radio, this phenomenon burgeoned with the advent of television as a mass medium in the post–World War II era. Williams observed that, thanks to these media, "for the first time in human history, a majority of the population [has] regular and constant access to drama, beyond occasion or season." Moreover, drama "is built into the rhythms of everyday life," having become a "habitual experience"—indeed, a "basic need"—of modern life.[1]

In the early postwar years American television broadcasters quickly developed an approach to drama that was hailed as an innovative use of the new medium. Like television's other early dramas, its first plays dealing with the Holocaust focused on affect rather than context, on individuals rather than whole communities. These dramas offered viewers an understanding of the Nazi era through the histrionic demonstration of psychological insight, and the resolutions they presented of the Holocaust's moral dilemmas were modeled on the denouements of Western dramatic literary tradition. Despite changes in television drama over the years, especially the transition from live telecasts of studio productions to dramas prerecorded on location, the dramatic idiom that coalesced during the medium's early years has continued to shape more recent productions. Because of their formal accessibility as much as their extensive audiences, television dramas of the late 1970s, 1980s, and 1990s have informed more Americans' understandings of the Holocaust than any other representation of this subject. Consequently, other responses to the Holocaust, even those with alternative approaches, are obliged to reckon with assumptions rooted in television drama.

Extensive as their influence has been, the Holocaust dramas televised during the first postwar years also reflect the sensibilities of the period. In particular, they manifest a very different relationship between the Holocaust and the American Jewish community. The image of Jews in American Holocaust television dramas has changed over the years, responsive to the development of televsion drama as a forum for cultural politics. Thus, apart from their value as works of Holocaust remembrance, these dramas offer a telling measure of the position of Jews in mid-twentieth-century American public culture.

Prime-time Playhouses

Drama anthology series were at the forefront of American television's early successes, especially in the eyes of media critics. Gilbert Seldes, for example, hailed these series as being at the "top of the prestige pyramid" and as the medium's "most honorable accomplishments."[2] More than any other genre, the dramatic anthology series earned American television of the 1950s its much-vaunted status as a "golden age." These weekly series presented live performances of dramas — original scripts as well as adaptations of stage plays and works of fiction — during the evening hours that had become broadcasting's prime time.

By the early 1960s, live dramas had all but vanished from the networks' regular weekly broadcast schedule, eclipsed by the advent of episodic programming prerecorded on film or the new medium of videotape. Yet despite its brief heyday, live television drama continues to be cited as an early high-water mark of American television broadcasting. Having enabled the medium to achieve its first popular and critical successes while demonstrating a sensibility that distinguished it from radio, film, and theater, these series are still hailed as demonstrating "the real purpose behind the invention of the medium."[3]

Veteran television producer Fred Coe observed that the first postwar efforts to "bring Broadway to America via the television set" proved untenable.[4] However, broadcasters quickly conceived of the television play as a new dramatic genre. By the mid-1950s, a number of writers—Paddy Chayefsky, Horton Foote, Reginald Rose, Rod Serling, and Gore Vidal, among others—achieved renown for their television scripts. Unlike other writing for the medium, the original television play acquired the cachet of a serious art form. Collections of selected scripts were published, and television playwrights and critics philosophized in print on the nature of the new format. This special attention accorded to television plays has invited their consideration not merely as a component of corporate productions of popular culture, but as the artistic output of a single *auteur*.[5]

During the first postwar years, critics, producers, and writers alike saw in television drama singular opportunities for making personal statements. They regarded the speed with which television presented scripts to a growing national audience and the seeming immediacy of viewing television broadcasts as enabling a new kind of creativity. The distinctive aesthetic of the television drama was deemed ideal for examining individual, psychological responses to issues of topical relevance. Vidal, for example, praised television dramas' unrivaled ability to reach large audiences simultaneously: "If you did a good show on 'Philco,' you would walk down the street the next morning and hear people talking about your play. . . . Writers—at least my kind of writer—want as large an audience as [they] can possibly get, to do as much damage as they can to the things they think stand in want of correction to society."[6]

Central to its champions' notion of what made the television play novel and distinctive, even revolutionary, is the medium's intimate scale: the privacy of television viewing, primarily in the home; the small size of most television screens; and the limited proportions of early television studios. Television playwright and historian Erik Barnouw wrote that, as a result, "close-ups became all-important. . . . The human face became the stage on which drama was played."[7]

Television's small scale was regarded as less a limitation than a virtue, enabling a new kind of drama that, in Barnouw's words, "depends more on character than on action." Television, he argued, freed plays from the constraints of stage sets: "Cameras can be constantly on the prowl, showing us always new vistas and juxtapositions. . . . Objects and details of settings can swim into view at strategic moments, entering and leaving the spotlight like characters. . . . And television can, even within a single set, handle time more flexibly than the theatre." In one of Chayefsky's essays on the art of writing television drama, he made similar claims for the medium's virtues: "Scenes can be played as if the actors were unaware of the audience. The dialogue can sound as if it had been wiretapped." Authors of television plays "can write about the simplest things, the smallest incidents." Chayefsky saw the television drama as particularly appropriate to the self-reflexive spirit of the modern age: "These are strange and fretful times, and the huge inevitable currents of history are too broad now to provide individual people with any meaning to their lives. People are beginning to turn into themselves. . . . The jargon of introspection has become everyday conversation . . . , and the drama of introspection is the drama that the people want to see." Television, he suggested, "may well be the basic theater of our century."[8]

Chayefsky also pointed out what he considered to be the medium's limits, noting that "the big story is not for television," and that its "basic limitation . . . is time." Like other observers, he linked these limitations to the commercial nature of the medium—for example, the production of programs of uniform length, regularly punctuated by commercial breaks. At the same time, Chayefsky characterized coping with these commercially driven constraints as a valuable, formative experience: "Television is the greatest place to learn cutting because of the time limitations. They simply do not have time for indulgence. . . . My own rules are very simple rules. First, cut out all the wisdom; then cut out all the adjectives."[9]

Barnouw conceptualized the rapid rise and fall of live television drama in terms of a conflict between its aesthetic ideals—which he summed up, citing Chayefsky, as an attraction to the "marvelous world of the ordinary"—and the commercial nature of its venue:

> Most advertisers were selling magic. Their commercials posed the same problems that Chayefsky drama dealt with: people who feared failure in love and in business. But in the commercials there was always a solution as clear-cut as the snap of a finger. . . . Chayefsky and other anthology writers took these same problems and made them complicated. . . . It made the commercial seem fraudulent.[10]

As was the case with much of early television programming, sponsors wielded considerable influence over the production of these series, often directly controlling the content of programs. Many of the drama anthologies were underwritten by a single corporate sponsor, as their names indicate: *Philco Television Playhouse* (NBC, 1948–1955), *Lux Video Theatre* (CBS, 1950–1954; NBC, 1954–1957), and *The U.S. Steel Hour* (ABC,

1953–1955; CBS, 1955–1963), among others. Other series, notably *Playhouse 90* (CBS, 1956–1960), were among the first television programs with multiple sponsors, each of which bought commercial time from the network on a "spot" basis known as the "magazine format." Under this arrangement, advertisers and their agencies wielded less direct control over actual production, which went to the series producer, usually an employee of the network. Drama anthology series figured strategically in the emergence of the producer as the driving creative force in television programming. Veteran producers such as Herbert Brodkin, Fred Coe, Worthington Miner, and David Susskind did some of their earliest television work on these series.

These live anthology series were thus highly contested venues, where producers, underwriters, broadcasters, and critics vied for the control of television drama as a forum for artistic expression.[11] In addition to grappling with competing aesthetic criteria and with the relationship of sponsors to artistic issues, this struggle involved the efforts of individual dramatists, who strove to use the new medium for the "drama of introspection" as it addressed a rapidly expanding public.

Toward "Jewish Self-awareness": *The Offscreen Drama of Postwar American Jewry*

Jews were prominent among the writers and producers who sought to use this new American art form to explore their sense of self. Indeed, the newness of television and the opportunities it presented were emblematic of the signal changes American Jews experienced in the years immediately after World War II. Some of these changes Jews shared with many other Americans: large-scale movement from the working class to the middle class; extensive internal migration, especially from ethnic urban enclaves to more integrated suburban communities; rapid rise in religious affiliation, especially with large, corporate movements; and expanded access to professional, educational, and cultural opportunities that were previously restricted.

At the same time, American Jews experienced changes that set them apart from their fellow citizens: confronting the news of Nazi persecution of European Jewry and its consequences; watching the struggles to establish and maintain a viable Zionist state in Palestine; and realizing that America was now home to the world's largest and oldest continuous diaspora Jewish community, albeit by default. Literary critic Irving Howe described the life of American Jews at this time as "inherently 'schizoid.'" While they experienced "a growing sense of ease, comfort, security" at home, Europe loomed as the site of "the greatest horror in the history of mankind. . . .

How were these two elements of Jewish experience to be reconciled? The only honest answer was that they could not be."[12]

Indeed, American Jewish responses to their postwar circumstances were anything but uniform. Although generally characterized as a period of American Jewish silence on the Holocaust,[13] the immediate postwar years saw a considerable amount of activity in response to this as-yet-unnamed subject: pioneering historical scholarship, the writing of the first of hundreds of personal and communal memoirs, the establishment of the earliest memorials.[14] Most of these efforts were confined to the survivor, refugee, and immigrant Jewish communities.

At the same time, much of the public work of the American Jewish Committee, the American Jewish Congress, and the Anti-Defamation League of B'nai B'rith during this period offered a very different response to the Holocaust within their larger commitment to the intergroup relations movement. Historian Stuart Svonkin has noted that these and other American Jewish organizations played a leading role in the nation's "ecumenical effort to eliminate racial, religious and ethnic bigotry." During this heyday of American Jewry's "liberal universalism," these organizations conceptualized anti-Semitism—and the Holocaust, its most extreme consequence—as a "model prejudice, closely connected to all other forms of intolerance" and, moreover, as "a problem that could be solved, or at least alleviated, through propaganda, education, and legal action."[15]

These various responses to the Holocaust were situated within a larger cultural dynamic that poet and essayist Judd Teller characterized as "a shifting posture from Jewish self-consciousness to Jewish self-awareness." This change in sensibility was manifest in a wide range of cultural activities: the growth of organized religious movements proffering a distinctly American style of Judaism, major social science studies of American attitudes toward Jews and of the nation's Jewish communal and religious life, a spate of publications devoted to the "lost" culture of prewar East European Jewry, and the emergence of a new American Jewish literature that was neither "apologetic nor accusatory" but was in search of a "Jewish myth and Jewish idiom in which it might strike root."[16]

Postwar American television served as one venue for realizing this emergent self-awareness, in part by presenting some of American Jewry's earliest efforts to deal with the Holocaust in large, mainstream public forums. Here, too, the response was not consistent. While Jews were no more than a peripheral presence in most of the first documentaries on American television that dealt with the Holocaust, Jewishness figured much more centrally in early dramas on the subject. At the same time, Jewish identity and its relation to the Holocaust did not appear as forthrightly during the early postwar years as it has in more recent presentations of the Holocaust on

American television. Rather, the subject was broached more circumspectly, reflecting anxieties that some of television's first playwrights and producers shared with many of their fellow Jews over their public place in postwar America. Indeed, the struggle over the significance of Jewish identity became the central conflict in a number of early Holocaust dramas.

At the same time, the subject of the Holocaust raised particular challenges for the new genre of television drama: How to relate an event of vast proportions in a medium regarded as ill-suited to "the big story"? How to deal with the moral complexities raised by the subject in a medium that writers feel requires them to "cut out all the wisdom"? How to present a Jewish story, especially one about anti-Semitism, to an audience largely composed of non-Jews, during a period when American Jews are particularly circumspect about being distinguished as Jews? How to tell a story involving the complex particulars of European history, politics, and society to American viewers, especially in a medium understood as demanding brevity and simplicity?

A Test of Faith: Holiday Song

Paddy Chayefsky's *Holiday Song,* presented on *Philco Television Playhouse* on 14 September 1952, is perhaps best recalled as the first hour-long television script by "the first playwright to achieve fame through the television medium."[17] It is also one of the earliest television dramas to feature survivors of the Holocaust among its characters and to deal, albeit obliquely, with the American Jewish response to the destruction of European Jews.

Chayefsky situated the Holocaust on the drama's periphery; his script centers on the question of affirming religious faith in a postwar American Jewish community. The play begins with a crisis of belief experienced on the day before Rosh Hashanah by Leon Sternberger (played by Joseph Buloff), the pious cantor of a suburban Long Island congregation. Following an act of anti-Semitic vandalism on his synagogue, the cantor becomes despondent, wondering, "What sort of a God is it who would allow this?"[18] Sternberger announces to his friend Zucker (Herbert Berghof) and his niece Naomi (Frances Chaney) that he has lost his faith in God and cannot lead his congregation in prayer when the Jewish New Year begins the following day.

At the others' urging, Sternberger takes a train to New York City to consult with Rabbi Marcus, a respected sage. The cantor becomes confused in the unfamiliar subway station and, after asking a subway guard for directions to the city, winds up on a Brooklyn-bound subway. The only other passenger is a young woman (Irja Jensen) who is about to attempt suicide. Sternberger stops her from jumping off the train car and takes her back to her apartment, where she reveals that she is a survivor of Auschwitz, living

Cantor Sternberger (played by Joseph Buloff, right) seeks the advice of the rabbi (David Kerman) on how to deal with a crisis of faith in Paddy Chayefsky's *Holiday Song*, aired on *Philco Television Playhouse* in 1952. (Globe Photos, Inc.)

without her parents or her husband, whom she believes to have died during the war.

The cantor returns home, his mission unfulfilled, and goes to his syna-gogue to tell the rabbi (David Kerman) to find another cantor for the upcoming holiday service. The rabbi insists that Sternberger return to New York and discuss his problem with Rabbi Marcus. Once more the cantor sets out for New York; once more the subway guard misdirects him and he winds up on the line to Brooklyn. Again he meets a solitary passenger—a man (Werner Klemperer). Also a recently arrived émigré, he is looking for his wife, who had been interned in Auschwitz while he was in a labor camp. Sternberger realizes the man must be the husband of the woman he met earlier. He finds a telephone, calls the woman, and reunites the couple. When he returns to the train station, the cantor discovers that the guard who misdirected him earlier is no longer there—nor, in fact, was anyone who fits the guard's description working there all day. Sternberger recognizes that his encounter with the two survivors was an act of providence. His faith in God restored, he returns to his family and congregation to celebrate the arrival of the new year.

Chayefsky adapted *Holiday Song* from "It Happened on the Brooklyn Subway," a 1949 *Reader's Digest* feature labeled a "Drama in Real Life," which relates an actual chance encounter that led to the reunion of two Holocaust survivors. Chayefsky transformed the original incident into a drama about faith restored by recasting the original hero, a Hungarian-born photographer named Marcel Sternberger, as a cantor. In his preface to the published script, Chayefsky explained that the original story

> has only one dramatic meaning, and this is: there is a God. . . . If in the beginning of the play there was a character who didn't believe in God, then this incident could prove to him that there is a God. Of course, the character would have to be someone who would accept such a symbolic interpretation of the incident. . . . So then he must be a deeply religious man who has lost his faith.[19]

This transformation also enabled Chayefsky to situate the story more explicitly in a contemporary American Jewish community. In the *Reader's Digest* piece the Jewishness of the people involved went unmentioned. But the playwright's decision to (re)Judaize his protagonist was not a straightforward process. David Susskind, then a member of the *Philco Television Playhouse* production staff, reportedly told Chayefsky that his script was "'too Jewish' and urged him to rewrite the central character as a priest or minister." Chayefsky reluctantly acquiesced, only to have series producer Fred Coe later urge him to change the protagonist back to a Jewish cleric. Chayefsky subsequently described the decision to make Sternberger a cantor as circumstantial, almost involuntary, and yet connected to his own identity and ongoing artistic interests: "I happen to be Jewish, and my understanding of the religious emotion is limited to the Jewish ritual, so my leading character automatically became Jewish."[20]

Just as the playwright characterized his hero's Jewishness (and his own?) as incidental to *Holiday Song,* so does the Holocaust figure as an oblique presence in the drama. Though the Nazi persecution of European Jewry represents a powerful, extreme moral breach in the script, it is alluded to only vaguely and elliptically. As embodied by the two survivors, the Holocaust has a ghostly presence in Chayefsky's script. Originally the central figures in the *Reader's Digest* feature, the author makes them nameless, barely articulate phantoms. They are reminiscent in manner, if not in appearance, of the ghostly image of concentration camp survivors shown in the newsreels reporting their liberation. In *Holiday Song* the survivors exist as agents of a divine drama demonstrating that the redemptive power of God still exists. Chayefsky's play centers not on the survivors' stories but on the lives of American Jews, both immigrants and their children, and on their concerns with maintaining Jewish community and family life.

The redemptive, life-affirming conclusion of *Holiday Song* may exemplify what literary scholar Lawrence Langer has characterized as a distinctively—and problematically—"American vision of the Holocaust," which insists on "solace," "redeeming truth," and "hope that so many millions may not have died in vain," while evincing a "deafness" to "the horror."[21] In more recent years, much of American Holocaust television has focused increasingly on its horrors. But *Holiday Song* and other early television dramas appear to have responded to a quite different need: not so much remembering the events of the Holocaust as ameliorating its immediate consequences. At the end of the twentieth century, concern that younger generations are ignorant of the Holocaust motivates much of its memory culture. But during the first years after the end of World War II, few took comfort in their temporal proximity to this catastrophe. Chayefsky's *Holiday Song* offered solace with a story of faith lost and restored, affirming the redemptive power of the divine in the face of what might well have been seen as overwhelming evidence to the contrary.

What's in a Name: Walk Down the Hill

As prime-time anthology series grew more adventurous in the late 1950s, the Holocaust appeared both more prominently and with greater frequency in American television dramas. *Playhouse 90,* widely regarded as the most ambitious of the drama anthologies, presented an average of one Holocaust-related drama for each of its five seasons.

Several of these dramas approached the Holocaust through an American connection. *The Refugee* (NBC's *Matinee Theatre,* 1956), based on a story by Thelma Nurenberg, explored American anti-Semitism and its links to anti-Communism through a romance between a non-Jewish American veteran of World War II and a half-Jewish survivor of a concentration camp. *The Ransom of Sigmund Freud* (*Matinee Theatre,* 1956) portrayed the renowned psychoanalyst's escape from Vienna with the help of an American student and the intercession of President Roosevelt. *Playhouse 90's Homeward Borne* (1957) dramatized Ruth Chatterton's novel about an American family's adoption of a young European Jewish refugee.[22] These plays also evinced a growing interest in the Holocaust as a paradigmatic, rather than merely topical, subject for a drama. The Holocaust often provided a venue for examining more general issues, such as the nature of identity or the appropriate response to stigmatization and persecution. Even when situated in Nazi-run ghettos or camps, these dramas spoke more to contemporary American life than to the war years in Europe.

For example, the personal struggles of an American Jew with the significance of his Jewishness is at the center of a play cited as "the first television drama about a concentration camp."[23] In fact, Nazi concentration camps figure only offscreen in Ernest Kinoy's *Walk Down the Hill,* presented by CBS's *Studio One* on 18 March 1957.[24] Set in a German prisoner-of-war camp during World War II, the drama examines the challenges of being stigmatized as a Jew in terms that apply more to the situation of Jews in mid-twentieth-century America than to their contemporaries in Europe.

Walk Down the Hill focuses on the plight of American POWs in one of the camp's barracks, especially their barracks leader, Private Bernard Linton (played by William Smithers). Linton and another barracks leader, Private Al Rossi (Don Gordon), inform the men that the German officers will not distribute food rations until all POWs are registered. The camera pans around the crowded barracks and cuts to close-ups of the men—hungry, cold, and ill, some of them so weak that they need to be fed by others.

John Wills (David Lewis), an older man who taught philosophy in a university before entering the army, listens as Linton confesses his anxiety about being registered. The Germans are supposed to ask only for name, rank, and serial number, notes another prisoner. Linton considers their dog tags and reads his aloud, including the letter *H*, which stands for *Hebrew*. "You know, that's officially me," Linton muses. "It's amazing, boy, how quickly the sounds stop meaning anything at all. It's the first thing the army did—they nail your name on you . . . a convenient handle to grab you with."

As the POWs line up to be registered, the chaplain (Lonny Chapman) informs them that, in defiance of the Geneva Convention, the Germans are asking for the soldiers' army unit, next of kin, and religion. This last item causes consternation among the Jewish POWs. Goldstein (Stefan Gierasch) comments that when he tells the Germans his name, he's as good as told them his religion. When Wills asks Linton if he's concerned about the *H* on his dog tag, Linton replies that his last name "sounds neutral"; then he mentions seeing "those men at the rail yards, with the concentration camp stripe and the star," adding cynically that their destination is not "the reservation desk of a fancy hotel." Later, when the Germans ask for his religion, Linton answers "Protestant"; the word is punctuated by a harsh blare of brass on the sound track. Once outside, Linton surreptitiously drops his dog tags in the snow.

William Smithers, Don Gordon, and David Lewis (foreground, left to right), as American soldiers in a German POW camp, grapple with the consequences of anti-Semitism in Ernest Kinoy's *Walk Down the Hill,* presented on *Studio One* in 1957. (CBS Photo Archive.)

Back in the barracks, Rossi announces the commander will not distribute rations until all Jewish POWs are relocated to Barracks 39. Rossi reads the commander's list of registered Jews and those "he thinks have Jewish names": Goldstein, Cohen, and others are named, but Linton is not. Cohen (David Mason) remarks that being put on such a list is "like taking a perfectly ordinary word and suddenly saying it's dirty." Goldstein comments wryly on their possible fate by recalling a joke that his father told him when he was drafted. He translates its Yiddish punchline: " '*Denkst ikh bin meshuge? Kenst derharget vern dort!*'—You think I'm crazy? You can get killed out there!"

Later, Wills and Linton go to visit the Jewish POWs in their separate barracks, where they hold services for the beginning of the Sabbath. One of the POWs leads the service, chanting blessings over candles, wine, and bread. Then he recites the Kaddish, the prayer traditionally said by mourners in memory of deceased relatives, "for the men in the division who got it before we were captured." The camera pans out from the middle of the circle of men praying to Wills and Linton, eventually closing in on Linton's face, as string music swells on the sound track.

Back in the first barracks, Linton tells the chaplain that he's worried about the soldiers in Barracks 39; he confesses that he registered with the Germans as a Protestant and explains that his is "not a Jewish name." The chaplain attempts to offer Linton spiritual counsel—"I suppose anyone would feel doubt if he thought he was denying his faith"—but Linton explains that his is not a question of a religious commitment to being a Jew: "That's not a part of me. . . . Does God want a man forced into faith with a loaded pistol at his head?" The chaplain, concerned but confused, apologizes to Linton for not being able to help him.

Rossi reports that the Germans are sending some of the POWs from the camp to an unknown destination. In addition to using the opportunity to get rid of "undesirables" and "troublemakers," the camp commander put all of the POWs in Barracks 39 on the list of men to be shipped out. Rossi adds that he was told to put one name from this barracks on the list as well, and that he chose Lawton (Frank Sutton), a POW earlier accused of stealing from other prisoners. "Nobody knows what's gonna happen to those guys," Lawton protests, and he asks why Rossi didn't pick Linton, claiming that he should be "down in the Jewish barracks anyway."

Rossi assures a troubled Linton that no one expects him to join the other Jewish POWs if it is avoidable. Wills also urges Linton to stay: "You don't have to be pushed into something your mind can't believe because of . . . some kind of primitive guilt down in the glands." But Linton admits that, in part, Lawton's accusation has persuaded him that "it's easy to disguise cowardice as intellectual independence." He tells Wills that the service that they attended in Barracks 39 is somehow "mine—even if I don't know the words . . . , even if I don't want to know them. It has nothing to do with theology. I'm part of those people. . . . I don't know why exactly, but I'm going down there—I'm a Jew." Linton makes his way to the door through the crowded barracks. The camera cuts to a shot of Linton walking outside, following him as he walks down the hill to Barracks 39, as the drama concludes.

The POW camp in *Walk Down the Hill* figures as a forum for debating the appropriate response to larger events that are set in motion and take place beyond its boundaries. The close confines of the barracks setting intensifies the intimate scale of the dramatic action. Much of the play is filmed in close-up or in deep-focus shots that juxtapose a foregrounded individual with others in the background. For example, one scene concludes as Catholic soldiers make a novena on behalf of the Jewish POWs who have been segregated. As they recite the rosary, the camera cuts away to a series of close-up shots of various men in their bunks, who either chant along with them or stare silently toward the camera. The final shot shows the men kneeling in prayer, behind a close-up of an anxious Linton.

Kinoy's drama of conflicting philosophies and personalities set within this tight, closed setting recalls *Stalag 17,* the popular Broadway play (1951) and Hollywood film (1953) about American soldiers in a German POW camp.[25] The particular ordeals faced by Linton and his fellow prisoners in *Walk Down the Hill* also resemble the experiences of some actual Jewish GIs — including, perhaps, the playwright himself, who was an American POW interned in a slave labor camp in Berga, Germany, during the war. Details in Kinoy's script match the recollections of other American Jewish POWs in Nazi custody, who recall being forced to identify themselves as Jews, being segregated from other prisoners, and sometimes hiding their dog tags to escape detection as Jews.[26]

Moreover, *Walk Down the Hill* places American Jews in a situation that parallels the plight of many European Jewish communities living under Nazi rule: first stigmatized, then segregated, and finally deported to an unknown destination and an uncertain fate. Linton's pointed reference to "men at the rail yards, with the concentration camp stripe and the star" articulates the connection. It is questionable whether a private in the United States Army would ever have witnessed such a scene before the final days of the war. Rather, Linton's remark evokes an image much more likely to be familiar and powerfully resonant for an American television audience in 1957; by then, many viewers would have seen the Signal Corps footage of liberated concentration camps in newsreels or documentaries.

But while the ordeal faced by the American Jewish POWs in Kinoy's drama evokes the experiences of European Jews under Nazi persecution, Linton's response resembles the struggles of contemporary American Jews with the problematics of identity. His ability to "pass" as a gentile, and the moral consequences of his decision to do so, revisits a theme explored most famously during the early postwar years in the 1947 Hollywood film *Gentleman's Agreement,* based on Laura Z. Hobson's novel about American anti-Semitism, in which characters uncomfortably straddle the boundaries between Jew and non-Jew.[27] By focusing on Linton's dilemma of whether or not to declare himself a Jew, Kinoy places the arbitrariness of Jewish identity at the center of the drama.

In this respect, *Walk Down the Hill* recalls anthropologist Melville Herskovits's discussions of the problematics of Jewish identity in the middle decades of the twentieth century. In his 1927 article "When Is a Jew a Jew?" he reflected on his own attenuated sense of Jewishness in the American context. Pursuing a "Jewish least common denominator," Herskovits exhausted a series of paradigms — race, national group, linguistic group, religion, culture, character — before concluding that there may be no more satisfactory definition than a self-reflexive equation of the identity with the act of identification: "*A Jew is a person who calls himself a Jew, or who is called Jewish by others.*" Herskovits reiterated this in a second essay on Jewish identity, which appeared in 1949: While noting that Jews "represent a historic continuum" and "have survived as an identifiable, yet constantly shifting series of groups," he concluded that "no word . . . means more things to more people that does the word 'Jew.'"[28] Similarly, the protagonist of *Walk Down the Hill* contemplates the meaning of Jewishness as a spiritual, ethnic, familial, or communal identity, only to conclude that the act of voluntarily calling himself a Jew — his final words in the drama — is its ultimate significance.

Language — in particular, the arbitrary nature of signification — figures strategically in Kinoy's exploration of the question of Jewish identity, which is first articulated through personal names. Goldstein and Cohen are avowedly Jewish by virtue of their behavior and conviction, but also by dint of names that leave no doubt in their minds, or the minds of others, as to their identity. Linton's sense of self as a Jew is as ambivalent as his surname, which he regards as an ambiguous sign of the Jewish identity thrust upon him. Cohen and Goldstein also perform their Jewishness linguistically, especially through their use of Hebrew and Yiddish to pray, tell jokes, explain rituals, and describe home life (at one point, for example, Cohen reminisces about how his mother cooked *kugel* and *tsimmes*). Throughout the play Cohen and Goldstein gloss their use of Jewish languages for Linton's benefit — and, of course, for many in the television audience. Ultimately, Linton transcends the limitations of language as a link to anti-Semitic stigmatization and internal parochialism. His final embrace of Jewishness comes even though he doesn't "know the words," but as a response to something nonverbal and nonrational — what Wills derides, perhaps with a hint of anti-Semitism, as "primitive guilt down in the glands."

Like *Holiday Song*, *Walk Down the Hill* responds to the same need for an amelioration of recent memories of the Holocaust, albeit with a secular vision of redemption. Here the protagonist transcends the historical context of the Holocaust to defy what many viewers know to be its consequences through a symbolically heroic act. Although based on actual wartime experiences, *Walk Down the Hill* presents the American Jewish viewer with the fantasy of choosing to be a noble victim of history — rather than an anxious, self-interested bystander, who survives by denying his Jewishness — regardless of how nominal or ambivalent one's identity as a Jew might be.

"All Things to All Men":
In the Presence of Mine Enemies

The arbitrary nature of identity figures centrally in other American Holocaust television dramas of the late 1950s. Irving Gaynor Neiman's adaptation of Michel del Castillo's autobiographical novel *Child of Our Time*
(*Playhouse 90, 1959*) follows young Tanguy Legrand during World War II
and the immediate postwar years as he moves from being mistaken for a
Jew, and imprisoned in a German concentration camp, to an orphanage,
where he is falsely suspected of being a Communist.[29] The following year,
Rod Serling examined the same issue in one of American television's earliest
dramatizations of the Warsaw Ghetto uprising. Aired on 18 May 1960, *In
the Presence of Mine Enemies* was the last new drama broadcast by *Playhouse 90*.[30] Serling's play transformed the Warsaw Ghetto, which had been
identified during the war years as a definitive locus for Holocaust memory
culture, into a forum for exploring the arbitrary nature of identity and the
ethics of spiritual versus physical resistance. This tension is reflected in the
stylistic dissonance between the heightened language of Serling's play and
its squalid setting. Unlike Chayefsky's "wiretapped" dialogue, the text of *In
the Presence of Mine Enemies* is self-reflexive and, like its biblical title (a
citation from Psalms 23:5), elevated in tone. The physical production of
Serling's drama evoked the crowdedness and poverty of the ghetto in a
maze of tight, dingy rooms, twisting staircases, and narrow passageways.[31]

Typical of Serling's other early television plays, *In the Presence of Mine
Enemies* centers on a unifying moral issue. The drama's characters present
the relationships among Jews, their German captors, and their Polish neighbors as a study in the ethical implications of racial intolerance and self-
hatred. The central character, Rabbi Adam Heller (played by Charles
Laughton), is both a spiritual leader within the ghetto and the focal figure
of the drama's moral debates. The elderly rabbi lives with his children,
Rachel (Susan Kohner) and Paul (Arthur Kennedy), both young adults. The
passivity of the rabbi's commitment to traditional spirituality and piety is
juxtaposed against the activism of his son, a member of the ghetto's resistance movement. Heller and his son also clash over the rabbi's relationship
with Josef Chinik (Oscar Homolka), a Pole, who steals into the ghetto to
bring his old friend food and play chess with him. Paul denounces their
friendship in light of the Poles' history of anti-Semitism and their current
indifference to Jewish suffering: "They were killing Jews in Poland long
before Germany was a country; they made an art of it."

The relationships between Jews and Germans are examined through two
German characters, Captain Richter (George Macready) and Sergeant Lott
(Robert Redford). Disturbed by the sergeant's apparent reluctance to treat

Jews with sufficient harshness, Richter explains to Lott the "morality" of anti-Semitism as a "clue to survival. Nations can feed on it, they find their strength in it. . . . But there must be an object of hatred. Suddenly, in front of us, out steps a Jew. He can be all things to all men—moneylender, Communist, world banker, revolutionist—an unassimilated foreigner in our midst. And so we hate him, and in the process we are unified."

The captain, alluding to his sexual needs, orders Lott to bring the rabbi's daughter to him, and the sergeant reluctantly complies. When Paul learns that Rachel has been raped, he leaves the ghetto to seek revenge. The rabbi, stunned by the news, experiences a crisis of faith. Richter is found strangled to death, and German officers enter the ghetto to apprehend his killer, who was seen returning to the building where the rabbi lives. Josef decides to sacrifice his own life to save the rabbi and his family. "*Mea culpa,* my sin," Josef explains. "The sin of every human being who has ever hated another, or the identical sin of standing by as a witness to hatred, saying nothing, doing nothing." With this he leaves the rabbi's home, announces that he is the murderer, and is shot dead.

After a series of mass deportations from the ghetto, Paul tells his father that the resistance movement will soon start their uprising. Lott returns to see Rachel. Telling her that he knows of the imminent revolt, he offers to rescue her from the ghetto's destruction by leading her to safety through the city's sewers. Lott asks Rachel and the rabbi for their forgiveness and declares his love for her: "If things were different, if there were not a war . . . , if we were just two people, Rachel, who met, . . . I am not a German, and you are not a Jew, . . . I shall tell you that we would have fallen in love."

Paul returns home and, seeing the German officer, attacks him. Rachel separates them, and the rabbi points an accusing finger at his son, denouncing his hatred: "You look for Nazis? How about this one! . . . He's the one who must be the Nazi; there's no one else in the room except victims, . . . except the young one who finds it in his heart to help us." The rabbi explains to Paul that Rachel is pregnant from the rape—"but it is a life, and this is precious"—and therefore, Rachel should try to escape. At his father's request, Paul joins the rabbi in wishing her a "safe journey and the protection of God." Rachel and Lott depart, arm in arm.

Gunfire signals the start of the uprising, and Paul takes up his rifle. The rabbi joins his son, picking up a holy book, proclaiming that "faith is a weapon, too. And we have never lacked for faith—not in this ghetto, nor in the thousands of ghettos before this." The sound of gunshots mixes with the chanting of the hymn "Ani ma'amin" (first heard at the drama's opening) as the scene fades to black.[32]

Serling's earlier works for *Playhouse 90* had been among the most highly praised productions in the series, especially *Requiem for a Heavyweight*

Set in the Warsaw Ghetto, Rod Serling's *In the Presence of Mine Enemies,* presented on *Playhouse 90* in 1960, examines the nature of identity and the origins of intolerance. The cast includes (from left to right) Arthur Kennedy as Paul Heller, Charles Laughton as Rabbi Adam Heller, Susan Kohner as Rachel Heller, and Robert Redford as Sergeant Lott. (CBS Photo Archive.)

(1956) and *The Comedian* (1957), each of which earned the author an Emmy award for television writing. Yet *In the Presence of Mine Enemies* proved a controversial finale to *Playhouse 90*'s roster of original dramas. Both network censors and the program's sponsors found the subject "too downbeat, too violent, and too dated." Serling's play was reportedly produced only because a strike by the Writers Guild of America had left the series with no other scripts ready for production.[33]

The telecast of *In the Presence of Mine Enemies* also generated controversy, as Jack O'Brian observed in his review for the *New York Journal-American*: "Some felt it was too grim . . . a memory to be dangled where light entertainment is king. Others felt it was a reminder properly always in season, a case history of despair and evil." Serling's script drew considerable negative response, especially for "the gross indecency of including a sympathetic Nazi."[34] Among those who objected to the drama was author

Leon Uris, who denounced it as "an insult and defamation of the Jewish people. . . . The historical inaccuracies, the caricature of characterization and absolute false conflicts were a crying deception of the public. Joseph Goebbels himself could not have produced such a piece of Nazi apologetics." Uris demanded that the network destroy the film and "publicly apologize for the scandal."

In his response to Uris, Serling explained that "he never intended to provide a history lesson, only tell a human tale."[35] Indeed, his script makes generous use of archetypal characters and situations—especially the love interest between a young, attractive, persecuted Jewish woman and a noble-minded gentile man, à la Sir Walter Scott's *Ivanhoe*—to create a universalized moral reading of life and death in the Warsaw Ghetto. Serling also strips of its historicity virtually all discussion of the nature of racial hatred, the oppression it generates, and the ensuing responses of both the oppressed and the bystanders who witness it. The ideological milieu of traditional Christian anti-Semitism, Fascist nationalism, and Aryan race science in which the Nazis' anti-Jewish doctrines were forged goes unmentioned. Rather, by distilling specific social conflicts to yield universal moral lessons, Serling's script suggests that anyone could be either a persecutor or a victim.

Toward this end, the playwright characterizes ethnic identity—whether Jewish, Polish, or German—as arbitrary. In one of the play's first scenes, Rachel reminds her father to wear his armband, on which a Star of David is printed, as he prepares to go out into the street. "Of course," he jokes wryly. "How else would anyone know I was Jewish?" When Josef first sneaks into the ghetto he puts on a similar armband to avoid being arrested by German officers. The script extends this image of identity as superficial, something literally worn on one's sleeve, to Nazism. When Paul speaks of his desire for vengeance, his father responds, "I have a son now who talks like a Nazi? I have a son who wears a swastika?" to which Paul replies, "Fine! Let the Nazi wear the Star of David. Let him rot in the ghetto!" Serling reiterates this relativization of identities in characters' discussions of the nature of racism: Richter's dehistoricized "morality of hating Jews," Josef's universalized declaration of "*mea culpa,*" Lott's idealized vision of meeting Rachel in a world without racial distinctions.

The casting of Laughton and Kennedy as the rabbi and his son underscored this sense of ethnic identity as arbitrary. This was especially the case with Laughton's performance; though costumed and made up to look something like an observant East European Jew, the actor made no attempt to simulate an analogous accent or gestures. Instead, he gave his character a rhetorical largesse that owed more to the conventions of the British stage and to Laughton's own distinctive on-screen persona than to any effort at verisimilitude. Yet elsewhere the production relied on ethnic archetypes. Homolka's delivery was inflected with a Slavic intonation, while Macready and Redford affected German accents. Complementing Redford's blond good looks, Kohner was an archetypical dark "beautiful Jewess."[36]

Serling's abstracted treatment of Nazi anti-Semitism and its consequences in the Warsaw Ghetto may have been responsive to larger contextual issues: broadcasters' concerns about reaching an ever-expanding national television audience, or the apprehensions of Jews in the American television industry about appearing to be particularist. In addition, *In the Presence of Mine Enemies* resonated with concerns particular to the playwright himself, who had a complicated, ambivalent sense of self as a Jew. The son of Jewish parents, Serling joined the Unitarian Church as an adult and was married to a non-Jew. His biographers have described the subtle anti-Semitism that pervaded Serling's hometown of Binghamton, New York, as having been a formative influence. One biographer observed that, "while never ashamed of his Jewish background, Serling felt it was important not to be categorized as a Jew." In Serling's family "there would have been no other reason to talk about . . . what it meant to be a Jew had it not been for the events in Germany. He understood Jewishness almost solely because of his father's regular tirades about Hitler and the growing Nazi threat."[37]

Undaunted by the negative reactions to *In the Presence of Mine Enemies,* Serling reexamined Jewish responses to Nazi anti-Semitism in subsequent works for television. In keeping with his interest in extracting moral issues from the Holocaust, Serling revisited the subject after he had moved from the gritty verism of early television drama to the otherworldly realm of *The Twilight Zone.* The Holocaust proved an even more enduring inspiration for Herbert Brodkin, the producer of *Walk Down the Hill, Child of Our Time,* and *Judgment at Nuremberg,* as he turned to other television genres, including the episodic series *The Defenders,* the miniseries *Holocaust,* and the made-for-television movie *Skokie.* Brodkin's Holocaust dramas contributed to his reputation as a seminal figure in American television broadcasting, especially as a "producer of the provocative." A 1985 tribute to his career hailed him as a "major architect" of television's "Golden Age" who pioneered the presentation of "controversial subject matter" and as a "dedicated man who thumbs his nose at censors and ratings-watchers and definitely marches to a different drummer." Like the hero of many an American television drama, Brodkin was championed as the lone individual fighting established, institutional forces for his principles, among which was his belief in the morally transformative power of television. Indeed, Brodkin himself described his work in the medium as "a matter of using it not only to entertain the world but to save the world."[38]

The Sunday Ghetto

During the years that drama became a celebrated fixture of American television's prime time, plays were also aired at other, less prominent hours in the weekly broadcast schedule. Of special importance for Holocaust remembrance are dramas produced for ecumenical series shown during the daytime on Sundays: *Directions* (ABC, 1960–1984), *The Eternal Light* (NBC, 1958–1985), *Frontiers of Faith* (NBC, 1951–1970), *Lamp Unto My Feet* (CBS, 1948–1979), and *Look Up and Live* (CBS, 1954–1979). The aesthetics of Holocaust dramas presented on these series resembled those shown on prime-time playhouses—in fact, some playwrights wrote scripts for both venues. Yet the particular circumstances of their production and the context in which they were presented enabled those dramas written for ecumenical series to make distinctive statements about the Holocaust, identifying it as a powerful moral exemplar for America's postwar ecumenism.

Beginning in the early postwar years, ecumenical series were a staple of the commercial networks' public service broadcasting for decades. Produced by television networks in collaboration with theologians, rather than commercial sponsors, these programs epitomized the American broadcasting industry's efforts to demonstrate their commitment to the public interest by presenting programs that edify rather than entertain. Along with news analysis, public affairs, and other cultural programming, these series were aired on Sunday morning and afternoon, not only because of the day's traditional association with spiritual reflection, but also because this was a period in the networks' weekly schedules that had proved to be relatively unprofitable during the heyday of radio broadcasting. Within the television industry this time period came to be known as the "Sunday ghetto."[39]

The networks produced and underwrote programming for their ecumenical series in conjunction with mainstream Protestant, Catholic, and Jewish institutions. The leading coproducer of Jewish broadcasts during the early postwar decades was the Jewish Theological Seminary (JTS), the rabbinical academy and intellectual center of the Conservative movement, which was then the fastest-growing branch of organized Judaism in the United States. JTS's first regular venture into broadcasting was the weekly radio series *The Eternal Light,* which NBC began airing in 1944. From the late 1940s through the early 1980s, the seminary also coproduced hundreds of episodes for ecumenical television series shown on ABC, CBS, and NBC, including a televised version of its radio series.

During the early postwar years the Jewish episodes of these ecumenical series constituted the one venue where Jews and topics of Jewish interest were presented regularly and forthrightly on American television. The series offered original dramas as well as musical performances, interviews, and panel discussions, and dealt with a wide range of subjects: Jewish history from biblical times to the present; traditional Jewish ritual and lore; biographies of Jews accomplished in the sciences, politics, and other fields; the work of modern Jewish artists, musicians, and authors; and reflections on ethical issues of general concern to contemporary Americans.

Uniting these diverse subjects and genres was an overarching commitment to the ideals of America's postwar ecumenism. For Jews, this meant demonstrating that Jewish particularism, whether realized in ancient rites or modern history, is incidental to the fundamental universalism of Judaism, and that Jewish values and principles are compatible with those of all other Americans. Addressed to non-Jewish viewers at least as much as to Jews, JTS's broadcasts portrayed American Jews as loyal and well-integrated fellow citizens. Through the domestic media of radio and television, Jews in effect invited themselves into the homes of their gentile neighbors for a Sunday social call.[40]

By involving the talents of contemporary writers, composers, choreographers, and performers (both Jewish and non-Jewish), these broadcasts also strove to demonstrate that American Jewry's heritage could be presented with dignity and taste in performances that validated the compatibility of religion and "high" art. In 1947 Rabbi Louis Finklestein, president of JTS, hailed the artists and religious scholars that ecumenical broadcasting had brought together in order to "co-operate to translate ancient, abstract ideas into effective modern dramatics" and thereby pioneer a new mode of religious expression.[41]

The complex of agendas at work in ecumenical broadcasting posed particular challenges for creating dramas that deal with the Holocaust. In addition to the difficulty of presenting so disturbing a subject in a venue committed to respectability, there was the daunting task of discussing the origins and consequences of anti-Semitism in an ecumenical venue self-consciously committed to promoting tolerance. Even so, some early Holocaust dramas presented in the "Sunday ghetto" dealt with the issue of Jewish identity in terms similar to plays then aired during prime time.

"Being Myself, Being a Jew": Anne Frank: The Diary of a Young Girl

Ecumenical broadcasting's distinctive response to the Holocaust was already evident in one of JTS's earliest telecasts—Morton Wishengrad's *Anne Frank: The Diary of a Young Girl*, which was presented on *Frontiers of Faith* on 16 November 1952. Aired only a few months after the diary was published in English translation, this half-hour play was the first

American dramatic presentation of the life and writings of the Jewish victim of Nazism who would become most familiar to the nation's television audiences through an array of documentaries and dramas. Wishengrad's adaptation of what was already regarded as "an extraordinary document of adolescence"[42] bears some resemblance both to Frances Goodrich and Albert Hackett's authorized dramatization, *The Diary of Anne Frank,* which the *Frontiers of Faith* version predates by three years, and to the adaptation drafted at about the same time by Meyer Levin.[43] Like these other two works, Wishengrad's script juxtaposes the familiar story of a middle-class adolescent's struggles with her immediate family against the extraordinary circumstances of Europe's Jews fleeing Nazi persecution. Given the limits of the broadcast's time limit, Wishengrad achieves this with deft economy. At one point, for example, after Anne has quarreled with her mother, her father admonishes her: "Outside . . . there's a world full of hate. Human beings are taking other human beings and loading them into cattle cars. At least here let there be no hate and no enmity and no misunderstanding."[44]

Elsewhere, Wishengrad fashions from Anne Frank's reflections dialogue that resonates with the concerns of many Jews in postwar America. A diary entry in which Anne contemplates the fate of Jews under Nazi oppression becomes part of a scene depicting Anne's budding romance with Peter van Daan, whose family went into hiding with the Franks. Wishengrad's dialogue also incorporates a discussion of the nature of Jewish identity that is more attuned to sensibilities of postwar American ecumenism than of Jews in Nazi-occupied Europe:

> *Anne:* . . . We have to wait calmly for it to end. Jews and Christians wait, the whole earth waits; there are many who wait for death, Peter, but we have to wait for life because we are Jews.
> *Peter:* I didn't ask to be a Jew. What's the good of being one?
> *Anne:* Maybe it's because of our religion, from which the world and all peoples learn good that that's the reason we have to suffer now. And later, if any of us are left, instead of being doomed, we'll be held up as an example.
> *Peter:* I don't want to be an example.
> *Anne:* I guess I don't either. I want to be myself. But I guess being myself also means being a Jew.[45]

Anne's profession of Jewishness in her diary entry of 11 April 1944, on which this scene is based in part, is more forthright, more specifically European, and—most significant—a collective rather than individual proclamation:

If we bear all this suffering and if there are still Jews left, when it is over, then Jews, instead of being doomed, will be held up as an example. Who knows, it might even be our religion from which the world and all peoples learn good, and for that reason and that reason only do we have to suffer now. We can never become just Netherlanders or just English or any nation for that matter, we will always remain Jews, we must remain Jews, but we want to, too.[46]

As in the Hackett and Goodrich version, Wishengrad's drama concludes with the sound of Anne's disembodied voice after the audience has learned of her fate. Here, her final words articulate her wish to be a writer, so that she might "go on living even after my death." Anne thanks God for "this gift, this possibility of developing myself and of writing, of expressing all that is in me."[47] Thus, her diary and her life are offered as testimony to the compatibility of religion and art, in keeping with JTS's agenda for ecumenical broadcasting. Moreover, by championing the virtues of self-development and self-expression as God-given, this ending suggests that "being a Jew" also means "being oneself."

A Symbol of Freedom: The Final Ingredient

As the Holocaust became a more familiar setting for morally charged dramas broadcast on prime time during the late 1950s, they also appeared with increasing frequency on ecumenical programs in the "Sunday ghetto." Notable among these is *The Final Ingredient,* another half-hour drama produced by JTS, first aired on 19 April 1959 on ABC.[48] Its author, Reginald Rose, had already achieved considerable renown for several television plays presented on prime-time anthologies, most notably *Thunder on Sycamore Street, Twelve Angry Men,* and *The Remarkable Incident at Carson Corners,* all of which were broadcast on *Studio One* in 1954. *The Final Ingredient* bears thematic and formal resemblance to these works, which examine the dynamics of social conscience in abstracted contemporary American settings, yet Rose's Holocaust drama also offers a distinctly ecumenical response to its subject.

Set in the Bergen-Belsen concentration camp in 1944, this half-hour play begins with a shot of Aaron (played by John Cassavetes), a young Jewish inmate, looking through a barbed-wire fence. He stares at a bird in its nest, perched in a tree just on the other side. Next to him stands another prisoner, Eli (Martin Balsam), who speaks cryptically of a plan that he and the other prisoners have made for later that day; they are counting on Aaron's participation. With another inmate, Max (George Voskovec), Aaron speculates on the bird's freedom and wonders what he would do if he were free. Max comments that, for birds, "freedom is in their wings. For us . . . ," and he points to his head, "this is where our freedom is."[49]

John Cassavetes portrays a Jewish concentration camp prisoner in Reginald Rose's *The Final Ingredient,* aired on ABC in 1959. Photographer: Maurey Garber. (Ratner Center Archives, Jewish Theological Seminary of America.)

The scenes that follow show other Jewish inmates plotting what appears to be a revolt or escape. They collect a cache of short, stout wooden sticks, which are discovered by German guards during an inspection. The prisoners claim that they have only been gathering firewood. When one of them refuses to capitulate to the German captain's insistence that the sticks are weapons, the prisoner is beaten. Later, another short scene shows women inmates smuggling something to the male prisoners through a barbed-wire fence.

Aaron encounters his elderly father (Sam Jaffe), also a prisoner, who is trying to grow some small plants in tin cans outside the barracks. Aaron's father reinforces the others' pleas that his son help them, even though his ideas "are so far away" from theirs. Wondering whether the young man is afraid, his father recalls an incident from Aaron's childhood, when he overcame his fear of heights to climb up a tree and fix a bird's nest that was in danger of falling out of the branches. "I haven't known you very well in a long time—not until we came here," his father confesses. "Please, be with your people," he implores, and the two embrace.[50]

Night falls and the inmates put their plan into action. A group of prisoners stages a fight in order to create a distraction, and two German guards in a watchtower turn their searchlights on them. Meanwhile, Aaron uses an improvised ladder made of rope and the sticks of wood seen earlier to breach the camp's fence. He climbs up to the bird's nest that he was seen staring at in the drama's opening scene. Then he scrambles back over the fence to the others, only to be fatally shot by a guard. Aaron's father holds his son in his arms. "He didn't believe," says the father, "and he did this." Eli responds, "Now he believes." Aaron's father urges his son to say the Sh'ma (a prayer that Jews traditionally recite on their deathbeds), but the young man does not respond.

Back inside their barracks, Eli informs the other prisoners that Aaron is dead. "He brought this back," Eli continues, displaying a small egg. "Well, what are we waiting for?" he asks, and exits, followed by the others. Max, the last one to leave the barracks, picks up a half-eaten loaf of bread and recites, "Any leaven which remains in my possession, and which I have not seen nor removed, shall be as if it were not, and of no more account than the dust of the earth." Then he tosses the bread out the door and onto the ground.

The inmates gather outside and sit in a circle. One of them distributes skullcaps, which the men place on their heads. "Our women sewed these for us—they expect that we will wear them proudly," Eli announces, and he proclaims the beginning of their Passover seder. In turn, each inmate produces one of the ritual's traditional symbolic foods: "unleavened bread . . . baked from a handful of stolen flour"; "bitter herb, the grass on which we walk in slavery, as our fathers did in Egypt"; "harosseth, not apples, cinnamon and nuts, but a handful of the earth, to make us remember the clay out of which our fathers in Egypt wrought bricks." The plants that Aaron's father was seen tending earlier are produced: "This is our parsley, the fruit of the earth, for which we give thanks." Another inmate produces three grapes, "bought with the gold from our teeth. . . . This is our wine." Eli displays the egg: "This egg is a symbol of our immortality. A man gave his life that we could have it. Remember him till the day you die!" Aaron's father comes forward. "We sacrificed a lamb in Egypt once. We place a shankbone on our tables to remember this. Tonight a lamb was sacrificed. He was my son. This was his belt. This is our shankbone!"

"This year our seder is held on the bloody earth of Belsen," Aaron's father continues. "Next year in Jerusalem! Now here is the way I want it to begin . . . with the hymn of gratitude." As he leads the others in the Hebrew song "Dayenu" (which is sung in the middle of the traditional seder), a group of guards marches on. They come to a halt. A close-up of the captain's face shows him to be astonished, perhaps even moved, by the inmates' behavior. In the drama's final tableau, the guards stand upstage and watch the inmates continue to sing, as the credits begin to roll.[51]

Like some of the early prime-time television dramas, *The Final Ingredient* transforms a Holocaust site—here, a Nazi concentration camp—into an arena for dramatic debate on questions of faith, freedom, and redemption. The studio setting is austere, consisting of sparse elements (a tree, a fence, the facade of a barracks) set against a blank cyclorama. In this spare environment, Jewish characters spend most of their time philosophizing. The inmates are not costumed in camp uniforms, but in old clothes nominally distressed with smears of paint. Their "gaunt" appearance, as called for in Rose's stage directions, is signaled by a brief episode near the beginning when an inmate faints from hunger, and by the prisoners being described by the guards as "skeletons," rather than by the actors' actual physical presence.

The spare aesthetic of *The Final Ingredient* was as much a product of the agenda to abstract a historical locus into a universal, moral proving ground as it was, no doubt, a result of the limitations of producing studio drama on the modest budgets of public service programming. Differences among the Jewish characters are likewise drawn along the lines of the drama's ethical debate and not according to the distinctions of nationality, region, language, class, generation, politics, and so forth that characterized the diverse European Jewish population during the war. (Nor, for that matter, are there either signs of or allusions to the presence of non-Jewish prisoners in the camp.) Instead, *The Final Ingredient* addresses the question of Jewish survival under Nazi persecution solely in spiritual terms.

Rose's script does not credit as its source any documentation of observant Jews' actual responses to the challenge of celebrating Passover while in Nazi captivity. Nor does the drama deal with the complex questions of traditional rabbinic law concerning the celebration of Passover under the extreme conditions of a concentration camp, with which observant Jews did struggle during the war. In fact, rabbis interned in the actual camp where the drama is set composed a prayer for fellow inmates "who were compelled to violate the laws of Passover."[52] Instead, *The Final Ingredient* dramatizes the observance of Passover in the concentration camp as an affirmation of faith more than as a commitment to maintaining traditional observance—a choice more in keeping with the drama's ecumenical venue.

The broadcast of *The Final Ingredient* took place on the day before the start of Passover, thereby underscoring the connection between this holiday and the Holocaust. A critic reviewing Rose's play for *Variety* described it as "a blend of drama and ritual that had an added sock with the first day of the holiday upcoming tonight."[53] This was no innovation; symbolic connections between Nazi persecutions of European Jewry and Passover were first articulated during the war, especially in the wake of the Warsaw Ghetto uprising, which had begun on the first night of the holiday in 1943. Rather than merely analogizing the modern Jewish struggle against Nazi oppression with the ancient Hebrew narrative of slavery and redemption, *The Final Ingredient* subsumes the Holocaust within the Passover ritual. By organizing the drama's narrative around the preparations for the seder, culminating with its performance, Rose conceptualizes Jewish resistance against Nazi persecution in terms of religious faith and observance of a holiday that, as historian Jenna Weissman Joselit has observed, had become the American Jewish "domestic occasion par excellence."[54]

Moreover, Rose's drama articulates notions of faith using symbols and language more appropriate to American ecumenism than Jewish tradition. The most striking example of this is the drama's climax, Aaron's death. The symbolic equation of Aaron with a sacrificial or paschal lamb evokes both the biblical story of the binding of Isaac and the Exodus narrative. However, Aaron's sacrifice resonates much more powerfully with Christian theological readings of these biblical narratives, which identify them as prefiguring the crucifixion of Jesus, than it does with Jewish lore. Moreover, suggesting that there is something valid, even noble, in risking one's life to secure an egg for a seder challenges traditional Jewish notions of proper acts of martyrdom, as does the drama's privileging of spiritual resistance over self-defense.

The redemptive vision of Rose's play is typical of other Holocaust dramas presented on ecumenical television series. Certain features of *The Final Ingredient* are reminiscent of Joseph Mindel's *In the Beginning,* aired on *Frontiers of Faith* in 1956. This drama makes similar use of a site of Holocaust geography (the Warsaw Ghetto) and a Jewish holiday (Simhat Torah) as the setting for exploring spiritual and moral issues, by juxtaposing the naïve—and ultimately triumphant—faith of a Hebrew-school teacher against the cynical agnosticism of a resistance fighter. The ecumenical series celebrated positive relationships between Jewish victims of Nazism and non-Jewish rescuers in dramas about Swedish diplomat Raoul Wallenberg's efforts to rescue Hungarian Jews and the Danes' evacuation of their Jewish citizens to Sweden. Other programs presented on the ecumenical series focused on children as archetypal "innocent" victims of the Holocaust and commemorated the artistic reponses that it engendered. In addition to Wishengrad's dramatization of Anne Frank's diary, there are episodes of these Sunday series devoted to Janos Korczak's efforts to protect children in the Warsaw Ghetto and to the poetry and artwork created by children in the Terezín concentration camp.[55] As was the case with Anne Frank's diary (the official stage version of which was first televised in 1967 on *ABC Sunday Night at the Theatre*), some of the other subjects that were first presented to American audiences in dramas by the ecumenical series later proved to be staples of American Holocaust fiction, film, and theater.[56]

The ecumenical series' celebration of the arts' transformative power to combat the adversities of the Holocaust was demonstrated most elaborately in 1965, when ABC presented an operatic adaptation of *The Final Ingredient*. The hour-long work, with original music by David Amram to Arnold Weinstein's libretto, further abstracts the historical setting of the work as it situates the drama in the elevated, declamatory world of *opera seria*. Philosophical asides in Rose's play become arias, and the singing of "Dayenu" at the play's conclusion is replaced with a choral performance in a setting of Handelian grandeur.[57]

Within the confines of the "Sunday ghetto," broadcasters and theologians addressed the challenge of dramatizing the Holocaust for American television by linking the edifying sensibilities of ecumenism and "high" art. In doing so, they created some of the first popular articulations of Holocaust theology, which, as later defined by Emil Fackenheim, views the experience of European Jewry under Nazi-led persecution "as a world-historical event" that "poses new problems for philosophical thought."[58] The foregrounding of ethical and theological issues raised by the Nazi era in these dramas came, however, at the expense of its complex history and in defiance of those who understood the Holocaust as rooted in particular political, social, intellectual, and economic realities.

The ecumenical context in which these dramas were created and presented intensified their elevated, universalized vision of the Holocaust. In this setting, the Holocaust acquired its enduring value because American Jews offered it up as a moral exemplar to share with their fellow citizens. Despite this transcendent impulse, these dramas were, like their prime-time counterparts, very much artifacts of their time. Indeed, the sensibility that values the Holocaust as an ethical case study for universal edification marks these Sunday daytime dramas as examples of Holocaust remembrance of early vintage.

Trial by Document

Abby Mann's docudrama *Judgment at Nuremberg* may be the best-known example of American Holocaust television from the early postwar years, even though it is much more familiar in the expanded cinematic version of 1961 than in its original form as a television play aired live on *Playhouse 90* on 16 April 1959.[59] Based on one of the war crimes trials convened in Nuremberg shortly after World War II, *Judgment at Nuremberg* engages several key issues raised by American mediations of the Holocaust during the 1940s and 1950s: the role of vintage images as facilitators of vicarious witnessing of the Holocaust, the distinctive ability attributed to television to offer intimately scaled psychological dramas, and the challenges of examining this chapter of history in the United States during the first years of the cold war. In addition, *Judgment at Nuremberg* is the first major work of American television to examine the Holocaust through the format of a trial—an approach subsequently pursued in other dramas, documentaries, and news reports.

Judgment at Nuremberg engages these issues through the hybrid genre of docudrama. While this term is of recent coinage, the intermingling of cinematic devices conventionally associated with either documentary films (e.g., vintage photographs or motion picture footage) or dramatic features (performances by actors) predates the advent of television and, in fact, runs throughout the history of filmmaking. During the early post–World War II years, film scholar Jack Ellis has noted, such generic hybrids were common: American documentaries made substantial use of reenactments and other "dramatic" devices, while the spate of Hollywood features on social problems evince the influence of "documentary" film sensibilities. Indeed, Raymond Williams cautioned, the notion of documentary and drama as "absolutely separated categories" is a convention that "seems to depend on a fiction about reality itself." Williams suggested that docudrama, often considered problematic due to its hybrid nature, nonetheless has "positive consequences," particularly the way that it makes use of "what is taken as an intrinsic element of television: its capacity to enter a situation and show what is actually happening in it."[60]

In *Judgment at Nuremberg*, liberation footage plays a strategic role in realizing this attribute of docudrama. The teleplay's use of vintage images is much more elaborate and forceful compared to their conventional function in historical documentaries as illustrations of a spoken narrative. Instead, vintage images figure as icons of historicity, occupying a privileged status within a semifictional work as signs of the past or of "actuality." Moreover, the act of witnessing liberation footage—established as a galvanizing experience for American audiences at the end of World War II—is imbued with moral significance both within the virtual world of the drama and within the actual context of television viewing. In *Judgment at Nuremberg*, seeing liberation footage does not merely function as a pivotal moment of the drama's plot, as an illustration of Nazi war criminals' "trial by document"; for viewers, this also transforms watching the television program into an act of witnessing the Holocaust.[61]

Abby Mann's docudrama *Judgment at Nuremberg,* aired on *Playhouse 90* in 1959, dramatizes one of the war crimes trials convened before an American tribunal in occupied Germany during the immediate postwar years. The cast includes Paul Lukas (standing, third from left) as former Reich minister of justice Ernst Janning and Maximilian Schell (seated, left) as his defense counsel. (CBS Photo Archive.)

Judgment at Nuremberg does not retell the story of the first and most widely publicized of the Nuremberg war crimes trials, which was convened before an international tribunal beginning in 1945. Rather, it presents a fictionalized version of one of the dozen subsequent trials held in the U.S. Zone of postwar Germany before a panel of American jurists, in accordance with Control Council Law No. 10, a ruling of the Allied Control Council in occupied Germany enacted in December 1945. Case No. 3 was known as the "Justice Case," as all fourteen defendants were "judges, prosecutors, or ministerial officers of the judicial system of Nazi Germany."[62] This case provided the basis for Mann's drama, which features four defendants: a minister of justice, two judges, and a public defender, who all served during the Third Reich. By focusing on men who prosecuted or adjudicated cases in accordance with the laws of the Nazi regime, *Judgment at Nuremberg* approaches the war crimes trial as a morally charged case study of one group of jurists passing judgment on another and, more generally, of the nature of justice as a social institution.

Mann's script employs fictitious situations and invented characters, some of whom are loosely based on prosecutor Telford Taylor and less well known participants in the "Justice Case." Even before the play begins, *Playhouse 90*'s presentation of *Judgment at Nuremberg* similarly straddles conventional distinctions between the fictive and the historical. At the start of the broadcast Taylor appears on the screen, wearing a tuxedo, to introduce the drama. Announced as "former brigadier general and chief counsel for the prosecution at the Nuremberg war crimes trials," Taylor (who is also listed in the credits at the program's conclusion as a technical consultant) explains that the script is based on the records of one of the Nuremberg trials: "The plot and characters are, of course, fictional, but this play re-creates the atmosphere of the Nuremberg trials, the difficult legal and moral problems they involved, and the terrible events with which they were concerned." Taylor's presence, both as speaker of the prologue and as a consultant, gives *Judgment at Nuremberg* the imprimatur of authenticity.[63] At the same time, Taylor—dressed as if for an opening night at the theater rather than, say, in his general's uniform—assures viewers that the broadcast is, "of course, fictional," although its historical essence is genuine.

Following a commercial break, the drama proper begins with an introductory sequence featuring vintage footage of the first Nuremberg trial of 1945–1946. In what amounts to a miniature documentary, a narrator recalls the trial's most notorious defendants, the charges brought against them, and their sentences; he then explains that this first trial was followed by another twelve cases, which tried 177 members or supporters of the Nazi regime. Viewers next see an exterior establishing shot of a house in postwar Nuremberg—again, vintage footage—followed by an interior shot of the house, actually a set in a Hollywood television studio, as the first live scene of *Judgment at Nuremberg* begins with the arrival of the drama's protagonist, Judge Haywood (played by Claude Rains). Haywood, an American jurist, has been brought to Germany by the United States government to adjudicate the next round of trials. In this scene he learns that one of the defendants is Ernst Janning (Paul Lukas), a former Reich minister of justice. Janning was once renowned for his juridical erudition; indeed, Haywood himself admired Janning before the rise of Nazism.

The drama's integration of film footage from various sources with live studio action becomes more elaborate as the exposition progresses. Following the opening session of the trial, Haywood asks his military aide, Captain Byers (Martin Milner), to take him to see "something of the town, something of the people." In the ensuing scenes, live action and documentary footage are closely integrated to simulate the witnessing of historical incidents and their recollection. Establishing shots of postwar Nuremberg in ruins cut to a studio set of a sidewalk alongside a bombed-out building.

Haywood and Byers walk on; as they survey the city, the scene cuts to vintage footage of a pan across the ruined cityscape. Pointing out the former main street of Nuremberg, Byers explains, "I remember being here once as a child. . . . Nuremberg was a great toy center. It was also the anti-Semitism center. Storm troopers used to ride down the street on trucks shouting, putting up signs on shops." As he speaks, the image cuts away from the two actors back to the postwar cityscape, which then dissolves to vintage prewar footage, originally filmed for German newsreels, of a group of Nazis carrying flags and riding down a city street in a truck.[64] More vintage footage of Nazi activities in the early 1930s follows — short sequences showing Nazis beating or hauling off civilians and putting up signs on shop windows that call for the boycott of Jewish businesses. This dissolves back to the long shot of the city in ruins and then cuts back to Haywood and Byers as the latter comments sarcastically, "I guess for the Nurembergers they were the good old days."

Next, the two men visit Zeppelin Field, where large Nazi Party rallies were once held. Haywood turns around and looks up as Byers explains, "They'd start with the pageantry — the horns, the drums," and the screen cuts to an overhead shot looking down at Haywood, who gazes upward. This is followed by a cut to an image of a sculpture of a stylized eagle, which dissolves to an image of a similar eagle perched on a wreathed swastika. The sounds of marching, trumpets, and drums is heard. This is the beginning of a sequence culled from *Triumph of the Will,* Leni Riefenstahl's documentary film about the Nazi Party convention of 1934. For the next two minutes, viewers of *Playhouse 90* watch scenes of Adolf Hitler's arrival before an enormous crowd in Nuremberg; his delivery of a fiery speech (which is neither dubbed into English nor translated in subtitles), intercut with the handsome faces of German youths; and a torchlit procession at night, with Hitler leading the vast crowd in chants of "*Sieg Heil! Sieg Heil!*" This final image of Hitler dissolves back to the first eagle, then cuts back to Haywood looking up. "That's enough for one day," he tells Byers as the scene ends.

These sequences employed narrative principles of montage that are conventional in the cinema (such as cutting from an establishing exterior shot, which is often taken from stock footage, to an interior shot, often filmed on a sound stage) but were unusual for live television drama. As demonstrated by such productions as *Walk Down the Hill* and *In the Presence of Mine Enemies,* live television drama relied heavily on close-ups, tightly composed group shots, and intimate, confined settings. Rather than capitalizing exclusively on these conventions, *Playhouse 90*'s production of *Judgment at Nuremberg* challenged the limits of "live" drama by extending the action beyond the spatial and temporal frame of the television studio. The scenes described above drew on the established notion of vintage film as a historical record and the association of watching such images with the act of remembering the past.

The scenes of Haywood's Nuremberg walking tour integrate three distinct groups of shots: live action in the television studio (1959), footage of postwar Nuremberg in ruins (ca. 1946–1947), and footage of Nazi activities in prewar Germany (ca. 1933–1934). The postwar vintage footage is used to situate live scenes in historical settings and to show viewers what characters "see" as the actors portraying them look beyond the range of the sets in the studio. The footage from the 1930s represents a shift from the drama's postwar virtual present to its prewar past and from the interaction between the judge and his aide to the internal realm of memory. This is articulated in the dialogue (e.g., Byers remembers the prewar Nuremberg that he visited as a youth) and through the use of the dissolve, a convention of cinematic narrative long familiar to movie-goers as a signal of a shift away from the dramatic present to some other state of consciousness: dream, vision, memory, fantasy, and so on.[65]

It is likely that members of the television audience watching *Judgment at Nuremberg* in 1959 had seen some of these prewar images before. Like footage of liberated concentration camps, these scenes of Nazi Germany had appeared in commercial newsreels and propaganda films produced by the United States government, as well as in documentaries and other programs made for commercial television.[66] (It is even possible to imagine the characters portrayed by Rains and Milner having seen this footage in their respective virtual pasts.) But rather than call viewers' attention to the various origins of the prewar footage, the structure of the teleplay integrates it, along with vintage scenes of postwar Nuremberg, into the narrative line of a "live" drama.

As *Judgment at Nuremberg* proceeds, courtroom scenes alternate with scenes set in the American judges' chambers or in Haywood's private quarters. In both formal trial proceedings and informal discussions outside the courtroom, Haywood debates the moral issues of the trial with the other justices and with American military personnel: Are the trials meaningful, given the lack of public interest? Are they politically expedient, in light of rising tensions between the Soviet Union and the West? (In this regard, Mann's script resembles *Playhouse 90*'s adaptation of *Child of Our Time*, aired earlier in the season, in the way that it obliquely links the ethical issues raised by the Holocaust with the moral challenge posed by American anti-Communist activism in the 1950s.)

Midway through *Judgment at Nuremberg*—following the testimony of witnesses whom the defendants had prosecuted in accordance with the Third Reich's laws against political dissidents, Jews, and those who consorted with Jews—Chief Prosecutor General Parker (Melvyn Douglas) concludes his case. He introduces a witness to testify about the conditions in concentration camps, which were the destination of many victims of the defendants' rulings. Explaining that there are no words to describe the horrors of the camps, Parker presents "a mute but eloquent witness . . . the camera's eye. I now respectfully request the tribunal to view what the camera saw. These are official films taken by the Allied army upon entering Germany."

As Parker speaks, American officers set up a movie screen and darken the courtroom. A projector is turned on, and the movie screen is lit up with the title card *Nazi Concentration Camps,* the name of the film shown at the actual first Nuremberg trial. As a map of Europe appears on the movie screen, which now completely fills the viewer's television screen, a narrator intones, "This map shows the number and location of concentration camps under the Third Reich." Footage of uniformed prisoners in Buchenwald appears as the narration continues: "There was a motto at Buchenwald: Break the body; break the spirit; break the heart." The television screen image cuts away from the documentary footage to a shot of the three American judges in the darkened courtroom, watching the film. Haywood, who sits in the middle, swallows. The narrator continues as the screen image returns to footage of the camp's cremation ovens, followed by a display of "by-products of Buchenwald," which was shown to local German civilians: the skin of the camp's victims used as canvas for pornographic drawings, the shrunken heads of two Polish inmates, a human pelvis used as an ashtray. During this sequence the screen image cuts back to a closer shot of Haywood, who is visibly disturbed.

The documentary footage continues with images of children displaying their tattooed arms and piles of emaciated corpses as the narrator mentions inmates used as "human guinea pigs" in medical experiments. During this sequence there is a reaction shot of the German jurists on trial. Shot in profile—unlike the American justices, who are shown in full face—the defendants appear stoic. The documentary continues with images of the gas chambers at Dachau as the narrator describes the procedure for the mass gassing of inmates. This is followed by footage of Bergen-Belsen, showing piles of bodies being bulldozed into mass graves. "Who were the bodies? Members of every occupied country of Europe. Two thirds of the Jews exterminated—more than six million, according to reports compiled from the Nazis' own figures."[67] As the narrator speaks, the image of the mass of corpses is slowly cross-faded with a close-up of Janning, looking distraught. "But the real figures—no one knows," the narrator intones as the scene goes to black. A commercial for Ansco cameras follows, showing a family taking snapshots on their vacation.

The act of viewing the documentary footage from *Nazi Concentration Camps* provides the catalyst for the drama's turning point. Following this scene, Haywood grows firm in his resolve that the defendants are guilty of war crimes and merit punishment for their deeds, while Janning's denial of his culpability in wartime atrocities begins to break down. Haywood refers repeatedly to the atrocities depicted or described in *Nazi Concentration Camps* in the course of his subsequent discussions with fellow justices and with Byers. In the final scene of *Judgment at Nuremberg,* which takes place after the defendants have been pronounced guilty and sentenced to prison terms, Haywood refers to the film when he visits Janning in prison. The American justice describes viewing the atrocities depicted in the liberation footage as an experience that not merely informed his ruling but proved to be personally transformative: "I'll never forget the things I've seen here as long as I live."

The screening of *Nazi Concentration Camps* appears at the conclusion of the prosecutor's case in *Judgment at Nuremberg,* unlike its presentation at the first actual war crimes trial, which took place early in the prosecution's case. Situating the documentary's presentation within the climactic courtroom scene transforms the screening of the footage into the equivalent of a performance by a dramatic character. The prosecutor introduces *Nazi Concentration Camps* as the testimony of the ultimate in a series of witnesses — that is, the anthropomorphized camera, which implicitly sees with its own "eye" independent of human facility. Just as the camera is simultaneously "mute" and "eloquent," the photographed images that it produces are both the result of a dispassionate technical process and possessed of an ability to offer testimony that supersedes human eyewitnesses.

The dramatic power that these images effect is due in part to the privileged status of documentary footage in general and in part to the particular, graphic horrors that this footage depicts. Moreover, its role as the agent of the drama's climactic action is prefigured by the use of other vintage film clips in earlier scenes of *Judgment at Nuremberg.* The teleplay's prologue both establishes the historical context of the ensuing courtroom drama and validates the authority of documentary images as embodiments of history. The vintage footage employed in the scenes of Haywood's walking tour of Nuremberg signifies both history and memory. Remembering is presented as more than simply the ability to recall the past; in these scenes, remembering also entails the ability to testify about the past and to pass moral judgment on it. Thus, having portrayed the camera as the ultimate witness, *Judgment at Nuremberg* invokes the authority invested in documentary footage to dramatize how seeing "what the camera saw" transforms viewers into witnesses. The act of witnessing is shown endowing viewers with the recollective powers of the photograph and ultimately enables them to pass judgment on what they, too, have "witnessed."

The impact of watching *Nazi Concentration Camps* at the climax of *Judgment at Nuremberg* is extended beyond the virtual world of the drama to its actual American television audience. In accordance with the conventions of montage, the intercutting of reaction shots indicates to television viewers that they are actually watching what the characters in the virtual world of the drama are (apparently) watching. This sequence invites television viewers to join dramatic characters in the process of sitting in judgment of the testimony offered by these images and, at the same time, to judge their own reactions to the footage against those of the two protagonists, Haywood and Janning.

For the audience of *Judgment at Nuremberg,* the dramatic conceit that equates watching with witnessing is extended further — to view the act of witnessing is to become a witness oneself. Like the first newsreel presentations of this footage, *Judgment at Nuremberg* also juxtaposes the virtuous witnessing of morally stricken Americans against the culpable witnessing of stoic Germans. The teleplay thus provides its audience with a dramatic framework for viewing the documentary footage that gives historical significance, affective direction, and a moral charge both to what they see and to the act of seeing it.[68]

The complex integration of documentary and dramatic conventions in *Judgment at Nuremberg,* which creates this morally transformative act of witnessing, contributed to the drama's critical acclaim. A review in *Variety* praised the broadcast as "a gripping, frequently shocking, semi-documentary" in which "the cold, documentary flavor was tempered and enhanced throughout with character studies of intense understanding and compassion, and yet this element of compassion was never allowed to interfere with the objective tone of the drama, even in its retrospective status. It was a stunning balance of drama and documentary," especially "the smooth integration of film clips into the tape." The unnamed critic went on to lament "one jarring note" in the broadcast, when the American Gas Association, one of the sponsors of *Playhouse 90,* "chose to meddle in a work of this stature" by pressuring CBS into "blanking out four or five references to Nazi 'gas chambers.'" *Variety*'s critic denounced this as "an act so childishly outrageous and inconsistent with the high moral tone of this drama as to be worthy of serious public protest."[69]

This "blanking-out" incident has become one of the most oft-mentioned episodes of the early American television industry. In a 1981 interview, Herbert Brodkin, who produced *Judgment at Nuremberg,* recalled that the network yielded to the American Gas Association's demands after he had refused to make requested changes in the script: "Although the program was televised live, CBS delayed its transmission for a few seconds, long enough for an engineer to bleep on the word gas each time it was mentioned."[70] This incident has been frequently cited as a quintessential example of the degree to which sponsors interfered in programming during the early years of television.[71] Annette Insdorf began her study of Holocaust film with this episode to illustrate what she deemed to be the inherently problematic nature of "the Hollywood version of the Holocaust," in which commercial interests routinely get "in the way of authenticity."[72]

Though the "blanking-out" incident has usually been characterized as an outrageous violation of artistic integrity on behalf of venal interests, it was nonetheless part of the viewing experience for *Judgment at Nuremberg*'s first audience—in fact, it has been preserved in the kinescope record of the broadcast for future viewers.[73] The incident thus constituted a broadcasting counterdrama to the live drama being performed on *Playhouse 90*, a cybernetic duel that undid the integration of virtual and real worlds so admirably executed by the producers of *Judgment at Nuremberg*. As the *Variety* critic noted, "It is ironical that such sound-track snipping occurs in a play that criticizes the immature meddling with men's minds of an infamous era of the past."[74] Indeed, within the context of a drama that champions the power of mediated images to serve as enduring witnesses in the service of justice, the "blanking-out" incident reveals instead the vulnerability of mediations. The incident demonstrates the limits of the mediation as an instrument of testimony and its dependence on presenters who can shape its use—or erase it—according to their agendas.

There is another noteworthy interaction between advertising and drama in the telecast of *Judgment at Nuremberg*, but, unlike the "blanking-out" incident, it appears to have passed without critical comment. Immediately following the drama's climactic scene, in which the camera offers its "mute but eloquent" testimony, comes another drama of the camera as witness in the form of the commercial for Ansco cameras.[75] Viewers might, conceivably, have found the juxtaposition of these cheery, banal scenes of an American family photographing their summer vacation with the preceeding images of genocide to be offensive—or, at the very least, ironic.

But no such comments seem to have been made, at least publicly, at the time—perhaps because the photographic record of the Holocaust, like the Holocaust itself, has come to be regarded as having an ontologically privileged status, somehow transcending the mechanical means of its production, which links liberation footage with family snapshots and all other photography. In contrast to the evanescence of the "photo opportunity" in daily life, the Holocaust is widely regarded as having yielded up images that defy temporality, for they document an event understood as having taken place beyond the normal flow of time. Indeed, observations that the images documenting liberated Nazi concentration camps were somehow singular are among the first expressions of the notion that the Holocaust is an event situated at the "limits of representation." One of the best known examples was offered by photojournalist Margaret Bourke-White, who photographed Buchenwald shortly after its liberation. At the time, she commented to her editors at *Life* magazine that "the sights I have just seen are so unbelievable that I don't think I'll believe them myself until I've seen the photographs."[76]

Such elevated claims for the value of Holocaust representation did not situate the subject beyond the scope of television, despite the medium's newness or its attributes of intimacy and familiarity. By the late 1950s, American television had already fashioned a variety of presentations of this subject according to the medium's own emerging sensibility, and it had begun to establish a relationship with viewers as a distinctive venue for encounters with the Holocaust.

Two years after *Playhouse 90*'s production of *Judgment at Nuremberg* was aired, American television presented viewers with another war crimes trial—and, moreover, with another body of visual testimony about the Holocaust. Unlike Abby Mann's drama or other previous programs, these telecasts presented the Holocaust in the context of news coverage of an event many have considered to be the first major watershed in Holocaust memory culture after the immediate postwar years. Like *Judgment at Nuremberg*, this trial used the medium of television to invite its viewers to sit in judgment of the indicted—and of themselves.

part two 1961–1978
Into the Limelight

Among the hundreds of examples of American Holocaust television, two events stand out as major watersheds: the medium's coverage of the war crimes trial of Adolf Eichmann, convened in Jerusalem during the spring and summer of 1961, and the premiere telecast of the *Holocaust* miniseries, which took place in April 1978. Differences between them testify to television's wide range as a medium of memory culture. The Eichmann trial's presence on television extended over a period of several months and embraced news reportage, public affairs broadcasts, documentaries, and docudrama; the *Holocaust* miniseries was a single nine-and-a-half-hour drama aired over four consecutive evenings. Both events stand as landmarks of America's television industry. Telecasts of the Eichmann trial were the first broadcasts of actual courtroom proceedings to an international audience. *Holocaust* was one of the earliest as well as most widely seen and discussed American television miniseries; its impact also reached far beyond the nation's borders.

These two events demonstrate the dynamics of American Holocaust remembrance and the changing role that television plays in shaping public memory. Scholars and critics have long recognized the Eichmann case as a threshold event in America's Holocaust memory culture in the United States; they often identify the trial as marking the end of a period of "silence" on the subject. Yet the role that television played in enabling millions to observe Eichmann and the Israeli government's proceedings against him is seldom given more than passing attention, and the televised record of the trial has been rarely seen in the United States. Whereas the impact of television on Holocaust remembrance has been largely ignored in the case of the Eichmann trial, it was the focus of attention following the broadcast of the *Holocaust* miniseries seventeen years later. Indeed, much of the extensive discussion of the miniseries centered on whether the medium was, by its very nature, an appropriate forum for addressing this subject.

The seventeen years between these two events produced no single broadcast to rival their impact, but from 1961 to 1978 the Holocaust appeared with increasing frequency on American television in documentaries, dramas, even science fiction and comedy programs. These telecasts played a crucial role in establishing the Holocaust as a regular presence in American public culture. In particular, the occasional appearance of the Holocaust on episodic programs—dramatic series about lawyers, detectives, newspaper reporters, or space travelers—helped establish this subject in the nation's popular repertoire of moral concerns.

Television's role as a public forum for addressing America's moral crises was transformed during the 1960s and 1970s, largely in response to the civil rights movement and the war in Vietnam. Televised presentations of both these issues occasionally invoked the Holocaust as a moral paradigm. The Holocaust was also entering the "time consciousness of American historians" during these years and becoming "an established article in the creed of what has been called 'Jewish civil religion.'"[1] Yet, at the same time, questions also arose about the implications of the Holocaust's increased visibility in American public culture, thanks in part to television, even before the extensive discussion that followed the *Holocaust* miniseries. As early as 1972, author Elie Wiesel claimed that "the theme of the Holocaust is no longer taboo. It is now discussed freely—sometimes too freely and too much," and he wondered whether the Holocaust, having found recognition in public culture, was then "doomed to remain in the limelight."[2]

four

The Man in the Glass Box

At five, at exactly five . . . Hattie and I sit before the TV and we become a silent movie. . . .

A small-faced man narrates. His voice weak and light. An advertisement disguised as not an advertisement from a Jewish real-estate firm.

None of that seems to matter. I begin to sweat. My heart pounds. . . . We sit on hard kitchen chairs drawn up before the TV, watching. As if putting ourselves to school.

The eyewitnesses, their faces designed into masks, wrinkled. . . . Their voices, in translation, disembodied.

There is something . . . about the way we both move — or don't move — while we are watching.

Hattie and I are an experimental, silent film reacting to a film on TV. The old speeded-up, slowed-down, silent film.

—Norma Rosen, *Touching Evil*

Televising Eichmann

In the spring and summer of 1961, many Americans joined these two characters from Rosen's novel and sat in front of their television sets to watch the war crimes trial of Adolf Eichmann. These broadcasts constitute a major landmark in the chronicle of American Holocaust television. It was the first time that the Holocaust received extended television coverage, in the form of news reports, public affairs programs, documentaries, and dramas aired over a period of months. The Eichmann case provided the first opportunity for television networks to deal with the Holocaust in the context of reporting a major news story. In fact, American television audiences are most likely to have first heard the word *Holocaust* used to describe the Nazi persecution of European Jewry during broadcasts of the trial.[1]

The courtroom set up in Jerusalem's Beit Ha'am for the war crimes trial of Adolf Eichmann, 1961. (UPI/Corbis-Bettmann.)

The Eichmann trial—which consisted of 114 sessions in the Jerusalem District Court, from 11 April through 14 August 1961—was the first major public effort to conceptualize the Holocaust as a discrete chapter of history, distinguished from larger narratives of World War II or the Third Reich, and defined as a phenomenon centered around Nazi efforts to exterminate European Jewry.[2] Telecasts of and related to the Eichmann trial are also landmarks in the annals of American television. As the medium's first presentation of the actual proceedings of what Robert Hariman has distinguished as a "popular trial," broadcasts of the Eichmann case raise larger questions about such events as "a genre of public discourse," their performative nature, and the impact of television on their presentation to the public.[3] The Eichmann trial's coverage also prompts questions about how television broadcasters conceptualize "history" in the course of reporting current events.

Televised presentations of the Eichmann trial continued to invoke the trope of witnessing as a morally charged act. At the same time, the Eichmann case provided the occasion for the first extended contention over the significance of the Holocaust as a moral paradigm in America, and televi-

sion figured strategically in the debate. The Israeli government, which organized the proceedings, conceived the Eichmann trial as an occasion for presenting the Holocaust as a distinctly Jewish phenomenon and structured
the trial as a public event validating the new Zionist state's unique historical and political agenda. However, American conceptualizations of the
Eichmann case, including those offered in television programs, usually presented the Holocaust as a paradigmatic investigation, having universal significance, of the limits of human morality.

Historians and critics have frequently described the Eichmann case as
generating new interest in the experiences of European Jewry during the
Nazi era. The ensuing spate of important works of literature and film are
widely regarded as the first popular works of American Holocaust memory
culture. Scholars and journalists often acknowledge television's role in
bringing the trial to many millions of viewers. However, they have rarely
analyzed the impact that the medium had on how the Eichmann trial was
presented, observed, and discussed. Nor have they considered the televised
presentations of the Eichmann case as examples of Holocaust memory culture—even though, as the excerpt from Norma Rosen's 1969 novel at the
opening of this chapter illustrates, these broadcasts had a distinctive
and powerful impact on viewers, drawing them into the process of mediation itself.

"The Man in Charge of Exterminating the Jews": *Background of the Eichmann Case*

The Nuremberg trials of 1945–1948 were far from the last occasion for
official public hearings on the wartime atrocities of Nazis and their collaborators. During the immediate postwar years governments throughout
Europe conducted other war crimes trials, and both government-sponsored
and private forces in Europe, the United States, and Israel sought other suspected war criminals who had eluded capture. Anticipating the eventual
apprehension of war criminals by its own agents, Israel enacted its Nazis
and Nazi Collaborators (Punishment) Law in 1950. Among the most
sought-after war criminals was former SS officer Adolf Otto Eichmann,
who had been the highest-ranking official in the Nazi hierarchy specifically
charged with facilitating the extermination of European Jewry.

Born in Solingen, Germany, in 1906, Eichmann became a member of the
Nazi Party in 1932. He soon joined the SS and in 1935 began work in the
Jewish Section of the SD (Secret Service). By 1938 Eichmann had come to
be regarded as an authority on the Jewish community and had begun to
execute Nazi policy on compulsory Jewish emigration from Germany and
Austria. The following year he was appointed director of the Reich Center

for Jewish Emigration in Berlin. In March 1941 Eichmann was named the head of the Gestapo's Section IVB4, which oversaw the treatment of Jews under Nazi rule; later that year he was promoted to the rank of *Obersturm-bannführer* (the equivalent of lieutenant colonel). In this capacity Eichmann supervised the forced relocation of Jewish communities as the Nazis established Jewish ghettos in East European cities of occupied countries, and he administered the transportation needs of the *Einsatzgruppen* (mass killing squads). Following the decision made at the Wannsee Conference of 20 January 1942 to implement the mass gassing and cremation of Jews, Eichmann was charged with arranging their transport to extermination camps, which he oversaw until the final months of the war. During this time Eichmann also supervised the transport of other civilian populations targeted for incarceration in forced labor and concentration camps or for extermination.[4]

According to Attorney General Gideon Hausner, who led the prosecution of the case against Eichmann, the defendant's role in the Nazi hierarchy came to be fully understood only in the war's aftermath. During the postwar trials of other Nazi war criminals, Eichmann's name "was mentioned more and more. . . . The International Nuremberg Tribunal branded him unanimously as 'the man in charge of the extermination program of the Jews.'" At the time Eichmann had successfully escaped detection in various Allied prisoner-of-war camps and eventually fled the continent. In 1950 he made his way to Argentina, where he lived under a false identity with his wife and children.

Hausner wrote that, with the end of the Nuremberg trials and the "courting of Germany" as the cold war escalated, the Allies' official pursuit of Nazi war criminals was, in effect, over.[5] However, private individuals and organizations around the world continued the search for former Nazis who had escaped prosecution. Among these efforts, the capture of Eichmann had special significance for Jewish survivors of the Holocaust. Israeli journalist Tom Segev has noted that "Eichmann did not make policy—he carried it out." While Eichmann was not the most senior officer in the Third Reich's extermination program, "he was the highest Nazi official who had direct contact with Jewish leaders. To them he seemed omnipotent."[6] During the postwar years Eichmann was sought by the Jewish Agency as well as by independent Nazi hunters based in Europe. Eventually the Israeli Secret Service took up the pursuit of evidence documenting Eichmann's whereabouts. By the spring of 1960 Eichmann was traced to a suburb of Buenos Aires, where he lived under the name of Ricardo Klement. His true identity confirmed, Israeli agents kidnapped him and smuggled him out of Argentina.[7]

On 23 May 1960 Prime Minister David Ben-Gurion announced to the Knesset that Israeli agents had captured Eichmann and brought him to

Israel, where he would be tried before an Israeli court. Almost one year later the trial opened in Jerusalem on 11 April 1961. Eichmann was formally charged with committing "crimes against the Jewish people," "crimes against humanity," and "war crimes," as well as with "membership in a hostile organization."[8] During the intervening months a special unit of the Israeli police interrogated Eichmann extensively, and they undertook an exhaustive research effort to prepare the case against him.[9] Working under the supervision of Teddy Kollek, the director-general of the prime minister's office, other Israeli government officials selected and prepared the venue, procedure and personnel for the trial. With Eichmann's approval, Israel engaged as defense counsel Dr. Robert Servatius, a German laywer from Cologne who had defended a number of Nazis at the war crimes trials in Nuremberg. The three jurists who would adjudicate the case were also named: Justice Moshe Landau, of the Supreme Court, the trial's presiding judge; Justice Benjamin Halevi, president of the Jerusalem District Court; and Justice Yitzhak Raveh of the Tel Aviv District Court.

During these months, the agenda and protocols of Eichmann's case were widely debated in public forums, both within Israel and internationally. The extensive pretrial publicity generated considerable interest in the case, and its singular nature raised a number of key questions: Could Eichmann be tried for these crimes in accordance with laws enacted after the crimes had been committed? Could Eichmann be tried for these crimes in Israel, a country other than the scene of their perpetration or his place of residence at the time of his arrest—moreover, a country that did not even exist at the time that the crimes were committed? Could Eichmann, who was accused of attempting to destroy the Jewish people in its entirety, be given a just trial before a tribunal of Jews in a Jewish state? Could Eichmann be justly tried by a nation that had forcibly abducted him for the purpose of bringing him to justice? The debate over these questions fostered the anticipation that the proceedings would address issues much larger than the culpability of Adolf Eichmann.

"A New Wailing Wall": Debating the Eichmann Case

From the start, discussions of the Eichmann case conceptualized it as a symbolic performance, its significance linked variously to Jewish history, Israeli politics, human psychology, or universal ethics. In Jerusalem the news of Eichmann's arrest came, by coincidence, within the context of another symbolic performance staged with international—and especially American—audiences in mind. At the time, thousands of Israelis filled the city's streets to appear as extras in the Hollywood film version of Leon

Uris's novel *Exodus*. While reenacting the historic announcement on 29 November 1947 that the United Nations had voted in favor of the partition of Palestine, the crowd was abuzz with "only one topic of conversation — the capture of Eichmann by Israel's Security Service."[10]

Participants in the controversy surrounding the Eichmann trial itself often described it as a performance. As Hariman has noted, the perception of a trial as a "performance of the laws" in the "national theater" creates a dilemma: "The more a trial appears to be a scene or product of public controversy and rhetorical artistry, the less legitimate it appears. . . . It seems that good law and powerful rhetoric do not mix."[11] Yet Israel's supporters and detractors alike invoked the notion of "trial as performance" when discussing both its effectiveness — in which the trial's performative nature was often acknowledged, sometimes championed — and its legitimacy, in which defenders as a rule rejected critics' notions of the Eichmann case as a mere "show trial."

This debate began as soon as the Israeli government announced its intention to try Eichmann in Jerusalem. The legitimacy of Israel's claims on Eichmann not only were formally raised in the forum of the United Nations, but also were widely discussed in the international press.[12] Hausner wrote that, with Ben-Gurion's announcement of Eichmann's capture, "Israel itself was on trial. The whole world seemed to be watching to see how we acquitted ourselves of the task we had undertaken." The prosecutor noted that this " 'trial' of the trial" continued as an international audience observed the proceedings in Jerusalem.[13]

While the deliberations at the United Nations were limited to the question of Israel's abduction of Eichmann from Argentina, the press served as a forum for a much broader debate over whether the promised proceedings would serve justice with dignity and fairness, or if they would devolve into either an act of vengeance or a politically manipulated show trial. Israel's detractors were not limited to its traditional opponents. The plan to try Eichmann in an Israeli court was criticized publicly by, among others, Joseph Proskauer, honorary president of the American Jewish Committee; Nahum Goldmann, president of the World Zionist Organization; and Jewish philosopher Martin Buber, a resident of Jerusalem.[14]

Some critics of the trial warned of an event whose performative nature would preclude its claim to serving justice. In April 1961 the *Tulsa Tribune* described the trial as "a new wailing wall — a show and spectacle carefully stage-managed to wring the maximum sympathy out of a dramatic exposure of Nazi genocide."[15] The *National Review* cautioned its readers that they were in for a "prolonged and exhaustive treatment" that not only raised troubling legal questions, but also threatened to be unsatisfying as social ritual: "There is no more drama or suspense in store for us than there would be if the trial and ultimate exoneration of Dreyfus were to be repeated." Moreover, the editorial argued, the Eichmann trial promised to be an inappropriately "lurid extravaganza" that would ultimately prove ineffective: "Overfamiliarity with bestiality can dull one's sense of horror. The diary of Anne Frank did more to bring out the horror of Buchenwald than the trial of Eichmann will do."[16]

Ben-Gurion responded by validating, rather than denying, the notion of the Eichmann trial as a performance, arguing that the proceedings would effectively and appropriately fulfill a larger agenda. In a December 1960 interview he outlined Israel's motives: "We want to establish before the nations of the world how millions of people, because they happened to be Jews, . . . were murdered by the Nazis." The nations of the world, he stated, "should know that anti-Semitism is dangerous, and they should be ashamed of it." Moreover, Ben-Gurion hoped that the Eichmann trial would help "ferret out other Nazis—for example, the connection between Nazis and some Arab rulers." He also championed the trial as a means of educating "the generation of Israelis who have grown up since the Holocaust" about Nazi persecutions of European Jewry. Indeed, with regard to the matter of the defendant's culpability or punishment, Ben-Gurion appeared to be dismissive: "I don't care what verdict is delivered against Eichmann. Only the fact that he will be judged in a Jewish state is important."[17]

Hausner, too, was sensitive to the trial's performative aspects. While preparing his case, he felt that the extensive documentary evidence that had been compiled for prosecuting Eichmann was limited, because it would fail "to reach the hearts of men." Instead, Hausner sought to present "a living record of a gigantic human and national disaster." In selecting which of many possible witnesses to call upon to testify at the trial, Hausner not only sought effective performers, choosing those who seemed "less tongue-tied" after a "preliminary sifting" of candidates, but also made dramaturgical choices as to how different individuals might present similar evidence:

> I asked a plumber to give evidence on the events in Bialystok, an important Jewish center. After his statement was recorded, a well-known writer, a leader of the underground in the same place, volunteered to give evidence on the same events. By many standards the latter witness might have been preferable. But I wanted to have the plumber tell his story in his own simple words; so, finally, I kept him on the list and summoned him to court, regretfully forgoing the evidence of the author.[18]

"The Whole World Could Watch": Televising the Eichmann Trial

The special concern for the Eichmann trial as a performance extended to preparations for its worldwide audience. Despite the extensive controversies surrounding the case, the Israeli government planned the trial with a large press presence in mind. Segev has noted that "in those days many Israelis had an almost mystic faith in the power of the international media to harm Israel or help it, and they deeply desired to win its support and favor."[19]

Israel's decision to televise the Eichmann trial epitomized this investment in the power of mass media. An apparently unprecedented move, this, too, provoked controversy. When Eichmann's defense counsel argued against allowing cameras in the courtroom, the prosecution made its case by citing precedents that championed publicity as a guarantor of a fair trial.[20] Israeli judges who ruled in favor of the prosecution cited British law on the subject of witnesses and publicity: "Where there is no publicity there is no justice. It keeps the judge himself, while trying, under trial. The security of securities is publicity."[21]

Rather than convening the trial in a courthouse, the Israeli government held the proceedings in Beit Ha'am (literally, "the house of the people"), a large public theater and community center in western Jerusalem that was under construction at the time of Eichmann's capture. This was done, in part, so as to accommodate the large number of journalists expected for the trial. The four-story building was surrounded with a ten-foot-high fence and renovated to meet the trial's special security needs. These included the quarters to which Eichmann was confined for the duration of the proceedings and a bulletproof glass enclosure surrounding the dock in which he sat, flanked by armed guards, throughout the trial.[22]

Beit Ha'am was also remodeled to provide hundreds of print and broadcast journalists with work space and telecommunications services. The "$1 million press facilities" featured "$350,000 worth of new transmission facilities, including banks of teletypes staffed by Jerusalem housewives hastily recruited and trained," according to a feature in *Time* magazine. The spectators' section of the auditorium in Beit Ha'am was to be separated from the "stage" on which the trial proceedings took place by a sheet of bulletproof glass similar to the material that surrounded the defendant's dock. Of the 756 seats in the spectators' section, 474 were reserved for members of the press (whereas initially only about 20 were set aside for the public). The Israeli government provided reporters with transistor radios that received simultaneous translation of the trial—which was officially conducted in Hebrew—into English, German, or French; mimeographed copies of the court's daily proceedings were also made available in these four languages. In addition, journalists were able to watch the trial proceedings live on closed-circuit television in the press room.[23]

Although Israel had no broadcast television at the time, the government arranged to record the trial on videotape—"so that the whole world could watch," according to Hausner.[24] (With the exception of the 570 people who daily obtained admission to nearby Ratisbonne Hall—an old French monastery, where the trial was shown live on a thirteen-foot screen via closed-circuit transmission—most Israelis followed the trial by listening to live radio broadcasts of the proceedings and reading newspaper coverage.)[25] The major American networks and several European national television systems had each requested permission to set up its own cameras in the courthouse. Unable either to accommodate this many broadcasters or to provide pool footage of its own, and concerned that "the filming must not interfere with normal and proper trial procedure," the Israeli government decided in November 1960 to contract with one American company to create a comprehensive video record of the trial.[26]

Israel awarded the contract to Capital Cities Broadcasting Corporation, then a relatively small, independent company based in New York City. The arrangement stipulated that "the company was not an 'agent' of Israel and that it had no rights or exclusivity to the recording." Capital Cities agreed to provide footage of the proceedings to all interested television networks and newsreel producers and to turn over any profits from the fees charged for the use of the footage to a charity designated by the Israeli government. Although American networks protested this arrangement when it was announced in early 1961, they eventually complied, each paying $50,000 for an hour's worth of footage per day for the course of the trial. In addition, each network used its own cameras and personnel to supplement Capital Cities's trial footage with material recorded outside the courtroom. A *TV Guide* feature on coverage of the trial noted that "the camera crews interview counsel, bystanders, victims of the Holocaust, as the extermination of the 6,000,000 has come to be known in the State of Israel—and when things are dull they interview each other."[27]

According to Milton Fruchtman, an executive producer with Capital Cities, footage of the trial was used by thirty-eight countries, and an estimated "80 per cent of the world's viewers have seen shots of the trial." *New York Times* media critic Jack Gould noted that television coverage of the Eichmann trial promised "to be the most sustained and extensive attention that TV ever has accorded a single news story, partly because what will be one of history's most celebrated trials will be the first to be televised on home screens around the world."[28]

Indeed, some described the televising of the Eichmann trial as an important precedent for international television coverage of future major events. Fruchtman predicted that the videotape record of the trial would be "one of the great reckoning points of television" and might eventually lead "to a worldwide network."[29] He also envisioned videotape facilitating the creation of "visual case histories," which would become a valuable resource for jurists and law schools: "Video tapes will tell them not only *what* the

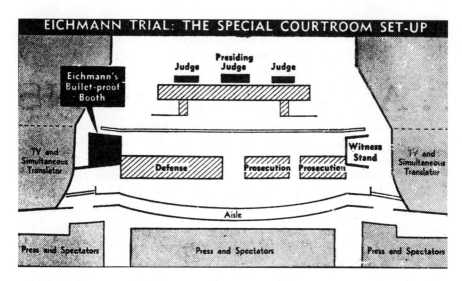

This diagram of the Eichmann trial courtroom appeared in the *New York Times* as the proceedings were about to begin. Note the placement of television cameras in enclosed areas on the left and right sides of the stage. (Copyright © 1961 by The New York Times Company. Reprinted by permission.)

witnesses said, but *how* they said it and *how they looked* when they said it."[30]

Although filming the proceedings was considered an important venture, the cameras' presence in the Jerusalem courtroom was masked. Capital Cities set up four cameras in Beit Ha'am, which were concealed in booths located to the left and right of the stage on which the tribunal sat. "Only because you have been informed of the presence of the cameras do you know they are at work in the courtroom," a feature in *TV Guide* explained. "The cameras, mounted in recesses of the wall, shoot through a fine wire screen. The screen does not seem to hurt the quality of the picture. You have to look carefully about the room to see the cameras."[31]

The recording of the trial proceedings involved a crew of two dozen men, supervised by Capital Cities's Leo Hurwitz, who had been director of television news and special events for CBS from 1944 to 1947. (A director of politically charged documentary films—*Heart of Spain,* 1937; *Native Land,* 1942; *Strange Victory,* 1948—Hurwitz had also been the victim of anti-Communist blacklisting during the early postwar years.) The filming of the Eichmann trial evolved its own aesthetic criteria during the course of actual proceedings. "You can't follow mechanically," Hurwitz explained in an interview. "You can't simply follow a witness all the time he speaks, and then put the camera on Eichmann when his name is mentioned. You have to have a sense of the event, a sense of following the case as it is built up against Eichmann."[32] As Hurwitz's team was the only production crew filming the trial, their choices—camera angles, composition and length of shots, camera-to-camera editing—became a fixed part of the trial's official visual record.

While copies of tapes of complete sessions of the Eichmann trial repose in archives in Israel and the United States, most of this footage has never been aired on television in any country.[33] At most, broadcasters presented an hour of trial footage daily during the run of the proceedings; most offered much less. A *TV Guide* feature outlined the daily procedure of recording, selecting, and distributing the trial footage: Following the end of each morning and afternoon court session, "the tape is studied and enough for a 30-minute showing is processed by a network pool. . . . Two sound tracks are recorded: one in the original language spoken in the court, the other in translation from the simultaneous translators' booths." Then crews set about the "monumental task" of transporting the selected footage to dozens of countries around the world: "If the tape is considered routine it is sent by one of the many airlines leaving Lod airport, 90 minutes' fast driving from Jerusalem. All the airlines are cooperating to speed the tapes and films to their intended destinations. Now and then, when a network producer thinks the tape is 'hot,' he will charter a small plane to fly to Lod airport."[34]

Television coverage of the Eichmann trial thus represents a transitional stage in international telecommunications. Videotape facilitated a more efficient handling of footage than film, but getting the footage to European and American audiences still required shipping videotape copies by air. On at least one occasion, "America's television networks were left without expected films of the Eichmann trial . . . because of a failure in flight connections."[35] While the next-day presentation of footage of the Eichmann trial was an advance over newsreels, which took several days to process and distribute, this achievement would soon be eclipsed by simultaneous global broadcasting via satellite.[36]

Over the course of the two years between Eichmann's capture and his eventual execution on 31 May 1962, his case appeared repeatedly in the multichannel flow of American television in a variety of configurations and venues.[37] Although these presentations do not meet all of media scholars Daniel Dayan and Elihu Katz's criteria for what they have defined as "media events," the televised coverage of the trial and related programming might be considered a forerunner of these "high holidays of mass communication." Telecasts of or about the Eichmann trial were not broadcast live, but they did interrupt the broadcasting routine; the coverage was preplanned, in part, by forces outside the broadcasting industries and pre-

sented with some "reverence and ceremony." The televising of the Eichmann trial was a "hegemonic" celebration of Israel's "establishment initiatives" and was proclaimed, by Israelis and others, as "historic." The
broadcasts engaged large audiences and generated an intense level of interest, stimulating people to "tell each other that it is mandatory to view."
Like the more recent media events that Dayan and Katz have analyzed (e.g.,
the Apollo moon landing in 1969, Anwar el-Sadat's visit to Jerusalem in
1977), the Eichmann trial telecasts demonstrate the role that television can
play in forming political constituencies and shaping civil religion by creating transformative viewing experiences, celebratory rituals in which viewers take a collective and often active role: "These broadcasts integrate
societies in a collective heartbeat and evoke a renewal of loyalty to the society and its legitimate authority."[38]

   While pursuing the larger common agenda of presenting the trial as a
landmark event of history, news, and broadcasting, American television
offered coverage of the Eichmann case that differed from one broadcaster
to another. All three national commercial networks featured reports on the
case in their nightly prime-time news programs over the course of the proceedings, and all three presented a variety of special programs dealing with
the trial near the time of its opening and closing. Of the three networks, ABC
offered the most extensive regular coverage, broadcasting weekly one-hour
summaries nationally and presenting nightly half-hour highlights of the previous day's proceedings to viewers of its flagship station, WABC-TV (Channel 7)
in New York City. The weekly hour, aired on Sunday at 4:00 P.M., and the
daily broadcasts, aired Monday through Friday from 6:30 to 7:00 P.M., were
hosted by news anchors Jim Bishop and, later, Quincy Howe. "Daily videotapes" were also presented in New York on WNTA (Channel 13), which
advertised "the most complete coverage" of the Eichmann trial. This independent station scheduled broadcasts of "the full available hour of the Eichmann affair" at noon, which was reaired after midnight Tuesday through
Saturday.[39]

   Special programs broadcast on American television during the week that
the Eichmann trial began included public affairs programs focusing on the
case itself as well as documentary and dramatic programs offering background on Nazism and the Holocaust. Public affairs programs discussed
historical, juridical, and moral issues raised by the case with legal scholars,
clergy, West German government officials, and veterans of the Nuremberg
war crimes trial. Among the special documentaries aired during this week
were ABC's *Israel and Eichmann,* which sought to "assess the mood in
Israel just prior to the proceedings," and the first installment of NBC's *Trial
of Adolf Eichmann,* a series of news specials narrated by Frank McGee.
Other documentaries broadcast as the trial commenced focused on the
careers of Adolf Hitler and Nazi doctor Joseph Mengele.[40]

In addition, the Eichmann trial was the subject of the week's episodes of news and documentary series. Walter Cronkite and Winston Burdett reported on the trial on CBS's weekly news analysis series *Eyewitness to History,* while ABC's *Bell and Howell Close-up* presented the documentary *I Remember,* in which Simon Gutter, an American Jewish survivor of eight concentration camps, revisits Auschwitz, Bergen-Belsen, and other sites of his European past.[41] CBS also rebroadcast *Engineer of Death: The Eichmann Story,* an episode of *Armstrong Circle Theater* first aired in the fall of 1960.

At the same time, the parameters of television coverage of the Eichmann case were articulated by what could *not* be broadcast. In the television column of the *New York World-Telegram and Sun,* comedians Marty Allen and Steve Rossi commented, "There's nothing you can really do with the Eichmann thing that is really funny." While they regularly drew on headlines for their humor—Soviet astronaut Yuri Gagarin's first space flight, for example, inspired one joke cited—the comedians confessed that "the crimes charged to Eichmann defy humor." They reported having heard Eichmann jokes (ending with such punch lines as "Ah, I'll bet he'll get off with a fine" or "I hear it's going to be settled out of court"), but, the columnist explained, Allen and Rossi "have no plans to incorporate them into their routines at the Copacabana . . . or on the Ed Sullivan Show. It would seem, thus, that the business of comedy, long accepted as an interloper where angels fear to tread, pulls up its reins at the point where horror manages to equal the imagination."[42]

A "Front Seat" in Beit Ha'am: American Television News Coverage of the Eichmann Trial

American broadcasters offered more extensive television coverage of the Eichmann trial than did any other nation. At the outset of the proceedings, broadcasting the trial was treated as a newsworthy item in itself; news coverage of the extensive press that the trial had attracted included details of the effort to televise the proceedings. However, the American press offered relatively little discussion of this unprecedented mediation of a major court case, in contrast with the extensive coverage of the trial itself. On the eve of the start of the proceedings, Jack Gould noted that a number of television programs on the Eichmann case had made comparisons between the upcoming Jerusalem trial and the postwar proceedings in Nuremberg, which "pointed up a little-noticed fact that could have a bearing on the future awareness of Nazi bestiality. In the fifteen years separating the Nuremberg and Jerusalem trials the medium of television was introduced." Gould was, in fact, one of the few observers to mention television's role in shaping the presentation of the trial to the American public and its response to the case. In this review he commented directly on the medium's impact on the subject only once, noting the problematic presence of commercials in an ABC broadcast, which "opened with an appropriately somber and serious summation of the meaning of the trial and then switched to a frothy and gay plug for a consumer product; the juxtaposition was jarring."[43]

Three days later, Gould reviewed the first of the New York local stations' regular broadcasts of daily footage from the trial proceedings. He found that the video record "reflected alert and competent camera work for the most part. There's no gainsaying that the sustained visual coverage affords a very real sense of presence at the courtroom drama in Jerusalem. . . . The close-ups of Eichmann in the glass-enclosed dock are especially good; the impassiveness of the man on listening to the indictment was chilling to watch."[44]

Television was, of course, not the only source that Americans had for learning about Eichmann's history and following his trial; the range of American news media treated the case as an important story. Regular reports appeared in the nation's major daily newspapers and newsmagazines; the trial was also covered in theatrical newsreels and news radio broadcasts. In addition to receiving heavy coverage in the American Yiddish, German-Jewish, and Anglo-Jewish press, the trial was also followed by the press of various Christian denominations.[45]

Nonetheless, televised coverage of the Eichmann trial was distinguished from that provided by other sources, offering a combination of the other media's attributes. Compared to newsreels and popular magazine features, television offered Americans reports that were more immediate, presenting footage of a courtroom session as quickly as twenty-four hours after it had taken place. Though newspaper and radio coverage were often just as prompt, television also offered the trial as spectacle, providing, as one telecast claimed, "the whole world" with "a front-row seat" in Beit Ha'am.[46]

Unlike any other medium, television fostered a sense of "live" contact between event and audience; its intimate scale and speed of transmission gave viewers a sense of proximity to the proceedings. Moreover, television could present the trial in segments of "actuality" that, while selectively edited, still ran much longer than film clips usually shown in newsreels. For those watching the trial coverage in New York, the daily reports appeared in serial installments that paralleled the trial's progress. Together, these elements of television broadcasting fostered an unrivaled sense of direct contact with the proceedings in Israel. "Thanks to the ingenuity of modern communications—particularly the urgent intimacy of television—the distance between us and the *Beit Ha'am* in Jerusalem is almost non-existent," wrote one American observer of the trial. "We, too, are present in the courtroom. We *listen* to the recitals of the prosecution. We *hear* the testimony of the witnesses. We *see* Adolf Eichmann."[47]

In this respect, the Eichmann trial was one of a number of contemporary events whose presentation on television marked the development of the medium as a vehicle for world news coverage. In fact, the opening day of the Eichmann trial vied for the television spotlight with another major news story of international interest, Gagarin's first space mission. A feature in *Variety* seized the occasion to describe the growing pains being experienced by television news:

> As Adolf and Yuri made news, prepared tv programs were dumped to make room for new ones, cues were lost, jet planes skittered across the Atlantic so that one or another of the network news departments might luckily score a two-minute scoop on an arch rival, experts were dragged out of bed or out of left field for "exclusive stories" and, in the past seven days, a great deal of airtime was consumed keeping listeners and viewers abreast of the times.[48]

Beginning in the late 1950s, Americans were becoming increasingly aware of the strategic role that television could play in reporting—and, moreover, in shaping—international news stories. Media scholar Mary Ann Watson has argued that, in 1960, "the television industry had something to prove" to the American public, prompting, among other developments, a signal change in the nature of television news reporting.[49] In the wake of scandals surrounding rigged quiz shows and corrupt FCC officials during the late 1950s, television networks made special efforts at the end of the decade to demonstrate their commitment to responsible broadcasting in the public interest. Prominent among these efforts was the development of new and expanded formats for news and public affairs programming. Within a year, the major networks all announced plans to introduce news documentary series—*CBS Reports* in 1959, and NBC's *White Paper* and ABC's *Bell and Howell Close-up* in 1960.

These developments coincided with the beginning of the Kennedy administration. His special regard for the medium earned Kennedy the nickname of "the television president." Kennedy believed that the medium "could help keep citizens informed about the activities of their government and should be allowed to do so. Documentary producers sensed they had a spokesman in the White House." During the years of the Kennedy administration, American television news departments also began "consolidating authority" as the nation's "preferred medium for news."[50]

The Journalist as Authority

Coverage of the Eichmann case demonstrates how these recent developments in television news shaped the mediation of a major event for the American public. During the spring of 1961, NBC presented a series of news specials on the Eichmann trial. The first to be aired after the proceedings had begun was broadcast on 23 April.[51] The half-hour program consists of excerpts from Capital Cities's trial footage and a series of interviews, with correspondent Frank McGee serving throughout as narrator and interviewer. McGee begins the broadcast while standing in front of Eichmann's vacant, glass-enclosed booth in Beit Ha'am. The courtroom is otherwise empty, except for an armed Israeli guard standing behind the booth. McGee sets the scene of the trial and discusses its "larger purposes," including the goal of understanding the Holocaust "so that the symptoms of madness can be isolated and recognized for all time to come."

Throughout the broadcast, McGee demonstrates the authoritative role journalists play in mediating the trial. He accomplishes this through his presence "on the scene" beside Eichmann's glass-enclosed booth, the trial's most distinctive and crucial locus, as well as through a series of interviews with other journalists and a segment dealing directly with the unprecedented scope of the trial's international press coverage.[52] These devices also link reporting on the trial with the news media's role of making sense of the event's "larger purposes."

After the introduction, images appear of Israelis listening to broadcasts of the trial over loudspeakers on the streets of Jerusalem, followed by footage of the trial's opening sessions. McGee explains Israel's mission to provide its Jewish citizens of non-European origin and its youth with an understanding of the Holocaust. In addition, he claims that Israel seeks "to impress on the conscience of humanity that these crimes . . . were committed in an enlightened age — against Jews this time, but could be committed against others in the future." As he identifies footage of Eichmann's defense counsel, McGee notes that while "legal procedures are scrupulously followed," it is common knowledge that the issue of Eichmann's culpability is "incidental to the larger purpose that has fallen to the Israeli prosecutor, Gideon Hausner."

At this point, an excerpt of Hausner's opening statement is presented; as he speaks in Hebrew, a translator recites: "I do not stand alone. Here with me at this moment stand six million prosecutors. But, alas, they cannot rise to level the finger of accusation in the direction of the glass dock and cry out '*J'accuse*' against the man who sits there." Hausner articulates the paradigmatic value of the Eichmann trial as conceptualized by the Israeli government, which differs from the interpretation offered by American journalists. This conflict between these two visions of the trial's significance is apparent, if obliquely so, in the way that the NBC report presents Hausner's statement. McGee's narration over the trial footage, during which the Hebrew-language proceedings can be heard underneath, offers American viewers an interpretation of what are ostensibly otherwise impenetrable activities. McGee acknowledges the viewers as part of the world that is hearing "the voice of accused and accusor," but it is, in fact, only McGee's own voice and his explanation of the trial's significance that they can understand. Hausner's remarks ("I do not stand alone") are offered as corroboration of the narrator's analysis.

Although McGee's report differs from the Israeli vision of the Eichmann case, the broadcast presents Israel as a newsworthy subject in itself. Following the first courtroom sequence are interviews with two men who survived Nazi persecution, recorded at an Israeli seaside resort and a kibbutz in one of the country's "fertile valleys." These sequences not only extend the program beyond the confines of Beit Ha'am, but also incorporate daily life in the new Zionist state into the coverage of the trial. Both men are asked about the significance of the Eichmann case for the world at large, for Jews, for Germans, and for Israelis, especially the nation's youth. McGee cites some of the lessons that Israeli children report they are learning from the trial, including the observation of one teenager that "those Hitler called subhuman have formed a modern sovereign state where Eichmann can be treated as he never treated the Jews." This citation echoes Ben-Gurion's conflation of the validity of the trial with the legitimacy of the Zionist state, as it substantiates the program's linking of reports on the Eichmann trial with stories on life in modern Israel.

After another segment of trial footage, the NBC news special turns to the media coverage of the proceedings. A long shot shows a large room filled with rows of tables at which people sit typing. McGee legitimates the journalists' authoritative role, describing how the hundreds covering the Eichmann trial—more than the number who covered all the Nuremberg trials—transmit their reports to "the most distant corners of the world." Besides championing them as a crucial link between the trial and its international audience, McGee describes journalists as singularly charged both with the moral duty of complete and honest coverage and with the responsibility to serve as the trial's interpreters: "Some realize the trial will produce revelations embarrassing to their own governments. They say they will report these fully. Each in his own way is trying to reach the core of the trial's significance and report it to his readers, listeners, or viewers."

Interviews with three journalists follow. In addition to asking them professional questions (e.g., "Are you handling this like any other trial?"), McGee also raises personal issues. For example, he asks Carl Renz of the Cologne *Bildzeitung* for his reaction to the trial, in light of having served in the German army during the war. Through these interviews McGee also returns to the issue of the trial's greater significance. On this subject, Takeshi Murumatsu of Japan's Mainichi Newspapers explains that while there is no anti-Semitism in Japan, other forms of racism—"the problem between the Chinese and the Korean people and the Japanese"—do exist. The Eichmann trial therefore provides a "very good opportunity to reflect on our attitudes . . . and to reflect on our crimes during the war." McGee thus situates journalists, rather than the trial or its participants, at the center of the story. Reporters, he claims in his final remarks to the television audience, "realize *they* have been given a responsibility" to "distill and transmit the essence" of the proceedings "if the larger purpose of bringing Adolf Eichmann to trial is to be realized."

History as News

The NBC news special evinces one of the challenges that the Eichmann trial posed to news programs—the coverage as "news" of an event so extensively rooted in "history." Many observers of the trial have noted that it presented relatively little in the way of information about the Nazi persecution of Jews that had not already come to light during the Nuremberg trials or in some other public forum. As Israeli leaders, journalists, and others reiterated, the trial was staged in large measure to present these past events to those ignorant of them—especially those too young to know them through direct experience. It was the act of retelling, rather than what was told, that made the Eichmann case "news," and yet the two were easily conflated. Thus, one of the Holocaust survivors interviewed by McGee explains that, among his cohorts, the Eichmann trial "brought [them] back sixteen years. . . . All that they went through is new again today."

The challenge of what to present as "news" (and as "new") that television broadcasters faced in covering the Eichmann trial was further compounded by the purported immediacy of their medium. Rather than simply providing simultaneous coverage of the Eichmann trial, television offered a complex integration of past and future events. Videotape and jet planes made it possible for Americans to see excerpts from the trial proceedings within twenty-four hours of their occurrence. In addition, evening news programs in the United States were able to report on what had taken place during the trial earlier in the day of the broadcast. Because of the time difference between Jerusalem and New York City, where the news broadcasts were produced, anchors could read stories sent to them on the same date over the wire services. Reporters were also regularly briefed as to what was scheduled to take place at upcoming sessions— who would be testifying, what evidence would be submitted, and so on— which further complicated the sense of time in the trial coverage. Moreover, journalists offered background reports on the Nazi era and speculated as to the eventual outcome of the trial and its implications in the course of covering the daily proceedings.

This conflation of divergent layers of time into television's ongoing present is evident in a sample broadcast of WABC's daily half-hour coverage of the Eichmann trial, aired on Friday, 7 July.[53] News anchor Jim Bishop begins with a report on what took place in court "earlier this morning," the first day of Hausner's cross-examination of Eichmann. Bishop then turns to introducing footage, recorded the previous day, of defense counsel Servatius's direct examination of Eichmann regarding his role in transporting Hungarian Jews to Auschwitz. After Bishop reminds the audience of Eichmann's earlier testimony, the trial footage appears on the screen, showing Eichmann in his booth with Servatius seated nearby. As Eichmann speaks, the camera occasionally cuts away from him to close-ups of others in the courtroom, including Servatius, the woman sitting next to him, and members of the prosecution staff. Repeatedly the image returns to Eichmann, who is sometimes shown in full face, sometimes in profile, sometimes in medium shots that include the structure of the glass-enclosed booth in which he sits, other times in close-ups that exclude the booth's framework. The cutaway shots of others in the courtroom generally last only a few seconds, much shorter than the shots of Eichmann.

Eichmann stops speaking, and then his testimony is heard, translated simultaneously into English and Hebrew. The English, delivered in a female voice, is heard louder than the Hebrew, which is spoken in a male voice. This was specially engineered for American telecasts; in the courtroom, one would have heard the Hebrew translator and could have listened to the simultaneous English translation only on headsets. During the delivery of the translations, the camera continues to focus on Eichmann, with occasional brief cutaway shots of others in the courtroom. In most of the shots of Eichmann, he appears sitting still; sometimes he cocks his head to one side, adjusts his headphones, makes notes, or examines papers before him. The translated section lasts considerably longer than the previous sequence, during which Eichmann was heard (and seen) speaking in German.

At the conclusion of the translation sequence—which, together with the sequence of Eichmann testifying in German, presents some eight minutes of footage from the trial—Bishop reappears on the screen to offer some analysis: "The prosecution appears to be jubilant, and the defense appears to be grim. I can't understand why it is that a man would say he'd publicly hang himself for his part in a crime with which he is charged if he felt no sense of guilt. . . . However, he's fighting . . . as though he stood a chance of winning."

After a commercial break, Bishop introduces an interview (by an unidentified ABC reporter) with Joel Brand.[54] A leader of the Jewish community in Budapest, Brand had met with Eichmann in 1944 to discuss a proposal to purchase the freedom of Hungarian Jews by supplying the Nazis with trucks and other equipment.[55] Bishop explains how the "trucks for Jews" deal fits in the larger trial narrative, reminding viewers of what they have seen and heard in previous broadcasts. He also directs their attention to particular details of the ensuing footage: "Notice in particular his reference to the machinery at Auschwitz."

Following the interview, Bishop reappears to set up more footage from the previous day's proceedings, linking it to reports on Eichmann's testimony heard earlier:

> Eichmann is now using this story of "trucks for Jews" as a basis for defense. He will now tell you in a moment that it was his idea—and you may remember the other day, when we first heard this news, and before we got the tape, a wave of laughter swept the court when he said it was not Himmler's idea, as we thought all along; it was Eichmann's idea, and it was his idea to make himself a big man with his Nazi superiors. . . . Unfortunately, the cameras miss the wave of laughter that swept the court when he first said that "I thought it up."

More footage is shown—again, a relatively short sequence with Eichmann speaking, followed by a longer sequence of him sitting during the translation of his testimony. Cutaway shots in this sequence show a group of elderly spectators, perhaps survivors of the Holocaust; a reporter wearing transistor earphones and picking his nose; and a younger spectator, among others. At the end of this sequence, Bishop reappears to conclude the broadcast. He returns to the current day's proceedings, the start of Hausner's cross-examination of Eichmann ("which I hope will be here as part of our report on Monday"), and reenacts some of their exchange:

> Eichmann admitted that he was anti-Semitic. But then he went on to say, "I do not admit to being an accomplice in the murder of Jews from a legal viewpoint." So Hausner responded to that by saying, "Do you in your own heart find yourself guilty as an accomplice in the murder of millions of Jews: yes or no, yes or no." "Yes, from the human point of view, yes," Eichmann replied.

Before bidding the audience good night, Bishop philosophizes on the case as well:

> All of our criminal procedure all over the world is based on moral law, and moral law is based on God's law, and God's law is universally based on the Ten Commandments, so that there's hardly a line of demarcation where you can say, "Yes, I was morally responsible or I was humanly responsible, but I certainly am not legally responsible." This is a very, very fine, delicate point, and I don't subscribe to it.

Critics generally praised the broadcast of reports of the Eichmann trial on local television, and they placed special value on the medium's presentation of exceptional actuality in the course of their coverage. Jack Gould characterized it as "viewing not to be missed," and *TV Guide*'s Jay Michael wrote that "television had never before offered programs more powerful in their impact, more numbing in their horror of the events they recounted." Howard Thompson's review of *Operation Eichmann*—a feature film based on Eichmann's wartime career and postwar experiences up to the time of his capture by Israeli agents—dismissed it as "standard melodrama with factual trimmings" and stated that, for "staggering impact," nothing could equal "the television vignettes and the expressionless figure in the glass booth." *Variety*'s review of the broadcasts hosted by Bishop characterized them as "not especially professional but frequently interesting and informative." While noting Bishop's limitations—"the burden of . . . the nightly half-hour occasionally leaves him with some relatively limp things to say"—the critic considered the trial coverage "fascinating watching for the most part" and praised the host for having "a purpose in mind that is commendable: To give design, other than that supplied by the random chronology of the trial itself—he's been tying together pieces, which to him, give distinct insights into the many facets of the former Nazi assassin."[56]

In Bishop's efforts to reconfigure the trial's complex temporal structure into an "interesting and informative" narrative for his viewers, his commentary continually shifted: from the historical past (the wartime events being recounted) to the trial's present; from the footage of "yesterday" to the news of "today" to the anticipated events and videotape of "the next day"; from describing what had happened or would be seen (or should have been seen but was "missed" by the cameras) to reenacting the words or thoughts of Eichmann and Hausner, to offering conjectures and judgments about both past and future events. While this jumble of tenses, voices, and discursive modes may have been, in part, the consequence of a news report hastily assembled and broadcast live, it also testifies to the trial's complex of agendas and the conflation of past(s), present(s), and future(s) inherent in its coverage.

The temporal complex of Bishop's nightly reports on the Eichmann trial is exemplary of what media scholar Mimi White has described as television's "peculiar relationship with history," which she has characterized as "hyperhistory." White has argued that, in contrast to conventional notions of history as ordered and closed, television offers a vision of history that is "fragmentary, multiple, and contradictory." Thus, televised events "are both past and present, there-then and here-now, ended and open-ended; they are already historicized as stories, and yet to be finalized." White has noted that news and public affairs programs, in particular, often proclaim that we are "witnesses to 'history in the making.'" While this is understood to mean that events are "momentous rather than historic," it also suggests that what "is not yet a closed sequence of events with a beginning, middle, and end . . . can be—must be—'historic' if it is in the process of being recorded by television."[57]

The Eichmann trial itself constituted a kind of hyperhistory, by virtue of its self-conscious performance of the past as "historical" in its multiple meanings. The trial's notions of history included not only the period of Nazi persecution of European Jewry, but also the much larger sweep of Jewish experience as conceptualized by Zionist ideology—for example, Hausner's evocation of figures from the biblical prophet Joel to Captain Alfred Dreyfus in his opening statement to the court. Later, Hausner wrote of the trial that "in the air were Biblical phrases, which had foreshadowed the event over twenty-five centuries before: 'The delivered shall come up on Mount Zion to judge the Mount of Esau.'"[58] The televising of the trial compounded the hyperhistory of the event by simultaneously creating a videotaped record of the trial "for history" as well as an instant, international audience of "witnesses to history."

Witnessing for Tomorrow

The notion that witnessing mediations of the Holocaust is a morally transformative experience, first articulated in the newsreels of April and May 1945, also played a strategic role in the televising of the Eichmann trial. Witnessing figures as a motif throughout *Verdict for Tomorrow,* a half-hour documentary on the trial produced by Capital Cities Broadcasting Corporation after the conclusion of the proceedings and aired on American television during the fall of 1961, as the presiding Israeli judges prepared their verdict.[59]

The documentary opens with newsreel footage of the 1930s showing Nazis driving through the streets of a German city and putting up boycott signs on Jewish shops. The sound track plays a vintage radio broadcast by Lowell Thomas, a renowned newscaster for CBS during the 1930s, reporting the news of anti-Semitic violence in Germany. Next, Thomas (who in 1961 was a major stockholder in Capital Cities) appears on the screen and addresses the camera:

> I wonder if you recall that news broadcast of mine of November 10, 1938. It was the climax of the opening chapter of one of the most shocking news stories of our time, of all time—the infamous *Kristallnacht,* or "Crystal Night," when Nazi mobs smashed the windows of Jewish shops, plundered synagogues, and beat up Jews in Germany and Austria. This was the beginning—the ending involved the murder of six million Jews as part of Nazi Germany's Final Solution to the Jewish problem.

As Thomas continues his narration of the Nazis' efforts to exterminate the Jews of Europe, vintage images reappear on the screen: footage of German officers directing civilians onto cattle cars is followed by films recorded in liberated concentration camps, including shots of an empty stretcher being pushed into a crematorium oven, of the charred remains of a corpse inside an oven, and of an emaciated corpse lying on the ground.

"The last chapters of this unforgettable nightmare are now being written — written by newsmen crowded into Jerusalem's Beit Ha'am," Thomas continues as images of the trial appear on the screen, beginning with a long shot of the courtroom interior. Eichmann is shown in his glass-enclosed booth; on the sound track a male translator asks in English how the defendant pleads, and he responds in German. A female voice translates Eichmann's reply into English: "In the spirit of the indictment, not guilty." As Eichmann continues to respond to each of the counts against him with identical answers, the program's title and opening credits appear on the screen.

This prologue to *Verdict for Tomorrow* offers, in effect, a capsule summary of what was coming to be known at this time as the Holocaust. As presented here, the Final Solution occupies the narrative's climactic center, flanked by temporal boundaries of the rise of Nazism (with *Kristallnacht* figuring as its own climax) on one side and the Eichmann trial as its resolution on the other. Radio, newsreel, and television news reports not only serve as the instruments of narration, but also embody the creative force behind the narrative's conception and articulation. "Newsmen" are described as forging "the last chapters" of this epoch, just as journalists — including Thomas himself — authored its opening chapters. Indeed, Thomas first describes the narrative in journalistic terms, as "one of the most shocking news stories of our time."

By using vintage prewar and wartime images, much of which was familiar to American audiences from newsreels or early television documentaries, *Verdict for Tomorrow* invokes the iconic role of these images as virtual witnesses. Their privileged status is implicitly extended to the television footage of the trial that follows. After the opening credits, the documentary offers a chronological overview of the Eichmann trial. Thomas narrates excerpts from Capital Cities's videotapes of the proceedings to review the indictments against the defendant, the judges' initial consideration of the legitimacy of the charges and of the decision to conduct the trial in an Israeli court, the prosecution's presentation of its case, Eichmann's defense and cross-examination, and the summations by Hausner and Servatius.

Early in this chronicle Thomas addresses the significance of witnessing the proceedings, linking it to the role of mass communication: "More than just a man was on trial — the conscience of the entire world was being called to account for allowing such inhumanities ever to have occurred. It was of paramount importance, then, that the whole world see, hear, and understand the causes and the consequences — the price that must be paid should this ever be allowed to happen again. This job could only be done

Director Leo Hurwitz (seated second from right, wearing headphones), executive producer Milton Fruchtman (standing behind Hurwitz), and other employees of Capital
Cities Broadcasting Corporation in the television control room at Beit Ha'am, recording
the Eichmann trial proceedings for international broadcast. On the wall, left, is a row of
monitors carrying the continuous feed from each of the four cameras in the courtroom;
the uppermost monitor shows which shots were recorded on videotape as they were
selected. Photographer: Werner Braun. (National Jewish Archive of Broadcasting, the
Jewish Museum, New York. Reprinted with permission of the photographer.)

by a world mass communications medium." As the screen fills with shots of
the television control room in Beit Ha'am, Thomas continues: "Through
the eyes of the television camera and by means of videotape, the whole
world had a front-row seat in the Beit Ha'am. The cast was complete. The
historic courtroom drama was about to begin."

Like the early postwar newsreels in which Americans first saw images of
Nazi death camps, *Verdict for Tomorrow* contrasts virtuous and culpable
witnessing. Here, survivors who testified about their wartime experience of
Nazi atrocities for the prosecution are juxtaposed against Eichmann, the
sole defendant and the one witness for the defense to appear in court. *Verdict for Tomorrow* presents a sequence of excerpts from five prosecution
witnesses' testimony. As they describe various gruesome acts of sadism, torture, and murder, the camera cuts away to show Eichmann listening impas-
sively, his mouth occasionally twisted to one side in a smirking tic.

These reaction shots show a dispassionate Eichmann amid some of the most well-known moments of the trial: A witness describes how a Nazi officer stopped a woman as she tried to hand her baby over to others for safekeeping; the officer "shot her twice, then took the baby in his hands and tore him as one would tear a rag." In contrast to Eichmann's undemonstrative, inscrutable mien, the cameras cut away here to show a woman in the audience bury her face in a handkerchief. Yehiel De-Nur (who wrote some of the earliest popular works in Hebrew on the Holocaust under the pen name Ka-Tzetnik 135663) is shown collapsing after his agitated and rambling effort to testify about his experiences at Auschwitz. Again, reaction shots of Eichmann show his apparent indifference. Another witness, Rivka Joselewka, dabs her eyes with a handkerchief as she describes her survival of a mass execution by an *Einsatzgruppe*. As she recounts seeing others shot and then being shot herself, the image cuts to Eichmann and then returns to the witness. This sequence not only contrasts Eichmann's detached appearance with Joselewka's emotional testimony, but also suggests that she might be testifying against the defendant as though he were the man who had actually shot her — thereby realizing Hausner's agenda of presenting Eichmann as "the central pillar of the whole wicked system."[60]

Thomas concludes the documentary by distinguishing television's contribution of creating an international audience for the trial and facilitating its ultimate purpose of transforming each viewer into a morally engaged witness: "What is truly important is that the trial was held at all; that, by means of the television camera and videotape, this trial has been seen by thinking men thoughout the world. . . . We trust it has caused you to stop and think, to render your own final verdict — a personal resolve . . . that this shall never be allowed to happen again."

Watching Eichmann

Compared to viewing liberation footage during the final months of World War II, which was rooted in wartime propaganda, watching the Eichmann trial on American television was tied to an agenda both more universalized and more individuated. In the mainstream American media, witnessing the courtroom proceedings focused less on the Nazi era and more on general concerns about human psychology and morality, advancing the notion of the Holocaust as an intellectual and ethical paradigm in American public culture.[61] The ability to watch the trial on television contributed to this shift of attention from the events of the Holocaust to the presence of the man accused of their realization. This is borne out in the extensive discussion of the trial and its broadcast, as well as in television dramas, aired at the time, that address the Eichmann case.

"He Looks Like a Human Being": Eichmann, the Body of Discourse

Even before Americans saw the first televised images of the Eichmann trial, broadcasters had encouraged them to conceptualize watching the proceedings as a morally charged act of witnessing. For example, a full-page advertisement run by WABC-TV in New York City's daily newspapers on 12 April 1961 stated, under the heading "The judgment of Eichmann":

We are, we have reason to think, creatures of reason.

Yet the evidence, in numbers and in pictures, of this man's crimes defies all reason, rejects all belief.

How, then, do you judge a man accused of murdering millions? . . .

Who indeed is being judged?

Is not the judgment of an Adolf Eichmann, in its final sense, the judgment of an entire generation, of twenty-five years in which the world itself took leave of reason? . . .

We are that generation grown older, grown forgetful. Humanly so.

Yet, in the cause of this humanity, let us now remember what we would most forget. And let us now watch the judgment of Eichmann, by sitting in judgment of ourselves.

In so remembering, we may best keep vigil on the future. In so judging, we may best make sure our children, and their children, need never sit in similar judgment.[62]

Watching the Eichmann trial on television not only offered American audiences the unprecedented opportunity to observe, albeit remotely, the trial of an actual war criminal. By focusing attention on the presence of the trial's sole defendant, this act of witnessing emerged as an individuated and self-reflexive act. As conceptualized in this advertisement, watching Eichmann was ultimately an exercise in observing a fellow human being and thus constituted an invitation to sit in judgment of all humankind—including oneself.[63]

Journalists and others attending the trial were also preoccupied with watching Eichmann. Before his first public appearance in court, the lack of any vintage film footage and dearth of photographs of the defendant (which was said to have made his capture that much more challenging) intensified the public anticipation of laying eyes on him. On the opening day of the trial, Lawrence Fellows reported to the *New York Times* that "for nearly everyone in the courtroom, it was a first look at the man charged with having 'caused the killing of millions of Jews.'"

The act of seeing Eichmann was so important that looking, watching, and witnessing became central motifs of the trial's press coverage. Like most other print journalists, Fellows offered his readers a description of Eichmann's physical appearance and demeanor:

> Lean and partly bald, [he] was well groomed and poised throughout the first day's sessions. He had a fresh haircut and wore a dark gray suit that had been finished for him only yesterday. It was set off by a starched white shirt and black-and-white tie. There were only the smallest indications that he was at all restive. He frequently tightened his lips and wet them from time to time. He swallowed often and rubbed his right thumb against his left forefinger.[64]

Such descriptions demonstrate a fixation on the ordinariness of Eich-mann's appearance — which extended close-ups on television only magni-fied — in stark contrast to the enormity of the crimes for which he was on trial. More charged accounts of the defendant's appearance, which appeared in the American Jewish press, explored the significance of seeing Eichmann. Elie Wiesel's description of the first day of the trial appeared on the front page of the *Jewish Daily Forward*:

> "His face was somewhat pale, but he had been kept from resting." All 560 correspondents in Jerusalem's Beit Ha'am underscored this in their reports yesterday. And they uttered this with a certain tone of surprise, of disbelief, even more — of impossibility. It was as if they had expected something differ-ent: a man who is a murderer six million times over *can't* be perceived as nor-mal people are. He *must* have a different appearance: he *must* display some sort of nervousness, some sort of hatred, some sort of madness, that would mark him as different from other human beings.[65]

As Wiesel suggested, descriptions of Eichmann's physical presence were closely linked to efforts to understand the defendant's inner psyche or his significance in the larger goals of the trial. Many journalists also character-ized his appearance as other than human, describing his demeanor as "snakelike," resembling a "robot," or suggesting "some bleak, canted ora-cle out of a half-forgotten world." Eichmann's physical presence in the courtroom inspired a range of symbolic associations. Leyb Rakhman, another reporter for the *Forward*, presented a vision of Eichmann as the metonym for generations of anti-Semites: "I felt as though not only were he standing before the Jewish court, but that behind him stood the hundreds of our enemies and persecutors of many generations — Torquemada and Chmielnicki, Haman and Hitler, their shadows filled Eichmann's glass cell." And, in an effort to demonstrate how the Eichmann trial had become a "Kafka nightmare," *New York Times* editor C. L. Sulzburger described the defendant as being "himself more 'Jewish looking,' according to con-

Adolf Eichmann, surrounded by Israeli military guards, testifying in the glass-enclosed defendant's dock. (UPI/Corbis-Bettmann.)

ventional definitions, than the two sunburned Israeli guards who sit with him inside a bullet-proof, glass courtroom cage."[66]

Accounts of Eichmann's appearance also sought revelations about the "Nazi character," the human condition in general, or the nature of evil as a metaphysical force. In their quest for insight into Eichmann—and all that he had come to embody—through their attention to his body, observers scrutinized his presence for revealing minutiae, his behavior for involuntary betrayals of inner monstrosity. As Tom Segev has noted, even Gideon Hausner engaged in this pursuit. The prosecutor, who first saw Eichmann when the trial began, subsequently wrote that the defendant "had 'disconcerting eyes,' which during the cross-examination 'burned with a bottomless hatred.' A closer look, the attorney general wrote, revealed that he also had 'hands like talons'—a photograph of his fingers was published in the press and was, Hausner said, 'frightening.'"[67]

Journalistic scrutiny of Eichmann's physicality lasted throughout the trial and continued well after its conclusion. Martha Gellhorn began a retrospective essay on the case with a close description of the defendant's appearance—his "thin neck, high shoulders, curiously reptilian eyes"—and habits:

"He changes his glasses frequently, for no explicable reason. He tightens his narrow mouth, purses it. Sometimes there is a slight tic under his left eye. He runs his tongue around his teeth, he seems to suck his gums. . . . People, coming fresh to this courtroom, stare at him. We have all stared. . . . We are trying, in vain, to answer the same question: how is it possible? He looks like a human being."

Gellhorn, like many other journalists, included a description of the glass-enclosed dock — which the defendant never left during the course of the trial, except to be escorted back to his living quarters — as part of her portrait of Eichmann.[68] She compared the structure to "the prow of a ship" and, as did many others writing about the trial, "a cage."[69] Another commentator remarked that a number of American observers likened the structure "to the glass cage used in televised quiz shows."[70] The association with television, especially by Americans, is telling. Correspondents such as Gellhorn, who attended the trial in person, could also watch the proceedings on closed-circuit monitors in the press room of Beit Ha'am. Moreover, they were doubtless aware that many of their readers watched telecasts covering the proceedings, and that their minute descriptions of the defendant's appearance and demeanor would resonate with readers' own experiences of scrutinizing extended close-ups of Eichmann.

Over the course of the trial, reporters' comments on the defendant's appearance became more self-reflexive, as making sense of the face-to-face encounter with the visually unexceptional, undemonstrative Eichmann proved an increasingly frustrating exercise. In the *Forward,* Rakhman described the ordeal he and fellow journalists faced, articulating the challenge in terms of the trial as performance — or, more specifically, of Eichmann as performer: "Our eyes never leave him, and he remains for us an impenetrable psychological riddle. Where did he get such cold nerves? Why doesn't he break out in screams? Let him curse, swear, or weep, or yell! But — once and for all — do something! . . . Let us at least see one pulsation of an artery behind this heavy mask!"[71]

Indeed, the failure of this scrutiny of Eichmann's physical presence to yield satisfactory insight into his (or the general "Nazi") character became a subject of discussion in itself. Patrick O'Donovan wrote in the *New Republic* that nearly "every journalist worth his own carbon paper" made a stab at an insightful description of Eichmann, including a French reporter "who wrote that he could see a gas chamber in each of his eyes. Most took the easy way out, which was to describe him as some version of a mean bureaucrat or a little clerk of a man." Such analogies were "rough on honorable trades, but it is possible to see for what the baffled press was groping." Similarly, T. S. Matthews suggested in the *Saturday Evening Post* that Eichmann's "face presents an enigma which each observer interprets according to his fancy."[72]

These discussions extended beyond contemplating Eichmann's physical presence to include his viewing of documentary images of the Holocaust. As in Abby Mann's *Judgment at Nuremberg,* witnessing liberation footage figured as a privileged, if not pivotal, moment in the course of the Eichmann trial. Deciding that "words no longer conveyed their full meanings," Hausner concluded his presentation of evidence by screening excerpts of liberation footage, similar to what was shown at the Nuremberg war crimes trials.[73] Defense counsel Servatius at first objected to the screening but eventually agreed, provided that he and Eichmann could preview the films before they were shown in court. Eichmann's response to the footage was the subject of considerable interest among print journalists covering the trial. Recalling the "withering effect" that screening such films had had on the defendants at the first Nuremberg war crimes trial, Homer Bigart speculated in the *New York Times* that this "could be more devastating than any unpleasantness Eichmann might encounter under cross-examination later in the trial."[74]

But witnessing liberation footage apparently failed to provoke in Eichmann the uneasy or remorseful responses that it had in other war criminals, whether actual defendants at Nuremberg or the fictitious jurist Emil Janning in *Judgment at Nuremberg*. Bigart reported two weeks later that during the trial "Eichmann sat through eighty minutes of filmed horror . . . without flinching or batting an eye." Whereas "the presiding judge, Moshe Landau, appeared ashen and ill as he hurried from the court during a recess called after the movies," Eichmann appeared unmoved. He "never took his eyes from the film, never raised his hands to his face. The man who said he could not bear the sight of blood . . . was the very model of composure."[75]

Eichmann's failure to be demonstrably moved by these images, which had come to be codified as embodying the morally charged act of witnessing the Holocaust, was variously taken as further evidence of his inscrutability, sheer arrogance, mental instability, or lack of humanity. Newsweek contrasted Eichmann's stolid—and, therefore, culpable—response with the virtuous witnessing of Judge Yitzhak Raveh, who "covered his face with his hands as the film showed the bulldozer blades thrusting into piles of skeletal corpses."[76] The reporter for *Time* offered this glib account of the defendant's stoicism: "Chin in hand, Eichmann watched the filmed record of victims being shot and dumped into ditches, barrel after barrel of severed heads. Throughout 90 minutes, Eichmann scarcely moved—except that once he picked his nose. When the lights came on, Eichmann rose, bowed to Dr. Servatius, walked straight back to his cell, and so to bed."[77]

This was one of several incidents during the trial that centered on watching Eichmann watch someone or something. Reports of these incidents sought some insight into Eichmann not by scrutinizing him—which had proved a frustrating and unenlightening activity—but by observing his interactions with others or even by interacting with him. For example, the *New York Times* recounted a "duel of glares" between Eichmann and prosecution witness Dr. Gustave Mark Gilbert, a prison psychologist. While most other witnesses were apparently incapable of looking at the defendant, Dr. Gilbert "took a long, cool and calculated look" at Eichmann while on the witness stand and took notes on his reaction. Gilbert was "barred from giving a professional appraisal of Eichmann's character" in court but later shared his observations with the press that the defendant "was obviously suffering from schizoid apathy, insensitivity and a lack of empathy."[78]

Although these reports on Eichmann as both an insensitive watcher and an impenetrable object of watching do not mention the televising of the trial, they illuminate the problematic nature of the Eichmann trial as a television event. Telecasting the proceedings was vaunted as facilitating for millions the edifying and morally transformative act of witnessing. However, the televised image of Eichmann only compounded the problematic presence described by journalists who watched him in court. Viewers saw an image that was challenging to begin with—a man in a glass box, whose eyeglasses often "reflected light from the neon lamps in the ceiling"—refracted further through another set of lenses (those of the television camera) and another glass box (that of the television screen).[79] Rather than making him more present—and ostensibly more comprehensible—television only made the frustration of watching Eichmann that much more apparent. Close-ups of him did not provide the television viewer with an advantage over the courtroom spectator, but only emphasized Eichmann's inscrutable ordinariness and made his presence seem that much more remote.

The refracted spectacle of Eichmann on trial was further disjointed by the audial component of the telecasts. Whereas journalists attending the trial were able to hear Eichmann speak when he testified (albeit via a microphone), American television audiences heard relatively little of Eichmann's voice, but listened instead to his testimony in translation. During these sequences, viewers watched Eichmann sit—perhaps listening, perhaps merely waiting—as an interpreter delivered translations of his testimony. The spectacle of Eichmann as a rare specimen, enclosed in glass and subjected to extensive scrutiny by television cameras, clashed with his displaced audial presence. On American television, Eichmann was most often heard in a voice other than his own, often that of a female translator, speaking in a language that he did not know, and doing so when he himself was not talking but was silent. Rather than enhancing Eichmann's visual presence on television, the broadcasts disrupted their purported immediacy by undoing the synchronized image and sound that is fundamental to television's simulation of a continuous present.[80]

As T. S. Matthews noted in the *Saturday Evening Post,* this multilingual trial "could not possibly have been conducted without the microphones, recorders and hearing aids of our electronic age. And these 'aids,' of course, help to slow down the proceedings." The trial's sequential translation between Hebrew and German also articulated what Robert Hariman has described as the "competing forms of speech" that are always at play in the "rhetorical context" of all trials.[81] For its American television audience in particular, the translation process complicated the trial's narrative flow with an intricate multilingual dynamic.

Although American television and print coverage often mentioned the trial's multilingual format, they seldom considered its ongoing impact. Print journalists rarely commented on the subject after the trial's opening session. Television coverage obscured the trial's multilingualism through the selection and editing of Capital Cities's footage, which showed less of Eichmann speaking in his native German, and through the reengineering of the sound track, which made the English translation the dominant language. As presented to American viewers, the trial was, in effect, an event that took place in English. Yet while the subtleties of the trial's multilingual format might well have been lost on the majority of its American viewers, the audial presence of Hebrew, German, and Yiddish was accessible, even when these languages could only be heard "under" the English translation. Thus, the significance of each language as part of what literary scholar Benjamin Harshav has called the "semiotics of Jewish communication" was available to the cognizant viewer, irrespective of what was being said in each language.[82]

It is quite possible that the telecasts of the Eichmann trial presented most Americans, as well as other international viewers, with their first substantial encounter with the sound of modern Hebrew. As the official language of the State of Israel, it was also the language of record for the trial. Conducting the proceedings in Hebrew reinforced the commitment, despite considerable objections, to try Eichmann in an Israeli court. The use of Hebrew demonstrated Israel's sovereignty and the nation's ability to serve the ends of justice. Moreover, conducting the trial in Hebrew made the proceedings — at least symbolically — accessible to all Israelis, not merely those of European descent, thereby presenting the Holocaust as a defining event for the country's diverse ingathering of diaspora Jewish communities. The language also marked the trial as being, first and foremost, an event for an Israeli audience. This was occasionally evident in the American television coverage. Viewers of *Verdict for Tomorrow,* for example, watched scenes of Israelis crowded outside Beit Ha'am to listen to the proceedings, which were broadcast live over loudspeakers in the surrounding streets. Thus, Israel was shown as a land that resounded with the sound of the trial, a performance that united territory and language.

The Israeli government could, in theory, have easily conducted the Eichmann trial in German. Most of the documentary evidence was written in German; not only was this the native language of the defendant and his counsel, but it was also that of all three judges who sat on the tribunal, and Hausner was a fluent German-speaker as well. Indeed, during Eichmann's testimony and cross-examination the judges—who, in accordance with Israeli law, were permitted to question the witness directly—sometimes addressed Eichmann in German, thereby circumventing the official translation process. This prompted C. L. Sulzberger of the *New York Times* to comment in an editorial that "the real language of this trial is German." He noted that the chief prosecutor's and the judges' "colloquies and interrogations are directly in that tongue whose very sound once terrified the people of this ancient-modern nation." But while the judges and the defendant speak the same language, "they do not understand the same moral language."

As Sulzberger intimated in his editorial, the trial stigmatized German as the language of evil; like Eichmann, the language epitomized the amorality of the Nazi regime. At the start of the trial, the Israeli government provided journalists with a ninety-six-page book of Nazi terminology. It described the language of the Nazis as having "a most specific sound and nature" and characterized many terms as "linguistic monstrosities."[83] Journalists' reports on the proceedings sometimes linked German syntax with Eichmann's efforts during cross-examination to evade moral responsibility through obfuscating bureaucratese: "Some of his sentences ran to 250 words, and at one point Judge Landau broke in wearily and said to Eichmann's counsel: 'If we are to understand him properly, he must speak shorter sentences. Of course, we know that in German the verb always comes at the end, but he is making us wait too long for it.'"[84]

Other reports linked associations of the texture of Eichmann's speech with evil. Martha Gellhorn described Eichmann's voice as "ugly, with a hard *R,* a sound that makes one think of a hammer and a knife. . . . The cold snarl, the bark that many of the witnesses remembered was there, one tone beneath what we heard."[85] Televised presentations of the trial reinforced this association by frequently showing Eichmann speaking German without simultaneous translation. In these sequences the language was offered to American audiences as an inaccessible, evil noise, similar to its presentation in earlier documentaries and dramas, which show Hitler or other Nazi leaders speaking at public rallies without translating the text of their speech.

Although not an official language of the proceedings, Yiddish also figured in the multilingual dynamics of the Eichmann trial. Indeed, the marginalized presence of Yiddish, the language most widely spoken among Jews before World War II, signified an Israeli effort to displace diaspora Jewry as the authoritative voice on the Holocaust before an international forum. Whereas the Israeli government provided journalists covering the trial with simultaneous oral translation in English, French, and German, and issued daily bulletins on the trial in these languages as well, it made no effort to offer these services to the considerable number of journalists covering the case for the international Yiddish press. When confronted by reporters for Yiddish publications, the Israeli government first claimed that they were unable to prepare the daily bulletins in Yiddish. Asked how the Israeli government could overlook the "language of Eichmann's victims," an official replied that "Yiddish journalists ought to know Hebrew, and that they can translate on their own from the other languages," as did Yugoslavian or Polish journalists covering the trial.[86] Eventually, an abbreviated version of the trial's daily bulletins was issued in Yiddish.

During the proceedings, a number of witnesses for the prosecution testified in Yiddish. Among them was Rivka Joselewska, the sole survivor of her community, who described being shot by a Nazi killing squad and buried alive in a mass grave. As can be heard in the excerpt of her court appearance included in *Verdict for Tomorrow,* her testimony was rendered into Hebrew translation, delivered out loud in the courtroom. This symbolically erased Yiddish as the language of Holocaust survivors, as well as its victims, and replaced it with the official language of the Zionist state. However, Yiddish was sometimes heard in American television coverage of the Eichmann trial produced outside of the courtroom. In the aforementioned NBC news special of 23 April, for example, Frank McGee explains in his interview with a Holocaust survivor that, although he "understands English, he preferred to speak in Yiddish—the language, he said, of so many who died." Thus, the Eichmann trial and some of its televised presentations exemplify a pervasive postwar conceptualization of Yiddish as being, according to literary scholar Anita Norich, "itself a sign of rupture and loss," a signifier of the Holocaust.[87]

The audial and multilingual complexities that the Eichmann trial posed to its American audiences were compounded by other challenges. Complementing the frustrating, enigmatic spectacle of the trial's sole defendant was the displaced presence of the implicit plaintiffs—the millions of Jewish victims of Nazi persecution whom Hausner claimed to represent in his opening address to the tribunal. These victims were invoked repeatedly throughout the proceedings, whether as an abstract number ("the six million"), as communities (the Jews of Hungary, the Jews of Warsaw), or as individuals, both named and anonymous. Their lives and deaths were represented by documentation, both statistical and narrative, including texts of their own authorship; by the oral testimony of survivors or scholars; and by displaying images of victims in documentary footage of concentration and extermination camps. Yet, in contrast to Eichmann's corporeal, if inscrutable, presence at the trial, "the six million" remained elusive. "Who were they?" Gellhorn wondered, as "their names, light as leaves, float through the days of testimony."[88]

Those writing about the trial frequently mentioned the disparity between these two divergent, antispectacular presences—the abstracted, unseen six million Jewish victims of Nazism and the enigmatic Eichmann, the sole individual charged with the onus of their horrific demise. Herbert Freeden wrote in the American Jewish Congress's bulletin that "there seemed to have been no connection between the cavalcade of cruelties and the impassive individual huddled in his glass box, so remote in appearance from the entire proceedings."[89] As a consequence of the disparity between the unfathomable six million and the inscrutable individual defendant, the trial often proved disappointing as an engaging performance, both for those attending the proceedings in Jerusalem and for those watching on television around the world. In fact, dissatisfaction with the trial as compelling watching increased when, after weeks of testimony by a series of witnesses for the prosecution, Eichmann took the stand. Homer Bigart reported that during Hausner's presentation "the trial appeared to be more like a folk opera than a legal case, with poets and lecturers fainting and with much time devoted to painting the lurid background of the holocaust. Now suddenly it has become a dull spectacle with no assault on emotions, with Dr. Servatius and Eichmann conducting their dialogue not for the gallery's benefit but solely for the ears of the three Israeli judges."[90]

The general American press reported that Israeli spectators apparently found Eichmann's testimony "extremely boring," at times falling asleep in the spectators' gallery or leaving well before the court had adjourned for the day.[91] In West Germany many viewers found Eichmann surprisingly "lackluster," and they stopped watching the regular broadcasts.[92] By this point in the proceedings, American television audiences may have also found watching the trial less than compelling, especially in comparison to the succinctness of regular newscasts or the tightly constructed cohesion of television courtroom dramas.[93]

In general, telecasts of the Eichmann trial may well have seemed slow, diffuse, and extensive beyond the medium's limits. They were, indeed, unlike anything else American television had ever offered. The trial's televised presentation consisted of a generic olio of news reports, public affairs programs, news specials, and dramas; it was both exotic and universal, both news and history, both special and routine. Structurally, the telecasts often waffled from past to present to future and back again. The content of the trial itself veered from the histrionics of Jewish "folk opera" to the deadliness of Nazi "bureaucratese." The great majority of the plaintiffs were invisible, and their absence became only that much more palpable with every effort to invoke their presence. The trial's archvillain, accused of unfathomable atrocities, was banal, puny, enigmatic, and boring. His anti-spectacular presence matched the trial's visually austere setting—a converted assembly hall that was neither playhouse nor courthouse. The trial's most eye-catching element was the glass box in which the defendant sat throughout the proceedings. This glass box—with its contradictory promises to display and to protect—came to epitomize the frustrating enigmas of the trial.[94]

While those commenting on the trial rarely scrutinized its presentation on television per se, the issue of the trial as a performance figured prominently in their analyses.[95] Some American critics of the trial faulted it as an ineffectual performance. Others denounced the proceedings for aspiring to be a performance, which they deemed incompatible with the pursuit of justice, despite the endorsement of the trial as a performance of great importance for the State of Israel by its leadership. A review of American press coverage of the case noted that while some newspapers denounced the trial in terms such as "'the worst stage-managed circus in modern history,' equipped with 'every hysterical and sensational device,'" the vast majority "found that the trial had been conducted with 'impressive dignity,' 'remarkable restraint,' scrupulous fairness.'"[96] The notion of the trial as a performance thus straddled conflicting understandings of the Eichmann proceedings as an event whose effectiveness was, on one hand, linked to its affective impact on the public and, on the other hand, gauged by the extent to which it appeared to be dispassionate.

Among American Jewish intellectuals, much of the discussion of the value of the Eichmann trial centered on Hannah Arendt's controversial analysis of the proceedings. First printed as a series of articles in the *New Yorker,* it was eventually issued in book form in 1963 as *Eichmann in Jerusalem: A Report on the Banality of Evil.*[97] Irving Howe described its appearance as an event that not only affected his own thinking enormously but also aroused "overwhelming" passions in other New York Jewish intellectuals. Reflecting on the publication of Arendt's work years later, Howe admitted, "I still have just as sharp an objection to that book. . . . I cannot think of anything since then that harassed me so much except perhaps the Vietnam War."[98]

Early in *Eichmann in Jerusalem,* Arendt critiqued the effectiveness of the trial as an act of justice by faulting its performative elements, beginning with its participants and setting:

> There is no doubt from the very beginning that . . . Judge Landau . . . is doing
> his best . . . to prevent this trial from becoming a show trial under the influ-
> ence of the prosecutor's love of showmanship. Among the reasons he cannot
> always succeed is the simple fact that the proceedings happen on a stage
> before an audience, with the usher's marvelous shout at the beginning of each
> session producing the effect of the rising curtain. Whoever planned this audi-
> torium in the newly built *Beit Ha'am* . . . had a theater in mind, complete
> with orchestra and gallery, with proscenium and stage, and with side doors
> for the actors' entrance. Clearly, this courtroom is not a bad place for the
> show trial David Ben-Gurion . . . had in mind when he decided to have Eich-
> mann kidnapped in Argentina and brought to . . . Jerusalem.

Arendt continued to delegitimate the trial as a performance, with references
to Ben-Gurion as "the invisible stage manager of the proceedings"; to
Hausner's "frequent side glances into the audience, and the theatrics char-
acteristic of a more than ordinary vanity"; and to his indulgence in
"putting oneself in the limelight." She also mentioned the judges' reluctant
presence, "seated at the top of the raised platform, facing the audience as
from the stage in a play," and ultimately proclaimed "the play aspect of the
trial" to have been a failure. (Her one reference to the proceedings' presentation on television was a passing expression of contempt for the commercials: "The American program, sponsored by the Glickman Corporation, is
constantly interrupted—business as usual—by real-estate advertising.")[99]

Eichmann in Jerusalem provoked extensive and passionate critical
response. Most of Arendt's detractors rejected her conceptualization of the
trial as a "lesson" in the "banality of evil," and they condemned her for
portraying European Jews as largely passive victims of Nazism and even, at
times, willing collaborators in their fate. In the process of denouncing her
reading of Nazi anti-Semitism and the Jewish response, Arendt's critics
faulted her devaluation of the Eichmann trial as a just undertaking and
rejected her description of it as an untenable performance.

Jacob Robinson, one of the most prominent of her early critics, found
Arendt's claim that Ben-Gurion had masterminded the proceedings as a
show trial to be unsupported and dismissed the significance that she
attached to the trial's setting in the converted Beit Ha'am. Robinson, who
had served as an advisor to the Israeli government on the documentation
and law connected with the Eichmann trial, also refuted Arendt's charges
that Hausner indulged in histrionics or inappropriately pursued the limelight. In his efforts to catch inconsistencies in *Eichmann in Jerusalem,*
Robinson attacked Arendt for denouncing the theatrics of the proceedings,
on one hand, and for criticizing the trial because it "never became a play,"
on the other. Yet he, too, offered contradictory testimony on the effective-

ness of the trial as an affective performance, citing both Telford Taylor's praise for the Israeli tribunal's "meticulous and dispassionate assessment of the evidence" and Hugh Trevor-Roper's hailing the proceedings as "a wonderful performance."[100]

Although Arendt's writings and the controversy that they engendered dominated the discussion of the Eichmann trial in the mid-1960s, other American Jewish intellectuals offered reflections on the trial's significance as well. Some of these writings dealt more centrally with the performative nature of the trial and did so with greater nuance. Harold Rosenberg identified the issue of the trial as performance as being crucial to understanding both the motives behind the Eichmann case and its consequences. He characterized Ben-Gurion's enumeration of the Israeli government's agenda for the trial as merely "a rationalistic disguise for the irresistible demand for a tragic retelling" and described the event itself as "a way of giving public shape to a tormenting memory."

Rosenberg argued that while the Eichmann trial set out to fulfill a legitimate and universal need—"that of social therapy, perhaps, or of patriotism, or of progress toward a better world"—the conventions of the trial as a narrative genre thwarted this end, because it attempted to undertake "the function of tragic poetry . . . on a world stage ruled by the utilitarian code." Not only were the officials concerned with the case "under pressure to have the Trial 'make sense'; they were obliged also . . . to participate in incongruities by the legal situation itself."

In particular, Rosenberg suggested, the trial setting required that Eichmann "be allowed to compete with the survivors" by offering his own Holocaust narrative along with theirs. This gave the defendant "the opportunity to become one of the most memorable figures of this century." It also problematized the nature of his culpability and his defense by making Eichmann's personality "central to the question of his guilt." This enabled him to defend himself, "like Hitler before him, as the little man, the put-upon 'front soldier,' the . . . 'cog in the machine.'" Rosenberg concluded that while the Eichmann trial presented "an indispensable account of the tragedy of the Jews in this era," it was "an account marred in the telling and needing to be gone over and interpreted again and again."[101]

In reviewing one such retelling—Rolf Hochhuth's 1963 play *Der Stellvertreter* (The deputy)—Susan Sontag also reflected on the performative nature of the Eichmann trial. She conceptualized the proceedings as a work of performance art that epitomizes the place of tragedy in the modern age. No longer confined to the virtual world of the theater, she argued, tragedy has become "a form of history. Dramatists no longer write tragedies. But we do possess works of art (not always recognized as such) which reflect or attempt to resolve the great historical tragedies of our time. . . . As the supreme tragic event of modern times is the murder of the six million European Jews, one of the most interesting and moving works of art of the past ten years is the trial of Adolf Eichmann in Jerusalem in 1961."

Noting the analysis of Arendt and others on the questionable legitimacy of the trial as a juridical procedure, Sontag suggested that "the Eichmann trial not only did not, but could not have conformed to legal standards only." Like Rosenberg, she saw the role in which Eichmann was cast as crucial to the problematic nature of the trial: "It was not Eichmann alone who was on trial. He stood trial in a double role: as both the particular and the generic; both the man, laden with hideous specific guilt, and the cipher, standing for the whole history of anti-Semitism, which climaxed in this unimaginable martyrdom." Sontag also echoed Rosenberg's argument that the trial format thwarted its agenda as a cathartic performance of memory: "The trial is a dramatic form which imparts to events a certain provisional neutrality; the outcome remains to be decided; the very word 'defendant' implies that a defense is possible. In this sense, though Eichmann, as everyone expected, was condemned to death, the form of the trial favored Eichmann. Perhaps this is why many feel, in retrospect, that the trial was a frustrating experience, an anticlimax."[102]

Morality Plays:
American Television Dramas and the Eichmann Trial

Across the range of responses to the Eichmann trial, many hailed it for having achieved its goals of educating new audiences about the Holocaust or of validating Israel's sovereignty. Yet even some of the trial's champions faulted the proceedings for failing to provide psychological insight into the Nazis' attempt to annihilate European Jewry. Yale Newman, who covered the trial for ABC, later commented that, while the trial succeeded in chronicling "for the first time . . . man's inhumanity to man and put it on a global scale, making the audiences face it," he regretted Hausner's inability to "get inside the mind of Adolf Eichmann."[103] In an essay printed shortly after Eichmann's execution, John Ciardi raised this question in his critical reflections on the death sentence, wondering "what Israel has gained in exacting its six-million-to-one vengeance on the sorry flesh that was Eichmann." Ciardi thought it would have been better if Eichmann had instead been sentenced "to a lifetime of close study by a panel of analysts and clinicians," arguing that "the world needs to know its monsters."[104]

Such judgments exemplify what Michel Foucault described as the "psychiatrization of crime" in the modern age, which requires not only that a criminal be proved the agent of a transgression, but that a psychologically convincing motive for the crime be established in order to mete out satisfactory justice. Beyond the criminal's admission of guilt, "there must be confession, self-examination, explanation of oneself, revelation of what one is," in order to satisfy those who sit in judgment. Moreover, Foucault argued, the issue of establishing motive as part of the trial process has become so important in modern criminology that it is now "more solid and more real" than the crime itself, which must be "drawn aside in order to reveal the only thing which is now of importance, the criminal."[105]

Eichmann's inscrutable presence in televised excerpts of the proceedings may well have contributed to the sense that the trial failed to reveal the defendant's motive or character. The contrast between the stoic, enigmatic presence of the actual Eichmann and fictional portraits in television dramas aired around the time of the trial may have only heightened this frustrating sense of a lack of insight or resolution. Indeed, these broadcasts exploited the affective power of drama to offer American viewers a vision of Eichmann, or an Eichmann-like villain, that satisfied the desire, left unfulfilled by the trial, for psychological insight into his crimes.

Engineer of Death: The Eichmann Story exemplifies this desire to probe the inner workings of the criminal mind.[106] The hour-long docudrama, presented on CBS's *Armstrong Circle Theater,* begins in a darkened room inside a safe house, where Eichmann is held prisoner by Israeli guards. As the camera pans slowly around the head of the actor playing Eichmann (Frederick Rolf), an off-camera narrator explains that once Eichmann's name brought "a shudder of terror from the victims of his savagery. But when he was captured, millions the world over did not even recognize the name, and they said, wonderingly, 'Who is this man?'"

CBS first aired *Engineer of Death* on 12 October 1960, several months after Israel announced Eichmann's capture and abduction, and rebroadcast it during the first week of the trial. Typical of other episodes of this series, *Engineer of Death* fuses elements conventionally associated with documentary and drama to present a current news story. The trappings of news reportage frame the docudrama. The 12 April 1961 rebroadcast is introduced by series host Douglas Edwards, who was then also the anchor of CBS's national evening newscasts. He reminds viewers that the announcement of Eichmann's capture "electrified the world. It was as though Hitler himself had been found alive." The credits shown at the end of the broadcast acknowledge as sources "exclusive reporting by correspondents of *Time,* the weekly magazine, and French, Hebrew, and Yiddish documents furnished by the newspaper *Day-Jewish Journal.*"

Throughout the broadcast, dramatic scenes are interwoven with narration, animated maps, vintage film footage, and radio broadcasts to chronicle Eichmann's career as a Nazi and recount the story of his capture. Like other docudramas, *Engineer of Death* exploits both the authoritative imprimatur of the documentary genre and the demonstrative power of drama to create a psychohistory of the protagonist, who is portrayed as an extravagantly sadistic villain. A series of early episodes explain Eichmann's criminal anti-Semitism as the consequence of his own sense of shame in being falsely identified as a Jew. In one scene Eichmann approaches a group of fellow Nazis in a tavern. They remark that they think he is a Jew and comment on his accent and features ("the hair — dark, oriental almost," "the thin face," "the nose"). When Eichmann is unable to produce evidence of his Nazi party membership, they rough him up and douse him with beer. After they depart, Eichmann cries, "They did this to me — the Jews! The damn, rotten Jews!"

Engineer of Death chronicles Eichmann's career as an SS officer through reenactments of testimony by Nazis on trial for war crimes at Nuremberg. Scenes of the escalation of the Nazi persecution of Jews at the hands of Eichmann alternate with scenes of postwar testimony by SS Captain Dieter Wisliceny (Telly Savalas) and Rudolf Hoess, commandant of Auschwitz (Carroll O'Connor). They describe Eichmann as being fanatical in his pursuit of the Jews, above and beyond the commitment of his comrades. A series of scenes tracing the evolution of the Nazis' anti-Jewish policies — expulsion, the deployment of killing squads, the establishment of death camps — portrays Eichmann as the primary driving force behind their development. He appears as a zealous and unrepentant murderer of Jews until Germany's defeat. While planning their escape at the war's end, Wisliceny asks Eichmann if he is afraid of dying; Eichmann replies, "Believe me, when my time comes to die I'll leap into the grave laughing — happy that I've killed six million Jews."

Documentary and dramatic elements complement each other throughout *Engineer of Death*. Narration and vintage footage contextualize individual scenes and move the narrative forward, while dramatic sequences complete the documentary record with affective detail. The resulting presentation offers both the hallmarks of historical authenticity — the omniscient narrator, the citation of dates and other factual details, the use of maps and vintage actuality, even the re-creation of courtroom testimony — and an emotionally satisfying psychological completeness. The dramatic idiom makes manifest "hidden" motives or "lost" explanations in the broadcast's master psychological narrative. These scenes do not merely rest on the assumption that if one had been at the scenes re-created, the actual participants would have talked and behaved thus. They also intimate that an eyewitness to the actual events portrayed would have been able to see and hear the psychological motives behind Nazi crimes.

In 1960, *Engineer of Death* suggested to its first viewers that the forthcoming telecasts of the Eichmann trial would also provide the same intimate, psychological drama. At the same time, the docudrama identified

Eichmann as "the other Adolf"—a reminder that Eichmann was, ultimately, a surrogate figure. By presenting the evolution of the Nazis' anti-Jewish policies in terms of one person's motives and actions, *Engineer of Death* deviated from what was known of the advent of the Final Solution as a complex corporate enterprise. However, the drama's narrative paralleled the Israeli agenda to try Eichmann as the metonym for all Nazi war criminals, dead or missing, who collaborated on the plan to annihilate European Jewry. While *Engineer of Death* anticipated the trial's principal strategy, the docudrama also offered a psychological coherence and completeness that would be found lacking in the portrait of Eichmann presented during the proceedings in Jerusalem.

Another television drama of this period that relates to the Eichmann case, albeit less explicitly, presents a similar portrait of a Nazi war criminal as a thoroughly depraved sadist who delights in the torment of his victims. Aired on 10 November 1961, after the trial had already concluded and the Israeli tribunal was preparing its verdict, this drama offered viewers an imaginary war crimes trial that delivered swift, unambiguous, and demonstrative justice, thereby satisfying impulses that television's presentation of the actual Eichmann trial left unfulfilled for many.

   Although the drama is ostensibly set in the present, in and around the former concentration camp of Dachau, it also transports viewers "to another dimension, a dimension not only of sight and sound, but of mind, a journey into a wondrous land whose boundaries are that of imagination . . . the Twilight Zone." "Death's Head Revisited," written by the series's creator, Rod Serling, appeared on *The Twilight Zone* (CBS, 1959–1965) during its third season.[107] Like other episodes of the science-fiction series, it uses supernatural settings and events, realized through a variety of special-effects techniques, to explore social and ethical issues relevant to contemporary American audiences in the form of otherworldly "morality plays."[108]

   The half-hour drama begins as a former SS captain named Lutze (played by Oscar Beregi) returns to the town of Dachau seventeen years after the end of World War II. Lutze plans a nostalgic visit to the former concentration camp, his "old haunts." "What he does not know," Serling narrates, "is that a place like Dachau cannot exist only in Bavaria. . . . By its very nature, it must be one of the populated areas of the Twilight Zone."

   Lutze arrives at the deserted camp. As he strolls about its landmarks—former gallows, barracks, and offices—ghostly images of inmates, dressed in striped uniforms, fade into view and disappear. Lutze's sadistic reminiscences are disrupted by the sudden appearance of a man (Joseph Schildkraut) in a striped prisoner's uniform, who stands in front of one of the camp buildings. He welcomes the astonished Lutze, addressing him as "Captain": "We've been waiting." Lutze recognizes the man as Alfred

"Death's Head Revisited": Victims of Nazi persecution at Dachau rise from the dead to try one of their tormentors for crimes against humanity in this 1961 episode of Rod Serling's *Twilight Zone*. (Rod Serling Archives, Ithaca College.)

Becker and tells Becker to stop calling him "Captain," as he is no longer a soldier: "That's all in the past. . . . It's utterly ridiculous to dwell on these things. You did as you thought best and I . . . functioned as I was told." The wind howls; Becker informs Lutze that it is the sound of his victims, protesting his dismissive apology: "Ten million human beings were tortured to death in camps like this. . . . And you wonder that the misery that you planted has lived after you?"

A nightmarish sequence follows, in which Lutze finds himself surrounded by a group of stern-faced men in prison uniforms. Among them is Becker, who announces that the inmates of Dachau will try Lutze for "crimes against humanity." As his trial begins, Lutze loses consciousness. When he awakens, Becker informs Lutze that the trial is already over; he has been found guilty and a sentence has been handed down: "From this day on you shall be rendered insane."

Lutze runs for the gate to the camp; Becker appears suddenly at his side. "At this gate you shot down hundreds of people with machine guns. Do you feel it now, Captain? Do you feel the bullets smashing into your body?" The sound of machine-gun fire is heard; Lutze writhes in pain and staggers across the courtyard. Becker continues to lead Lutze from one part of the camp to another, describing the suffering of the Nazi's victims at each site. Lutze screams, reels from place to place, and eventually falls to the ground as if he were having a violent seizure. Becker stands over the tormented man and concludes: "If there's still any portion of your mind that can function, take this thought with you: This is not hatred, this is retribution. This is not revenge, this is justice. But this is only the beginning, Captain. . . . Your final judgment will come from God."

The epilogue to "Death's Head Revisited" fades up on a shot of policemen, a taxi driver, and a doctor standing over a heavily sedated Lutze. As two men pick him up and carry him off, the doctor and the driver wonder what could have turned Lutze into a "raving maniac" in the two hours since the driver left him at the gate. The doctor surveys the camp and asks, "Dachau . . . Why do we keep it standing?" As the camera pans around the camp, Serling responds off camera: "All the Dachaus must remain standing . . . because they are a monument to a moment in time when some men decided to turn the earth into a graveyard. Into it they shoveled all of their reason, their logic, their knowledge — but worst of all, their conscience. And the moment we forget this . . . then we become the gravediggers. Something to dwell on and to remember — not only in the Twilight Zone, but wherever men walk God's earth."

The fictitious villain of "Death's Head Revisited" is a metonym for Nazism, similar to the role the actual Eichmann played in the Jerusalem trial and that of the virtual Eichmann in *Engineer of Death*. (Serling's script hints at the parallel between Eichmann and Lutze through the occasional detail, such as his changing his name and seeking refuge in South America after the war.) Unlike the psychohistory of the *Armstrong Circle Theater* drama, "Death's Head Revisited" explains the origins of Nazism as a supernatural, absolute evil, stripped of its ties to history, whether personal or global. The *Twilight Zone* drama further simplifies and abstracts the complex particulars of the Eichmann trial by reducing it, in effect, to a contest between two men.

Moreover, thanks both to the technical capabilities of television film and to the liberating possibilities of the science-fiction genre, "Death's Head Revisited" offered viewers the compelling spectacle of the victims of Nazism rising from the dead to bring their persecutor to justice. Unlike Eichmann's much-debated fate — the international press was full of suggestions as to how he might be appropriately sentenced by the Israeli court — Lutze's punishment provided viewers with the satisfaction of seeing the depraved tormentor become the victim of his own tortures.[109]

Both "Death's Head Revisited" and *Engineer of Death* conclude by transforming their dramas of the evils of the historical past into lessons for an abstracted future. Yet these dramas admonish audiences with morals that run counter to the thrust of their narratives. After spending an hour performing a psychohistory of Eichmann that shows him to be the prime mover behind the Nazi persecution of European Jewry, *Engineer of Death* concludes that its protagonist is "less a man than a symbol of the ultimate horror of tyranny." Similarly, after portraying the evils of Nazi war criminals and the possibility of bringing them to justice as the stuff of otherworldly nightmares, Rod Serling argues that the potential to become Nazis—to say nothing of becoming their victims—lies within all people, "not only in the Twilight Zone, but wherever men walk God's earth."

Toward "the Cinéma Vérité of Due Process": The Eichmann Trial and Holocaust Memory Culture

The Eichmann case is widely cited as a marking a threshold in American awareness of the Holocaust, generating "renewed engagement" and "heightened historical consciousness" as well as serving as a catalyst for a spate of American Holocaust literature, television programs, and feature films.[110] However, telecasts of the trial—despite Sontag's suggestion that it be regarded as a "work of art"—did not emerge as a fixture of American Holocaust memory culture. While televising the Eichmann trial played an essential role in establishing the proceedings as a landmark of American Holocaust consciousness, the broadcasts and their reception also indicate the limits of this consciousness—and of media literacy in general—at the time.

Journalists, pollsters, communications scholars, Jewish community leaders, and others began to consider the impact of the trial on the American public well before Eichmann's execution. A number of studies assessing press coverage and public opinion of the case appeared during the early 1960s. These include a series of Gallup polls taken in the spring of 1961, a survey of American media coverage of the trial published by the American Jewish Committee in 1962, and *The Apathetic Majority: A Study Based on Public Responses to the Eichmann Trial*. Prepared by the University of California's Survey Research Center with funding from the Anti-Defamation League of B'nai B'rith, this study was begun during the trial and published in 1966.[111] These various efforts gauged the extent of public awareness of facts related to the Eichmann trial and the Holocaust, and they examined public responses to the range of prevailing concerns surrounding the case: the appropriateness of Eichmann's capture, the legality or fairness of the trial, the justness of Eichmann's sentence, the larger impact of the trial, and the ethical lessons that it imparted.

The surveys paid special attention to any indications of change in Americans' attitudes about Jews, Germans, Germany, and Israel in the wake of the trial. For example, the University of California study asked informants whether they agreed or disagreed with such statements as "One trouble with Jewish businessmen is that they stick together and connive, so that a Gentile doesn't have a fair chance at competition," and "I can hardly imagine myself marrying a Jew."[112] While paying some attention to which of their informants followed the Eichmann trial on television as opposed to other media, these studies offered no analysis of the impact that television might have had on responses to the case. The research did indicate that television had contributed significantly to the public's awareness of the Eichmann trial. According to *The Apathetic Majority,* 68 percent of the informants for the University of California study, who were all residents of the San Francisco Bay area, said that television news reports were one of their sources of information on the Eichmann trial, and 25 percent cited television specials as a source (compared to 78 percent for newspapers, 65 percent for radio news reports, 41 percent for conversation, and 36 percent for magazines). Aside from providing these statistics, however, *The Apathetic Majority* only questioned the value of the trial's television coverage. The study concluded that "what most distinguishes the knowledgeable from the unknowledgeable is the tendency of the former to rely on the written word, rather than the broadcast media, as a source of information."[113]

Literary scholar Sidra Ezrahi has argued that telecasts of the Eichmann trial did help galvanize American writers in the 1960s by "forcing its entry into the homes of all Americans who committed the minimal act of turning on their television sets." In literary responses to the Holocaust, which were "catalyzed" by the trial, American writers such as Arthur A. Cohen, Irving Feldman, Arthur Miller, Sylvia Plath, Charles Reznikoff, Norma Rosen, and Isaac Rosenberg focused not so much on the events that took place during the Nazi era but on "the moral options which prevailed in those times and which could be repeated under similar circumstances." Influenced by Arendt's notion of understanding Nazism as a manifestation of the "banality of evil"—which served as "the filter through which most Americans were able to conceptualize what was otherwise a morass of indigestible, unintegrable facts"—American writers tended to relate to the Holocaust "not primarily as a historical event," Ezrahi has suggested, "but as a complex of psychological possibilities."[114]

In the months following the trial, the Eichmann case also continued to inspire new television documentaries, dramas, and news affairs broadcasts. These, too, demonstrate how the trial served as a point of entry for addressing a range of larger issues, including the history of Nazism and efforts to save European Jews during World War II, as well as Germany's postwar response to the Nazi era and anti-Semitism.[115] But major histories of American television or news broadcasting do not mention the Eichmann trial coverage, despite claims made in 1961 that telecasts of the proceedings were a milestone in the development of international broadcast journalism.[116] And despite its landmark status in the history of Holocaust documentation and commemoration, the trial telecasts have had a less enduring impact on American Holocaust remembrance than have either other contemporary phenomena—such as the film version of *Judgment at Nuremberg* or the English-language edition of Elie Wiesel's *Night,* both of which appeared during 1961—or more recent televised presentations of the Holocaust. And, while American Jews have turned to Israeli culture for an authoritative response to the Holocaust in more recent decades, they are much more likely to encounter Israel's relationship with the Holocaust in local Yom ha-Sho'ah commemorations, visits to the Yad Vashem memorial in Jerusalem, or group tours of former extermination camps in Poland that conclude with a visit to Israel (such as the March of the Living) than through any institutionalized recollection of the Eichmann trial.[117]

That telecasts of the Eichmann trial did not become a fixture of American Holocaust memory culture might be rooted in an inherent contradiction between the electronic media and the law, which, according to legal scholar Ethan Katsch, "would not be possible without the special properties of print."[118] At the same time, the problematic aspects of the trial as performance might also be attributed, in part, to the nature of trials as social rituals. Political scientists Lance Bennett and Martha Feldman have written that for trials to "make sense to untrained participants, there must be some implicit framework of social judgment that people bring into the courtroom from everyday life." To that end, Bennett and Feldman have argued, criminal trials in America and other Western democracies are organized around the quotidian activity of storytelling. Through presenting evidence in the form of narratives, the participants in the modern courtroom "engage some parallel form of social judgment that anchors legal questions in everyday understandings."[119]

In the case of the Eichmann trial, a number of factors complicated, perhaps even confounded, the ability of storytelling to provide the public with accessible and persuasive arguments for the guilt or innocence of the defendant. The Israeli government's ambitious, multivalent agenda for the trial presented one set of challenges. The overall question of what story was to be told, why, and by whom was debated not only before but also during the trial. In the course of the proceedings, numerous complaints arose, some of them from the Israeli judges hearing the case, about the relevance of testimony, particularly during the weeks of stories offered by dozens of survivors of the Holocaust.[120]

The multiple audiences that the trial addressed also challenged the effectiveness of its storytelling. From a legal perspective, the proceedings were directed solely at three men—the Israeli judges who sat on the bench and eventually handed down the verdict. As a public event, however, the trial was generally acknowledged to have a wide array of audiences, both within Israel and around the world. Catering to these various audiences posed a challenge to the prosecution in determining what stories to tell, who should tell them, and how they should be told.

The trial's repeated identification of the Holocaust as an atrocity unrivaled in scope, its events beyond description, was no doubt intended to impress listeners with the exceptional horror of the event. Yet this also implicitly challenged the ability of trial participants to use storytelling as an effective means of bringing about justice. The rambling, incoherent testimony of Yehiel De-Nur and his eventual collapse on the witness stand — one of the most often shown moments from the trial footage — presents viewers with the spectacle of the *inability* to offer narrative. Arendt wrote that this incident, "to be sure, was an exception, but if it was an exception that proved the rule of normality, it did not prove the rule of simplicity or of ability to tell a story."[121]

By presenting the Holocaust as an event that tests the boundaries of human communication, ethics, and justice, Eichmann's prosecutors in effect challenged the ability of the trial, and the stories that it told, to fulfill its agenda of serving justice. The fact that Eichmann was successfully prosecuted and eventually executed did not mitigate the sense of the trial's "failure" as a performance. Many observers considered the conviction ineffectual, anticlimactic, or a confirmation of the inability of justice to make amends for the enormity of these crimes.

Disparities between the agendas of the Israeli government conducting the Eichmann trial and of American and other foreign journalists covering the event further complicated the trial's effectiveness as an adjudicating narrative and as a landmark of Holocaust memory. Israel envisioned the trial as an opportunity to articulate its authority over the Holocaust and thereby legitimate its sovereignty as a Jewish nation. Therefore, it was essential that the prosecution present the Nazi persecution of European Jewry as a phenomenon both central and exceptional within the full range of activities of the Third Reich. However, journalists reporting on the Eichmann case to general American audiences repeatedly conceptualized the trial as an event primarily of universal significance, raising questions about the nature of evil in the individual psyche and humankind's universal moral responsibility.

This expansive presentation of the Eichmann case may have been a bid to attract a largely non-Jewish audience to watch the proceedings — in effect, to script a role that American spectators might play in this public performance. American television's approach to covering the Eichmann case also evinces the industry's larger concern, during the early 1960s, with rehabilitating its tarnished reputation by asserting its role as a moral voice for the nation. Yet American television did not simply mediate the trial's already ambitious symbolic agenda, but further complicated its meaning as a social drama.

In 1961, the decision to televise the Eichmann trial was considered both novel and controversial. While some hailed the notion of broadcasting the proceedings on international television as a valuable and forward-moving effort, others expressed concern that the very presence of cameras in the courtroom would violate the trial's integrity and dignity. As a concession to these concerns, the Israeli government limited the number of cameras permitted in the courthouse to those of one production company, and their presence, while no secret, was concealed from view. Indeed, Capital Cities's executive producer, Milton Fruchtman, prided himself on having rendered the location of his cameras invisible. As a colleague recalled, Fruchtman "said that neither the judges nor a corps of experts were able to detect where the cameras were placed when they made pre-trial tours" of Beit Ha'am.[122] The decision to conceal the cameras placed the television crew in the posture of a hidden surveillance team. Their absence from the spectacle — in contrast, say, to the visibility of camera crews and photographers at press conferences or public hearings — indicates the court's inability to acknowledge the connection television provided to spectators beyond the confines of Beit Ha'am, let alone to recognize the implications of the camera's presence.

Aside from the issue of courtroom decorum, the decision to conceal the cameras evinces a general innocence, among the press as well as the Israeli government, about the impact of television as a cultural force on the trial as a public event. Reporters covering the Eichmann trial usually characterized the decision to make footage of the proceedings available to international television broadcasters as an act that, in effect, enlarged the gallery of Beit Ha'am to include millions of television viewers from several dozen countries. The press reported the televising of the Eichmann trial, along with the coverage of early American and Soviet space missions, as an achievement of the television industry and a measure of general technological advance. By contrast, journalists presented Israel's lack of television at the time to be primitive, as illustrated by the following oft-reported anecdote about Israelis watching the trial on closed-circuit television in Jerusalem's Ratisbonne Hall:

> As it happens each morning, the picture fluttered into focus with the bailiff peering from the courtroom toward the judges' chambers to wait for the three men to emerge in their solemn, black robes. When the judges came into sight the bailiff spun around to call the spectators in court to order. "Beit Hamishpat!" he barked (the words mean "court" in Hebrew). Without stopping to think that they were more than a block away from the courtroom, the attorneys [who were watching the trial] in Ratisbonne Hall jumped respectfully to their feet.[123]

But whereas these Israelis, watching live television for the first time, naïvely failed to distinguish the virtual from the actual (much like the first audiences of silent film at the turn of the century, who jumped from their seats to avoid being hit by the image of a locomotive heading toward them), many Americans were still naïve in their acceptance of television coverage of the trial as a simulation of the actual experience of sitting in Beit Ha'am. Not only did the trial footage offer viewers images—such as close-ups of Eichmann's face or hands—unavailable to courtroom spectators, but American television then transformed this "actuality" through the process of selecting and editing excerpts of the footage, reengineering its multilingual soundtrack, and contextualizing it through reporters' commentary and supplementary coverage. Knowing that millions were able to watch Eichmann also shaped the prosecution's case, which was addressed more to its invisible legion of auditors and viewers than to the adjudicating tribunal. Awareness of the trial's vast television audience in the United States affected the way American journalists and others discussed Eichmann and his case, directing the focus away from the historical events of the Holocaust or the Israeli context of the trial and onto the defendant's physical presence and the proceedings as a performance. Thus, Eichmann's inscrutable, antispectacular presence may have made Arendt's explanation of the case as a lesson in the "banality of evil" seem a particularly apt way of understanding the trial and the historical events that it recounted.

As the first major televised presentation of actual courtroom proceedings, the Eichmann trial anticipated by three decades the advent of Court TV, the American cable channel devoted exclusively to presenting scenes of courtroom actuality from current trials along with commentary and other related features, which began transmitting in July 1991. Discussion of the effectiveness and legitimacy of Court TV have retraced key issues debated in 1961, such as whether the presence of cameras in the courtroom compromises its dignity or otherwise adversely affects the proceedings. Yet the discussion has also demonstrated a more sophisticated level of media literacy, as commentators consider the aesthetics of what one of them has dubbed "the cinéma vérité of due process."[124] In contrast, the lack of consciousness of television's impact on the Eichmann trial—understandable, perhaps, in light of the novelty of the enterprise—may have prevented American viewers from thinking of it as an enduring, culturally defining "media event."

Thanks in considerable measure to television, the Eichmann trial aroused extensive American interest in the Holocaust and inspired a range of works of Holocaust memory culture. However, the trial's presentation on television did not itself become a fixture of the nation's public memory. Indeed, rather than enhancing the Eichmann trial's potential to become a fixture of American Holocaust remembrance, television coverage contributed to its problematic status as a cultural landmark. At the time of the Eichmann trial, the issue of presenting the Holocaust on American television barely arose as a subject of discussion—and would not do so until late in the next decade.

five
A Guest in the Wasteland

The years between the Eichmann trial of 1961 and the premiere broadcast of the miniseries *Holocaust* in 1978 constitute a transition in televised presentations of the Holocaust. Critics have often characterized American television programming during these years as routinized, lacking the innovativeness of the 1950s, and, at its worst, having devolved into a cultural "wasteland." At the same time, the 1960s and 1970s witnessed the rise of television to a preeminent status among America's mass media. Similarly, while this period offered no major works to rival the landmark broadcasts at its boundaries, the years between 1961 and 1978 saw the Holocaust become an increasingly frequent, even routine, presence on American television.

In programs ranging from news documentary to science fiction, the Holocaust emerged during these years as a regular, if occasional, subject within American television's repertoire. These broadcasts help establish a distinct Holocaust iconography and recurrent thematic approaches to the subject. In particular, American television used the Holocaust as a point of entry into more general issues—the limits of justice, the consequences of intolerance, or the nature of evil—demonstrating the development of the Holocaust as a moral paradigm in general American culture. The programs of this period also indicate changes in how American Jews understood the Holocaust, responsive to their increasing distance from World War II and to the stabilization of both a strong postwar community in the United States and a viable State of Israel.

Although histories of American broadcast media rarely mention televising the Eichmann trial as one of the major events of 1961, they do often recognize this year as a watershed in the medium's development. Coinciding with the start of John F. Kennedy's presidency, 1961 inaugurated "the expanding vista" that television offered as mediator and shaper of national and world news. The year also marked television's arrival as a major force in American culture, dominating the nation's "republic of mass culture."[1]

But 1961 is perhaps most distinguished in the annals of the medium as the year in which Newton Minow, then newly appointed as chairman of the FCC, proclaimed much of American television "a vast wasteland." According to media scholar William Boddy, this phrase "crystallized the accumulated public and critical disenchantment with commercial television and immediately entered the vocabulary of public debate."[2]

During the 1960s the three major commercial networks consolidated their control over the most popular national broadcasting venues, standardizing schedules, genres, and other conventions of American television programming. This was a period of "accommodation and adjustment," in which programming demonstrated a "slow evolution of types," rather than "any revolutionary change."[3] During the 1960s critical concern mounted over the quality of television's wide-ranging broadcasts. Erik Barnouw described the "bizarre juxtapositions" of popular situation comedies and "other Nielsen pacemakers" with news specials of the era as seeming to come from "two worlds" that were often "incompatible."[4]

Presentations of what was coming to be known as the Holocaust on American television during these years responded to developments in the broadcasting industry. New opportunities to broadcast documentaries appeared, as the commercial networks inaugurated news documentary series and public television (then called "educational television") emerged as an important venue for airing independently produced films. Among the documentaries dealing with the Holocaust televised during the 1960s were *The Last Chapter* (1962), a portrait of East European Jewry on the eve of Wold War II; *Trial at Nuremberg* (1964), a chronicle of the first international war crimes trial; *Who Killed Anne Frank?* (1964), an installment of the CBS series *The Twentieth Century;* and *Change My Name to Life* (1966), a program on American responses to the needs of Displaced Persons.[5]

At the same time, live drama anthologies, which presented many of television's first Holocaust plays, disappeared from prime time, to be replaced by prerecorded, episodic drama series. Original Holocaust dramas continued to be broadcast on Sunday daytime ecumenical series, which also provided an early public forum for prominent individuals associated with the Holocaust, including author and activist Elie Wiesel and Simon Wiesenthal, the most renowned pursuer of Nazi war criminals.[6]

The Holocaust as Episodic

The appearance of the Holocaust on occasional installments of episodic drama series best characterizes the subject's presence on American television during this period. By the early 1960s, episodic programs had become the mainstay of prime-time television entertainment. Most of these offered a series of what amounted to self-contained dramas of a particular genre (e.g., court or police cases, espionage, westerns), which were linked together by the presence of continuing roles and locations (e.g., doctors, reporters; classrooms, spaceships). While rooted in consistent characters, plots, and settings, these series afford opportunities for guest performers in occasional roles, and, similarly, the appearance of "guest" locales and topics. The Holocaust figures as such a "guest" on a number of these series and even appeared on the occasional science-fiction program or situation comedy.

The creation of these episodes was part of a larger effort, which began during the early 1960s, to deal with contemporary social issues on primetime dramatic series in a manner similar to original teleplays aired on the earlier anthology programs. In addition to attracting viewers by offering them "provocative involvement with relevant themes," producers hoped that such programming "would counteract the assessment of television as a vast wasteland."[7]

Episodes featuring the Holocaust were also part of a larger phenomenon of occasional guest appearances by Jewish characters or issues on American television series. Following the demise of the ethnic working-class family situation comedy of the 1950s, major networks' prime-time schedules as a rule eschewed Jewish characters in episodic programs.[8] The characters on American television identified as Jews in the 1960s and 1970s either were comic foils or appeared as guests in single episodes that were sometimes devoted to a Jewish subject.

Jewish (and, similarly, black or Asian) guest appearances introduced variety into the routine of continuing characters and conventionalized plots and dialogue. Some of these episodes also addressed social issues of contemporary concern, such as the question of racial tolerance. Media scholar J. Fred MacDonald has noted that "at least one 'racial' story appeared on each of the major dramatic programs in the 1963–1964 season."[9] Within the television industry, some have characterized the existence of these guest appearances by ethnic characters as being the result of a social struggle that took place off camera. Shimon Wincelberg, who wrote scripts for television programs from the 1950s through the 1970s, introduced Jewish characters on episodes of a number of dramatic series, including the western series *Have Gun Will Travel* (CBS, 1957–1963). He described this in interviews as achieved in spite of network policies and tastes at the time: "They rationed you: one Jewish character a year, one black a year. . . . The producers make you feel that they are doing you a great favor by throwing you a bone." Wincelberg also noted that, by virtue of their repetition, the occasional appearance of these characters often became conventionalized: "Back in the 60s, there was a sort of informal quota on television westerns, police shows, detective shows; they let you do one Jew a year, usually as the innocent victim of the bad guys. The Jewish character made the hero look good because the hero was tolerant of him." Similarly, he noted, in the late 1970s and early 1980s, "the escaped Nazi-war-criminal was a popular stock heavy, kind of a nice change from drug-dealers and terrorists."[10]

Episodes that featured a Holocaust "guest appearance" at this time typically centered around an individual character or isolated incident that related the subject to a contemporary social concern of American audiences. An early example is "The Avenger," a 1962 episode of *The Defenders* (CBS, 1961–1965).[11] This series, set in New York City, followed the practice of a father-and-son team of attorneys, Lawrence and Kenneth Preston (played by E. G. Marshall and Robert Reed). Produced by Herbert Brodkin and created by Reginald Rose, the series was based on a television play that Rose had written for *Studio One* in 1957. Celebrated for dealing with provocative issues of the day—including abortion, euthanasia, and anti-Communist blacklisting in the entertainment industry—*The Defenders* was, in part, an extension of the kind of socially conscious dramas that Rose had written and Brodkin had produced for live television during the 1950s.[12]

The title character of "The Avenger" is Meyer Loeb (played by Ludwig Donath), a survivor of a Nazi concentration camp in Königshapfen, Germany. At the episode's beginning, Loeb fatally shoots Dr. Gerhard Prinzler, a highly respected scientist. Loeb freely admits to having killed Prinzler as an act of retribution. Loeb claims that during World War II the scientist had been a doctor in the camp at Königshapfen, where he was responsible for the deaths of Loeb's wife and son. Engaged as Loeb's counsel, the Prestons debate how to defend him. While the father argues for understanding the murder as a "justifiable homicide," the son describes it as "revenge, not self-defense." The elder Preston discusses with Loeb the possibility of a plea of temporary insanity, but Loeb demurs: "By resorting to any defense, you are allowing the legal code to set the conditions." When Loeb dismisses laws as mere "rules of a game," Lawrence Preston champions the law as "man's greatest single achievement—a system for self-regulation." Loeb responds by describing how Nazis used their own laws to maintain order in concentration camps, so as to ensure that inmates complied even in their own deaths, and he warns that the world "must prepare for the next time the man-made rules will not apply in the search for justice."

During the trial, witnesses and attorneys discuss the issue of choice—both Prinzler's choice to follow the Nazis' orders, and Loeb's wife's choice to die with her son when the boy had been selected for gassing. At the conclusion of the proceedings the jury returns and announces that it is unable to reach a verdict. "The problem is not a legal one," the foreman explains. "We could never begin to pass judgment on this case—it's beyond us." Nonetheless, the judge sends them back to deliberate further. "Is this the law's answer to a difficult question?" a skeptical Loeb asks the elder Preston, remarking that there are some things that the law apparently cannot deal with. "You're wrong," Preston replies. "The law and its processes have understood the nature of the case truly, and have given us a precious allowance — more time. . . . When all else fails, that's all we can hope for — more time." The episode ends with no verdict as to Loeb's guilt or innocence.

As is typical of courtroom drama, "The Avenger" relies on unexpected turns of plot to maintain suspense. However, the identity of the killer is not at issue. Here, law itself is on trial. Dramatic tension escalates with Lawrence Preston's efforts to prove the value of law as a social force, through a series of debates with his son, the district attorney, the defendant, and Dr. Prinzler's American-born widow. Just as these discussions further complicate the case, "The Avenger" offers no easy division between hero and villain. Loeb and Prinzler are both characterized as victims and as killers; Loeb's willful act of vengeance and his nihilism are set against his identity as a concentration camp survivor, just as Prinzler's postwar virtues are juxtaposed with his collaboration in war crimes.

Moreover, the episode does not conclude, according to the convention of courtroom drama, with an unambiguous resolution. The jurors' inability to rule suggests the program's creators wished to present the Holocaust as a subject that raises questions that are beyond simple answers but instead require continued discussion. Indeed, the case tried on "The Avenger" does, in effect, get another hearing on prime-time television a year later on another courtroom series, *Sam Benedict* (NBC, 1962–1963). In an episode entitled "Season of Vengeance," attorney Benedict (Edmond O'Brien) defends a widowed survivor of Dachau who has attempted to kill a renowned philanthropist responsible for informing on her husband and parents during the war. The Prestons reexamine the moral complexities of crimes associated with the Holocaust when they defend "the unpopular cause of a teen-aged American Nazi . . . accused of killing the aged caretaker of a New York City synagogue" in "The Indelible Silence," which aired on *The Defenders* in the fall of 1962. And the story of a virtuous doctor on trial for his murderous past as a Nazi war criminal was revisited in *QB VII* (ABC), a 1974 made-for-television movie based on Leon Uris's novel.[13]

In other television dramas of this period the Holocaust served as a paradigmatic case study in the psychology of evil.[14] These examples also approached the subject through stories of individuals, exemplified by dramas that explored the personal histories of neo-Nazis. Though they focused on marginal individuals in extreme situations, these episodes evinced a more general understanding of anti-Semitism and its relationship to the Jewish community at that time. The episodes also reflected, more broadly,

The Defenders: The Prestons (played by Robert Reed, left, and E. G. Marshall, right) defend an American Nazi (Dennis Hopper) accused of murdering an elderly Jew in "The Indelible Silence," an episode aired in 1962. (Photofest.)

contemporary notions of social intolerance as being rooted in the psychopathology of the individual.

Following the 1961 drama "Death's Head Revisited," Rod Serling's *Twilight Zone* reexamined the Nazi criminal mind in a 1963 broadcast entitled "He's Alive."[15] The hour-long drama, written by Serling, offers a portrait, part psychological and part supernatural, of Frank Vollmer (played by Dennis Hopper), a young member of an unnamed American neo-Nazi organization. As the drama opens, Vollmer's career as the spokesman for a small, struggling political movement that advocates driving foreigners, nonwhites, Jews, Catholics, and Communists out of the country is fraught with setbacks. When he is denounced and then beaten up by a hostile crowd after giving a speech on a city street corner, Vollmer retreats to the home of his only friend—an elderly Jew named Ernst Ganz (Ludwig Donath). Ganz, a survivor of Dachau, has looked after Vollmer since he was a little boy, the son of neglectful and abusive parents. While bitterly critical of Vollmer's activism in the neo-Nazi movement, Ganz nonetheless offers him compassion.

Dennis Hopper played Frank Vollmer, another neo-Nazi killer, in "He's Alive," a 1963 episode of *The Twilight Zone*. (Rod Serling Archives, Ithaca College.)

Vollmer's career as a neo-Nazi improves markedly after he makes the acquaintance of a mysterious stranger. This man, who always remains hidden in shadows, offers Vollmer effective advice on how to rouse his audience. Vollmer enters into a Faustian bargain with the stranger. Promising the young man success and immortality, the shadowy stranger tells Vollmer to order one of his fellow party members killed. The stranger instructs Vollmer to make the murder look like an attack by the party's enemies, thus turning the victim into a martyr for the neo-Nazis' cause. Next, the stranger demands that Vollmer prove his total commitment to the movement by killing Ganz, who has denounced Vollmer at one of his public meetings (Ganz tells the crowd, "I've seen it all before. . . . We can't let it happen again"). When Vollmer resists at first, the stranger emerges from the shadows—it is Adolf Hitler (Curt Conway). Soon after Ganz's death, the police come after Vollmer, charging him with complicity in the murder of one of his comrades. Vollmer tries to escape but is fatally shot by the police. As the shadow of Hitler's silhouette looms on the wall behind Vollmer's body, Serling narrates off camera:

Where will he go next, this phantom from another time, persecuted ghost of a previous nightmare? . . . Anyplace—every place—where there's hate, where there's prejudice, where there's bigotry. He's alive . . . so long as these evils exist. Remember that when he comes to your town. Remember it when you hear his voice speaking out through others. Remember it when you hear a name called, a minority attacked—any blind, unreasoning assault on a people or any human being. He's alive because, through these things, we keep him alive.

Serling returned to the subject of anti-Semitism and Jewish self-hatred again in 1966 with "Hate Syndrome," a half-hour script for the syndicated religious drama series *Insight,* first aired in 1961.[16] Billed in its opening credits as offering "stories of spiritual conflict in the twentieth century," *Insight* was hosted and produced by Ellwood E. Kieser, a Paulist priest. In this drama, the psychological interdependence between Jews and neo-Nazis is more intensely configured. The program follows the aftermath of an assault by Mr. Fine (played by Edouard Franz), an elderly Jew, on a young man named Joseph McWilliams (James Beggs), a deputy commander of the American Fascist Party. (Joseph McWilliams was also the name of the head of the Christian Mobilizers, an American anti-Semitic organization active in the 1930s and 1940s.) Fine, a teacher of Hebrew, attacked McWilliams in New York's Central Park after hearing him deliver an anti-Semitic speech. Fine explains to police detective Abraham Polansky (Harold Stone) that he was provoked not only by the content of McWilliam's oratory, but also by the young man himself. The Hebrew teacher recognized the neo-Nazi as Seymour Abelson, a "frightened kid" who had been a student of his in Hebrew school twenty years earlier.

When McWilliams recognizes Fine as his former teacher, he drops the assault charges and, in a confrontation with the old man, agonizes between guilt and self-hatred. Fine denounces the young man for his "gospel of poison" and for something "far worse—you have planted a seed of hatred in me that makes me ashamed . . . to present myself to God." McWilliams responds by recalling the pain he felt as a child about being a Jew: "I had to wear it like a hump. . . . When I was seven years old, I had a *nigger* say to me that I killed his Lord—a *nigger!*" The swastika, McWilliams explains, "comes with no tears and no wailing walls." Putting on his Nazi uniform, he looks at himself in a mirror and says to himself, "I am not a Jew! I am *not* a Jew!"

Fine visits McWilliams at a neo-Nazi meeting. The old man explains that he wants McWilliams to punish him: "I tried to kill you. I turned away from God." McWilliams hesitates, telling Fine to leave: "There are no Jews here to protect you." But when the other Nazis start to attack Fine, McWilliams stops them. Fine tells the remorse-stricken young man that he must look within himself to understand the source of his hatred: "I believe that men hate other men for one reason only—because there comes a point, deep in the pit, where they can no longer stomach hating themselves."

Just as the *Twilight Zone* episode depends on supernatural devices, Serling's script for *Insight* relies heavily on coincidence and parallel structures to relativize the moral dilemmas of Jews and neo-Nazis. Like Ganz and Vollmer, both Fine and McWilliams are attackers as well as victims; their respective Jewish self-hatred and Jewish desire for retribution are juxtaposed as equally deficient moral responses. This effort to present an ethical dilemma of "universal" (that is, Christian American) significance avoids and contorts the historical and cultural particulars of both sides of the conflict between American Jews and neo-Nazis in a balance that ultimately tests the limits of credulity.

Nonetheless, "Hate Syndrome" remains an illuminating, if unsettling, artifact of the psychology of Jewish self-hatred in the post-Holocaust era. The Hebrew teacher's attack on the neo-Nazi is, like Ganz's denunciation of Vollmer in "He's Alive," a retroactive effort to compensate for a perceived lack of Jewish resistance to anti-Semitic persecution during the Nazi era. As symbolic rescriptings of history, these plots intimate that if more Jews had acted like this in the 1930s, there would have been no Holocaust. But Fine's assault on McWilliams/Abelson also proves to be the attack of one Jew on another, in which the hatred of the teacher for his self-loathing former student mirrors the younger man's contempt for the older one and for his professional commitment to the furtherance of Jewish particularism. According to this configuration, not only is Nazism an externalization of Jewish self-hatred, but Jews bear responsibility for its perpetuation.

American neo-Nazism as one individual's extreme form of Jewish self-hatred was reexamined in a 1977 episode of *Lou Grant* (CBS, 1977–1982), a series about the staff of a contemporary Los Angeles daily newspaper and the local stories that they cover.[17] The episode, entitled "Nazis," begins with a newsroom debate over how to cover the story of a clash between a local Jewish rally in support of the State of Israel and a small group of members of the National Socialist Aryan American Party. Reporter Billie Newman (played by Linda Kelsey) investigates the neo-Nazi organization. She attends a party meeting, at which the film *Triumph of the Will* is screened, followed by an impassioned speech by the group's leader, Commander Stryker (Peter Weller), in which he explains that America must be returned to the "white Protestant pioneers" who built the country. Newman, struck by his zeal, asks Stryker for an interview, but he refuses.

Continuing her research, Newman discovers that Stryker's real name is Donald Sturner; she visits his parents' home, where she discovers a mezuzah attached to the doorpost. In a brief exchange with the Sturners,

Donald's father angrily tells her, "I said Kaddish for him years ago." When Newman reports this to her editor, Lou Grant (Ed Asner), he responds that her discovery in itself is not enough; the real story involves explaining "what turned this bar mitzvah boy into a Nazi with a swastika on his arm—how did it happen?" Newman interviews people from Donald Sturner's past, including a high school teacher who remembers him as a loyal patriot, "one of the few who kept faith with the country" during the late 1960s. She also speaks with a psychiatrist, who tells her that sometimes a victim will identify with his persecutors—he "can't bear to be a victim any longer, so he simply changes sides."

Newman confronts Stryker with what she has learned about his past. At first he threatens her; later he asks Grant not to print the story, offering the newspaper evidence about "homosexuals in the Ku Klux Klan" in exchange (thereby implying that one case of hypocritical bigotry is as good—or as bad—as another). Finally Stryker pleads, "I'll lose all my friends. . . . Everything I worked for will be gone." When Grant refuses to pull the story, Stryker storms off. The next day, the newspaper staff learns that Stryker has killed himself. Grant reassures a distraught Newman: "A man is dead—a sad, twisted, tormented man, but a human being, nonetheless. By writing about him, you've helped us understand about him and maybe ourselves a little bit."

Despite this profession of the redeeming value inherent in telling Stryker's story—a defense of its presentation both as provocative news story and as engaging television drama—the episode provides limited insight into the neo-Nazi phenomenon and the intolerance that is central to their ideology and practice. There are actual examples of neo-Nazis who turn out to be Jews or to have Jewish ancestors (e.g., Frank Collin, leader of the Chicago-based National Socialist Party of America, was the son of a Jewish survivor of Dachau), but these cases are as rare as they are extreme.[18] Like "Hate Syndrome," this episode of *Lou Grant* portrays Jews as implicit in their victimization. The episode presents the Stryker/Sturner story as a cautionary tale to Jews—and, by extension, others—of the dangers of self-loathing. The fatal consequences of internalized anti-Semitism, the program warns, await those who lack the kind of strong, positive Jewish identity performed by the pro-Israel demonstrators seen at the episode's opening.

These dramas suggest that the proper search for an understanding of Nazism or neo-Nazism lies in the psychohistory of the individual. The specifics of the historical, cultural, social, and economic context in which Nazism or neo-Nazism flourishes are deemphasized or ignored in these episodes, while insight into the individual is linked to a universalized approach to the human character. Consequently, these dramas offer conflicting understandings of the Jewish neo-Nazi: at the same time that he is a highly marginal figure, he epitomizes the notion that anyone—even a Jew—has the potential to become a Nazi.

The notion of an interdependent relationship between Jews and their persecutors was hardly new, having appeared in a number of seminal post-war reflections on anti-Semitism, such as Jean-Paul Sartre's oft-cited assertion that "it is the anti-Semite who *makes* the Jew." Such ideas also figured prominently in writings about the Holocaust by historian Raul Hilberg, philosopher Hannah Arendt, Zionist activist Ben Hecht, and author Robert Shaw, all published in the United States during the 1960s, which explored the notion that European Jews in some way collaborated in their demise at the hands of the Nazis.[19]

Complementing the self-loathing Jews who appear in the Holocaust episodes of American television's dramatic series are other characters—most of them non-Jews—who freely, sanguinely denounce or mock Nazis, both to their face and in passing reference, variously calling them "punks," "kooks" ("He's Alive"), or "little rat patrol" and "off-the-wall lunatics" ("Nazis"). Whereas these episodes portray neo-Nazis as cowardly, mentally unstable, of limited intelligence, and sometimes comically inept, their detractors appear to be of sound mind, fearless, and proud. Like the notion of a link between Jews and anti-Semites, this idealized vision of the proper response to Fascism was no innovation. Rather, it harkens back to propaganda films made in Hollywood during the Second World War, ranging from home-front dramas, epitomized by *Mrs. Miniver* (1942), to animated cartoons such as Disney's *Der Fuehrer's Face* (1943).[20]

At the same time, the characters in these television episodes who readily and fearlessly denounce Nazism resemble those who embody the torment of Jewish self-hatred, presenting a different kind of affective escape from a more complicated and painfully honest confrontation with the Holocaust. These morally forthright characters may have assuaged some American viewers' uneasiness over charges that the United States government did not do its utmost to prevent civilian fatalities in Europe during World War II, as publicized by Arthur Morse's *While Six Million Died: A Chronicle of American Apathy* in 1967.[21] These performances of decrying social injustice resonated as well with contemporary televised images of actual social activism in the nation's civil rights and antiwar movements.

The mockery of Nazis in these episodes is also an extension of the comic Nazi-bashing that persisted in American media beyond wartime propaganda, exemplified by Mel Brooks's 1968 film *The Producers* and the television series *Hogan's Heroes* (CBS, 1965–1971). This situation comedy, arguably not an example of Holocaust television, is nonetheless an interesting test case of the boundaries of the genre and offers a telling, if oblique, measure of the extent to which American television had evolved its own pro-

MAD magazine's 1967 parody of the situation comedy *Hogan's Heroes* ends with this panel, in which writer Larry Siegel and artist Jack Davis envision the setting of the series transformed from a World War II POW camp to a Nazi concentration camp. Despite its satirical exaggerations, the cartoon evinces a public sense of what constitutes an inappropriate Holocaust representation. (© 1967 E.C. Publications, Inc. All rights reserved. Used with permission.)

tocols with regard to the Holocaust by the mid-1960s.[22] While the series, set in a Nazi-run prisoner-of-war camp, portrayed the camaraderie among Allied POWs and their generally amicable relationship with charmingly bumbling German captors, many viewers misconstrued *Hogan's Heroes* as a comedy about a Nazi concentration camp when the program debuted, which generated considerable controversy.[23] A cartoon in *MAD* magazine in 1967 followed this discomforting confusion to its implicit end by offering readers a parodic vision of the series as a comedy set in Buchenwald.[24]

In addition to linking the Nazi era with recurring paradigmatic themes, the Holocaust's "guest appearances" on episodic television series demonstrate the codification of a Holocaust iconography in American popular culture. This association of various signs with the Holocaust enabled both its easy identification as a discrete subject and its ready application as a paradigm. The episodes discussed above identify their subject as the Holocaust and characters as Jews, Nazis, or neo-Nazis through a variety of semiotic codes—language, gestures, visual icons, music—some of which draw directly on symbols in use during the Holocaust period. Other codes are rooted in conventions of American television and film dramas. Occasionally these Holocaust episodes invent symbols for their fictitious neo-Nazi movements. In "He's Alive," for example, the neo-Nazis' uniforms bear the insignia of a flaming torch held by a hand (recalling the Statue of Liberty) pierced with a lightning bolt. Usually, however, these dramas make use of the iconography of the Third Reich: the death's-head and double-S insignia worn by members of the SS, portraits of Hitler and other prominent Nazis, and, above all, the swastika.

A number of these episodes introduce the Nazi era or neo-Nazism as a plot element by first showing a swastika on uniforms, on placards, or as a graffito before there is any reference to the subject in dialogue or narration. This device not only assumes the historical literacy of viewers, but also draws on—and sustains—the powerfully affective role that this icon has played as an element of Nazi ideology and practice.[25] Often the initial appearance of this sign of Nazism creates an emotionally charged moment. In the opening of "Hate Syndrome" Detective Polanski finds the case he has been assigned to investigate bewildering, until he sees McWilliams's jacket hanging on a coatrack. "This pretty much tells the story," he says as the camera cuts to a close-up of the jacket's sleeve, which bears a swastika patch. Other efforts to make dramatic use of the Nazi emblem were more expressionist, such as the plan for "He's Alive," eventually abandoned, to shoot an extreme close-up of Vollmer's face with a swastika glowing in the pupil of his eye.[26]

Signaling the Jewishness of characters is more complex, reflecting the multivalence and self-consciousness of articulating Jewish identity in post–

World War II America. The public demonstration with which the "Nazis" episode of *Lou Grant* opens, for example, features a melange of signs: the sound of a male voice chanting a text from the Bible in Hebrew, men wearing skullcaps, and demonstrators carrying placards bearing pro-Israel slogans and six-pointed stars. This fusion of Jewish scriptures, traditional religious practice, and Zionist political activism introduces Jews into the drama through signs representing them in terms readily recognizable by a contemporary American audience, albeit in a configuration unlikely to occur at an actual public event.

Whereas visual signs figure prominently in identifying Nazi and neo-Nazi characters, audial codes — language, sound effects, and music — play a more important role in signifying Jewish characters. Plangent, minor-mode background music, usually played on string instruments, regularly accompanies the appearance of Jews in these and other television dramas that deal with anti-Semitism, following an established convention of Hollywood film for signaling Jews.[27] When Billie Newman visits the Sturners' apartment in "Nazis," this music swells on the soundtrack as she looks at the doorjamb and the screen cuts to a close-up shot of the mezuzah. In "He's Alive," this musical convention is woven into the narrative: When Vollmer first walks up the stairs to Ganz's apartment, melancholy string music is heard; as the young man enters the apartment, Ganz is seen playing a cello. Later, when Vollmer fatally shoots Ganz, the cello music is reprised on the sound track. (Ganz's Jewishness is mentioned only once, toward the end of the drama; until then, were it not for this musical signal, one might be as inclined to think that he was a non-Jewish German who had been interned in Dachau.)

Produced before the word *Holocaust* was a fixture of general American discourse, these dramas rely on other words and signs to establish the subject. The names of major concentration and extermination camps, which had entered the American vocabulary during the final months of World War II and the early postwar years, figure as charged words evoking the larger phenomenon of Nazi genocide. Similarly, characters are often mutely identified as Holocaust survivors by the revelation of numbers tattooed on their forearms, recalling images that appear repeatedly in documentary photographs and footage from liberated concentration camps. For example, when Lawrence Preston first meets Meyer Loeb in "The Avenger," the attorney asks where and when Loeb's wife and son were murdered. Loeb responds by rolling up his shirtsleeve and thrusting his tattooed forearm in front of Preston in reponse, as harsh brass chords are heard on the sound track.[28] Set in the postwar era, these dramas evoke the Holocaust as a memory both for characters and for the audience. Indeed, the episodes assume a foreknowledge of the Holocaust that is rooted not in experience but in mediated encounters, whose point of entry is situated at the end of the war.

While the aforementioned episodes deal with the Holocaust in stories about marginalized individuals driven to extremes—victims of Nazism as haunted avengers, neo-Nazis as transgressive sociopaths or as self-hating Jews—the Holocaust figures as a symbolic event on a grander scale in some of its other "guest appearances" on episodic series of the period. In such instances, iconography plays a critical role in the dramatic realization of the Holocaust as a paradigm. "Patterns of Force" (1968), a typical episode of the science fiction series *Star Trek* (NBC, 1966–1969), offers an encounter between the inhabitants of fictitious planets and the crew of the starship *Enterprise*, who are mandated by an interplanetary federation to patrol the galaxy in order to gather scientific information and promote security.[29] Although set in the twenty-third century, these tales of interplanetary travel frequently resonated with social issues of concern to contemporary American audiences. In this episode the *Enterprise*, under the command of Captain Kirk (played by William Shatner), visits two neighboring planets: Ekos, reputed to be inhabited by "a primitive, warlike people in a state of anarchy," and Zeon, which "has a relatively high technology" and whose inhabitants are "peaceful." The *Enterprise* is looking for John Gill (David Brian), a prominent historian who was once Kirk's mentor and was sent to Ekos by the federation years earlier as a "cultural advisor" but hasn't been heard from for years.

Kirk and the *Enterprise*'s science officer, Mr. Spock (Leonard Nimoy), arrive on Ekos, where they discover, to their astonishment, that the planet has been transformed into a replica of Nazi Germany in the 1930s. Ekosians, wearing jackboots and swastika-adorned uniforms, have taken on the role of Nazi aggressors, while Zeons are the victims of the Ekosians' hatred and persecution. On a public "viewing screen" (i.e., a large outdoor television monitor), Kirk and Spock watch a news report announcing that "today the Führer has ordered our glorious capital to be made Zeon-free."[30] The broadcast ends with a salute to the "Führer"—whom Kirk recognizes as none other than John Gill.

Kirk and Spock resolve to find Gill and learn how he came to be the leader of this replica of the Third Reich. They disguise themselves as Nazis, only to be discovered and arrested. In prison they meet Isak (Richard Evans), a Zeon captive who is a member of an underground resistance movement. Spock asks Isak why the Nazis hate Zeons. Isak replies, "Because with no one to hate there would be nothing to hold them together. So the party has built us into a threat, a disease to be wiped out."

Spock and Kirk escape from prison with Isak, who introduces them to members of the resistance movement. Eventually they infiltrate Nazi headquarters and find Gill, who has been drugged into compliance by Melakon (Skip Homeier), the Nazi Ekosians' second-in-command. Roused from his drug-induced stupor, Gill explains that he "interfered" with the Ekosian culture because the planet was "fragmented, divided." He decided to take a "lesson from Earth history" and replicate the Third Reich, because it was the "most efficient state Earth ever knew." At first the plan worked, Gill explains, until Melakon took over and initiated a campaign of racial hatred against the Zeons. With Kirk's help, Gill broadcasts an announcement denouncing Melakon and canceling the assault on the Zeons. Melakon is assassinated by Isak, but not before the Ekosian fatally shoots Gill. As he dies, Gill tells Kirk, "I was wrong. The noninterference direction is the only way. We must stop the slaughter. . . . Even historians fail to learn from history. They repeat the same mistakes. Let the killing end." Before returning to the *Enterprise,* Kirk pronounces the planet to be "in good hands." Spock concurs: "With the union of two cultures, this system would make a fine addition to the federation."

The Nazi era is evoked with the appearance of swastikas, SS and Gestapo uniforms, and Nazi salutes; the dialogue is sprinkled with idioms associated with the Third Reich. But rather than signaling to viewers a drama set in the Nazi era or among a postwar neo-Nazi movement, here these elements are signs of a fictitious totalitarian culture—indeed, they are integral to its realization. Moreover, these Nazi terms and symbols signal the potential for universal adoption of the principles of the regime that they represent. Not only were Ekosians able to become Nazis in a matter of a few years, but both Zeons (who, out of uniform, are physically indistinguishable from Ekosians) and humans such as Kirk can pass as Ekosian Nazis. (When Kirk first dons his Gestapo disguise, Spock comments dryly that the captain "should make a very convincing Nazi.") In this science-fiction replication, Nazism is presented as a discrete and externally induced phenomenon—imported to this part of the universe by the "alien" John Gill—that on its own instigates strife between Zeon and Ekos. Other than what is reported about the respective "evolutionary" stages of the two planets' peoples, there are no apparent physiological, linguistic, or cultural differences that distinguish them, nor do they have a reported history of relationships, hostile or amicable.

Instead, "Patterns of Force" uses Spock, the series's resident alien, to dramatize the ordeal of difference. The son of a human mother and a Vulcan father, Spock has greenish skin, pointed ears, and prominently slanted eyebrows. His markedly different appearance figures strategically in this episode. When Spock disguises himself as an SS officer, Kirk comments that the helmet he wears "covers a multitude of sins." Later, while trying to enter Nazi party headquarters in search of Gill, they are stopped by a suspicious Ekosian superior officer. He orders Spock to remove his helmet, while Ekosian soldiers surround him with weapons drawn. As Spock complies with the order the camera closes in on his face, and ominous background music swells to a suspenseful climax as the scene ends.

Spock's physical appearance plays a focal role in a later scene that more directly evokes Nazi racial policies. When Kirk, Spock, and the resistance fighters infiltrate Nazi party headquarters in search of Gill, Kirk creates a momentary diversion by pretending to be a Zeon officer who has discovered an "alien" spy masquerading as a Nazi. He turns Spock over to Melakon, who, as an expert on the "genetics of racial purity," analyzes the specimen: "Note the sinister eyes and the malformed ears—definitely an inferior race. Note the low forehead, denoting stupidity—the dull look of a trapped animal." Melakon orders Spock executed, explaining that he wants "the body saved for the cultural museum. He'll make an interesting display." (Spock is, of course, rescued before any harm befalls him.)

Though viewers of *Star Trek* have variously understood Spock's archetypal "otherness" as analogous to that of African-Americans, Asians, and other cultural groups, here connections between Spock's alien identity and Jewishness seem deliberate.[31] Race science was a fundament of Nazi anti-Semitism, and the Third Reich had planned to exhibit Jewish culture after the war in a "Museum of the Defunct Jewish Race." Spock's unmasking in the earlier scene resonates with stories of Jews living under Nazi occupation who attempted to pass as non-Jews, only to be "betrayed" by physical distinctions. (Knowing that Nimoy is a Jew might further reinforce this association for some viewers.)[32] There are other references in the script that suggest the creators of "Patterns of Force" modeled the conflict between Ekosians and Zeons on the Nazi persecution of Jews. Zeons have names similar to those of biblical heroes—besides Isak, there are Abrom and Dovid—while the name *Zeon* itself suggests a play on *Zion*.

The image of Zeons rising up to defeat their oppressors may have recalled the triumph of modern-day Zion for some of the first viewers of "Patterns of Force," which was aired less than a year after the Six-Day War. However, the drama resonates even more powerfully with the United States' military involvement in Vietnam and the burgeoning American anti-war movement. During the 1960s American television audiences had been watching another drama of advisors who had originally been sent to observe a foreign conflict—in this case, presented on nightly news reports. By 1968, these advisors had actively intervened in the internal operations of the struggle and escalated the violence between North and South Vietnam, which compelled increasing numbers of Americans to protest. Gill's final words ("Let the killing end") seem less meaningful with regard to the immediate dramatic situation—indeed, he has already called off the attack on Zeon—than as a tragic figure's final, cautionary words of wisdom, addressed to the drama's audience rather than to other characters.

This and other episodes of *Star Trek* were part of an ongoing effort to "represent a mythic reworking" of America's experience in Vietnam in science fiction. These works offered "a vision of Americans' opportunity, in the midst of a fallen mythic landscape, to take control of their destiny by taking control of their national consciousness, and thus self-consciously work out the implications of the Vietnam experience for their larger journey through history."[33] "Patterns of Force" was also not the only American television broadcast to analogize the Holocaust with the war in Vietnam. In 1967, two different productions of *The Investigation* were televised. This drama by Peter Weiss, based on documentary records, deals with war crimes trials of Nazis who ran the Auschwitz death camp. Yet, as Erik Barnouw observed, the broadcasts of the drama were widely understood as offering "familiar echoes"; during these years, "every subject tended to become Vietnam."[34]

As the American public learned of its military's persecution of Vietnamese civilians and the United States government's covert policies to escalate its military role in Southeast Asia were exposed, analogies between the Holocaust and the war in Vietnam became more direct. In *Nuremberg and Vietnam: Who is Guilty?*, a news special coproduced by PBS and the BBC that aired on 7 June 1971, the first major public effort to come to terms with Nazi persecutions served as a moral paradigm for evaluating America's ongoing role in Vietnam. The two-hour broadcast, anchored by Robert MacNeil, included interviews with Albert Speer and Telford Taylor—whose book *Nuremberg and Vietnam: An American Tragedy* had appeared in the previous year—as well as a live discussion with jurists in New York, London, and Hamburg, linked by satellite.[35]

These programs invoked the Holocaust as an episode of recent history by which to measure the legal and moral implications of present policy, very much in the spirit of George Santayana's oft-cited words that "those who cannot remember the past are condemned to repeat it."[36] Yet "Patterns of Force" offers a striking departure from this sentiment, as Gill concludes that even historians can fail to learn from history. This is not simply more pessimistic, but subverts Santayana's faith in the social value of documenting and studying history. Indeed, history, as embodied by Gill, is a threat to *Star Trek*'s utopian vision of future interplanetary social harmony. The notion of "history repeating itself"—enacted here by vintage footage, costumes, gestures, and rhetoric—is understood as dangerous not because of a failure to learn from past mistakes, but because of a failure to escape the destructive power of history. Far from offering edification, history in "Patterns of Force" only provides the blueprint for genocide. All that prevents Nazi Ekosians from destroying Zeons are the universalist forces of good, embodied by the multinational crew of the *Enterprise* and the edenic model of the federation that they serve. In "Patterns of Force," the Holocaust — the consequence of Gill's misguided efforts to make a progressivist application of the lessons of history — is a kind of sociopolitical Flying Dutchman, careening through space and time, much like the immortal figure of Hitler in Serling's "He's Alive." Like Serling's "Hate Syndrome," the notion that the Holocaust is a paradigmatic phenomenon of human (and humanoid) behavior is embodied in the title "Patterns of Force."

Prime-time television's role as a public forum for debating provocative social issues expanded during the 1970s. Appearances of the Holocaust followed this development, figuring as a moral touchstone even in an occasional situation comedy — for example, "Archie Is Branded," a 1973 episode of the long-running series *All in the Family* (CBS, 1971–1983).[37] Like *Star Trek,* this situation comedy was renowned for dealing with social concerns in a popular entertainment genre generally regarded as escapist. *All in the Family* is set in the Queens, New York, home of Archie Bunker (played by Carroll O'Connor), a middle-aged, working-class WASP, whose conservative political and cultural views peppered his daily conversation. Each week Archie, his family, and their neighbors debated such topical issues as the war in Vietnam, feminism, gay liberation, and American race relations while running the paces of domestic misadventures typical of other situation-comedy plots.

"Archie Is Branded" begins on a Sunday morning, as Archie goes to get the newspaper — only to discover that someone has painted a large black swastika on the front door of his home. Archie assumes it to be the work of young pranksters and calls the police. But his daughter, Gloria (Sally Struthers), and son-in-law, Mike (Rob Reiner), think it may be more than an act of mischief — especially when they discover a note saying, "This swastika is just the beginning — we'll be back." Archie covers the swastika temporarily with an American flag, commenting, "This put the kibosh on the Nazis once before, it'll do it again."

A man comes to the door of the Bunker home, identifying himself as Paul Benjamin (Gregory Sierra), a member of the Hebrew Defense Association, or HDA.[38] He informs the Bunkers that their house was mistakenly targeted by an anti-Semitic group. They intended to attack the home of a neighbor, David Blum, whom Archie identifies as a "big-mouth liberal." Paul offers to help protect the Bunkers, because the vandals may still think that theirs is the Blums' house. Mike, an ardent liberal himself, denounces the HDA as "a strong-arm outfit" and "a vigilante group," but Archie accepts Paul's offer of protection. Mike engages Paul in a debate, with the former advocating for the importance of law and for encouraging dialogue between enemies, the latter arguing that humankind is essentially violent and that force must be met with force.

Another member of the HDA arrives and tells Paul that the anti-Semitic group now knows they attacked the wrong house. Telling the Bunkers that they are no longer in danger, Paul bids them farewell, saying *"Shalom,"* as he heads off for his car. Mike and Gloria are commenting on the irony of this salutation when a powerful explosion erupts. They rush to the door and look out: "Holy gee," says Archie in the episode's final shot. "That's Paul—they blew him up in his car." (Like the unresolved conclusion of "The Avenger," this break in the conventional happy ending of the situation-comedy genre indicates an understanding of the episode's subject as something exceptional.)

No neo-Nazis or other anti-Semites appear in "Archie Is Branded." Their sole visual presence is the swastika painted on the Bunkers' front door, which, when first seen, elicits both gasps and laughter from the studio audience present at the episode's taping. The limitation of Nazism to this one symbol facilitates dealing with the subject in the context of a situation comedy. Indeed, the swastika appears in the kind of chance mistake that is a staple of this genre. Archie Bunker's accidental identification as a victim of Nazism—and, therefore, his being mistaken for a Jew—offers a comic variation on the arbitrariness of stigmatization that was the grist of plots of Holocaust dramas televised during the 1950s. The notion that anyone can be the victim of anti-Semites is humorously confirmed when Archie— whom regular viewers of *All in the Family* know to bear some prejudice against Jews himself—takes on the Hebrew Defense Association as his ally.

"Guest appearances" by the Holocaust on episodic series have not been limited to television's entertainment genres. References to the Holocaust on installments of documentary series during the 1960s and 1970s have also enhanced its stature as a paradigm for understanding contemporary social and political concerns. For example, the Holocaust figures as an oblique presence in the 1960 documentary *Cast the First Stone*.[39] This inaugural episode of ABC's *Bell and Howell Close-up* series examines prejudice in contemporary America through a range of case studies: a profile of an American neo-Nazi; anti-Semitism in the exclusive community of Grosse Pointe, Michigan; and examples of discrimination against African-Americans in Chicago, Puerto Ricans in New York City, and Mexicans and Japanese in Los Angeles. These different instances of intolerance are equally condemned by the documentary, which evokes both American principles (citing the Declaration of Independence's "insistent, drumming demand for equality") and Christian values ("Let he who is without sin cast the first stone") to make its case for confronting this "vestige of the savage past." As it situates anti-Semitism and neo-Nazism within a broad spectrum of social intolerances that plague postwar America, *Cast the First*

Stone also implicitly invokes the Holocaust as a cautionary paradigm of the ultimate consequences of indifference to prejudice.

Television news documentaries on the State of Israel provide a measure of how the Holocaust became increasingly important as a point of entry for understanding Israeli history and culture. *Israel—It Is No Fable,* an hour-long *CBS News Special* aired in 1963 on the fifteenth anniversary of the country's founding, focuses primarily on how Israel deals with the challenges of integrating Jews from many different diaspora backgrounds into a nascent national Zionist culture.[40] With an eye, perhaps, to considering America's racial problems at a time when the civil rights movement was gaining wider national media coverage, *Israel—It Is No Fable* pays special attention to the lives of various Jewish immigrants from African and Asian countries of origin and to the circumstances of Israeli Arabs (whose presence "touches a raw nerve in a Jewish population sensitive for centuries to the rights of minorities"). Only a passing reference is made to the Holocaust in the telecast, when an anonymous farmer, who talks exclusively about the importance of settling the land, is identified as a "survivor of the Nazi Holocaust" and a "fighter for independence—the embodiment of Israel."

The Israelis, another *CBS News Special* aired ten years later, demonstrates both how the Holocaust became a much more significant part of many Israelis' discourse of identity over the course of the decade and how connections between the Holocaust and Israel came to be articulated in American culture.[41] Israeli journalist Amos Elon hosts the news documentary, one of a series on the national character of different countries. *The Israelis* was distinguished from these other documentaries by the coincidence of its production and broadcast with the Yom Kippur War of October 1973.[42] In his introductory remarks on what shapes the Israeli character, Elon notes that "almost a million Israelis have direct connections with the six million Jews slaughtered during World War II. . . . A colleague once wrote about Israel, 'Every day we fight the Arabs and win, but every night we fight the Nazis and lose.'" Over footage of a memorial service for Israeli soldiers killed in a recent battle with Arab neighbors, Elon narrates, "This war started in 1947 and it's not over yet—that's one generation. In Europe it started in the 1930s—that talk of extermination—and that's two generations. So no matter what your age in Israel, or how you disagree with your own government, your subconscious inevitably knows that there are foreign governments that want to kill you." Such sentiments do not merely conceptualize Israel's violent history since its founding as a continuation of the Holocaust. In this broadcast, aired several months after the last American troops had been evacuated from Vietnam, Elon's remark also distinguishes the sensibilities of young men and women serving in the Israeli military from those of many of their American cohorts.

• • •

Historian Leon Jick has suggested that, while the Holocaust gained the recognition of scholars and became a fixture of American Jewish culture during the 1960s, it still remained a subject "of which the broader society took little note."[43] Yet during the 1960s and early 1970s the Holocaust made regular, if occasional, "guest appearances" on television, which helped establish a readily identifiable iconography that facilitated using the Holocaust as a paradigm. Recurrent plots and themes in episodic series linked the Holocaust with universal moral issues as well as specific, contemporary social and political concerns of Americans in general and of American Jews in particular.

Holocaust television of the 1960s and 1970s also exemplified the American television industry's struggle with the challenge of addressing issues regarded as difficult, unpleasant, or controversial as it consolidated authority over a medium that had come to dominate national popular culture in a matter of years. Scholars have characterized the television industry during the 1960s as "uneasy about its standing in American society. Its leaders avoided offending any significant segment of the public. In terms of programming, that meant offering evenings of avoidance. At a time of racial turmoil, political murders, and a massive military intervention in southeast Asia, Americans viewed relentlessly escapist entertainment and rigorously 'neutral' news programming."[44] Television scholars have described the medium as lagging behind other cultural forces with regard to the quality or relevance of its content: "At a time when other expressions of American culture were experiencing flourishes of experimentation and expansion," television was mired in a "period of contraction and product rationalization."[45]

Yet within these limitations, the episodes in which the Holocaust made "guest appearances" on television during this era exemplify the strategies that broadcasters pursued in order to accommodate a desire to address serious, controversial issues while delivering a reliable, consistent product of broadest possible appeal. Subjects such as the Holocaust brought novelty and variety to episodic programs, at the same time that the protocols of these television genres shaped the way that the issues were presented. While the conceptualization of the Holocaust as a moral issue with universal significance challenged understanding the event in its historical context, this approach facilitated the inclusion of the Holocaust in television's growing canon of social concerns. Along with gender and race relations, poverty, government corruption, and environmental issues, television presented the Holocaust as a meaningful issue for all Americans.

Toward the end of the 1970s, American television's era of "accommodation and adjustment" reached a threshold, as did the nation's understanding of the Holocaust. These two developments coincided in a single event, during which television elevated the presentation of the Holocaust from the episodic to the epic.

six

The Big Event

By many accounts the premiere broadcast of the miniseries *Holocaust: The Story of the Family Weiss* on NBC constitutes the most significant event in the presentation of the Holocaust on American television. Aired on four consecutive evenings, 16–19 April 1978, it was seen, at least in part, by an estimated 120 million viewers nationwide.[1] Scholars and critics often cite the miniseries as a landmark of Holocaust consciousness in America. With this one event, many have claimed that the Holocaust "fully 'arrived' on the American scene."[2]

Beyond its impact in increasing American awareness of the Nazi persecution of European Jewry, *Holocaust* initiated extensive discussion of Holocaust television and other forms of Holocaust remembrance. The responses to the American broadcast premiere by and large deemed Holocaust television to be an inherently problematic genre. Subsequent discussion about mediating the Holocaust—on television as well as by other means, from videotapes of Holocaust survivors' testimony to the feature film *Schindler's List*—has continued the critical debate engendered by *Holocaust*.[3]

Reaction to the 1978 miniseries reflected ideas prevalent in the United States concerning both the medium of television and the subject of the Holocaust. Indeed, the first broadcast of *Holocaust* came during a period when both American television broadcasting and Holocaust memory culture were undergoing signal changes, marked by increased self-reflexivity and the recognition of the aging of one generation and the coming of age of its successor.

Holocaust Remembrance Comes of Age

By the mid-1970s the Holocaust had become a fixture of American Jewish consciousness, and greater numbers of non-Jewish Americans were aware of it both as a historical event and as a focus of Jewish memory, political activism, creativity, and scholarship. Increasing numbers of American Jews commemorated the Holocaust in public memorial programs, many of them tied to Israel's annual observance of Yom ha-Sho'ah, which had been decreed a national holiday in 1951. Holocaust survivors, who had been at the forefront of Holocaust memory culture since the early postwar years, had begun to emerge as figures of greater public authority. They continued to play key roles in organizing Holocaust memorials and in efforts to erect monuments to the Jewish victims of Nazism in American cities. In ever greater numbers, survivors published memoirs of their wartime experiences and spoke in public about their personal histories as well as the larger subject of the Holocaust.

These developments were responsive, in part, to the aging of the survivor community. The greatest number of Holocaust survivors were in their teens or twenties at the end of World War II. The mid-1970s marked a midlife threshold for many of them, who, having weathered the transition into their postwar lives, had learned new languages, found homes, begun careers, started families, and established community ties. Now approaching their senior years, survivors often had children who were entering adulthood and, in many cases, were beginning to raise children of their own. These Holocaust survivors were naturally poised to engage in the process of life review—an activity that had gained new respect in the eyes of social scientists and gerontologists such as Harry Moody, who argued that the reminiscences of the elderly serve as "generational links," which "*must* become public in order to shine through the natural ruin of time."[4]

In addition to personal motivations to examine and discuss their life histories, many Holocaust survivors were urged to do so by adult children seeking insight into their parents' early histories and their own childhood experiences, as well as by a larger community that had come to recognize survivors as the privileged bearers of the "legacy" of the Holocaust. The imperative to document the memories of the aging Holocaust survivor population before their passing also took on an urgency intensified by increased public attention devoted to Holocaust revisionists, deniers, and the presence of neo-Nazi movements in the United States and Germany.

By this time the Holocaust had come to figure more prominently in American Jewish public culture as a "prominent and powerful" mythic presence in what Jonathan Woocher has termed "American civil Judaism." Beginning in the mid-1960s, consciousness-raising and fund-raising efforts on behalf of Jewish *refuseniks* in the Soviet Union (notably Elie Wiesel's *The Jews of Silence*) and in support of the State of Israel—especially around the time of the Six-Day War in 1967—often invoked the Holocaust as a cautionary tale for American Jews.[5] At the same time, the Holocaust began to figure with increasing prominence in works by American Jewish prose writers and poets, and American authors outside the Jewish community began to demonstrate an interest in a vicarious literary engagement with the subject as well. Sylvia Plath's use of Holocaust imagery to describe personal anguish in *Ariel* (1965), her final collection of poems, engendered considerable critical controversy, foreshadowing more recent public debates over "rightful and credible claims" on the Holocaust as cultural property.[6]

The field of Holocaust studies also reached a threshold in its development. By the mid-1970s, the Holocaust had become a topic of study in venues ranging from Jewish schools and summer camps to public high schools and nonsectarian colleges. The decade witnessed a burgeoning of Holocaust scholarship in print—so much so that scholars felt less obliged to bemoan the lack of interest in the Holocaust as they had in the 1950s and 1960s. By the end of the 1970s David Blumenthal wrote that scholars of the Holocaust "are rapidly reaching the point where no one can read all the literature in the field, and I suppose this means that 'Holocaust Studies' has come of age."[7]

By this time concern in the academy had shifted from the quantity of attention paid to the Holocaust to its quality. Scholars began to analyze the dynamics of responses to the Holocaust in scholarship, literature, film, fine arts, and popular culture as phenomena of Jewish culture and of general American culture. Typically, they approached the issue in the form of an inquiry into the "abuse" or "deformation" of the Holocaust, thereby seeking to establish intellectual, political, aesthetic, and moral criteria for evaluating representations of the Holocaust as (im)proper, (ir)responsible, (in)appropriate, or (un)conscionable. As Holocaust scholars Alice and Roy Eckardt noted, "The very study of the Holocaust's aftermath becomes, inevitably, part of that aftermath."[8]

In an overview of American Jewish intellectuals' response to the Holocaust, historian Stephen Whitfield considered the limitations of the Holocaust's entry into American culture, given the distances of time, place, experience, and, above all, sensibility. Whitfield linked the dynamics of this response, moving from "muteness" to "explicitness," with the aging of witnesses to the Holocaust and the coming of age of their children: "Those who were there and are still alive cannot be expected to relive their most unbearable years for the sake of those who are unlikely to understand. Nevertheless, survivors, bystanders and their descendants will all be torn between the need to make the Holocaust intelligible, which risks trivialization, and the recognition of the incomprehensibility of the Holocaust, which risks oblivion."[9]

Television as "Elder"

Erik Barnouw, who structured his landmark history of the American television broadcasting industry in terms of the human life cycle, labeled the period from the early 1960s to the late 1970s as its "elder" stage. This followed a "toddler" period (from the 1920s to the end of World War II) and "prime" years (from the early 1950s to the early 1960s), and it yielded to an era characterized by the advent of television's "progeny"—video, cable, satellite, and so on—in the 1980s and beyond.[10] Thus, American television and Holocaust survivors—and, by extension, Holocaust memory culture—can be thought of as age-mates. At the same time that Holocaust survivors began to grow old and their children were coming of age, American television showed signs of a generational shift of its own.

Barnouw characterized both the *Roots* (ABC, 1977) and *Holocaust* miniseries as being "in the spirit of reexamination and rededication" in the United States, which followed the war in Vietnam and the Watergate scandal and was fostered by the American bicentennial in 1976.[11] At this time the American broadcasting industry also marked jubilees and commemorated its own achievements: NBC and CBS, the two oldest national networks, celebrated their fiftieth anniversaries in broadcasting in 1976 and 1977, respectively, and the Museum of Broadcasting opened in New York City in 1976.[12] Broadcasters' accomplishments were acknowledged outside the industry the same year with the establishment of an American Television and Radio Archives in the Library of Congress to preserve "the broadcasting heritage of the American people."[13] Members of the Jewish community undertook similar efforts in the United States and Israel, with the creation of major media archives devoted to Jewish subjects at the Hebrew University in Jerusalem (1970) and the Jewish Museum in New York (1979), as well as smaller collections established at schools and communal institutions.

At the same time, however, American public opinion surveys indicated unprecedented drops in television viewership and in the public's esteem for the medium.[14] In particular, many members of the "television generation"—that is, "the first generation in history to have grown up taking television for granted as an everyday, ubiquitous fact of life"—regarded the medium, in the words of two chroniclers of this generation, as "the idiot engine of the Establishment, electronic opiate of the consumerist masses, and thus a favorite object of ridicule and contempt."[15]

As viewers became more familiar with television, they often grew more critical of what they were watching and more sensitive to the ideological underpinnings of programming in general. Viewer activism increased steadily during the 1960s and 1970s, some of it following the lead of Nicholas Johnson, commissioner of the FCC from 1966 to 1973 and author of *How to Talk Back to Your Television Set*. The number of books written for the general reader on the state of the medium increased considerably during these years. While some authors expressed cautious optimism about the potential of television (for example, Anne Rawley Saldich's *Electronic*

Democracy), others denounced it as a social evil (notably Jerry Mander's *Four Arguments for the Elimination of Television*). The era also witnessed the emergence of the guerilla television movement and the work of underground humorists who satirized both the form and content of the medium.[16]

In addition, signal changes were taking place in the ways that American academics studied television. When it emerged as a national medium in the post–World War II years, social science and humanities scholarship was already, as a rule, unkindly disposed toward the mass media. But by the mid-1970s new calls for the academic study of television had been sounded in a variety of settings, from its established place in schools of communications and departments of sociology to new venues in cultural anthropology, literary criticism, and cinema studies. Responses to these appeals often challenged prevailing scholarly models and generated new approaches to the medium and its role in modern culture. Horace Newcomb, for example, argued for the development of a "television aesthetic," a humanistic approach to studying the medium that demands the "discovery of new laws, new relationships, new insights into drama, ritual and mythology." As Tania Modleski observed, it became the agenda of a new generation of scholars of television to "rescue" it from decades of "critical opprobrium."[17]

The Holocaust as Epic: The Holocaust Miniseries

At the time of its premiere broadcast, *Holocaust: The Story of the Family Weiss* was by far the most elaborate single presentation of the Holocaust made for American television, involving unprecedented numbers of performers and production staff and entailing unrivaled expense and promotion.[18] Even so, the response to its broadcast in the United States and abroad arguably proved to be a more noteworthy cultural landmark than the miniseries itself. Few critics championed *Holocaust* for making a significant artistic or intellectual statement about its subject—for some, its greatest virtue was that it was produced at all. Similarly, its many detractors often said less about the aesthetic or ideological foundations of *Holocaust* and more about the problematic nature of its very existence.

Created by Titus Films, an independent production company headed by veteran television producer Herbert Brodkin, *Holocaust* was first broadcast as part of NBC's weekly showcase for short-run, special programming known as *The Big Event*. During the late 1970s and early 1980s, *The Big Event* featured other made-for-television dramas and the broadcast debut of major films originally made for theatrical release, as well as concerts and television retrospectives—all part of a strategy to boost NBC's sagging ratings with regular offerings of spectacular or epic programs.[19]

Running nine and a half hours (including opening and closing segments and commercial breaks) over four days, *Holocaust* was distinguished from other "big events" as a miniseries. This television genre was fairly new to American commercial networks at the time; NBC initiated plans for *Holocaust* following the success of one of the first miniseries aired by a commercial television network in the United States, ABC's presentation of *Rich Man, Poor Man* in 1976.[20] The miniseries' novelty and large-scale format, as well as its origins in British television and American public television (for example, *The Forsyte Saga*, a 1967 BBC production aired on PBS in 1969–1970), endowed the genre with a cachet of prestige relative to the medium's other entertainment genres.

The unusual format of presenting *Holocaust* in prime time on four consecutive nights (i.e., Sunday through Wednesday evenings) imitated the premiere broadcast of *Roots,* a twelve-hour miniseries aired eight evenings in a row during the previous season. Based on Alex Haley's saga of an African-American family over the course of five generations, *Roots* proved to be an unexpected programming coup. The miniseries garnered unprecedented high ratings in audience size and share, and it earned extensive praise from educators, African-American leaders, and media critics, winning numerous awards and citations.

NBC envisioned *Holocaust* as an epic work analogous to *Roots*.[21] Gerald Green's script resembles Haley's book and its screen adaptation in the use of an extended family saga as the point of entry into the larger sweep of history. Whereas *Roots* offers a chronology spanning more than two centuries, *Holocaust* reaches across the geographic, political, and cultural expanse of the European Jewish experience during Nazi era. Like the nineteenth-century historical novels that serve as the model for this genre, the miniseries' intimate dramas of romance and family relations both complement and facilitate the presentation of warfare, class struggle, and the rise and fall of social and political movements.

In some respects, *Holocaust* also constitutes a culmination of three decades of American television dramas dealing with the subject. Green's script centers on the experiences of the cosmopolitan, upper-middle-class, German-Jewish Weiss family from the mid-1930s until the end of the war. Each family member's fate brings him or her to different sites that had come to be widely acknowledged as landmarks of the Holocaust's master narrative. Dr. Josef Weiss (played by Fritz Weaver) and his wife, Berta (Rosemary Harris), are deported from their home in Berlin (where they are witnesses to *Kristallnacht*) to the Warsaw Ghetto and from there to Auschwitz, where both perish. The Weisses' elder son, Karl (James Woods), is an artist, whose fateful path to Auschwitz takes him first to Buchenwald and then to Theresienstadt.

The other Weiss children are brought to key sites and events of the Holocaust narrative that were less familiar to American television audiences. After being raped by German soldiers, Anna Weiss (Blanche Baker) becomes deranged and is sent to the asylum at Hadamar, whose patients are gassed to death. The Weisses' younger son, Rudi (Timothy Bottoms), flees Germany, joins a partisan unit in the Soviet Union, and marries Helena (Tovah Feldshuh), a Czech Jew and a Zionist. Captured by German soldiers and taken to Sobibor, Rudi participates in the extermination camp's uprising. The only member of his immediate family to survive the war, he heads for Palestine at the drama's end.

These fictional characters mingle with actual historical figures, including Warsaw Ghetto resistance fighter Mordecai Anilewicz (Murray Salem) and Nazi leaders Reinhard Heydrich (David Warner), Heinrich Himmler (Ian Holm), and Adolf Eichmann (Tom Bell). Other characters are composites, notably Erik Dorf (Michael Moriarty), an aide to Heydrich, who is modeled in part on Nazi war criminal Otto Ohlendorf. Dorf and his family serve as dramatic foils to the Weisses; he, too, is employed to bring the drama to Holocaust landmarks previously unseen in television dramas — the Wannsee Conference, the killing operations of *Einsatzgruppen* in Eastern Europe, the massacre at Babi Yar.

Themes in Green's script frequently call to mind those of earlier Holocaust television dramas: Conflicts over the proper mode of resistance in the Warsaw Ghetto and the camps recall Rod Serling's *In the Presence of Mine Enemies* (1960) and the religious television dramas *In the Beginning* (1956) and *The Final Ingredient* (1959). Karl Weiss's artwork in Theresienstadt (his character is partly based on the artist Otto Unger) is reminiscent of the religious television drama *I Never Saw Another Butterfly,* a 1967 tribute to the artistic output of the camp's inmates, while Karl's marriage to a non-Jewish German, Inga (Meryl Streep), recalls the Jewish-gentile romance of the Serling drama. Green's portrait of Dorf's rise to power in the Nazi hierarchy, and the dramatic conceit of embodying Nazi anti-Jewish policy in the person of this one officer, resembles the psychological portrait of Eichmann in the 1960 television docudrama *Engineer of Death.*

Other devices employed in the miniseries conform to the protocols of American Holocaust television, which had been taking shape since the early 1950s. The focus on a bourgeois, assimilated West European Jewish family as the dramatic point of entry into the vast expanse of the Holocaust recalls dramatizations of Anne Frank's diary, while the use of romantic love to represent the dramatic antithesis of warfare, hatred, and genocide is reminiscent of *In the Presence of Mine Enemies* and Paddy Chayefsky's 1952 play *Holiday Song.* The incorporation of vintage footage from the Nazi era in *Holocaust* to articulate the historical progress of the plot — calling to mind

N Viewer's Guide to
HOLOCAUST

VIEWER'S GUIDE BY CULTURAL INFORMATION SERVICE

NBC issued this viewer guide when it rebroadcast the miniseries *Holocaust* in 1979. (Globe Photos, Inc.)

its use in *Judgment at Nuremberg* (1959) and *Engineer of Death,* among other television dramas — also demonstrates the wide recognition of these images both as signs of historicity and as morally charged icons.

With *Holocaust* NBC hoped to match, perhaps even best, the success of *Roots* in popularity, critical acclaim, and impact. The network prepared an extensive campaign to encourage viewers to watch and discuss *Holocaust,* which went well beyond typical public relations efforts for a television drama. NBC developed a viewer's guide for mass distribution to educators across the country and encouraged national organizations (including the Jewish Anti-Defamation League of B'nai B'rith and the National Council of Churches), as well as magazines and newspapers, to print their own guides to the program and its subject. Over a million paperback copies of the novelization of Green's script for *Holocaust,* published by Bantam Books, were in the nation's bookstores two weeks before the beginning of the broadcast, and the text was serialized in a number of American newspapers, including the *New York Daily News,* during early April. RCA Red Seal also produced a recording of music composed for the sound track of *Holocaust* by Morton Gould. In addition, the network arranged advance screenings of the program for Jewish and Christian clergy, thereby promoting the subject of the miniseries as the "topic of the week" in American churches and synagogues. The day on which the first episode of the miniseries was broadcast "was unofficially proclaimed 'Holocaust Sunday'" throughout the country.[22]

Thus, promotors of the miniseries conceived the act of viewing *Holocaust* as the culmination of days of advance preparation on a national scale in a variety of venues — from the press to the pulpit, from televised promotional announcements to word of mouth. Taking place in the days before the home VCR facilitated more fragmented and customized television viewing habits, the telecast of *Holocaust* was envisioned as bringing families across the nation together for a simultaneous, extended encounter with the story of the Nazi persecution of European Jewry. For many American Jews, the anticipated broadcast took on a special meaning above and beyond the network's appeals to a general audience. Besides dealing with a subject that had become increasingly important in American Jewish culture, *Holocaust* promised to offer a portrait of Jewish family and community life on a scale never before seen on American television. A feature on the miniseries in *Moment* magazine stated that "for Jews, the watching has about it the quality of a religious obligation."[23]

This association was reinforced by NBC's linking the broadcast to fixtures of the Jewish calendar. The miniseries aired the week before the celebration of Passover, and its final episode aired on the thirty-fifth anniversary of the Warsaw Ghetto uprising. The scheduling of *Holocaust* not only echoed established associations in postwar Jewish culture between this traditional celebration of ancient Israel's redemption from Egyptian slavery and modern European Jewry's struggle to survive Nazi persecution, but it also situated the Holocaust in the context of television's annual scheduling of special broadcasts commemorating Passover.[24]

At the same time, the broadcast of *Holocaust* coincided with events unforeseen by its producers. Several critics and scholars commented on the telecast's resonance with contemporary Jewish affairs. Literary scholar Ruth Wisse observed that "by an odd coincidence, the showing of Holocaust came at one of the lowest points in the political fortunes of American Jews since World War II."[25] During the week that *Holocaust* aired, the national news media gave extensive coverage to the anticipated visit of Israeli prime minister Menachem Begin to Washington, at which time he asked the Carter administration to cancel planned sales of American-made arms to Saudi Arabia. Wisse described Begin's unsuccessful mission as the latest in a series of episodes that marked the declining fortunes of Israel vis-à-vis its neighbors and various world powers since the 1973 Yom Kippur War, epitomized by the United Nations' 1975 resolution denouncing Zionism as racism.

The telecast of *Holocaust* not only culminated weeks of advance public relations and resonated with world history, Jewish ritual, and current events, but also initiated a much longer period of response. Reactions to the first American telecast of the miniseries were voluminous, prolonged, conspicuous, and contentious. Taking place over a period of months in a wide range of public forums, the discussion of *Holocaust* can be seen as constituting a "big event" in American culture above and beyond the miniseries itself. Although the debate over the miniseries took place, for the most part, in venues other than on television, the medium was often central to the discussion.

A wealth of articles about *Holocaust* appeared in the American press during the spring and summer of 1978. In addition to reviews by media critics, the miniseries inspired editorials and letters to the editor, reports on the extent of its audience, features on topics related to the Holocaust, and opinion pieces about the program's impact from a wide range of viewers. During the last two weeks of April, over twenty items on or related to *Holocaust* were published in the *New York Times* alone. These include two reviews by media critic John O'Connor and a sharply derisive essay on the miniseries by Elie Wiesel. The *Times* also offered articles about the extensive viewership of *Holocaust* and isolated instances of viewer protest of the broadcast, a brief historical overview of Nazi anti-Semitism, and features on the rising interest in Holocaust studies and on Christian-Jewish ecumenism, both of which mentioned the NBC program. Other articles discussed the reaction of Holocaust survivors to the program and reported on negotiations to arrange for the miniseries to be telecast in West Germany.[26]

In addition, the *Times* served as a forum for the public exchange of ideas about *Holocaust*. George F. Hoover, an NBC executive, wrote two letters to the editor in response to O'Connor's negative reviews. A week after the broadcast began, Gerald Green's "In Defense of Holocaust," a response to Wiesel's criticisms, appeared on the front page of the "Arts and Leisure" section. Wiesel replied to Green the following week in the "Arts and Leisure" section, which also printed sixteen letters to the editor on the subject. This was the largest of several selections published by the *Times* from among the many letters that the newspaper had received in response to *Holocaust* and its coverage. Some public figures used the broadcast of *Holocaust* as a point of departure for discussing other current issues. Senator William Proxmire advocated for the United States' long-delayed ratification of the United Nations Genocide Convention in a letter to the editor about the miniseries; in an op-ed essay referring to *Holocaust*, columnist William Safire spoke out against a lack of response to contemporary persecutions in Soviet slave labor camps, Uganda, Iraq, and Cambodia.[27]

During subsequent weeks and months a wide range of American periodicals continued to assess the impact and value of *Holocaust*. Editorials and opinion pieces on the miniseries appeared in many Jewish journals, among them the *ADL Bulletin, Jewish Frontier, Journal of Reform Judaism, Judaism, Lilith, Midstream, Moment,* and *Reconstructionist.* The *Jewish Daily Forward,* the nation's largest Yiddish-language newspaper, offered reviews, editorial analysis, and news reports on the program's impact during the week of its broadcast. A large number of Christian publications — including *The Episcopalian, The Lutheran, Commonweal, Christian Century, Catholic Star Herald,* and *Christianity Today* — discussed the program, its subject, and the moral questions that it raised. The miniseries inspired a variety of political commentaries, including an essay by William F. Buckley in the *National Review* and articles in *Near East Report,* the newsletter of the American Israel Public Affairs Committee (AIPAC). At the polar extremes of the American political spectrum, *The Daily World* decried the miniseries's portrayal of Ukrainians' involvement in the persecution of Jews during World War II, while the broadcast provided an occasion for neo-Fascists to denounce the Holocaust as a fiction in *The Voice of German Americans.*[28]

Discussion of the *Holocaust* miniseries in the American public forum was renewed the following year with reports on its broadcast in Israel, South Africa, and several West European countries: England, France, Austria, Italy, Spain, and especially West Germany. Consideration of the miniseries broadened to include not only the range of responses it engendered elsewhere, but also the notion of exporting an American vision of the Holocaust abroad.[29] (International broadcasts of the miniseries played a leading

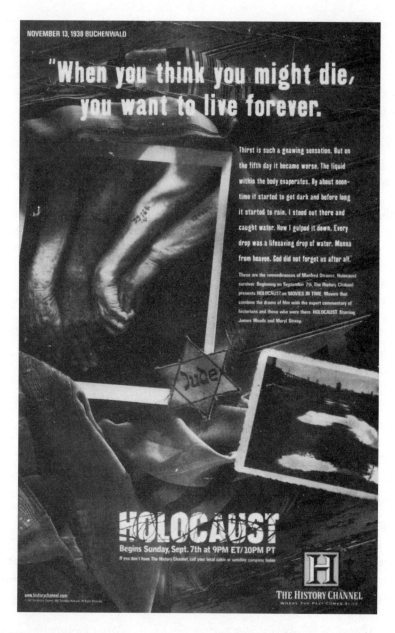

This full-page advertisement for a repeat presentation of the *Holocaust* miniseries in 1997 on the History Channel ran in the *New York Times*. The rebroadcast was supplemented by "the expert commentary of historians and those who were there." Appealing to a new generation of viewers, the advertisement links the miniseries with images and texts of Holocaust commemoration with which Americans have become increasingly familiar through television broadcasts, films, and Holocaust museums. (Courtesy of The History Channel. Reprinted with additional permission of Magnum Photos Inc., and Mark Seliger.)

role in popularizing the use of the term "Holocaust" for the Nazi persecution of European Jewry in other languages—French *le holocauste,* German *der Holocaust,* Spanish *el holocausto,* and so on.) The American Jewish Committee undertook a study of the program's impact on American audiences, and scholars analyzed both American and international reactions to the miniseries. Not surprisingly, there was particular interest in the consequences of bringing this American vision of the Holocaust to the former site of the Third Reich. The response to *Holocaust* in West Germany generated an extensive literature, both there and in the United States. Analysts of Holocaust media have also discussed the miniseries as a landmark work.[30]

NBC rebroadcast *Holocaust* in September 1979, a year after its original airing. Again, the program was scheduled to coincide with a historical date, this time marking the fortieth anniversary of the beginning of World War II. *Holocaust* has since been released on videocassette and has been rebroadcast in the 1990s on the CBN Family Cable Network and the History Channel. (Promotions for the former telecast, in April 1994, appealed to a new generation of viewers: "*Schindler's List* opened your eyes. *Holocaust* will touch your heart.") The miniseries was also reaired in 1993 in Germany, "in a bid to expose the horrors of racism" to the citizens of the recently reunited nation, faced with the rise of neo-Nazi groups and racist attacks.[31] Thus, *Holocaust* has remained a public presence in the United States and abroad for much longer than the four evenings in April 1978 when it captured the lion's share of the American television audience.

Popularizing the Catastrophe:
Assessing Holocaust Television

At the same time that *Holocaust* prompted millions to discuss the Nazi persecution of European Jewry, it also engendered an extended public exchange on the representation of the Holocaust on television—the first major discussion, if often an oblique one, of this genre. In the course of assessing the miniseries, critics frequently considered the challenges of mediating the Holocaust by other means or pondered the problems of commercial television drama in general. As a rule, participants in this discussion conceptualized Holocaust television as an essentially problematic genre, because it attempts to present its subject in a medium inherently unsuited to the task. This notion is rooted in a series of assumptions about the nature of both television and the Holocaust, which had taken shape during the three decades since the end of World War II.

"The word critics used on *Holocaust* was 'trivialize,'" screenwriter Paddy Chayefsky commented in a 1981 interview, "and in a sense that was unfair criticism, even though accurate. Trivialization *is* television."[32] Indeed, the most frequently offered explanation of why Holocaust television is inherently flawed has been that the medium, frivolous and superficial by nature, trivializes the enormity and gravity of the subject. Even critics whose assessment of *Holocaust* was essentially positive described the miniseries as having, in effect, defied the odds against succeeding, given the ill-fated combination of medium and subject: "At first it seems like an obscene idea. . . . American television has a tendency to trivialize almost everything it touches, and, of all important subjects, the Holocaust should be immune to such treatment. . . . Yet *Holocaust* demonstrates that TV's built-in limitations can become assets."[33]

In Elie Wiesel's seminal attack on the miniseries in the *New York Times,* which was entitled "Trivializing the Holocaust," he denounced *Holocaust* as transforming "an ontological event into soap-opera." Critics frequently directed this epithet at *Holocaust,* perhaps because it derided television in terms of the medium's own hierarchy.[34] The comparison suggested that the miniseries—commercial television's newly crowned king of its dramatic genres—was no better than the daytime serials widely regarded, by viewers and industry alike, as its lowest form of drama.

While most critics similarly used the comparison of *Holocaust* to soap opera to signal the unseemliness of the miniseries, British television director Dennis Potter reversed the conceit in his critique: "The case against Holocaust is not that it is bad soap opera, but worse—much worse—that it is very good soap opera. It was well made, often well acted, skillfully mounted, beautifully shot, and the score of naked extras quivering about the already open graves were sufficiently accomplished not to show their genitals to the cameras. Prime-time codes of behaviour, praise be, are still strong enough to over-ride Nazi edicts."[35] Potter's comment linked the issue of trivialization to another set of assumptions about the incompatibility of television and the Holocaust, namely, that the medium cannot convey the physical—and, therefore, the metaphysical—ugliness of the subject. Others similarly derided the production of *Holocaust* for softening or bowdlerizing harsh actualities. Critics condemned in particular the portrayal of extermination camps, where "everyone seems to be calm, well-fed, to have regular shampoos and freshly laundered clothes."[36]

Some critics of *Holocaust* dwelt more generally on the problematic aesthetics of contemporary television production. For example, the largely favorable review of the miniseries in *Variety* concluded with the suggestion that "the cinematographer Brian West should have photographed the miniseries in black-and-white. The hard-edged color gives a picture-postcard prettiness to scenes that cry out for the murky and somber tones of a 'Night and Fog,' Alain Resnais' brilliant 1955 documentary on Auschwitz." Similarly, Lance Morrow wrote in *Time* magazine that "the sometimes garish colors seemed to produce a falsification. If any world needed to be filmed in black and white, it was what French writer David Rousset called *l'univers concentrationnaire*. All that obscenity transpired in an absence of color: ashes and smoke were gray, the SS uniforms black, the skin ash white, the bones white. Franz Stangl, the commandant of Sobibor, used to greet the trains wearing a white riding costume."[37] These and other critics understood the Holocaust to have a distinct aesthetic, which American television does not easily accommodate. In "Trivializing the Holocaust," Wiesel considered "what the French call 'pudeur'" a more appropriate sensibility for mediating the Holocaust than the miniseries's attempt to show and to "tell it all," thereby implying that this sense of restraint is literally a foreign concept for Americans.

However, Wiesel also suggested that the effort to establish an appropriate aesthetic for mediating the Holocaust is impossible, because the subject defies aestheticization: "Art and Theresienstadt were perhaps compatible in Theresienstadt, but not here—not in a television studio. . . . A film about Sobibor is either not a picture or not about Sobibor." John O'Connor also faulted the miniseries's production effort, but not, as others had, for failing to create a verisimilitudinous spectacle. On the contrary, he suggested that any attempt to reenact scenes of the Holocaust according to the conventions of historical drama is incompatible with the extreme nature of the subject: "Incredible horror is reduced to 'effective' on-location settings in Austria and West Berlin. Unprecedented pain is mixed up with the choosing of 'correct' costumes. . . . If this were an ordinary television miniseries, . . . I could comment on several fine performances, . . . but performances, sets, costumes and the rest of the dramatizing paraphernalia are beside the point." In a similar vein, film critic Molly Haskell suggested that the attempt to create an artistic representation of the Holocaust constitutes nothing less than an act of sacrilege: "How can actors, how *dare* actors, presume to imagine and tell us what it felt like! The attempt becomes a desecration against, among others, the Hebraic injunction banning graven images."[38]

Haskell argued that *Holocaust* not only flirted with the limitations of representing something ineffable, but that any such enterprise would be compromised by the medium's small scale: "The Holocaust is simply too vast, the elimination of 6 million people from the earth too incomprehensible, to fit into any conceivable dramatic framework, particularly in the reductive context of the small screen." Other critiques of the miniseries focused on the disparity between the epic proportions of the Holocaust and the domestic scale of television, with regard to both the viewing context and the dramatic content. Paul Chedoff, a psychiatrist and scholar of the Holocaust, commented in a 1980 interview that television productions about the Nazi era "domesticate the horror, give it a family background" as a superficial substitute for the "sheer unadulterated horror" of genocide. In particular, critics faulted the miniseries's use of one family's experiences as the point of entry into the Holocaust's master narrative as a contrivance: "Too much appears to have been done by [the Weisses] to be credible."[39]

But not all observers found that the domesticity of television drama disqualified it from effectively presenting the Holocaust. Indeed, literary scholar Andreas Huyssen claimed that it was precisely the "audience's emotional identification with the individual members of a family" that enabled *Holocaust* to have such a tremendous impact on West German audiences when shown there in 1979. According to Huyssen, the "reception context" of television enhances this impact. "TV watching is after all a family affair," and so the story's "semantic structure" becomes more powerful as it moves "from family to family." Moreover, Huyssen questioned the dismissal of the miniseries's emotional appeal based on the "common assumption that a cognitive rational understanding of German anti-Semitism under National Socialism is *per se* incompatible with an emotional melodramatic representation of history as the story of a family."[40]

However, most critics faulted *Holocaust* as a misguided effort to use the conventions of popular entertainment to present a complex and disturbing topic. Even those who lauded the intentions behind the miniseries admitted that the presentation of the Holocaust on television necessitates the simplification of the subject, which has a reductive or distancing effect: "It seems to me petty to find television critics complaining that the concentration camp inmates were too healthy-looking for authenticity or that the uniforms they wore were too neatly pressed. They forget that all popularisation of human catastrophes inevitably diminishes the events and characters involved."[41]

Defenders of *Holocaust* responded by making the case for the miniseries as a valuable popularization of the catastrophic. They proposed, at times begrudgingly and with considerable reservations, that vulgarizing the Holocaust is essential for reaching uninformed and otherwise unreachable masses. In *The Nation*, Peter Sourian explained that Gerald Green "had to attract people in an escapist frame of mind to a real and repellant business. And thus, ironically, contradictorily, he had to make it in some sense or other *attractive*. . . . Green's *Holocaust* is thus, finally, false, yet it gets some of the important facts across, because in its falseness it moves the prime-time viewer who is otherwise uninterested, and carries him to the end. If it were not false, it could not do so."[42]

According to such arguments, television is a necessary evil—indeed, the fact that it does not conform to scholarly standards of historical accuracy is key to the process of popularization. Saul Friedman wrote that critics who denounced the miniseries for its "lack of realism" failed to appreciate the distinctive value of presenting the Holocaust in a commercial television drama, as opposed to a documentary film. For example, *The Eighty-first Blow,* a 1975 Israeli documentary on the Holocaust, had recently been aired on American public television "and received nowhere near the celebrity or audience of 'Holocaust.'" Friedman also cited Simon Wiesenthal, who had recently stated that the miniseries reached more people than he could in a lifetime of activism on behalf of Holocaust remembrance.[43] Such arguments suggest that aesthetically appropriate mediations (e.g., documentary film) and venues (noncommercial television) for the presentation of the Holocaust do exist, but what distinguishes them as appropriately dignified or serious also disqualifies them from effectively reaching mass audiences.

Others who challenged the virtue of popularizing the Holocaust on television argued that such attempts are inherently misdirected, as the subject resists conventional notions of representation. Claude Lanzmann, then at work on his documentary film *Shoah,* wrote with regard to the miniseries that the uniqueness of the Holocaust as a historical event "cannot be logically deduced from any . . . system of presuppositions"; hence, the subject defies dramatizations that employ conventional, chronological emplotment. Helen Yglesias concluded her review of Green's novelization of *Holocaust* by asking sarcastically, "If the auto industry, airports or the *shmatte* trade could be successfully 'researched' for mass entertainment, why not the holocaust?" Besides questioning the attempt to mediate the Holocaust in the same manner as other subjects, Yglesias also expressed repugnance at the idea of treating the Holocaust as a commodity. Similarly, James Wolcott claimed that "one of the most appalling things about the *Holocaust* phenomenon is the way it's being used as a weathervane for the future of television. . . . Television and advertising executives live by such mathematical obscenity—trying to calculate how many Nielsen shares can be garnered by the deaths of 6,000,000 Jews."[44]

In his overview of responses to the miniseries, Sander Diamond noted that the dozens of commercials aired during *Holocaust* were the frequent target of many critics' complaints.[45] As a rule, the routine presence of advertisements during a broadcast on commercial television receives little, if any, attention from media critics. Yet critics of *Holocaust* decried the commercial "interruptions" more than any aspect of the teleplay itself. Indeed, for many, the commercials epitomized the incompatibility of medium and subject.

Commercials were the focus of O'Connor's second essay on the miniseries for the *New York Times,* subtitled "Art Versus Mammon": "For the overwhelming majority of broadcasting executives, the bottom line of the profit is paramount. Content is secondary, a means to the monetary end.

Therefore, the medium's use or exploitation of serious material such as the Nazi holocaust must prompt profound reservations. . . . Despite noble intentions on the artistic side of the project, the process is inevitably reduced to marketing."[46] In his review of *Holocaust,* historian Henry Feingold expanded his critique of the commercials aired during the telecast into a larger discussion of the "commercialization of the Holocaust." By using the Holocaust to sell products, he suggested, the miniseries became one long commercial that hawked the Holocaust "much like toothpaste." Moreover, Green's formulaic dramatization of the subject reduced the Holocaust itself to a commodity, thereby depriving it of its singular stature. The Holocaust thus became one of a series of mass-produced dramas of "an ethnic grievance," which might also include "the saga of the American Indian, the Irish potato famine and the 'troubles,' or perhaps the suffering of Japanese Americans interned during the war." The miniseries's conventional format of historical fiction lent itself "to 'selling' almost anything." However, Feingold insisted, "the Holocaust is not just any event."[47]

Despite the widespread condemnation of the advertisements during NBC's presentation of *Holocaust,* critics varied in their assessments of the commercials' impact on the drama and its viewers. Whereas Bernard Martin found that the "incessant" commercials "utterly destroyed the mood" of the miniseries, Paddy Chayefsky noted that frequent commercial interruptions in fact structured the plot, albeit adversely, by imposing on the narrative a demand for "high emotional moments, regularly, because you have these damn ten-minute intervals all the time." In at least one instance, the presence of commercial breaks was defended: "I did not notice the commercials, for I permitted my 12-year-old son and 9-year-old daughter to watch all four nights," wrote Saul Friedman. "My wife and I used the commercial pauses to answer inevitable questions. I am certain that even experts and survivors could have used [this time] for discussion. Failing that, everyone could have made use of the pauses in this tale of horror for simple reflection."[48]

Critics more consistently complained about the juxtaposition of specific advertisements with the content of *Holocaust.* O'Connor, for example, described the effect as being at times "absurd," at other times "shocking in its insensitivity. A story that includes victims being told that the gas chambers are only disinfecting areas is interrupted by a message about Lysol and its usefulness in 'killing germs.'" In a similar indictment of the juxtaposition of commercials with the drama, Bernard Martin articulated their incompatability with the Holocaust in terms of technology, describing the "intrusion of advertisements for so many American products" as being "of the same technological capacity that produced Zyklon-B gas in Germany for expediting the 'final solution of the Jewish problem.'"[49] Implicit in Martin's critique is the notion of still another incompatibility between medium and subject: Television, by virtue of its positive associations with technology — as expressed, for example, when a broadcast is described as being brought to viewers by the "miracle" of television — violates the Holocaust, in which the associations with technology are generally negative — for instance, describing Auschwitz and other extermination camps as "death factories."

This sense of the disparity between television and the Holocaust also exemplifies what may be the ultimate expression of the incompatibility of subject and medium — that television's treatment of the Holocaust, far from enlightening audiences about this past evil and teaching them to guard against it in the future, instead constitutes a virtual repetition or perpetuation of the Holocaust itself. O'Connor expressed such sentiments in the conclusion of his "Art Versus Mammon" essay, writing that "a monstrous historical fact has been put through the peculiar process that is called commercial television. In its more extreme moments that processing proved to be almost as obscene as the holocaust itself."[50]

Indeed, some critics felt that the miniseries could unwittingly play into the hands of Holocaust deniers. Wiesel characterized the connection of medium and subject as a destructive combination: "Holocaust, a TV drama. Holocaust, a work of semi-fact and semi-fiction. Isn't this what so many morally deranged 'scholars' have been claiming recently all over the world? That the Holocaust was nothing else but an 'invention'?" Owen Rachleff also faulted the miniseries's "ambiguity of genre," epitomized by its promotion as "only a story" that "really happened." This, he suggested, could facilitate the presumption that the Holocaust itself "has been fictionalized in line with the assertions of certain revisionists and other more sinister groups who proclaim Jewish genocide to be entirely a lie. Possibly they can now cite this film to prove their point."[51]

Ruth Wisse offered yet another perspective on the notion that television, at least in this instance, perpetuated the Holocaust. She found that the effort of the miniseries's producers to present "a most balanced and *inoffensive* Holocaust," by dramatizing the experiences of an assimilated German Jewish family, created a "deracinated" drama. Wisse cited Green's description of his protagonists as "the equivalent of American Jews who think of themselves first as Americans," who would therefore "appeal to a broad audience." She regarded this choice as part of an ongoing "Hollywood image of accidental particularism" that has unsettling implications: "One of Nazism's most potent weapons was the myth of the Aryan for the sake of whose purity it was necessary to root out all the hook-nosed, swarthy aliens. Here we are told, with no apparent irony, that in the name of commercial expediency the Jew as Aryan was the only safe choice for a 'broad audience' that could not be expected to empathize with 'foreigners.'"[52]

Other critics of the miniseries described the use of television as a vehicle for remembering the Holocaust to be a violation of its memory, by virtue of the disparity between a uniquely ineffable subject and a medium regarded as pervasive and pernicious. According to Claude Lanzmann, the success of *Holocaust* was, "perhaps, the latest ruse of a kind of history that disposes of the Holocaust's singularity even as it claims to be portraying it." Because the subject "defies the resources of any fiction, *Holocaust* perpetuates a lie, a moral crime; it assassinates memory." For critic Jean Baudrillard, the miniseries exemplified how television, as disseminator of the "evil demon of images," has "imposed its own immanent, ephemeral logic" on reality, bearing within it "the extermination of its own referent." Baudrillard described the ostensibly worthy goal of the miniseries to recall the Holocaust and to teach a moral lesson from its history as subverted by the nature of television, "a medium which is itself cold, radiating oblivion, dissuasion and extermination in an ever more systematic manner, if this is possible, than the [extermination] camps themselves. TV, the veritable final solution to the historicity of every event."[53]

Although such critical responses to the miniseries implicitly defined Holocaust television as a problematic genre, they presented conflicting understandings of television's significance in contemporary American culture, hinting at greater discomforts with the medium. Critics often made contradictory judgments of television: it was too verisimilitudinous, or it was too sanitized; its commercials interrupted the drama, or they gave shape to the drama. However, critics were generally united in placing the burden of responsibility for this incompatibility on the medium. Even the one virtue most often ascribed to television—its unrivaled ability to reach mass audiences—was qualified by a series of caveats: the medium misinforms, it cheapens, it desensitizes. Indeed, some critics attributed to television the same power wielded by the Nazis to distort, degrade, dehumanize, and destroy, echoing the warnings of Frankfurt School critics Max Horkheimer and Theodor Adorno (themselves refugees from Nazi Germany) that the culture industry offers "enlightenment as mass deception."[54]

Yet, while critics of *Holocaust* assigned the onus of the flawed nature of Holocaust television to the medium, it was not television itself so much as what it had come to represent in American culture that they decried. Television functioned in this discussion as a sign for an array of sources of anxiety over modernity, a phenomenon that is, perhaps, intensified by discussing the medium in conjunction with the Holocaust. In disparaging television as simplistic or trivial, critics often used it as a metaphor for anxieties about the openness or historical shallowness of contemporary American culture or of popular culture in general. Complaints about the commercial nature of American television variously signaled concerns about modern culture's devaluation of the individual, its challenges to conventional notions of private and public, or its privileging of the material over the spiritual. In some instances, television also served as a metonym for the post–World War II era's transformative break with the past or symbolized America's postwar ascendence to a position of international political, economic, and cultural influence.

Holocaust *Postscripts*

In the years since the premiere broadcast of *Holocaust,* the scope of the "big event" that it generated has continued to grow. Historians, critics, filmmakers, and others regularly cite the miniseries as not merely a landmark, but a catalyst in American Holocaust memory culture. U.S. Senator John Danforth, for instance, who was the first elected official to propose a national day of remembrance for the victims of the Holocaust, said that he was inspired to do so in part after watching the miniseries.[55]

NBC attributed a number of consequences to the broadcast of *Holocaust* in an unusual "special news report" aired following the rebroadcast of the miniseries on 13 September 1979.[56] In *Holocaust: A Postscript,* Floyd Kalber reports that the series "triggered a wide range of opinion and debate. It had such impact that it became a news story. The ramifications were worldwide." Among the events that took place in the wake of international broadcasts of *Holocaust,* which NBC enumerates in a series of international field reports, were Pope John Paul II's visit to Auschwitz; the efforts of the President's Commission on the Holocaust, chaired by Elie Wiesel, to formulate plans for an appropriate Holocaust memorial for the United States; the unprecedented interest in the Holocaust in West Germany, evinced by such phenomena as a sharp rise in the number of visitors to Dachau; and the debate in the Bundestag on extending West Germany's statute of limitations for the prosecution of Nazi war criminals.

Holocaust: A Postscript also presents a range of responses from Jewish viewers in Israel and America. While the news report shows the miniseries, its reception, and its impact in a largely favorable light, it also airs dissenting views of the program's value. Several students at Tel Aviv University offer differing assessments of the miniseries and its impact, while John Cochran reports that "Israelis hope the American [Holocaust] memorial, along with repeat showings of the TV movie, will increase public support in the United States for Israel—support that Israelis say has diminished over the past year." In another segment Rabbis Wolfe Kelman and Mark Tannenbaum (the latter an advisor to the producers of *Holocaust*) and Sister Ann Gillen of the National Coalition of American Nuns debate Elie Wiesel's claim that the miniseries was "cheap" and "offensive" and offer their opinions of the program's potential impact on the American public. Citing an American Jewish Committee study reporting that *Holocaust* was shown in fifty countries and viewed by some 220 million people, Tannenbaum champions the extensive impact of the miniseries for providing so many "with some beginning of an insight which most of them did not have."

Yet others who have identified various phenomena as consequences of the miniseries have characterized them as an extension of the problematic nature of Holocaust television. In a 1980 overview of the popularization of the Holocaust in American culture, historian Paula Hyman described the advent of Holocaust simulation games and exercises at a number of American schools and summer camps as part of the effort to teach children about the Nazi persecution of European Jewry. (One Jewish educator whom Hyman cited described these practices as using "role playing 'to turn the classroom into a concentration camp.'") Questioning the appropriateness of such activities, Hyman invoked Elie Wiesel, who "holds the mass media responsible for making these misuses of the Holocaust seem legitimate. When Wiesel asked one teacher why she used simulation techniques, he was told, 'If NBC could do it, if they could create fake gas chambers for their audience, why can't we do it for children?'"[57]

The miniseries has also been cited as negative inspiration by the creators of other works of Holocaust media. Both Swiss director Markus Imhoof's 1981 film *Das Boot Ist Voll* and Edgar Reitz's *Heimat,* first shown on West German television in 1984, were reportedly conceived in part as responses to shortcomings in *Holocaust.*[58] But the largest corpus of Holocaust media identified as a response to the miniseries is doubtless the recording of hundreds of testimonies by survivors and other witnesses to the Holocaust on videotape. The Fortunoff Video Archive for Holocaust Testimonies at Yale University, one of the first and largest of several such efforts, began videotaping survivors in the late 1970s and had collected some 1,600 testimonies as of 1990. Initially a grassroots effort, the Fortunoff Archive was "born of the conviction that time is running out and that every survivor has a unique story to tell. It was felt that the 'living portraiture' of TV would add a compassionate and sensitive dimension to the historical record."[59]

At the same time that the project embraced video technology as a worthy means of documenting the Holocaust, the Fortunoff Archive rejected what its founders regarded as commercial television's approach to the subject. In her study of Holocaust memory culture, journalist Judith Miller has described how the project was inspired, albeit negatively, by *Holocaust:*

> Though the program scored record ratings and was widely credited with having prompted interest in the Holocaust among young Americans and Europeans, survivors in Connecticut and elsewhere were angered by what they saw as the program's trivialization of the searing experiences. "Everything

Videotaping an interview with a Holocaust survivor at the Fortunoff Video Archive for Holocaust Testimonies, Yale University Library. (Yale University Office of Public Affairs.)

had been taken from them. Now television was trying to take away their stories too," said [project manager Joanne] Rudof.[60]

Descriptions of the project's approach to mediating the Holocaust have repeatedly conceptualized it as a corrective response to the misbegotten genre of Holocaust television. Geoffrey Hartman, Yale University's faculty advisor to the Fortunoff Archive, commented that it provides an alternative to the "talk-show format, with the host gushing over the survivor, how strong, heroic, wonderful such a person must be. The very intimacy of the medium is as much a danger as its graphic and sensational impact. Yet our testimonies counter both this sensationalism and this trivialization."[61] Miller similarly juxtaposed the Fortunoff Archive's approach to mediating the Holocaust against the efforts of "Hollywood," describing the former as a low-budget, nonprofit enterprise that "operated on less than what is required for one made-for-television movie."

Miller argued that the Fortunoff Archive overcame the challenges of mediating the Holocaust by virtue of its focus on the survivors, thereby providing a moving and engaging spectacle of "human response" to the Holocaust's master narrative. She favorably characterized the Fortunoff Archive's videotapes—the work of "trained, noninterventionist interviewers" interacting with survivors who have come forward voluntarily to "bear witness"—as "the Holocaust of fact," as opposed to the "Hollywood" Holocaust "of imagination." Moreover, she suggested that these videos are not merely a remedy to the miniseries but also surpass other forms of Holocaust remembrance: "Thanks to the camera," survivors' testimonies "were no longer simply words on a page absent their teller."

Indeed, Miller identified the intimate and affectively engaging aspects of this medium, rather than what the survivors have to say, as being essential to the distinctive power of these testimonies. She observed that in the course of the interviews survivors "reached a point at which they could no longer find the words to describe what they had endured. It was then that the camera took over. It captured the hesitation, the averted glance, the ironic smile, the flash of pain at a memory, the fidgeting, the sighs, the errant tear, the silent search for the right phrase to translate the inexplicable." The aesthetic of videotaped interviews with survivors has thus become a hallmark of their authenticity, their visual austerity and unrelieved intimacy signifying a near-unmediated encounter with history. Miller described watching the tapes as coming "as close as those who have never experienced what [Holocaust survivors] did can come to understanding their world."[62]

Together with the diverse responses that it engendered, the *Holocaust* miniseries constitutes a threshold event in American television and American Holocaust memory culture with enduring implications. The program has been widely identified as the progenitor of a heightened awareness of the Holocaust. Yet the consequences of this awareness have been anything but simple or consistent. Rather than merely demonstrating, as champions of the miniseries asserted, that presenting the story of the Holocaust to great numbers of people constitutes a morally edifying encounter, *Holocaust* engendered a new discussion about the ability of the subject to be presented properly and effectively, especially on a grand scale and in a popular format.

Remarkably, the recognition of Holocaust television as an inherently problematic, even impossible, genre coincided with the initiation of efforts to identify and collect examples of the genre in various media libraries, archives, and educational centers. Moreover, despite numerous suggestions to this effect, the creation of works of Holocaust television has not desisted in the years since the premiere broadcast of the *Holocaust* miniseries. Indeed, the genre has flourished in the final decades of the twentieth century, not only generating works of greater quantity and variety, but also propelling the Holocaust to unprecedented prominence in American public culture.

part three 1979–1995
A Household Word

Despite widespread sentiments following the *Holocaust* miniseries that the medium and subject are inherently incompatible, American Holocaust television has burgeoned since the late 1970s. The inventory of these broadcasts has grown in quantity and variety, as have the venues for their presentation and reception. But the extent and range of these telecasts do more than simply demonstrate that the medium has played a leading role in bringing the word *Holocaust* into "virtual 'household' use."[1] During this period, television has also established itself as a mainstay of American Holocaust remembrance, elaborating the subject's public presence and enriching its value as a moral paradigm in the national culture. Moreover, television has made the Holocaust a household word in ways unmatched by other forms of memory culture, their greatly increased prominence during the final decades of the twentieth century notwithstanding.

This development has taken place at a time when television broadcasting has experienced unprecedented change, responding to rapid technological innovations and major shifts in the "marketplace of communication."[2] This period, shaped by what media scholar John Caldwell has called an "institutional and presentational crisis," has witnessed the rise of "narrowcasting," as the domination of television broadcasting by the three national commercial networks has been yielding to a multitude of specialized and localized cable channels. The advent of the home VCR has facilitated customized screening of prerecorded broadcasts as it has expanded the repertoire of what can be seen in the context of domestic viewing. The last two decades of the twentieth century have also seen a transformation of television's aesthetics, characterized by a "highly evolved intertextuality" and an "extreme self-consciousness of style."[3]

Just as the impact of these developments in the medium can be seen among the wealth of Holocaust television in the 1980s and 1990s, these broadcasts also reflect signal changes in American Jewish life. As part of the rapid growth of large-scale works of Holocaust remembrance in which

American Jews have been actively involved as creators, funders, audiences, and critics, Holocaust television of the 1980s and 1990s also testifies to the entry of American Jewry into the nation's public culture on a grand scale unprecedented in the community's history. As part of the expanding variety of telecasts—situation comedies, dramas, soap operas, public affairs programs, documentaries—in which Jews appear forthrightly as Jews, often engaging issues of special interest to Jews, these Holocaust-related programs demonstrate the extent to which many American Jews have embraced television as a medium for the performance of self.

The proliferation of Holocaust television, especially broadcasts tied to the historical or holiday calendar, has special significance for ritual behavior among American Jews. This is also true for the growing availability of Holocaust media on videotape, a phenomenon noted by both Jewish educators and scholars of Holocaust memory culture.[4] In the early 1980s Eric Goldman, then director of the Jewish Media Service, described the body of Holocaust dramas and documentaries made available on videocassette as constituting "a different *haggadah*," likening a family's viewing of these videos on their home television sets to gathering around the table to celebrate the Passover seder through an educational ritual of retelling. More recently, literary scholar James Young has described Holocaust film as a "celluloid *megilla*"; by invoking the scrolls of sacred books recited on Jewish holidays, he has raised for further consideration the impact of the availability of these media works, especially for repeated, ritualized, public presentations and commentaries.[5]

These recent developments in the production and reception of Holocaust media have come at a time when Holocaust memory culture has confronted perhaps its greatest challenge: the aging and eventual passing of the generation of survivors and other witnesses to the Holocaust. Much of the heightened self-consciousness about the use of media in recent Holocaust television parallels—and is responsive to—an intensifying concern for the loss of "unmediated" contact with the Holocaust through survivors. Whereas vintage documentary images were once distinguished as the most privileged form of Holocaust representation, survivors, both as individuals and as a community, have since come to be widely regarded as the subject's most affectively powerful and genuine resource.

This development is borne out not only in documentaries and dramas about the Holocaust but also in ways that this historical epoch is invoked with regard to current concerns, from American identity politics to interethnic strife in the Balkans. Remarkably, as the Holocaust recedes further into the past, it appears with greater frequency in television news reports.[6] Here, too, survivors appear in a variety of roles—as witnesses, authorities, activists, creators of memory culture, or the very embodiment of memory. Indeed, in much of the increasingly diverse corpus of Holocaust television, the Holocaust survivor figures as a unifying presence.

Yet at the same time that the medium assists in the survivors' ascent to this status, television also looks toward the other side of the generational threshold, when the ability of survivors to represent the Holocaust is eventually overtaken by mediations. Alongside the intense production of media works involving Holocaust survivors during this century's final decades, questions have arisen regarding the ability of the Holocaust to endure beyond the survivors' lifetime as a fixture of American Jewish civil religion and a moral paradigm in general American public culture.

seven

The Rise of the Survivor

Perhaps no other measure of the dynamics of American Holocaust memory culture over the past half century is more telling than the changing public image of the men and women now known as Holocaust survivors. During the immediate postwar years, survivors were the subject of considerable attention in the American media as witnesses to war crimes, as Displaced Persons seeking new homes, or as recent arrivals in the United States. But in the ensuing decades survivors as a group received little public notice in America. When they were the occasional subject of media attention—for example, in a 1960 Movietone newsreel reporting a reunion of survivors of Auschwitz—survivors were generally depicted as busy with new lives in their adopted homeland and raising children.[1] Occasional dramatic portraits of the individual survivor as a social misfit, haunted or tormented by wartime memories, appeared on American television and in film.[2]

Beginning in the mid-1970s, the community of Holocaust survivors attracted new interest on the part of the American public. Terrence des Pres's *The Survivor: An Anatomy of Life in the Death Camps* and Dorothy Rabinowitz's *New Lives: Survivors of the Holocaust Living in America,* both published in 1976, offered portraits of survivors that stress their special tenacity in the face of persecution and the success of their efforts to create new families and communities in the postwar period.[3] Critical responses to the *Holocaust* miniseries of 1978, which were often voiced by survivors or their relatives, inspired new works of Holocaust remembrance that located survivors at the center of activity and gave them unprecedented opportunities to appear in public as authorities on the Holocaust era. Some of these efforts, such as the founding of the Fortunoff Video Archive for Holocaust Testimonies at Yale University, situated survivors and their testimony as the antithesis of the televised presentation of the Holocaust. Increasingly, however, survivors have become mainstays of American Holocaust television. In the 1980s and 1990s their testimony has attained the status of ultimate authority on the Holocaust, surpassing all other forms of its representation, thanks in a considerable degree to television.

"I, Too, Am a Survivor of the Holocaust": Televising the Skokie Incident

Television played a leading role in bringing Holocaust survivors to the attention of the general American public during the late 1970s. Among the medium's most significant presentations of survivors at this time were news reports and other broadcasts, culminating in a made-for-television movie, concerning an event that came to be known as the "Skokie incident." This was, in fact, a sequence of related events that took place over the course of more than a year. From April 1977 through June 1978 a series of legal confrontations between members of the National Socialist Party of America (NSPA), a small neo-Nazi group based in Chicago, and the municipal government of the nearby suburban village of Skokie, Illinois, attracted national attention as a provocative test of American civil liberties. In response to NSPA leader Frank Collin's efforts to stage a public demonstration in Skokie, the village government issued a series of injunctions against the neo-Nazi group. The NSPA responded by engaging the services of the local office of the American Civil Liberties Union (ACLU) to sue the village of Skokie over violations of the neo-Nazis' First Amendment rights to freedom of speech and assembly. The subsequent court cases and appeals led to an eventual victory for the NSPA as a result of a ruling by the Illinois Supreme Court.[4]

Although the official parties in these disputes were the village of Skokie and the NSPA, American Jewish individuals and groups played a range of important roles in the incident. Skokie then had a population of some seventy thousand; about half of its residents were Jews, among whom were almost seven thousand survivors of the Holocaust.[5] The threat of a neo-Nazi rally in the village, widely acknowledged as a confrontational act targeting these Jews in particular, drew reactions from organizations ranging from the Jewish Anti-Defamation League (JADL) to the Jewish Defense League (JDL). When the Illinois branch of the ACLU agreed to take on Collin's case, thousands of the organization's constituents nationwide withdrew their membership and financial support in protest. Among these were many Jews, some of whom were particularly outraged that a Jewish lawyer, David Goldberger, represented Collin for the ACLU.

The Skokie incident received frequent coverage on both local and national television news programs, and it was occasionally addressed in other television forums.[6] For example, Goldberger appeared on an installment of the syndicated talk show *Donahue* in 1978. Three years after its resolution in the courts, the Skokie incident was reenacted in a "special presentation" produced for CBS by Herbert Brodkin's Titus Productions.[7] *Skokie,* a two-and-a-half-hour television movie, proved to be Brodkin's last television drama to deal with the Holocaust. The production reunited him with television playwright Ernest Kinoy—author of *Walk Down the Hill*, which Brodkin had produced for *Studio One* in 1957—and with producer Robert Berger, with whom Brodkin had worked on the 1978 *Holocaust* miniseries. *Skokie* also assembled an impressive cast for a television drama, including Kim Hunter, Carl Reiner, John Rubinstein, and Eli Wallach in leading roles; the drama featured Danny Kaye in his first dramatic role for television and a "special appearance" by veteran acting teacher and director Lee Strasberg.

In some respects, *Skokie* conforms to the conventions of the made-for-television movie as outlined by Todd Gitlin in his study of the genre: "Characters should be simple and simply motivated, heroes familiar, stories full of conflict, endings resolved, uplift apparent, and each act should end on a note of suspense sufficient to carry the viewer through the commercial break."[8] *Skokie* resembles some of Brodkin's earlier works of Holocaust television. In this drama the Holocaust engenders a debate over more general moral issues particularly relevant to an American audience, as was the case in *Walk Down the Hill* and *Judgment at Nuremberg* (*Playhouse 90*, 1959). *Skokie* also uses a story of family dynamics as the dramatic point of entry into a subject in which political and social forces figure strategically, recalling the *Holocaust* miniseries. Unlike these or any other television dramas dealing with the Holocaust, however, *Skokie* offers a forthright performance of American Jewish communal pride, in which the Holocaust figures as a central moral touchstone.

While Frank Collin (played by George Dzundza) and his fellow neo-Nazis are portrayed as rather conventionally unnuanced villains, *Skokie* offers one of the more diverse portraits of the American Jewish community ever shown on prime-time commercial television.[9] Around the neo-Nazis revolves a complex interaction among a divisive and contentious American Jewish community, including members of the JADL and JDL, Jewish leaders and supporters of the ACLU (who are themselves divided against each other), and the Holocaust survivor community.

Whereas all of the (non-Nazi) characters in the drama, Jews and non-Jews alike, are united in their contempt for the NSPA, they are deeply divided over the proper response to its threat to march in Skokie. Much of *Skokie* consists of a series of exchanges among the various groups drawn into the case. For example, attorney Herb Lewisohn (John Rubinstein), the character modeled on Goldberger, advocates that the ACLU should defend the NSPA on purely ideological grounds, citing Justice Oliver Wendell Holmes's injunction that the most valued principle in the United States Constitution is that of "free thought—not free thought for those who agree with us, but freedom for the thought we hate." Aryeh Neier (Stephen D. Newman), the head of the

Skokie: Holocaust survivor Max Feldman (played by Danny Kaye) stands up to decry a proposed neo-Nazi march through his home town in this 1981 television drama. (Photofest.)

national ACLU, argues that there is a more strategic political objective—the ACLU must defend the rights of the Nazis because this also constitutes an implicit defense of American Jews, black civil rights workers, and all other groups in America who risk having their freedom of speech suppressed on the grounds that their messages are hateful.

Within the spectrum of American Jewish voices presented in *Skokie,* the Holocaust survivor is distinguished as an individuated hero. The other characters involved in this debate are portraits of actual participants in the Skokie incident (some of them bearing their original names, others assigned pseudonyms), all of whom represent various larger interests. A single character, Max Feldman (Danny Kaye), similarly embodies the survivor community. Feldman is, in fact, a composite figure, modeled on several survivors involved in the actual Skokie incident. However, he is the only character in *Skokie* whose private life figures in the drama, distinguishing him as a sympathetic family man and not simply an advocate. A Skokie resident and owner of a small local business, Max Feldman is married to Bertha (Kim Hunter), another concentration camp survivor, and they are the parents of an American-born teenager, Janet (Marin Kanter). The only major character seen, to any extent, in the privacy of his home, Max Feldman is the empathic center of the drama, most closely resembling the middle-class, family-oriented private citizen assumed to be the archetypal viewer of this and most other prime-time television programs offered by the major commercial networks.

Unlike the other major characters, Max Feldman is not a member of an organization or a spokesperson for an institution. During a community meeting at which the NSPA's plans are first debated in public, he speaks up spontaneously and passionately from the audience, disrupting the presentation of official, prepared statements made by JADL representative Abbot Rosen (Carl Reiner), the local rabbi (Charles Levin), and village counsel Bert Silverman (Eli Wallach). Nor is Max an ideologue like members of the ACLU, the JDL, or the left-wing anti-Fascists who also appear in *Skokie*. Rather, he responds to the neo-Nazi threat out of personal conviction.

Above all, Max Feldman is distinguished from the other major characters as a witness to the Holocaust. When he first stands up to express his outrage at the response in Skokie to the NSPA, Feldman rolls up his shirt-sleeve to display the number tatooed on his arm. This iconic gesture renders the other characters' symbolic, ideological responses to neo-Nazism pale in comparison to Feldman's personal experience of Nazi persecution. Feldman's status as a Holocaust survivor figures as his rhetorical trump card in debates with all the other Jews with whom he clashes, as he announces, "I lived it. I know what I'm talking about." Even Lewisohn concedes that he can't argue with Feldman: "I'm not gonna try to give him logic and fancy law in the teeth of what he's been through," he tells Rosen. "When Max Feldman sees Collin . . . he sees his own past. He sees the *real* storm trooper."

On one hand, Holocaust survivors, as represented by Feldman, appear to occupy the moral high ground in this drama. Attorney Goldberger complained that the story "is told from the perspective of the survivors," and actor Rubinstein, who portrayed Goldberger's character in the drama, agreed that *Skokie* "shows all the heart from Danny Kaye's [i.e., Max Feldman's] point of view." On the other hand, *Skokie* deviates from the conventions of its genre by striving to present with equal conviction the validity of both sides of the legal case, an objective more in keeping with the conventions of "balanced" documentary filmmaking and news reportage. *New York Times* critic John O'Connor wrote in his review of *Skokie* that "if anything, it may be a touch too balanced, reaching that dramatically unsatisfying point, however accurate, at which nobody wins and nobody loses."[10]

This effort to present evenhandedly the complex moral debate surrounding the Skokie incident is tied to the drama's portrait of American Jewry. During one of the first scenes, when Skokie's mayor, Albert J. Smith (Ed Flanders), discusses with Silverman the NSPA's initial announcement of its plan to demonstrate in the village, the mayor refers cautiously to his concern for the town's residents "of Hebrew persuasion." "Jews—Jews, Al," Silverman interrupts. "It's all right—just say 'Jews.'" The public profession of Jewish identity, which was the torturous conclusion of Kinoy's protagonist in *Walk Down the Hill* twenty-four years earlier, is a statement delivered forthrightly from the beginning of *Skokie*.

Several times throughout the drama different characters proclaim their solidarity with fellow Jews, even despite ideological differences. Lee Strasberg plays Morton Weisman, a longtime active supporter of the ACLU who is identified as "a very politically conservative Republican" and a "native Chicagoan." Weisman comments to Lewisohn that, in addition, "as used to be suggested to me at various clubs and social events, I am a Jew." As he feels that he can "no longer in conscience support the organization," Weisman personally delivers a letter of resignation from the ACLU to Lewisohn and his supervisor. Weisman explains that he questions defending "those who, if they came to power, would deny the right to freedom, indeed, of life, to others," and he adds that "there is something monumentally inappropriate in a Jewish lawyer, financed by a membership disproportionately Jewish, to go into a court to defend the rights of a few hoodlums to go into a Jewish community and proclaim that it was too bad Hitler didn't finish the job."

This on-screen performance of American Jewish pride and moral rectitude was echoed off camera in several CBS press releases that featured comments by Kaye, Reiner, Rubinstein, and Wallach on their participation in *Skokie*. "We're talking here about the resurgence of racism in the world, and in our country," Reiner observed. "This is not an issue to be ignored, and 'Skokie' deals with it powerfully and dramatically." Wallach asserted, "I would have played any role in this script, just for the privilege of being in it." One press release mentioned the filming of the program on location in Skokie, using actual landmarks and residents: "Extras in many of the scenes at the city hall, a local temple, and in courtrooms participated in those same events in 1977 and 1978."[11] The village of Skokie thus figured not merely as a sign of the drama's authenticity, but as a tacit endorsement of the program by participating in the actual events reenacted.

Among Holocaust televison dramas, *Skokie* is further distinguished for its self-conscious use of the medium. Indeed, television is treated as one of the drama's protagonists. It facilitates dramatic moments—for example, scenes in which reporters interview various characters for local news broadcasts or cover public demonstrations related to the case—and is also a catalyst for dramatic confrontation. In a scene between Max and Janet Feldman, she competes for her father's attention with the television set as it broadcasts the latest local news report on Skokie's clash with the NSPA. Eventually shutting off the newscast, she berates her father for being drawn into the publicity that the case has attracted: "You get a kick out of it. You're having a great time with the interviews and the committees and the court cases." Janet vents her frustration with the disparity between herself and her parents wrought by the Holocaust, which she experiences, unlike them, via mediation: "I'm sorry I'm not dead, like the corpses in the pictures. . . . I can't suffer the way you did." In another scene, television watching serves as a catalyst for dramatic empathy, as Weisman explains to Lewisohn that it was while seeing Max Feldman in a news report that "it came to me—I, too, am a survivor of the Holocaust."

In its final moments, *Skokie* incorporates the program's viewers into its self-conscious use of the medium. The drama concludes with monologues by five of the principal characters—Collin, Rosen, Janet Feldman, Lewisohn, and Max Feldman—which are delivered to the camera as though each character were being interviewed for a television news report or documentary, thereby implicitly placing the viewer in the position of the interviewer. In their remarks, both Collin and Max Feldman refer to the importance of the media in the story. Collin waxes triumphant, proclaiming that he "beat the Jews" and noting that even though in the end the NSPA chose not to march in Skokie despite its legal victory, the incident "put me on television. . . . Millions of people heard me." Similarly, Max Feldman claims victory in the drama's final scene, as he is "interviewed" outside the local synagogue, draped in a prayer shawl. Not only did the survivors prevail against the NSPA's plans to march through their community, he notes, but "we told our story to the whole world. . . . We were witnesses."

Skokie invokes the formal conventions of television journalism and documentary as another sign of the authenticity of the drama. This device also enabled the drama's producers to offer a series of differing "final" statements instead of the single, unambivalent resolution that the genre usually demands. At the same time, the order in which the "interviews" are presented does literally give Max Feldman the last word, consistent with the survivors' status throughout the drama as ultimate authorities on the Holocaust. Max Feldman's closing words also indicate that while the survivors' unique stature is predicated on their actual experiences, their ability to realize their authority by offering testimony has become increasingly dependent on the power of mediation.

"To Tell and Retell":
Holocaust Survivors in Documentaries

Since the late 1970s, some telecasts have exoticized survivors, offering them as rare witnesses to extreme experiences—for example, a segment of the syndicated talk show *Geraldo,* aired in 1989, called "The Twins of

Auschwitz."[12] Others beatify survivors, featuring them as exceptional figures who have been ennobled by wartime ordeals. Most often, American television has presented survivors as distinctive voices of authority, especially in documentary films. Besides describing their experiences during the Holocaust, they sometimes offer testimony about postwar activities or recall Jewish life in Europe before the Nazi era. While some documentaries focus on an individual Holocaust survivor's particular experiences, in others—especially films about Jewish life before World War II—survivors figure as metonyms of the past. Occasionally their existence as survivors, both individually and collectively, is itself the documentary's focus.

During the same year that *Skokie* was broadcast, Holocaust survivors asserted their communal presence with a large-scale, public event of their own design—the World Gathering of Holocaust Survivors, which was convened in Israel from 14 to 17 June 1981. The World Gathering brought an unprecedented number of Holocaust survivors together at a single commemorative event; upward of five thousand from over twenty countries attended, accompanied by thousands of relatives, including hundreds of their children. During the course of the event, American television featured the World Gathering on national nightly news reports and on the ecumenical series *Directions*. New York public television aired daily reports on the proceedings and several months later presented highlights of this coverage in an hour-long documentary. Hosted by actor Martin Balsam, *Holocaust—The Survivors Gather: A Look Back* chronicles the four-day event, which it celebrates as a "historic occasion of the highest order."[13]

The World Gathering was an elaborately planned event, equally attentive to interests within the survivor community and to addressing its concerns to a larger public. This can be seen in the speakers, sites, and activities chosen for the World Gathering, which also reflect the planners' conceptualization of the significance of the Holocaust. Thus, as American Jews played a leading role in its conception, the World Gathering responded to and reinforced one of the basic tenets of American civil Judaism, according to Jonathan Woocher—that of "Holocaust and rebirth." Citing Jacob Neusner's observation that many American Jews understand recent Jewish history as "beginning in death, 'the Holocaust,' and completed by the resurrection or rebirth, 'Israel,'"[14] Woocher has argued that this conceptualization of modern Jewish experience offers "both a confirmation of the continuity of the present with the Jewish past, and a conviction that out of this present can emerge a radically transformed future."[15]

The symbolic value invested in the State of Israel as the locus of redemption was fundamental to the decision to convene the World Gathering in Jerusalem. Much of *Holocaust—The Survivors Gather* is devoted to several large public ceremonies, held at various Jerusalem landmarks, honoring the survivors and their families. These events repeatedly enact the mass presence of survivors as authoritative witnesses to the Holocaust, a role of privilege that also entails a special responsibility. "It is your duty to tell and retell the vivid evidence of your horrible experiences to your children and grandchildren, to your friends, comrades, colleagues," Israeli president Yitzhak Navon exhorts the crowd assembled at the formal opening of the World Gathering. "Document it, write it, tell it verbally—don't let it be forgotten." Both the opening and closing ceremonies are held in the square before the Western Wall in the Old City of Jerusalem. This setting, along with speeches by Navon and Prime Minister Menachem Begin and performances by an Israeli military chorus, elevate the World Gathering to state ritual. At the same time, these efforts link the moral authority of the international survivor community with the legitimation of the State of Israel.

Holocaust—The Survivors Gather complements these official, large-scale events with profiles of a few individual survivors' experiences during their visit to Jerusalem. These segments of the documentary are more intimate and informal; they offer richly detailed glimpses of the survivors' lives and their personal approaches to commemorating the past. For example, one sequence shows survivor Jack Bagelman, a delicatessen proprietor from Shaker Heights, Ohio, celebrating his bar mitzvah "forty years late" at the Western Wall. Bagelman is seen winding the leather straps of the *tefillin* over the number tattooed on his arm, as family and friends surrounding him document the event with cameras and tape recorders. When the Torah-reading ceremony is concluded, Bagelman and some of his fellow survivors sing a traditional Hasidic melody; then they abruptly switch to Hirsch Glik's "Partisans' Hymn," a secular Yiddish anthem celebrating resistance against Nazi persecution. The camera cuts away to show a group of young Hasidim standing nearby in prayer, apparently oblivious to the proceedings.

At the same time that the World Gathering honored the unique authority of Holocaust survivors, it also recognized the evanescence of that uniqueness. In response to the eventual passing away of the generation of Holocaust survivors—and with it, the ability of others to draw on their live, eyewitness testimony to the Holocaust—the World Gathering offered the survivors symbolic immortality. First, this came in the form of their children's public acceptance of their parents' "legacy" of the Holocaust and the accompanying onus of remembrance. The World Gathering featured children of survivors prominently at several of its public programs, and the gathering itself helped initiate plans to found the International Organization of Children of Survivors. Second, the World Gathering linked the promise of immortality that it extended to the survivors to the endurance of the State of Israel. As invoked by Begin, the Zionist state became, in effect, an eternal incarnation of Jewish survival—and, therefore, of the endurance of Holocaust memory—extending forward as well as backward in time: "Where is the emperor? Where is his might? Where is Rome? Jerusalem lives forever. We are here."

The increased public attention paid to the children of survivors, both as an emerging force in Holocaust memory culture and as a community with distinct concerns of its own, includes several documentary films made since the late 1970s and presented on public television, among them *In Dark Places: Remembering the Holocaust* (1978), *A Generation Apart* (1986), and *Breaking the Silence: The Generation After the Holocaust* (1988).[16] The intergenerational dynamics of Holocaust remembrance in the final decades of the twentieth century has also had important implications for the survivors. At the same time that filmmakers ask them with greater frequency to offer testimony about their experiences during the Holocaust, survivors are at a greater distance from the period. Moreover, those available to testify have increasingly limited recollections of the period, having been young children during the 1930s and 1940s. Nonetheless, survivors are often called upon in documentaries to invoke the broad sweep of history.

For example, two one-hour documentaries—*Forever Yesterday* (Fox, 1980) and *Holocaust: The Children* (ABC, 1981)—use the childhood memories of Holocaust survivors to trace the master narrative of the Nazi persecution of European Jewry.[17] Both films were made as a result of efforts within the survivor community to promote awareness of the Holocaust: *Forever Yesterday* was produced in association with the Holocaust Survivors Film Project (which eventually became the Fortunoff Archive at Yale University); *Holocaust: The Children* was produced by two survivors, Jack P. Eisner and Roman Kent, both of whom appear in the film.

In both documentaries, the survivors' testimonies are not framed by an authoritative, disembodied narration, nor do they complement other informants, such as historians or journalists; rather, their personal memories, spliced together, form a collective voice of authority. Both films intercut the survivors' testimonies with vintage photographs and other images—the artwork of survivors in *Forever Yesterday*, period footage in the case of *Holocaust: The Children*—which are used to illustrate or corroborate their words. In these documentaries, all formal elements—montage, camera-work, scripting, the use of supplementary visual and audial materials—reinforce the central, authoritative stature of survivor testimony.

Yet at the same time, the structure of these documentaries compromises the integrity of individual testimonies. While the different personalities of the various informants are not lost, their particular histories are subsumed by the documentaries' extensive intercutting of snippets of memory to construct a master narrative of the Holocaust. As historian Hans Kellner has observed, "The unprocessed oral reports of witnesses will tell us many things, but not about the Holocaust, because no one witnessed the Holocaust."[18] Some of the informants, however, seem to have conceptualized their personal memories as embodiments of a larger story. For example, in *Holocaust: The Children,* Eisner describes seeing Nazis beat an elderly Jew in the street: "And I recall that it felt like . . . the entire Jewish people are on that pavement right there, bleeding from the beating he got."

As these documentaries evince, presenting the Holocaust primarily from the vantage point of survivor testimony has distinct advantages as well as limitations. The interviews used in these films, all of which were recorded more than thirty-five years after the end of World War II, are, by and large, the memories of childhood or adolescent experiences. While this testimony is rich in affective detail — offering recollections of hunger and unsanitary conditions in the camps, of humiliation at being naked in front of others, of separation from family members and of witnessing death — it offers little information as to the larger social, political, or historical issues that shape the master narrative of the Holocaust. Told exclusively from the perspective of innocent childhood, the Holocaust becomes something akin to a collective nightmare that exists outside of a larger historical narrative, embodied in "memories that cannot be dimmed because they are forever yesterday."

Although Holocaust survivors are often regarded as exceptional people, their appearance as informants in documentaries made since the late 1970s generally conforms to the conventions of presenting authoritative figures in historical documentary filmmaking. Only occasionally have filmmakers broken with these conventions, doing so to try to convey the extreme nature of the Holocaust or the extraordinary challenges of its remembrance.

This can be seen, for example, in *Kitty: Return to Auschwitz,* a documentary made for Yorkshire Television in 1979 for a series on women in war, which was shown in the United States on both PBS and ABC in 1981.[19] The documentary begins and ends with conventionally filmed interviews of its subject, fifty-one-year-old Kitty Felix Hart, a radiologist living in Birmingham, England, who had been interned in Auschwitz from April 1943 to November 1944. But the center of the film, an extended documentation of Kitty's return visit to Auschwitz in the autumn of 1978 with her son, David, is filmed in *cinéma vérité* style. Long sequences, uninterrupted by narration or other images, show mother and son walking about the otherwise deserted camp. Neither Kitty nor her son directly addresses the camera during their visit to Auschwitz, and they are often filmed from behind, sometimes at great distance.

In contrast to survivor interviews that focus, sometimes exclusively, on the survivor's voice and face — thereby suggesting that their recollections stand on their own — *Kitty: Return to Auschwitz* presents the survivor's encounter with the environment of her wartime persecution as the touchstone of memory. Kitty is shown trying to get her bearings among the remains of long-abandoned buildings, which prompt memories of her experiences in the camp some three and a half decades earlier. A woman of great energy and in a heightened state, she strides about the extensive campgrounds, often talking animatedly, sometimes laughing or weeping. Her energetic delivery and gestures strive to animate the vast, empty spaces of Auschwitz with the thousands of people who once inhabited the camp. Kitty probes the environment aggressively, at one point poking with a stick at a puddle of wet ashes, which she identifies as the remains of people who had been gassed and cremated. Centered around the Harts' encounters with the environment of postwar Auschwitz, rather than her independent recollections or responses to an interviewer's questions, the documentary enables viewers to observe the process of memory as well as to hear the memories themselves.

In *Return to Poland,* a documentary presented on public television's series *World* in 1981, filmmaker Marian Marzynski turns the camera on himself.[20] The documentary tracks Marzynski's return to his native Poland after an absence of twelve years. In the course of revisiting the sites of his life in and around Warsaw, he tells the story both of his experiences during World War II as a Jewish child hidden with non-Jewish families and in a Catholic orphanage, and of his life in postwar Poland until he was forced to emigrate during the anti-Zionist purges of the late 1960s.

Throughout this chronicle, *Return to Poland* pays special attention to the roles that making, looking at, and keeping photographed images play in remembrance. In the documentary's opening scene, filmed aboard a train heading for Warsaw, a Soviet conductor covers his face when he sees the camera, wary of being photographed. Later, one of Marzynski's former neighbors in postwar Warsaw protests, "Don't take my picture looking this way." The filmmaker visits an exhibition of "forbidden images"—photographs of the Polish people's resistance against Soviet domination since 1956—and watches official May Day celebrations on Polish television with an old friend, who offers his own cynical commentary. Near the end of the documentary Marzynski incorporates "home movie" footage that he shot in 1969 as he and his wife packed up their possessions before leaving Poland.

Unlike other documentaries' more straightforward uses of vintage photographed images as glimpses of the past, *Return to Poland* calls attention to what has *not* been photographed and what was suppressed, suggesting that an understanding of the past often lies in contemplating what cannot be mediated or revisited.[21] Perhaps the most striking example of this occurs when Marzynski discovers that the house in which he and his family lived for twenty-four years after the war was torn down during their absence. As he walks around the lot where the house once stood, the camera following behind him, he says, "I feel a little like an archeologist, walking through bits and pieces of the past." Thus, Marzynski the survivor becomes part of one of the fragmentary images that Marzynski the filmmaker has collected, which document the limits of Holocaust remembrance.

The most widely discussed documentary on the Holocaust to have appeared in decades is Claude Lanzmann's *Shoah* (1985), which was televised on PBS in April 1987. Running nine and a half hours, it is not only one of the longest documentaries on any subject, but also one of the most aesthetically rigorous and relentless. *Shoah* consists almost exclusively of lengthy interviews with Jews who were once concentration camp inmates, Germans who had been officers during the war, and Polish civilians who were witness to the Final Solution. These are often difficult scenes to watch, not only due to their subject matter, but also because Lanzmann's interviews are conducted as demanding interrogations rather than occasions for the voluntary testimony of eyewitnesses.

Throughout the documentary, the filmmaker can be heard off camera, persistently pressing his informants to relate painful memories. In one oft-cited example, Lanzmann provokes Abraham Bomba—a former inmate of Treblinka who had been assigned the task of cutting women's hair before they were gassed—to describe his recollections of the experience. When Lanzmann asks Bomba about seeing his wife and sister before they were sent to the gas chamber, Bomba resists:

> [*Bomba:*] . . . I can't. It's too horrible. Please.
> [*Lanzmann:*] We have to do it. You know it.
> [*Bomba:*] I won't be able to do it.
> [*Lanzmann:*] You have to do it. I know it's very hard. I know and I
>   apologize.
> [*Bomba:*] Don't make me go on please.
> [*Lanzmann:*] Please. We must go on.[22]

Historian Nora Levin condemned this scene as an example of "Lanzmann's insistence on pushing survivors to a degree of torment that was unbearable, beyond that delicate line which they themselves had defined." Moreover, Levin suggested that Lanzmann had transgressed both a horizontal boundary of documentary filmmaking—by crossing the "delicate line" that articulates the implicit social contract between filmmaker and informant—and a vertical boundary that separates documentary from lesser forms of media. Lanzmann's interviewing tactics, she argued, are akin to "the ugly pressures of TV interviewers who want ready responses from survivors of destructive fires, murders, and, most recently, from relatives and friends of the crew of the *Challenger*." This approach to interviewing Holocaust survivors, Levin suggested, debased the elevated moral and aesthetic status ascribed to the documentary, and to the Holocaust, with the sensibility and principles of a lowbrow media genre.[23] At the same time, Lanzmann's relentless pursuit of his interviewees can be seen as a cinematic evocation of the breakdown of social contracts that occurred during the Nazi era and which culminated in genocide.

Few filmmakers whose subjects are Holocaust survivors have come near to challenging their informants as Lanzmann did. The great majority of these documentarians present the survivors' unrivaled authority as self-evident. Kellner has observed that "as the survivors pass, the dangers of representation become most intense. The highest ethical/rhetorical position in Holocaust representations belongs to the survivor." Moreover, he likens their evidentiary value to that accorded for decades to photographic images: "The intense listening to the words of the survivor parallels the interest Roland Barthes ascribed to the photograph—'that, there it is, lo!'"[24]

Indeed, other comparisons of survivor testimony with vintage documentary photographs or film of the Holocaust often implicitly place a higher value on the immediacy and orality of the former, in contrast with the remoteness and silence of the latter. Televised presentations of survivors' recollections seem intimate and vibrant in comparison to the relative temporal, geographic, and formal distance of excerpts from vintage footage. Set within a color news report or documentary, these black-and-white images become apparent as mediations, and the silence of their subjects—both living and dead—underscores the disparity between them and their viewers. The presence of these images in a documentary exemplifies what sociologist Paul Connerton distinguished as "inscribing practices" of memory—that is, they are among the range of "modern devices for storing and retrieving information . . . long after the human organism has stopped informing."[25] Although films and videotapes of interviews with Holocaust survivors are also inscribing practices, they are valued as simulations of what Connerton called the "incorporating practice" of oral culture, which requires direct contact among participants. As such, these "oral histories"—a term that itself strives to bridge the disparity between incorporating and inscribing practices—are embraced as a reassurance that contact with the survivor generation and its "legacy" will survive its passing.

But despite their purported immediacy and promises to endure, these interviews remain mediations themselves. Their contents reflect the particular agendas of the interviewers—what is or is not asked, how, and toward what larger goals. The interviews even have their own aesthetic—James Young, for example, has noted how the survivors' "well-groomed, outwardly mended" appearance contrasts with "the unassimilable images of the wretched dead and survivors" who appear in liberation footage.[26]

The identity of the young boy in the foreground of this well-known photograph, which was first published in the Stroop Report on the liquidation of the Warsaw Ghetto in 1943, is the subject of the 1990 documentary *Tsvi Nussbaum: A Boy from Warsaw.* (YIVO Institute for Jewish Research.)

Rather than superseding vintage photographs or other forms of Holocaust representation, the filming of Holocaust survivors' testimony has enabled them to become photographic evidence themselves.

The extent to which filming their testimony has drawn Holocaust survivors into the corpus of Holocaust mediations is borne out by a documentary that examines one effort to unite vintage photodocumentation and survivor recollections as mutually corroborating testimony. *A Boy from Warsaw,* made in 1990 by MTV Finland and Gamma TV France and subsequently shown on American television, examines the claim of Holocaust survivor Tsvi Nussbaum that he is the focal figure in a black-and-white photograph that is one of the most often reproduced images of the Holocaust.[27] The image, which was first published in the report by General Jurgen Stroop on the liquidation of the Warsaw Ghetto in 1943, shows a young boy at the front of a group of people standing in a street.[28] He and the woman next to him have their arms raised; behind them stands a German soldier, who points a rifle at the boy.

As *A Boy from Warsaw* reminds viewers, this photograph has achieved iconic status as a representation of the Holocaust. In the mid-1970s, Lucy

Dawidowicz observed that the image had become "the most concrete illustration" of the Nazis' commitment to the annihilation of the Jewish people. Reproduced in countless publications and documentaries on the history of the Holocaust, the photograph has inspired other works of Holocaust memory culture, such as Yala Korwin's poem "The Little Boy with His Hands Up." With its appearance in other contexts, such as Ingmar Bergman's 1966 feature film *Persona*, the photograph has been used, according to Susan Sontag, as an image "of total violence, of unredeemed cruelty."[29]

A Boy from Warsaw integrates Nussbaum's personal history with an investigation of his claim to be the boy in the photograph from the Stroop Report. Interviews with Nussbaum (who, at the time the film was made, was a physician residing in Rockland County, New York) as well as relatives, friends, and acquaintances who knew him and his family during the war years are intercut with vintage films and photographs, plus footage of contemporary Poland.

In the course of relating his wartime experiences, Nussbaum and the others situate the photograph at a moment within his personal history. Nussbaum and his relatives explain that he was never in the Warsaw Ghetto, which would seem to preclude his being the boy depicted. However, they claim that the photograph was taken in the "Aryan" section of Warsaw in July 1943 and that it, like some of the other images in the Stroop Report, is not an image of the Warsaw Ghetto per se or of its destruction. Nussbaum repeatedly tells interviewers that he remembers being told to put up his hands by a German officer, and he compares the face of the boy in the photograph with snapshots taken of him before and after the war. Others interviewed analyze fine points of the image, such as the significance of people in the photograph carrying baggage and wearing armbands bearing the six-pointed star, and they debate whether the Jews in the photograph were walking or standing still when the image was taken.

A Boy from Warsaw neither endorses nor dismisses fully Nussbaum's claim. The documentary includes an interview with another survivor, a historian, who argues that the photograph was taken inside the ghetto, and that Nussbaum is therefore not the boy in the image. At the same time, *A Boy from Warsaw* validates the power of this one photograph—and, implicitly, Holocaust photography in general—by repeatedly examining it and drawing out from it a series of meanings. These range from its value in Nussbaum's personal history to the insight it offers into the Nazi era in general. The documentary recounts how the soldier in the photograph from the Stroop Report was positively identified as Josef Blösch and explains how the image was used in his prosecution as a war criminal. In an interview, a Polish historian recounts Stroop's fondness for being photographed and for collecting photographs of his military accomplishments. The historian expands this into a general statement on the Nazis' predilection for documenting their exploits, which he regards as a sign that they believed they would never be held accountable for their actions by anyone outside of the Third Reich.

A Boy from Warsaw concludes with an interview with Nussbaum in his physician's office. On the wall over his desk hangs an enlarged print of the photograph from the Stroop Report, onto which he has pasted pictures of himself taken just before and after the war. He explains how the image helped him confront his reluctance to remember his wartime experiences, and how it has reinforced his commitment to Holocaust memory. While leaving unanswered the question of whether the boy in the photograph from the Stroop Report is Nussbaum, the documentary validates the meaning that attaching himself to the image has given to Nussbaum's sense of self as a survivor of the Holocaust.

Lost Between Two Worlds:
Holocaust Survivors in Television Dramas

In contrast to the presentation of Holocaust survivors as authoritative elders in documentaries, television dramas during the 1980s and 1990s have tended to offer portraits of survivors that hark back to teleplays aired during the medium's early postwar years. Indeed, a number of these portrayals appear in adaptations of literary works presented on vestiges of the drama anthology series that had their heyday in the 1950s: *The Cafeteria* (1984), a dramatization of a short story by Isaac Bashevis Singer; *The Ghost Writer* (1984), based on Philip Roth's eponymous novella; and *The Quarrel* (1993), adapted from a short story by Chaim Grade, all of which appeared on PBS's *American Playhouse;* as well as *Miss Rose White* (NBC, 1992) an adaptation of Barbara Lebow's stage play *A Shayna Maidel* for *Hallmark Hall of Fame.*[30]

The Quarrel enacts a philosophical dispute between two Holocaust survivors who meet by chance after the war. Once fellow students at a Lithuanian yeshiva in the 1930s, Chaim Vilner (played by R. H. Thomson) is now a secular Yiddish writer, while Hersh Rasseyner (Saul Rubinek) is the head of a yeshiva. Their quarrel over the possibility of a spiritual response to the Holocaust recalls similar debates in Holocaust dramas aired in the 1950s on Sunday ecumenical series and prime-time dramas. Both *The Cafeteria* and *Miss Rose White* present survivors as mentally fragile figures lost between two worlds—haunted by the terrors of the past, struggling to adjust to life in a new postwar environment. Similar to earlier pathologized portraits of the Holocaust survivor, they provide an occasion for histrionic performances by actresses (reminiscent of the nineteenth-century aestheticization of female insanity in bel canto opera), accompanied by flashbacks and, in the case of *The Cafeteria,* gothic hallucinations. Here, the title setting, a cafeteria on New York's Upper West Side, becomes a phantasmagorical chamber of Nazi horrors that drives the female protagonist (played by Zohra Lampert) to suicide.

Miss Rose White also recalls the earlier dramas that linked the Holocaust with postwar American Jewry's ambivalent sense of identity. Set in New York City in 1947, the drama centers on the title character (played by Kyra Sedgwick), an East European Jewish immigrant who came to America with her father (Maximilian Schell) before the start of World War II, leaving behind her mother and her sister Lusia (Amanda Plummer). Having anglicized her name from Reyzl Weiss, Rose strives to be "the 'all-American girl,' complete with a born-in-America boyfriend . . . and a promising career at Macy's." Rose's "comfortable world" is threatened by the news that Lusia has survived the war and is coming to live with her and her father. Lusia's arrival not only raises long-suppressed family tensions, but also forces Rose to "reconcile the truth of her past" in Europe with "the promise of her future" in America.

According to a *Hallmark Hall of Fame* press release, *Miss Rose White* "addresses many themes that are universal and is, at its heart, a family drama."[31] The ordeals of the Holocaust thus figure as the background for psychodynamic conflicts between father and daughter, sister and sister. The drama's denouement comes in a scene in which Lusia presents Rose with a letter written to her by their mother before her death, in which the mother expresses her love for her absent child; this gesture seals the bond between the two sisters and resolves Rose's conflicting feelings toward both her parents.

While *Miss Rose White* recalls an earlier generation of Holocaust dramas, there are noteworthy differences in this *Hallmark Hall of Fame* presentation. The psychological plight of the Holocaust survivor and the conflicted identity of the American Jew were treated as provocative, contemporary social problems in the 1950s. In *Miss Rose White* these dramatic subjects are revisited as time-honored, classic themes at the same time that they are sentimentalized and domesticated. And, in contrast with the clash between commercials and the disturbing content of televised Holocaust dramas that critics often decried in earlier decades, Hallmark punctuated this *Hall of Fame* presentation with advertisements for its greeting cards that are compatible with the sentiments of *Miss Rose White.* The resolution of each minute-long commercial drama centers around the giving and receiving of a greeting card as a life-confirming act, thereby reiterating in miniature the denouement of the larger drama, when Lusia gives Rose their mother's letter. Conversely, the juxtaposition of these commercial minidramas with *Miss Rose White*—which was broadcast two weeks before Mother's Day—transformed Lebow's play into a two-hour commercial for Hallmark cards.

In what is perhaps the most remarkable of Anne Frank's many appearances on American television, she, too, figures as a virtual Holocaust survivor in *The Ghost Writer*. Among the characters in this adaptation of Philip Roth's 1979 novella, which is set in the late 1950s, is a mysterious young woman named Amy Bellette (played by Paulette Smit), whom the work's protagonist and narrator, Nathan Zuckerman (Mark Linn-Baker), fantasizes is really Anne Frank. Zuckerman, a budding fiction writer, imagines that Anne survived the war, only to discover that, with the publication of her diary, she has been beatified as "a saint" in the postwar consciousness, "the incarnation of the millions of unlived years robbed from the murdered Jews." Moreover, the lessons embodied by her diary were deemed valid "only if she were believed to be dead"; hence, her need to assume a false identity.[32] *The Ghost Writer* offers provocative commentary on the singular status that Anne, her diary, and its dramatization by Frances Goodrich and Albert Hackett have attained in American Holocaust remembrance since the postwar years.[33]

Complementing these retrospective presentations of the Holocaust survivor as a wounded, isolated, or permanently displaced victim is the inclusion of survivors among the regular cast of characters populating continuing dramatic series. The earliest instance appears to be music teacher Benjamin Shorofsky (played by Albert Hague) in *Fame* (NBC, 1982–1983; syndicated 1983–1987), a series about students in New York City's High School for the Performing Arts. A more recent and more developed example appeared in *Homefront* (ABC, 1991–1993), a dramatic series set in a small midwestern town during the years immediately following the end of World War II.

One of *Homefront*'s several plotlines follows Gina Sloan (played by Giuliana Santini), an Italian war bride. In the series's initial episode, Gina arrives in her GI husband Mike's hometown of River Run, Ohio, pregnant with their child, only to discover that Mike was killed on his way back to America.[34] She is shunned by her husband's patrician WASP parents, who accuse her of having entrapped their son into marriage and who are put off by her being a foreigner. Gina then sets out on her own, aided by other returning GIs and their friends, to make a new home for herself and her child. Her identity as a Holocaust survivor is only briefly signaled in the series's premiere, in a scene that concludes with a close-up shot of a number tattooed on her bared forearm.

Homefront: Holocaust survivor Gina Sloan, portrayed by Giuliana Santini (standing, right), appears among the other regular cast members of this dramatic series, which premiered in 1991, set in a small midwestern town in the years immediately following World War II. Photographer: Bob D'Amico. (Photofest. © 1983 CBS Inc. All Rights Reserved.)

Gina's wartime experiences are explored in a later episode, in which she is haunted by memories of her internment, together with her mother, in Auschwitz.[35] Through a series of flashbacks, Gina recalls how her mother saved her life by teaching her to make lace for their Nazi captors, and how her mother sacrificed her own life so that Gina might survive. Gina's struggle to come to terms with her past is juxtaposed with another of this episode's subplots, involving the Davises, an African-American family. Mr. and Mrs. Davis (Dick Anthony Williams, Hattie Winston) sort through relics of the family past when elderly Grandmother Davis (Montrose Hagins) moves in with them. Among the mementos is a piece of lace that her own grandmother had made when she was a young slave working on a plantation, a skill that she passed down to Grandmother Davis. The common motif of lacemaking links the stories of the two women's past struggles to survive their respective adversities; at the conclusion of the episode both women find healing resolution of their past sorrows in the love of family and respect of friends.

The implicit analogy of African-American slavery with the Holocaust both looks back to earlier examples of this comparison made during the civil rights era and resonates with contemporary rhetoric concerning the "black/Jewish dialogue" in America—notably the 1992 documentary *Liberators: Fighting on Two Fronts in World War II*. Moreover, the analogy constitutes a symbolic act of inclusion, inviting Gina and her personal history into the multicultural, extended family inhabiting *Homefront*. Gina's presence as a recurring character in the series is a noteworthy departure from earlier "guest appearances" on American television by Holocaust survivors as highly marginalized figures. Gina, in contrast, is portrayed as a resourceful, responsible, and caring member of the community. Her character constitutes a belated gesture of offering survivors a sense of "at-homeness" in the postwar American heartland.

Elie Wiesel: "Witness for Life"

If a single figure is situated at the pinnacle of Holocaust survivors' public ascendance since the late 1970s, it is Elie Wiesel. Since his arrival in the United States in the mid-1960s, Wiesel's status as quintessential Holocaust survivor and voice of moral authority has risen steadily, to the point where he has been hailed as a "messenger to all humanity" and "witness for life."[36] Historian Peter Novick has noted a signal change in American Holocaust memory culture taking place in the late 1960s, epitomized by a "shift in the popular archetype of Holocaust victim: from Anne Frank (assimilated, universalist in orientation, sheltered by Gentiles) to Elie Wiesel (of Hasidic background, Zionist and particularist in orientation, abandoned by Gentiles)." Novick links the advent of Wiesel to "a generational shift in Jewish leadership: The replacement of those committed to an earlier, low-profile, 'don't make waves' posture, to a more assertive, younger generation which more often included—and the cultural difference is not insignificant—Jews of Eastern European rather than of German origin."[37] This development also constitutes a shift from a dead figure, who is the posthumous object of memory, to a living person who has played an active role in molding his iconic stature.

The rise of Wiesel's public stature can be traced through his recurring presence on American television, progressing from appearances on Sunday ecumenical series as early as 1967 to more highly visible venues. He has been featured as an authority on the Holocaust in documentaries and news reports, and the medium has presented his life story more than once.[38]

Television has also facilitated Wiesel's image as a public figure whose moral authority extends beyond the Holocaust. He has been seen several times in broadcasts as the recipient of important honors, including the United States Medal of Liberty and the Nobel Peace Prize in 1986.[39] In interviews by David Susskind (*Open Mind,* 1987), Bill Moyers (*Beyond Hate,* 1991), and Oprah Winfrey (*The Oprah Winfrey Show,* 1993), among others, television has also provided Wiesel with opportunities to philosophize on issues other than the Holocaust.[40] On such occasions, Wiesel has linked his status as Holocaust survivor with that of universalist humanitarian, thereby situating the Holocaust in a central, paradigmatic position within the contemporary discourse of morality.

An unusual example of this took place on 20 November 1983, when Wiesel was featured as a "philosopher, theologian, and author on . . . the Holocaust" on *ABC News Viewpoint: Nuclear Dilemma.*[41] This special broadcast followed the prime-time presentation of *ABC Theater: The Day After,* a three-hour, made-for-television movie portraying the hypothetical impact of a nuclear war between the United States and the Soviet Union on the residents of Lawrence, Kansas. Broadcast at a time when relations between the two superpowers seemed to be "at their coldest point since the Berlin blockade . . . or maybe even the Cuban missile crisis" and when the American antinuclear movement was at its peak, *The Day After* had become, in television journalist Ted Koppel's words, "a national event."[42] Koppel hosted the *ABC News Viewpoint* segment, which examined issues raised by the controversial drama through questions from a live studio audience and the comments of former and current high-ranking national officials (former secretary of state Henry Kissinger, former secretary of defense Robert McNamara, former national security advisor Brent Scowcroft, then secretary of state George Shultz), as well as input from conservative columnist William F. Buckley Jr., scientist and liberal activist Carl Sagan, and Wiesel.

Whereas the four officials address national policy on the arms race, past and present, and Buckley and Sagan voice opposing views of the popular debate over nuclear arms, Wiesel was, Koppel explains, "deliberately invited" to bring "a humanistic touch" to the discussion. Asked for his reponse to *The Day After,* Wiesel replies: "I'm scared because I know what is unimaginable can happen. I know that the impossible is possible." While watching the movie, he comments, "I had a strange feeling that I had seen it before. Except that once upon a time it happened to my people—and now it happened to all people. And suddenly I said to myself, maybe the whole world, strangely, has turned Jewish. Everybody lives now facing the unknown, we are all in a way helpless." Wiesel was hardly the first person to analogize the Nazi persecution of Jews and the mass destruction of human lives by atomic weapons. But in his Judaizing of the "nuclear holocaust," he equated being Jewish with being in an imperiled yet morally charged position, and he universalized Jewishness as a potential condition for all humankind.

The day after learning that he had received the 1986 Nobel Peace Prize, Wiesel was interviewed on the *MacNeil/Lehrer NewsHour* by anchor Charlayne Hunter-Gault.[43] She notes that the Nobel Committee hailed Wiesel as "a messenger of mankind—his message is one of peace, atonement, and human dignity," and she mentions his work on behalf of Holocaust education and his advocacy of rights for Soviet Jews and other oppressed groups. Hunter-Gault then adds that many know Wiesel best for remarks that he made at a White House ceremony the previous year. A short tape clip follows, in which Wiesel addresses Ronald Reagan on 19 April 1985, when the president presented him with the Congressional Gold Medal of Achievement.

Indeed, this incident, perhaps the most remarkable of Wiesel's numerous appearances on television, may continue to remain among the most memorable moments in his public career. Wiesel had used this occasion to continue his campaign to urge Reagan not to follow through on a plan, announced by the White House on 11 April, to make an official visit to a World War II military cemetery in Bitburg, West Germany, as part of ceremonies commemorating the fortieth anniversary of V-E Day on 5 May. The president's itinerary had triggered swift and angry protests from American veterans' organizations, Jewish groups, and others. They decried the White House's plan to honor German soldiers who had fallen in World War II, including a number of men who had served in the SS. Many also criticized the decision, announced earlier in April, that the president would not go to a concentration camp site during the course of his visit. Reagan's itinerary was planned to celebrate "a spirit of reconciliation" and emphasize "economic and military compatibility" between the two allies, rather than "reopening" Germany's sense of guilt over the Holocaust.[44] In the days following the 11 April announcement, Wiesel had made several public statements that were reported in the national media, in which he beseeched the president to reconsider his plan. On the day before the White House awards ceremony, Wiesel delivered another appeal to Secretary of State Shultz at the program for the National Civic Day of Commemoration of the Holocaust held by the United States Congress.[45]

"That place, Mr. President, is not your place." Elie Wiesel calls on Ronald Reagan not to pay a state visit to the Bitburg military cemetery in West Germany when the president presents him with the Congressional Gold Medal of Achievement at the White House in 1985. (As broadcast on MacNeil/Lehrer NewsHour.)

After Wiesel had presented Reagan administration officials with an advance copy of the speech he intended to give at the 19 April White House ceremony, aides to the president tried to compel Wiesel to cut his remarks from ten minutes to three and to delete critical references to the president, but they later relented. In an effort to keep Wiesel's speech "as low key as possible," the White House staff shifted the location of the ceremony from the East Room to the much smaller Roosevelt Room.[46] In response to mounting public outrage over Reagan's impending visit to the German military cemetery, the White House announced on 19 April that a stop at Bergen-Belsen would be added to the president's V-E Day itinerary, and Reagan met in private session with Wiesel immediately prior to the awards ceremony to discuss the situation.

Then, with White House press corps cameras rolling, Wiesel accepted the medal from Reagan and began his speech: "Mr. President, . . . I was very pleased that we met before, so a stage of reconciliation has been set in motion between us. But then, we were never on two sides. We were on the same side. We were always on the side of justice, always on the side of memory, against the SS and against what they represent." Toward the end of his remarks, Wiesel charged Reagan to reconsider his plan to visit the military cemetery in Bitburg: "May I, Mr. President . . . , implore you to do something else . . . to find another way, another site. That place, Mr. President, is not your place. Your place is with the victims of the SS."[47]

Excerpts of Wiesel's speech were featured in the lead stories on all three commercial television networks' national newscasts that evening, and this escalation of the Bitburg controversy continued to generate considerable attention for days afterward. Major newspapers reported Wiesel's challenge to the Reagan administration as a front-page story the day following the awards ceremony, and the incident fueled the debate over the president's plans for the V-E Day commemoration.[48] Wiesel continued to appear or to be mentioned regularly on national television news reports during the days leading up to the 5 May event. Newscasts also recalled Wiesel's 19 April speech at the White House in conjunction with an unrelated but similar news story. On 26 April another visitor to the White House, Mae Chee Castillo, a Navajo, seized the opportunity of receiving an honor from Reagan to criticize his administration's budget cuts in social services for Native Americans. This prompted national news reports on ABC and NBC to compare the incident to Wiesel's earlier confrontation with Reagan.[49]

Reagan ultimately followed through with the planned visit to Bitburg, despite the extensive controversy surrounding what journalist Hedrick Smith labeled "the most wrenching political episode of his Presidency" up to that point. The outcry against the trip to Bitburg eventually included published letters of protest signed by figures ranging from fundamentalist preacher Jerry Falwell to civil rights activist Coretta Scott King, the threatened resignation of the U.S. Holocaust Memorial Council (whose members were dissuaded from doing so by Wiesel, its chair), and a resolution passed on 30 April by Congress calling on Reagan not to visit the cemetery. The major networks announced plans to broadcast live satellite coverage of the commemorative events of 5 May, a sign that "the visit to the cemetery had taken on a significance far beyond the usual ceremonial tributes to war dead."[50]

Footage of the ceremonies in West Germany was aired throughout the day, together with images of protest against Reagan's visit and analysis of the controversy's impact on the president, international relations, and the American public. Of the three commercial networks, NBC offered the most extensive coverage of the day's events, beginning with the live broadcast of the ceremonies at 8:30 A.M. (Eastern time). At 12:30 P.M., NBC's public affairs program *Meet the Press* was broadcast from Bonn, where correspondents Marvin Kalb and Roger Mudd interview Assistant Secretary of State Richard Burt and Franz Josef Strauss, the prime minister of Bavaria and a political ally of West German prime minister Helmut Kohl.[51] During this half-hour broadcast the anchors debate the political implications of the Bitburg visit with the two government officials and also raise issues concerning the ceremony itself as a televisual event. In his introductory remarks, Kalb notes that the success of the president's visit depends to a considerable extent on the press, giving "some indication of the White House's attitude of the importance of television." Mudd characterizes Reagan as a leader who both "lives" and "dies" by the "photo op," and the journalist concludes the program by raising the question of the limits of the effectiveness of a single public event on international policy and public opinion.

At 2:00 P.M., NBC broadcast a news special showing highlights of the ceremonies at Bitburg and Bergen-Belsen. Later the network's national evening newscast opened with images of the president's "controversial" visit to the Bitburg cemetery, followed by reports of the White House staff's efforts to "minimize public relations damage" caused by the event and footage of American Jewish demonstrators in Bitburg. This was followed by scenes of Reagan at Bergen-Belsen (which had actually preceded the Bitburg visit), where he read aloud from Anne Frank's diary. Soviet reaction to Reagan's Bitburg visit was reported by anchor John Palmer, followed by scenes from New York of Jewish protest against the president at the annual March for Soviet Jews, as well as reports of protests by American veterans' groups. The six-and-a-half minute segment concluded with footage of Wiesel discussing the Bitburg issue with children.[52] (As was the case in the documentary-style conclusion of *Skokie*, the Holocaust survivor was again given the last word within the context of a "balanced" report.)

Reagan's visit to Bitburg, which the White House had planned as an ameliorative ceremony that would offer resolution to a troubling chapter of history, had become quite the opposite—a controversy that thrust a disturbing episode of the past into the present. Wiesel's televised remarks at the White House on 19 April in effect prefigured this transformation of the ceremonies of 5 May. The restraint of Wiesel's performance and the deference that he showed to the president honored the solemnity of the White House ritual at the same time that the content of his speech transformed the award's ceremony into a challenge of presidential authority. Television played a critical role in this process by presenting as news the spectacle of "made-for-television" rituals (both at the White House on 19 April and in West Germany on 5 May) transformed, scrutinized, and subverted by the medium for which they are staged—subverted, indeed, within the presentation of the rituals themselves.

More than simply reopening old wounds, Bitburg brought the issue of American Holocaust memory culture into the realm of international politics and its media coverage. Several commentators noted the critical role that television, as a vehicle for presenting official state "media events," played as a venue for the creation and undoing of memory culture. Thomas Elsaesser, for example, wrote:

> Making a media-spectacle out of what they could neither mourn, nor finally dared to celebrate, the elected representatives of the American and German people succeeded in re-presenting (making present) and commemorating (recalling to consciousness) not the specific historical moment in any of its manifold implications and consequences, but the processes by which in the very act of re-presentation, an event evaporates into an occasion, and history becomes the phantom signifier of endlessly interchangeable referents.[53]

Other critics, who were also concerned with the mutability of history and memory at the hands of those who make "media-spectacles," found the visit to Bitburg and its mediation to be an aptly cynical gesture. After stating that some American businesses had "actively collaborated with the Nazis" during World War II, Laurence Jarvik asked, "What better way to commemorate the 49th anniversary of the beginning of the cold war than a visit by the former spokesman for General Electric to the graves of Hitler's SS? What better and more honest statement of American values could the most imaginative novelist, screenwriter, or director devise?"[54]

Since the late 1970s Wiesel has offered occasional comments on the relationship between the Holocaust and television. Following the premiere of *Holocaust* in 1978, his denunciation of the miniseries emerged as a seminal critique of the program itself and of Holocaust television as a genre. A decade later, in an interview in *TV Guide,* Wiesel expressed a more complex view of the medium and its relationship to this subject. On one hand, he denounced television as "unthinkingly immoral" in its "casual treatment of violence" and expressed his fears that, as inhabitants of an "image-oriented world," modern humankind has regressed to "paganism." On the other hand, Wiesel acknowledged that television, a "two-edged weapon," has the power to do good as well. He cited the coverage of the war in Vietnam and of America's civil rights struggles of the 1960s as instances in which the medium "raises our consciousness," and he pointed out how, during events such as the assassination of President Kennedy and the *Challenger* explosion, television brought people together "and made us feel our humanity." Above all, Wiesel argued that the medium has "the obligation to bear witness." Had there been television during the Nazi era, he suggested, "I think it would have exposed Hitler . . . and millions of lives might have been saved. In that way, it is a wonderful tool. The camera cannot lie — not when it is always there."[55]

In the years since Wiesel expressed his belief that the medium might have made a significant difference in the fate of European Jewry during World War II, world events have put this notion—and Wiesel as well—to the test. At the same time, these and other incidents have tested the role of the Holocaust as a moral paradigm in contemporary American culture; here, too, television has often been both the venue for this contention and a catalyst in its formulation.

eight

The Master Paradigm

How did an American relationship with the Holocaust develop over the course of the half century following the end of World War II? One measure is provided by tracking the use of the term *Holocaust* itself. In 1959, historian Leon Jick noted, "a book called *Holocaust* was published in New York" that described a recent fire in a Boston nightclub in which hundreds of people perished.[1] This, he argued, demonstrates that the term *Holocaust* had yet to be associated with the Nazi persecution of Europe's Jews, which evinces the limited awareness of this historical epoch among Americans during the first postwar decades.

In 1988, Larry Kramer's *Reports from the Holocaust: The Making of an AIDS Activist* was published, another book in which the title word *Holocaust* referred to something besides the destruction of European Jewry during the Nazi era. In this instance, however, the author employed the term quite cognizant that it signifies both the Jewish Holocaust—a usage widely recognized by the late 1980s—and, more generally, any widespread destruction. Kramer deliberately invoked the double meaning of the term in order to characterize the impact of the AIDS pandemic on America's gay male community in the 1980s as being analogous to the Final Solution: "History recently made a pretty good attempt to destroy the Jewish people, and . . . I think history now has an opportunity to do (and is already doing) pretty much the same to homosexuals." As historian Peter Novick has observed, in recent years in America the Holocaust "is evoked as reference point in discussions of everything from AIDS to abortion."[2]

Beyond its use to identify other, more recent cases of genocide in Cambodia, Kurdistan, Bosnia, Rwanda, and Chechnya, the Holocaust now figures as a moral paradigm for a range of social conflicts in contemporary American life. So powerful is this paradigm that it is used with increasing frequency as a model for examining America's past; both the persecution of Native American tribes and the African slave trade have been termed an "American Holocaust."[3] The attraction to the Holocaust as a paradigm seems to have at least as much to do with its widely endorsed status as an exceptional, morally galvanizing, limiting case in human experience as it does with the particulars of its history. Thus, the Holocaust is distinguished as a master paradigm, situated above other ethical icons, models, and analogies.

Americans' use of the Holocaust as a master moral paradigm takes as many different forms as it has applications, appearing in venues ranging from bumper stickers and T-shirts to scholarly monographs and museums. But nowhere has the paradigmatic use of the Holocaust been effected more powerfully and extensively during the 1980s and 1990s than on television. This is not merely due to the large number and variety of programs related to this topic that broadcasters have presented to audiences of unmatched proportions; it is also a consequence of the medium's distinctive characteristics and its increasingly complex presence in American culture. In several instances, American television's paradigmatic use of the Holocaust has became the subject of great contention, demonstrating the medium's power as a cultural force and the extent to which how the Holocaust is represented has itself become a public concern. Television's influence can be seen on other forms of Holocaust memory culture as well, notably in major Holocaust museums that have opened in the 1990s. At the same time that the Holocaust serves Americans as a moral paradigm of unprecedented recognition and force, its presence on television nonetheless demonstrates the limits of its ability to effect change in the nation's responses to moral crises that are decried as "another Holocaust."

Moral Capital

Susan Sontag observed in her essay *AIDS and Its Metaphors* that "saying a thing is or is like something-it-is-not" is a fundamental activity of human cognition. Yet, while "one cannot think without metaphors," those that have become fixtures of public discourse are not exempt from critical scrutiny. Indeed, Sontag asserted that sometimes it is "correct to be 'against'" some metaphors and their significance. Certainly the Holocaust is now among the most scrutinized—and contested—subjects of metaphor in American public culture. As author Philip Lopate has noted, "The Holocaust analogy has the curious double property of being both amazingly plastic—able to be applied to almost any issue—and fantastically rigid, since we are constantly being told that the Holocaust is incomparable."[4]

The recent embrace of the Holocaust as a metaphor for an ever-widening spectrum of subjects has prompted questions as to both its propriety (that is, what constitutes "appropriate" or "just" use of the Holocaust) and its proprietary rights (that is, who are the "rightful" arbiters of "proper" Holocaust memory). Since the mid-1970s scholars have scrutinized a wide range of works—from revisionist histories to neo-Nazi propaganda, from avant-garde literature to pornography—with the intent of guarding the Holocaust against representations that are less than "proper" and represen- ters who are less than "qualified."[5]

Scholarly as well as popular concern about "protecting" the Holocaust against revisionist interpretations, outright denials of its facticity, and degrading representations extends to the use of the Holocaust as a para- digm in public culture. Historian Yehuda Bauer, for example, asked "Whose Holocaust?" in a 1980 essay in which he reflected on President Carter's statements about plans to create a Holocaust memorial in Wash- ington, D.C., as a result of proposals that had been submitted by the Presi- dent's Commission on the Holocaust. Bauer claimed that such a memorial would "submerge the specific Jewish tragedy in the general sea of suffering caused by . . . the Nazi regime. In the public mind the term Holocaust has become flattened in any case. Any evil that befalls anyone anywhere becomes a Holocaust—Vietnamese, Soviet Jews ('cultural Holocaust'), blacks in American ghettos, women suffering inequality, and so on."[6]

In an essay published with Bauer's, literary scholar Edward Alexander cited other examples of what he characterized as "stealing the Holocaust." Alexander focused on contemporary descriptions of the relationship between the State of Israel and Palestinians living in Israeli-occupied terri- tories that frequently evoked the Holocaust as a paradigm, using it to analogize Israel with the Nazis and the Palestinians with mid-twentieth- century European Jewry. When such a statement appeared at the Anne Frank House in Amsterdam, as part of an exhibition about the Palestine Liberation Organization, Alexander claimed that with "this obscene trav- esty, the wheel comes full circle." He argued that Jews "have been slow to recognize that failure to claim something that is rightfully yours is an invi- tation to others to lay hold of what is seen as valuable property, whether in land or—as in the case of Anne Frank—moral capital."[7] By likening the Holocaust to geopolitical territory (one assumes that he had in mind the territories occupied by Israel in the wake of the 1967 war), Alexander con- ceptualized a historical era and its public memory as something that is either in the hands of its "rightful" owners or is otherwise to be considered "stolen" goods.

More recently, Alexander expanded his discussion of "stealing" the Holocaust to include the efforts of intellectuals who, in his words, "cyni- cally" try to make "the actual Jewish victims of the Holocaust into metaphors," thereby expressing "a deep-seated wish to transform the Nazi murder of Jews, a crime of terrifying clarity and distinctness, into a blurred,

amorphous agony, an indeterminate part of man's inhumanity to man."
These misappropriations of the Holocaust have moral as well as political
consequences, Alexander argued, in that they serve "the designs of those
who wish to release the nations of the West from whatever slight burden of
guilt they may still bear for what they allowed or helped Hitler to do to the
Jews of Europe, and so remove whatever impediments of conscience may
yet stand in the way of the anti-Israel crusade."[8]

While many may find Alexander's position problematic or his rhetoric
extreme, the issue that he addressed has been of widespread concern among
Holocaust scholars, survivors, Jews, and other communities who have a
stake in Holocaust remembrance. The matter of proprietary rights to the
Holocaust resonates with a series of other provocative contemporary
issues: the nature of Jewish particularism and continuity, as well as general
debates on multiculturalism, the limits of historical authority, moral rela-
tivism, identity politics, and the culture of victimhood. Consequently, the
notion of the Holocaust as cultural property has played a defining role in
problematizing recent instances of Holocaust memory culture, ranging
from efforts, eventually abandoned, to establish a Carmelite convent at
Auschwitz to contentions over the representation of Armenians and Gypsies in Washington's Holocaust museum.[9]

As broadcasts related to the Bitburg incident of 1985 demonstrate,
television has served as a forum for contention over the propriety of
Holocaust remembrance. Since the genre came of age with the broadcast
of the *Holocaust* miniseries, Holocaust television has itself been the subject of debates over the proprietary rights to the Holocaust. Two television presentations in particular—the 1980 broadcast of Arthur Miller's
drama *Playing for Time* and the telecasts of the documentary *Liberators:
Fighting on Two Fronts in World War II* in 1992—generated extensive
public discussion that centered around the issue of who is entitled to represent the Holocaust, in what contexts, and toward what ends.[10] These
two programs entail confrontations with separate controversies: support
for Israel versus Palestinians in the case of *Playing for Time,* relationships
between African-Americans and American Jews in the case of *Liberators.*
These programs and their attendant debates demonstrate the distinctive
role of television as both a forum for and a catalyst in debates over the
proprietary rights to the Holocaust. In both cases, the medium opened
the virtual boundaries that ostensibly separated the programs themselves
from the contexts in which they were created and presented, enabling
complex, multilayered readings of their significance. This openness, in
turn, challenges the notion that the Holocaust ought to—or even can—
be designated as the property of one community to the exclusion of
others.

"An Artist and Only an Artist":
Playing for Time

The wartime experiences of Fania Fénelon, a French Jew who was a member of the orchestra of inmates in the women's camp at Auschwitz, first came to the attention of many Americans in 1978, when a segment of the CBS newsmagazine *60 Minutes* presented a report entitled "The Music of Auschwitz." This profile of Fénelon, which includes a sequence showing her return to the site of the extermination camp, appeared the year after the publication of the English-language translation of her memoir, entitled *Playing for Time*.[11] In the summer of 1979 CBS announced that it would broadcast a dramatization of the memoir, adapted by playwright Arthur Miller, some time in the 1979–1980 season.

The news that Fénelon would be portrayed by Vanessa Redgrave—an actress as well known in the United States for her ardent anti-Zionist, pro-Palestinian political activism as for her performances in films and on the stage—generated extensive protests from Jewish groups and individuals. Among the organizations that denounced the casting of Redgrave were the American Jewish Committee, the Jewish Anti-Defamation League, the Simon Wiesenthal Center for Holocaust Studies, and the Synagogue Council of America; individuals protesting CBS's decision included Fénelon herself, who at one point threatened to sue the network.[12]

Reported to be concerned over the impact of the controversy surrounding Redgrave, CBS postponed the broadcast of *Playing for Time* until the following season. In an effort to avert further negative publicity, the network arranged special preview screenings for Jewish groups. Linda Yellen, the producer of *Playing for Time*, defended the casting of Redgrave as a decision based solely on the actress's artistic talents. Herself the child of Jewish Holocaust survivors, Yellen explained that, while ignorant of Redgrave's politics at the time of the casting, she subsequently saw no reason for dismissing the actress: "That would have been anathema to me, given what I knew about blacklisting and the McCarthy era. I believe her performance is extraordinary, and speaks for itself." On 19 August 1979 *60 Minutes* reaired "The Music of Auschwitz" together with "Vanessa," a profile of Redgrave, first broadcast in April, that focuses on her political activism. These reports were followed by interviews with the two women, in which they discuss the upcoming broadcast of *Playing for Time*.[13]

Despite these efforts, CBS reportedly found it difficult to sell the advertising time available during the broadcast of *Playing for Time*. Sponsors were not only put off by the controversy surrounding Redgrave, but were also loath to feature their products "after scenes which consistently end on such a remarkably low point." The cost of commercial spots during the

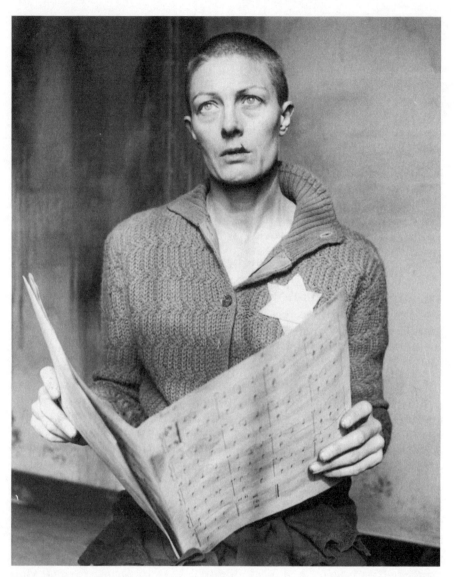

Playing for Time: The casting of Vanessa Redgrave, a controversial activist on behalf of Palestinian nationalism, as the lead in Arthur Miller's 1980 television drama proved more provocative than its subject, the women inmates' orchestra at Auschwitz. (Photofest. © 1983 CBS Inc. All Rights Reserved.)

drama were considered low for prime time, and CBS did not release the names of advertisers sponsoring *Playing for Time* in advance press for the drama, reflecting the network's qualms about generating adverse publicity for its sponsors. Two weeks before the broadcast, twelve actresses who appeared in *Playing for Time* with Redgrave issued a statement voicing their concern that the controversy over her politics had "come to over-shadow the film's content." Asking both Jewish groups and advertising agencies to support the drama, they wrote: "Our varied heritages lead us to feel and to say that all peoples would be proud of this film, and that no one should attempt to defeat a project that can only alert the world to a horror that must never happen again."[14]

Aired on 30 September 1980, *Playing for Time* earned considerable crit-ical praise and, although it was met with protest by Jewish groups at sev-eral local affiliate stations, was viewed by a "wide and enthusiastic audience." Media critics generally lauded Miller's dramatization—"the best script he has written in years"—as well as Daniel Mann's direction and Arthur Ornitz's cinematography, which "cast a gray, subdued spell over the entire production." The cast, which includes Jane Alexander, Marisa Berenson, Shirley Knight, Viveca Lindfors, and Melanie Mayron, also received praise, not only for giving moving performances but also for their commitment to the physical ordeal of being transformed into like-nesses of concentration camp prisoners "with utter authenticity."[15]

The highest of accolades were reserved for Redgrave; critics hailed her portrayal of Fénelon as "remarkable, restrained"; one of "intensity . . . unflagging from beginning to end. Even minor details are mesmerizing"; an effort of "profound force and intelligence." *Newsweek* featured Redgrave, her head shaved and scarred for the role, on its cover during the week of the telecast and presented an extensive profile of her career as activist and artist. Though calling her "the most politically controversial performer of our time," the cover story asserted that "as we watch Redgrave" in the role of Fénelon, "the TV screen seems at last to expand until it frames the shape and fatality of truth"—thereby suggesting that Redgrave's artistry tran-scends her politics.[16]

Reviewers of *Playing for Time* also seem compelled to address the provocative impact of Redgrave's presence in the drama's lead role, even if only to dismiss its significance. The controversy surrounding the produc-tion "cannot detract" from the worthiness of her performance and of the film as a whole, insisted Kay Gardella in the *New York Daily News;* "Fénelon should be proud," Richard Corliss concluded in his review for *Time.* "The various causes of the uproar surrounding this drama are almost irrelevant after one has viewed it," argued Arthur Unger in the *Christian Science Monitor.* John O'Connor, however, wrote in the *New York Times* that the "ironies" surrounding the broadcast "are little short of dizzying." While acknowledging that the network had been "insensitive" with regard to casting Redgrave, the critic observed that those denouncing *Playing for Time* for this reason "find themselves opposing a film of infinitely more sensitivity and power" than the 1978 *Holocaust* miniseries, which many of these detractors had championed.[17]

The Redgrave controversy also prompted a spate of essays on *Playing for Time* in Jewish periodicals, which took umbrage at the actress having been cast as Fénelon. ("Wagner was an artistic genius with an evil mind and so is Vanessa Redgrave," began a notice in AIPAC's *Near East Report*.) Several of these articles recalled, in tones ranging from the ironic to the outraged, the actress's appearance on television a few years earlier in a documentary film on the Palestinians, which Redgrave helped finance, in which she "was shown dancing for the PLO, waving a rifle above her head."[18]

In particular, these articles assailed Miller's unflattering portrayal of a Zionist prisoner as exemplifying the drama's "wrongheaded . . . philosophical interpretations." The author of a letter to *Reconstructionist* stated that "the only Zionist in the script, a minor character in the orchestra, is ridiculed whenever she mentions Israel. . . . I am not surprised that Vanessa Redgrave had so little trouble reconciling her political beliefs with her appearance in 'Playing for Time.'" Although this character was, presumably, scripted by Miller in advance of the casting process, some viewers apparently linked Redgrave's presence as Fénelon to the portrayal of the Zionist character. Such "negative stereotyping provides a clue to the thinking of the people who brought you Vanessa Redgrave in the role of one of the people whose human rights she is even now working to deny," claimed Joseph Hochstein, editor of the *Jewish Week*.[19]

Another critic found the casting of Redgrave to be "in a perverse sense . . . appropriate," analogous to "the Nazis' grotesque use of art in the midst of, indeed as part of, their most monstrous crime." Others similarly dismissed efforts to distinguish Redgrave's performance from her politics; at the same time, these critics rejected other political contextualizations of the Redgrave controversy, which condemned those who denounced her being hired to play Fénelon. After citing Miller's defense of Redgrave's casting— "Turning her down because of her ideas was unacceptable to me; after all, I suffered the [anti-Communist] blacklist myself"—*Hadassah* magazine's critic, Hannah Goodman, concluded that the playwright's argument amounted to "injecting false issues into the controversy . . . , substituting sloganeering for thinking."[20]

Evaluating the merits of *Playing for Time* as an example of Holocaust memory culture or of American television drama was thus enveloped in a debate over proprietary rights to the Holocaust as a moral paradigm. In addition to reexamining the issue of the Holocaust as a specifically Jewish versus universal subject, the debate over the Holocaust as cultural property invoked competing analogies. The discussion both revisited comparisons of the Holocaust with American anti-Communist blacklisting of the McCarthy era, one of the earliest uses of the Holocaust as a moral paradigm, and touched on the more recent invocation of the Holocaust on behalf of Palestinians living under Israeli occupation. Moreover, the discussion of *Playing for Time* generated a metadebate over whether it was legitimate to raise the question of Redgrave's politics in evaluating her, or others', artistic achievements. In this respect, the offscreen dissension surrounding *Playing for Time* resonated with one of the principal conflicts in Miller's script—the clash of sensibilities between Fénelon and Alma Rose (played by Jane Alexander), the niece of Gustav Mahler and leader of the female inmates' orchestra in Auschwitz. Whereas Fénelon agonizes over the moral dilemmas prompted by their situation, Rose insists that, in order to survive the camp, "you will have to be an artist and only an artist. You will have to concentrate on one thing only . . . to create all the beauty you are capable of."[21]

Both *Playing for Time* and its attendant controversy suggest that Rose was mistaken. Works of art are not hermetically sealed off from the contexts in which they are created and presented. Indeed, in the case of the debate surrounding CBS's presentation of Miller's drama, television facilitated the leakage of "life" into "art." The producers' decision to engage Redgrave to play Fénelon engendered a complex interrelationship between the two women, each of whom embodied a complex of personas. Redgrave exemplifies Richard Dyer's observation that a well-known performer's very presence on-screen, invoking previous performances and ongoing public reputation—what Dyer termed the "star text"—contributes to an audience's reading of a performance.[22] Fénelon, while not a star, figured in *Playing for Time* and the debate surrounding it as both a character created by Miller and an actual woman, known to audiences through other public presentations—notably her appearances on *60 Minutes*—and as the author of her memoir. Neither woman could exist, whether in actual life or in the virtual world of the drama, as "only an artist." Just as the action of *Playing for Time* centers around the limits of the artist situated within the Holocaust, the drama's presentation on television tested the limits of creating a work of Holocaust art independent of notions of "proper" and "wrongful" possession of the subject.

"History Doesn't Come Packaged So Neatly": Liberators

More than a decade later, another American television program provoked extensive controversy over the proprietary rights to the Holocaust. In this instance, television facilitated repeated presentations of the program in different venues, and the competing agendas behind these presentations fueled contentions over the proper use and control of the Holocaust as a moral paradigm.

Liberators: Fighting on Two Fronts in World War II, a documentary film produced by William Miles and Nina Rosenblum, was first aired on 11 November 1992 as part of the PBS series *The American Experience. Liberators* recounts the experiences of African-American soldiers who fought in Europe during World War II, among whose missions was the liberation of Nazi concentration camps. For the most part, the documentary examines the struggles of African-Americans in the armed forces during World War II. At this time the United States military was segregated; African-Americans were largely restricted to menial support assignments and were barred from becoming officers or engaging in combat. *Liberators* situates this issue in the larger context of race relations in the United States during the middle decades of the twentieth century. The documentary also calls attention to the contribution that the achievements of individual African-American servicemen and all-black military units made toward the eventual integration of the U.S. Armed Forces, at the order of President Truman in 1948, and the postwar civil rights movement.

Using vintage images and recent interviews with African-American veterans, *Liberators* chronicles the wartime experiences of two all-black units, the 761st Tank Battalion and the 183rd Combat Engineers. The documentary presents these units' participation in the liberation of Buchenwald and Dachau, among their final wartime actions, as a transformative encounter for the soldiers; one veteran describes the experience as "the shock of my life."[23] Jewish Holocaust survivors, in turn, variously describe their encounters with African-American liberators as meeting "black giants," "angels," and "givers of life." *Liberators* highlights the liberation of concentration camps as galvanizing the African-American soldiers' personal experiences of discrimination and enriching their larger understanding of racism in the United States.

Even before its completion, Miles and Rosenblum presented *Liberators* not merely as the documentation of a moment in history, but as a moral exemplar that would offer contemporary audiences powerful instruction on the evils of intolerance and provide Americans with an ennobling model of interethnic fellowship. One of the first public screenings of a portion of the documentary took place on 30 April 1992, as part of a public program offered by the Jewish Museum of New York in conjunction with its exhibition "Bridges and Boundaries: African Americans and American Jews."[24] Among those who spoke at the event were the documentary's producers, as well as several of the veterans and Holocaust survivors who appear in the film. Also present was basketball player Kareem Abdul-Jabbar, one of a

Liberators: Holocaust survivor Benjamin Bender (center) returns to Buchenwald with E.
G. McConnell (left) and Leonard "Smitty" Smith (right), two African-American veterans
of World War II, in this 1992 documentary. Photographer: Simon Chaput. (© Simon
Chaput. Reprinted with permission.)

group of producers who had acquired the dramatic rights to *Liberators,*
and it was announced that they were planning to make a television movie
based on the documentary.[25]

The focal event of the public program was the screening of a rough cut
of a scene from *Liberators.* Filmed in 1991, it shows E. G. McConnell and
Leonard Smith, two veterans of the 761st Tank Battalion, and Benjamin
Bender, a Jewish Holocaust survivor, visiting the grounds of Buchenwald,
where Bender had been interned as a young man. He recounts to the two
former GIs his memories of liberation and recalls his grief on discovering
that his brother, also a prisoner in Buchenwald, had died shortly before the
arrival of Allied troops. The three men are shown examining different areas

of the former concentration camp, including the crematorium and a room where prisoners were hanged. McConnell and Smith recall their reactions to encountering the evidence of these atrocities, which they describe as "the ultimate end of slavery" and "lynching by the dozens." At the end of the scene, Bender walks away from the two veterans to leave a small bouquet of flowers at the site of one of the barracks.

In their remarks at the public program, the filmmakers and those who appear in the documentary reiterated their conviction that *Liberators* presented contemporary Americans with a powerful moral lesson on the importance of fighting prejudice and promoting interracial harmony. This message not only resonated with the subject of the museum's exhibition, but was also charged with a special urgency in light of recent local events. On 19 August 1991 interethnic violence had broken out in the Brooklyn neighborhood of Crown Heights, when an automobile driven by Yosef Lifish, a twenty-two-year-old Lubavitcher Hasid, accidentally struck and killed Gavin Cato, a seven-year-old Caribbean-American boy and injured another black child. In the course of an ensuing riot that erupted in response to the automobile crash, a twenty-nine-year-old Hasid, Yankel Rosenbaum, was fatally stabbed; sixteen-year-old Lemrick Nelson Jr., a Caribbean-American, was arrested in connection with this attack. Random rioting and organized public demonstrations in Crown Heights continued throughout the week, involving hundreds of people and eventually resulting in dozens of arrests.[26]

After the violence and demonstrations ceased, questions arose regarding the response of New York mayor David Dinkins and the police department to the hostilities; some voiced dissatisfaction with the legal actions brought against Lifish, who was not indicted by a grand jury, or those brought against Rosenbaum's attackers. Many people outside the neighborhood came to identify the Crown Heights incident as emblematic of a deterioration in the relations between blacks and Jews, or of the city's interethnic strife in general. More than one speaker at the Jewish Museum's preview of *Liberators* invoked Crown Heights in their remarks to the audience.

The contentions surrounding the Crown Heights incident resurged at the end of October 1992, when a jury found Nelson not guilty of killing Rosenbaum. Mayor Dinkins, the object of sustained criticism for his handling of the riots, chose a gala honoring *Liberators* to defend his record on combating anti-Semitism and to express his sorrow over Rosenbaum's death. Speaking at the documentary's world premiere screening at Lincoln Center on 9 November, the mayor officially declared the day "Liberators Day in New York" and then commented on the connection between the subject of the film and recent events. He invited the audience to consider the premiere of *Liberators* as "a step along the road to mutual understanding and respect. And when we see those brave African American soldiers freeing Jewish prisoners of concentration camps, let us remember all that binds us together."[27]

Two days later, *Liberators* received its national broadcast premiere on PBS. Reviews were generally favorable —"an eloquent, frequently riveting work," "a remarkably illuminating documentary"—and in several instances, critics remarked on the value of its message for a racially divided New York. Praising *Liberators* as "a searing history told with formidable eloquence," *Wall Street Journal* critic Dorothy Rabinowitz commented that it was "a pity someone didn't show that to the crowds of black men running through Crown Heights last year yelling 'Hitler was right' and 'Kill the Jews.'"[28]

In an unusual programming decision, *Liberators* was rebroadcast locally on New York City's public television station WNET (Channel 13) only a few weeks after its original, nationwide presentation. On 17 December 1992 the documentary was incorporated into an evening-long live telecast of a public program convened at the Apollo Theater in Harlem. Devoted to "healing racial wounds and tensions" in New York City, the program was organized by prominent African-American and Jewish activists, with Reverend Jesse Jackson playing a leading role, and was underwritten by Time Warner, Inc. In conjunction with this special broadcast of *Liberators,* volunteers from Mayor Dinkins's office circulated among organized groups of viewers, who gathered "in synagogues, churches, community centers and private homes" throughout the city, in order to "facilitate group discussions. A special [telephone] hot line was established to assist residents who needed assistance in organizing community forums to discuss the significant implications of the film and its positive effect on racial tensions."[29]

The public program at the Apollo Theater was attended by an audience of twelve hundred; among them were leading figures of New York's African-American and Jewish communities, such as Reverend Al Sharpton, activist Betty Shabazz, New York's former mayor Abraham Beame, and financier Felix Rohatyn. The presence of consuls from the missions to the United Nations of Germany, Israel, and Jamaica was also publicly acknowledged. The program began with speeches from, among others, Mayor Dinkins, Congressman Charles B. Rangel, District Attorney Robert Morgenthau, Reverend Jackson, and, via videotape, Elie Wiesel.

Speakers repeatedly invoked *Liberators* as embodying a valuable lesson for contemporary New Yorkers. Dinkins commented that "images and words have been used to great harm; our task is to use images and words to heal."[30] Morgenthau, who proclaimed the event to be a "night of remembrance and reconciliation," said that the documentary "speaks volumes about racism in the United States," reminds viewers of the "unspeakable horrors of the Nazi regime," and, "most of all, speaks to our common human bonds." Jackson hailed *Liberators* as a "great story of shared suffering. . . . The bond between liberators and Holocaust survivors is an American treasure." He endorsed the presentation of the documentary as "a vehicle for reconciliation," saying, "The walls that came down in Dachau and Buchenwald must not be resurrected in Crown Heights or any place."[31]

Liberators was then screened in its entirety for the Apollo Theater audience, simultaneous with its broadcast on WNET; at the conclusion of the documentary, the live telecast from the Apollo resumed on the PBS station. Producers Miles and Rosenblum addressed the audience, and some of the Holocaust survivors and African-American veterans appearing in the film were introduced. It was announced that plans were under way to distribute copies of the documentary on videotape, along with study guides, to every junior and senior high school in New York City. "Every child must see this," Jackson urged. In a closing prayer, Reverend James A. Forbes, of New York City's Riverside Church, proclaimed, "We have been gathered in this place by history. . . . We pray that what we have seen will remain in our spirits."

A tent was pitched outside the Apollo Theater so that, following the program, members of the audience could "dialogue" about the film and the city's problems while partaking of a "kosher/soul food party."[32] WNET followed the conclusion of the program at the Apollo with a special installment of *Neighbor to Neighbor,* a local public-affairs program, broadcast live from the station's New York studio. The program, moderated by talk-show host Charlie Rose, featured a panel of local African-American, Jewish, and other civic leaders who debated solutions to the city's interethnic tensions.

The televised presentation of *Liberators* at the Apollo Theater, together with its attendant speeches and additional programming, testifies to television's special ability to incorporate other media — including other telecasts — and re-mediate them in different contexts, thereby enriching, controverting, or otherwise transforming their significance. Echoing the documentary's evocation of witnessing the liberation of Nazi concentration camps as a morally transforming experience, the program at the Apollo Theater hailed the act of collective witnessing and metawitnessing of *Liberators* as a catalyst for changes in consciousness and behavior. Thus, Peggy Tishman, a former president of the Jewish Community Relations Council and one of the evening's hosts, exhorted the audience to "symbolically re-enact" the black soldiers' liberation of concentration camps, an act "of reconciliation and brotherhood."[33]

However, reactions to the program at the Apollo Theater revealed a sense that this singular presentation of *Liberators* would have less than the desired impact on its audience. The first page of the "Metro" section of the *New York Times* on 19 December bore the headline, "After a Night of Unity at the Apollo, Optimism Wavers." The article following featured interviews with some of the participants in the Apollo program—many of whom acknowledged it as a genuinely moving experience—who nonetheless characterized its effectiveness "in the colder light of day" as being limited at best. Significantly, they expressed these sentiments in language that implicitly equated the evening's dramatic, mediated format with a lack of substance, variously describing it as "a catharsis," "just cosmetic," "mostly 'symbolism,'" "a circus," "an extravaganza," "a media bite."[34] The detractors of the public program at the Apollo Theater were less ready, or willing, to attribute the shortcomings of the event to other possible factors. Besides avoiding any potentially problematic aspects of the presentation itself, the critics cited did not address the complex and divisive cultural and political dynamic between New York City's blacks and Jews—in particular, the black and Jewish communities in Crown Heights—that this act of witnessing was intended to transform.[35]

Several weeks after the public program at the Apollo Theater and its citywide telecast, *Liberators* was once again at the center of a controversy. At the same time that the documentary was nominated for an Academy Award, questions were raised about the veracity of the film's depiction of the 761st Tank Battalion as liberators of Dachau and of the 183rd Combat Engineers' role in liberating Buchenwald. Doubts about *Liberators* were voiced in articles in the *New York Guardian* and the *Jewish Press* and on WBAI-FM by radio host Jim Dingman; journalist Jeffrey Goldberg pursued the story in articles for the *Forward* and the *New Republic*.[36]

According to Goldberg, historian Robert Abzug found *Liberators* and its eponymous companion volume to have "violated" his sense of "historical accuracy." Although Abzug is listed in the documentary's credits as an advisor, he told Goldberg that the producers never contacted him regarding their research; moreover, he felt that the filmmakers had been "taken in by the romance of the thing."[37] Goldberg also cited interviews with some survivors of the camps in question, who reported that "they were no longer sure when they first saw black soldiers." Similarly, some African-American veterans of the two units in question expressed various doubts about the timing or extent of their presence at the camps.

Goldberg wrote that the focus of *Liberators* on these events of questionable veracity seemed "all the more perplexing" in light of the uncontested achievements of the all-black units, which include the 761st Battalion's liberation of Gunskirchen, a small concentration camp near Mauthausen. He also reported that filmmaker Rosenblum "angrily denounced the film's critics as Holocaust deniers and racists," and he noted that despite these questions about its accuracy, *Liberators* was still supported by "a number of influential Jews." Among these was Peggy Tishman, one of the organizers of the program at the Apollo Theater, who questioned the motives of those

who "want to exploit the idea that [*Liberators*] is a fraud. . . . We're trying
. . . to make New York a better place for you and me to live. . . . There are
a lot of truths that are necessary. This is not a truth that's necessary."[38]

In February 1993, WNET, which helped produce *Liberators,* first issued
a statement asserting its "absolute confidence in the veracity" of the documentary. But shortly thereafter, the station announced its plans to with-
draw the film from further circulation, pending a review of its accuracy.
This decision was prompted in part by a report prepared for the American
Jewish Committee by Kenneth Stern, who found the claims that the 761st
and 183rd had liberated Dachau or Buchenwald to be considerably out-
weighed by evidence to the contrary.[39]

In September 1993 WNET announced that the review board, which it
had convened to scrutinize *Liberators*, had concluded that "the film's
account of the liberation of Dachau and Buchenwald was seriously
flawed." According to U.S. Army records, the review board reported, neither battalion was in the vicinity of the two camps on their dates of liberation. While some members of the units may have visited the camps during
the days following, they did not meet the military's criterion for being designated liberators, which is restricted to "those units that arrived within 48
hours of the initial Allied penetration of the camp." WNET explained that
these and other "factual inaccuracies" found in the documentary would
have to be corrected before *Liberators* would be shown again on PBS. The
station also announced the institution of a new policy "requiring producers
to demonstrate proof of their claims before financing is provided. . . . The
station's contracts would also be amended to specifically make producers
responsible for the content of their films."[40]

Some observers have assessed the *Liberators* controversy as a "clash of
good intentions and journalistic procedures." Documentary filmmaker
Morton Silverstein, who oversaw the review process for WNET, faulted
Miles and Rosenblum for a "paucity of research" and noted that they had
depended too much on the oral histories of informants who were "hazy
about details." Other observers have noted that the connection of the documentary with the provocative subject of contemporary black-Jewish relations and "the sacred nature of Holocaust history" turned the controversy
surrounding *Liberators* into an ideologically driven issue. Following the
report of WNET's review of the documentary, Goldberg characterized the
film as a wrong-minded effort "to make a social and policy point." As a
result of the filmmakers' "honest desire" to ameliorate black-Jewish relations, he argued, "they left the track a bit. . . . It was all too pretty a pack-
age. History doesn't come packaged so neatly." Rosenblum and Miles
rejected WNET's findings and accused the station of censorship. The
review process, they stated, "only serves to denigrate the courageous concentration camp survivors and their heroic liberators."[41]

The controversy surrounding *Liberators* is, in part, illustrative of a much larger tension between those who view documentaries as bearers of "truth and objectivity" and those who see them as vehicles for defining "the most important issues for public debate" and bringing about "positive social change."[42] At the same time, this controversy constitutes a case study in the debate surrounding the proprietary rights to the Holocaust. Some commentators have questioned the filmmakers' motives for linking the story of the experience of African-American servicemen during World War II to the Holocaust. Richard Cohen wrote in the *Washington Post* that this chapter of the "African American experience . . . has a power independent" of any such connection. Yet in an essay for the *Forward,* Joel Lewis wondered whether *Liberators* would have "received as much public attention" if it had not focused on the all-black units as liberators of Dachau and Buchenwald. Lewis argued that the film's presentation of liberation as a "bond" between African-Americans and American Jews is "a little naive." It is "not evidence of two communities' unity; it is simply a poignant fact of our shared history."[43] Cohen, who "laments the controversy" surrounding *Liberators,* agreed that the role of the African-American servicemen was misrepresented: "They were not off on some humanitarian mission on behalf of imperiled or doomed Jews. . . . They were functioning as American GIs."

With regard to the questions raised about the veracity of *Liberators,* Cohen argued that "it hardly matters" whether some or all of the soldiers in the all-black units were liberators of Dachau and Buchenwald. Abzug, however, expressed concerns that the inaccuracies in *Liberators* might "become fodder for the Holocaust-denial folks." Others also attached greater weight to this issue, arguing that "the moral edifice embodied in remembrance can crumble if history is handled casually, or distorted to fit current needs — and nothing having to do with the places whose names resonate with the century's worst crimes can be dismissed as a 'detail.'"[44] News reports and opinion pieces about the documentary's factual accuracy frequently mentioned the use of *Liberators* as a symbol of or catalyst for black/Jewish solidarity, citing its screening at the Apollo Theater on 17 December 1992 or the plans announced then to distribute the film to New York City schools. In doing so, reporters and commentators linked the issue of the propriety of Holocaust memory culture — the exceptional challenge of its proper representation as a singular "moral edifice" — with that of proprietary rights to the Holocaust, that is, the question of its appropriateness as a paradigm for other subjects.

The connection between these two contentions was forged in the content and structure of *Liberators* and then strengthened by the unusual series of contexts in which the documentary was presented. The Holocaust figures in the documentary, as its full title indicates, as part of the story of the liberators — who were themselves the victims of oppression — as opposed to the story of the liberated. As *Liberators* situates the Holocaust primarily as an event within African-American, rather than Jewish, history, liberation marks a triumphant moment prized by many African-American soldiers as a demonstration that their skills, bravery, and patriotism were indistinguishable from those of white Americans. This conflicts with the significance of liberation for many American Jewish viewers, regardless of their feelings toward the African-American community, as the moment that confirmed the catastrophic loss of families, communities, and entire cultures.

The central role into which *Liberators* was cast for the 17 December 1992 program at the Apollo Theater further complicated the documentary's significance as a contested invocation of the Holocaust as a moral paradigm, as did the controversy surrounding the documentary's accuracy. This also challenged the notion of the Holocaust as "sacred history" by raising questions about the status of eyewitnesses to the Holocaust and the trustworthiness of their testimony. According to Goldberg, Abzug had advised the publisher of the book version of *Liberators* "to put some sort of cautionary statement in the introductions about the nature of war stories and the way veterans recall war stories," but his advice was not taken.[45] Military records not only contradicted the recollections of liberators, who had attained a privileged status both as eyewitnesses to the evidence of Nazi atrocities and as embodiments of America's point of contact with the Holocaust, but also challenged the testimony of Holocaust survivors, including such prestigious figures as Samuel Pisar and Elie Wiesel, who both recalled seeing African-American soldiers when liberated from Dachau and Buchenwald, respectively.[46]

The presentations and discussions of *Liberators* exemplify how television facilitates the dissemination of a program via broadcast and (potentially, in this case) videocassette distribution and thereby transforms its significance through repeated public showings in shifting contexts. At its broadcast premiere, *Liberators* was presented on Veterans Day as part of the PBS series *The American Experience*, which has offered independently produced documentaries since 1988 on topics ranging from profiles of Duke Ellington and the Kennedy family to histories of the Last Stand at Little Big Horn and the amusement parks of Coney Island. *The American Experience* contextualized *Liberators* as a work of general American interest, one of a multicultural family of works validating the loyalty and accomplishments of the nation's diverse citizenry. Aired on Veterans Day, the documentary also paid implicit tribute to military service as a patriotic act and to the armed services as a proving ground for one's worthiness as an American citizen.

In contrast, the special rebroadcast of *Liberators* as part of the public program held at the Apollo Theater situated the documentary as an exceptional work of particular interest to two local minority communities at an especially tense moment in their relationship. Within the context of a larger special event that was broadcast live, watching *Liberators* was endowed with a sense of urgent value for the immediate present. The organizers of the evening at the Apollo tied the act of viewing the documentary on television, which is generally a private experience, to its being seen by the spectators gathered at the Harlem theater. These public viewers, whose ranks included prominent government figures and respected leaders of both the black and Jewish communities, became, in turn, the objects of watching as well. As part of the public spectacle televised from the Apollo Theater, these African-Americans and Jews came together, honored and embraced each other, "dialogued" under one roof, and ate each other's ethnic foods. The broadcast extended the symbolic power of this performance to the dozens of viewing groups set up around the city that evening as well as to thousands of private viewers. Moreover, this special broadcast's galvanizing impact was envisioned as an experience to be continually replicated, facilitated by the distribution of videocassettes of *Liberators* to New York public schools.

The champions of *Liberators* regarded the television set as an essential tool for forging a vital and enduring link between New York's African-Americans and Jews. It is impossible to know to what extent *Liberators* might have succeeded in imparting the lesson that its producers and supporters envisioned had the controversy over its accuracy not led to its withdrawl from circulation. However, by virtue of its content, the history of its public presentation, and the contentious discussions it engendered, the documentary has offered other lessons—albeit more complex and less comforting ones. These lessons concern the differences between contemporary African-American and American Jewish sensibilities and the challenges of using the Holocaust (and, by extension, other historical events) as a moral paradigm to resolve such disparities. The problem posed by *Liberators* is exemplified by the scene of the visit to Buchenwald by Bender, McConnell, and Smith, which points up the disparities between their wartime experiences as it shows the men struggling to acknowledge the very different meanings that the visit has for the others. Indeed, this use of returning to the site of liberation in order to promote fraternal bonds between African-Americans and American Jews also proves as powerful a demonstration of the gap between the two groups' understandings of the Holocaust.

Video Heads

Television's influence on American Holocaust memory culture has become so pervasive that it now informs other forms of Holocaust remembrance.

As scholars of the medium have suggested, television can be thought of as more than the proliferation of broadcasts; it can be conceptualized as a cultural force or sensibility rooted in the medium's distinctive properties and in the roles that it plays in modern life. Thus, scholars have variously characterized television as a "cultural forum," "gathering place," or "electronic hearth" and have described it as fulfilling a "ritual" or "bardic" role in contemporary culture. Moreover, the "imbrication" of television's distinctive intimacy, immediacy, ubiquity, and flow "into the textures of daily life" can be found in a wide variety of cultural phenomenon.[47]

Contemporary Holocaust memory culture offers a number of examples in which approaches to remembrance reflect the distinctive sensibility of Holocaust television or are debated along lines of argument as framed by discussions of this genre. For example, Jewish singles tours of Poland, which include visits to Holocaust landmarks, invite participants to realize the dramatic trope of finding romance in the wake of genocide, a trope encountered repeatedly in works of Holocaust television from the presentation of Hanna Kohner's life story on *This Is Your Life* (1953) and Rod Serling's Warsaw Ghetto drama *In the Presence of Mine Enemies* (1960) to more recent dramas and documentaries. The controversy during the mid-1990s over plans to build a shopping mall adjacent to the grounds of the former extermination camp at Auschwitz echoed the running debates about the problematic proximity of commercials to televised Holocaust dramas and news reports. As anthropologist Jack Kugelmass has observed of the ethnic "rites" of many late-twentieth-century American Jews, including their Holocaust memory culture, "Rather than television replicating culture, it is culture that replicates the world of television."[48]

The broader impact of television as a cultural force on American Holocaust remembrance is most elaborately illustrated by two major Holocaust museums that opened their doors to the public in 1993: the United States Holocaust Memorial Museum in Washington, D.C., and Beit Hashoah/Museum of Tolerance in Los Angeles. In addition to television's influence on defining the notion of what constitutes an artifact in these institutions, the medium figures in their installations as an iconic presence and a narrative sensibility.

Both museums, especially the one in Washington, have proved to be widely popular attractions and have become the subject of extensive discussion.[49] Yet, while scholars and critics often mention the prominence of media in the institutions' displays, little has been said about the implications of these installations beyond either a general admiration for this "state-of-the-art approach" to exhibition planning or, conversely, a derision of the application of media technology to the Holocaust as *"Shoah* business."[50]

Like many other museums, these two employ video displays in part as a response to ongoing concerns within museology. Increasingly, as museums have pursued a range of alternatives to the traditional exhibition of material artifacts, the use of video displays has become more common. Their functions within museum display have grown more complex, ranging from presenting vintage footage as a historical artifact to offering viewers curatorial interpretation in the form of short documentaries or interactive video displays.[51] The use of media in the Washington and Los Angeles Holocaust museums also raises concerns specific to their subject, including the choice of materials used to represent the Holocaust and the challenge of relating the subject's complex and disturbing narrative in the museum setting.

Media displays are prominent in both museums' installations. There are approximately one hundred screens of various sizes and formats, including interactive monitors, in the main installation of the Washington museum and that many, if not more, in the Los Angeles museum. But the impact of television as a cultural force in the new Holocaust museums extends beyond the presence of numerous monitors. Indeed, the considerable differences between the two institutions' approaches to representing the Holocaust can be described, to a considerable degree, in terms of the distinctions between their respective televisual sensibilities.

In many respects the approach to representing the Holocaust in the Washington museum resembles the conventions of a historical documentary, especially with regard to the aesthetics of authority. Built with private funds on land donated by the United States government and now run under federal auspices, the museum carries the authoritative weight of a national institution, situated among the capital's central monuments, government buildings, and cultural repositories. The aesthetics of the Washington museum's architecture (critic Edward Norden described James Ingo Freed's otherwise much-praised design as "self-consciously highbrow") and the design of its installation (by Ralph Appelbaum Associates) are uniform in their gravity and dignity of form, from the building's facade to the choice of typefaces for display panels and captions.[52]

The solemn sensibility of the Washington museum's design extends to the use throughout the building and installations of somber tones, predominantly gray and black. This recalls the aesthetic convention that motivated critics to fault the 1978 *Holocaust* miniseries for its use of color as being inappropriately "picture-postcard pretty" or "garish." The museum's palette also resembles Steven Spielberg's decision to film *Schindler's List* in black and white. Inspired by the tones of vintage photographs and footage of the era, the director described this choice as being appropriate to "the real experience" of Holocaust representation: "I've never seen the Holocaust in color. I don't know what Auschwitz looks like in color. Even though I was there, it's still black and white in my eyes."[53]

The main exhibition within the Washington museum building—which also houses archival and educational resource centers, an auditorium, special exhibition spaces, and a chapel-like Hall of Remembrance—occupies three floors. Using a running narrative in the form of text panels and an extensive assemblage of vintage images, documents, and material relics (clothing, utensils, architectural elements, etc.), this section of the museum presents the "Holocaust story" in an authoritatively univocal, linear, largely chronological fashion. This reflects the institution's emphasis, according to museum director Jeshajahu Weinberg, on "attempting to tell comprehensively the story of the historical events to which [its] collections . . . relate," thereby distinguishing it from "most traditional history museums, which usually . . . collect, preserve, and selectively display objects relating to history," rather than striving to "teach history."[54]

Unlike most museums, which allow visitors considerable freedom of movement among their various displays, Washington's Holocaust museum obliges visitors to its main exhibition to proceed along a prescribed route through its three floors, starting at the top and working their way down. Historian Hans Kellner has argued that the "linear narrative force" of such representations of the Holocaust reinforce the notion of its magnitude: "Great events have great causes, and chance is unacceptable on moral grounds."[55] Indeed, the controlled, linear, largely chronological route of the exhibition simulates the narrative line of a conventional historical documentary—a reflection, perhaps, of the professional sensibilities of Martin Smith and Raye Farr, the two principal planners of the Washington museum's main exhibition. Smith and Farr, both documentary filmmakers, had previously worked on *The World at War* (1974), a twenty-six-episode series chronicling World War II, produced by Thames Television. The two filmmakers also collaborated on *The Struggles for Poland* (1988), a documentary series on Polish history produced by an international consortium, which included a segment (*A Different World*, directed by Farr) on Polish Jewry through 1943.[56]

Aspects of the design of the Washington museum's main installation reinforce the visitor's sense of walking through a historical documentary film; some design elements are particularly evocative of television watching. After arriving in the museum, for example, visitors watch a short video "preview" of the main exhibition—similar to a promotion of "coming attractions" before a television broadcast—on monitors installed in the elevators that transport museum-goers up to the beginning of the exhibition. While the main installation is extensive, its scale encourages an intimate encounter with the displays as they unfold along narrow passageways. The size of the type on the extensive item labels and text panels is small, drawing the visitor close, as does the placement of most television monitors and video screens, which accommodate only a small number of viewers at a time.[57] Barriers prevent younger visitors to the exhibition from seeing some of the more graphic footage on display—such as Nazi medical experiments performed on concentration camp inmates, mass executions by *Einsatzgruppen,* and the exhumation of mass graves following the Allied liberation of camps— which also allow adult visitors to choose to avoid these images. The effect of these barriers resembles another distinctive feature of television watching: the warnings posted before some broadcasts that a program "contains material that may be unsuitable for children and other sensitive viewers."

If the sensibility of the Holocaust museum in Washington resembles a somber, authoritative, historical documentary, Beit Hashoah/Museum of Tolerance, built and operated under the auspices of the Simon Wiesenthal Center in Los Angeles, seems more inspired by the idiom of "tabloid" television news programs and other emotionally charged media genres. Well before the museum opened to the public, its organizers' plans to exploit "the intersection of Hollywood and the Holocaust" were the subject of considerable controversy. Indeed, Rabbi Marvin Hier, the founder and director of the Wiesenthal Center, was unusually forthright in his embrace of media as critical to the realization of his institution's educational goals: "Young people today don't read, . . . so you have to give them information about this period and its moral lessons in a form that they are used to receiving it—the tube."[58]

While the two main sections of the Los Angeles museum—the Tolerancenter and Beit Hashoah—make extensive use of media, each draws on different aspects of television as a cultural force according to its particular agenda. The Tolerancenter, the first section of the museum that visitors are directed to after their arrival, is set up somewhat like a video-game arcade. Museum-goers circulate among a variety of displays in this "workshop of human behavior," which is designed to call visitors' attention to how "we are bombarded with messages that enforce negative attitudes toward certain people" as part of the "American experience." By calling visitors' attention to these "building blocks of hatred," the Tolerancenter strives to promote "tolerance through education."[59]

This section of the Los Angeles museum focuses on questions of tolerance—or, more accurately, intolerance—in contemporary American life, rather than during the Holocaust. Almost all of the displays in the Tolerancenter rely on some form of electronic technology, and many of them are interactive. ("This is not a place for observation at a distance," explains the museum's guidebook.)[60] Interactive video screens enable visitors to access computerized databases through a series of menus. For example, the display entitled "The Other America" provides information on various "hate groups" (the Ku Klux Klan, neo-Nazis, white supremacists, etc.) that are active throughout the United States, including details on their locations and activities.

A more elaborate use of touch-screen technology is applied to the Tolerancenter's display on the Los Angeles riots of 1992. Looting and violence erupted in neighborhoods throughout the city on 29 April of that year in response to a verdict acquitting four white members of the Los Angeles Police Department of brutalizing an African-American, Rodney King, when the officers arrested him in 1991. The display provides a brief film about the riots, which replays a videotape of King's beating (an amateur recording that figured as a crucial piece of evidence in the officers' trials), related television news coverage, and timelines tracing the course of events from King's arrest through the city's response to the ensuing riots. The display also poses a series of multiple-choice questions to visitors, asking for their opinions about the cause and nature of the riots ("Can the beating of Rodney King ever be justified? Did the looting look like fun? Were store owners right to take up arms?"). A computer program instantly tabulates each visitor's responses to these questions and displays statistics that "show how your feelings compare with those of other people."[61] This device, which includes basic demographic information on respondents' race and sex, resembles flash polls on topical issues presented on nightly news telecasts.

There are dozens of television monitors in the Tolerancenter. Not only do they facilitate the display of information (for example, a short documentary on the American civil rights movement), but their mass presence becomes iconic, reinforcing the museum's agenda of calling to visitors' attention the extent to which "media images" shape "our attitudes" about different groups of people. A multiscreen display in the Tolerancenter flashes the message "Who is responsible?" and the reply "You are" in over a dozen different languages across a wall of about fifty monitors. Beneath these is an additional row of television screens, which provide an indication of what constitutes "responsibility" in this context by displaying black-and-white footage of public demonstrations for a range of unidentified social causes from around the world.

Near the entrance to the Tolerancenter, an anthropomorphic sculpture composed of nine television screens introduces museum-goers to "The Manipulator," who serves as "your 'charming' video host" while visiting this section of the museum. This character, enacted by an unidentified young white male performer, appears on these and other screens located throughout the section. The Manipulator serves as "an ongoing reminder" of the ability of the mass media he embodies to "entic[e] you into a state where he can easily direct and control you. . . . The Manipulator assumes he has caught you in his web of words and that you are now in his power. . . . His voice echoes periodically in the exhibit area, constantly challenging and provoking your thoughts." In another display, Video Heads—white plastic sculptures of stylized human bodies with television monitors instead of heads—present the inner thoughts of archetypal role models (named Joe Cool, Miss Uptight, and Mr. Normal) on their screens. Their "on-screen thought processes . . . reflect the heavy influence of advertising and other media."[62] While these uses of the television monitor as a compositional element of the human figure bear some formal resemblance to Nam June Paik's avant-garde video sculptures of the 1970s and 1980s, they also embody the worst fears of the Frankfurt School and their followers regarding the power of mass media.[63] In these Tolerancenter sculptures, television transmission and individual reception are completely fused. The human head has become one with the broadcasting receiver, and its brain has been replaced by videotape.

At the same time that the Tolerancenter presents the cultural force of television as a leading culprit in fostering intergroup prejudice, this section of the museum also displays the media as a strategic vehicle for the defeat of intolerance. The Global Situation Room, a "state-of-the-art newsroom connected to international news services, news wires and electronic research networks," monitors "the activities of human rights violations" around the world. Through a glass wall museum-goers can watch—but not interact with—staffers working at computer terminals, handling videotape cassettes, and so on. Outside the room, television monitors replay recent news telecasts and display wire service stories on "bigotry, anti-Semitism, prejudice, and intolerance around the globe."[64]

After leaving the Tolerancenter, visitors to the Los Angeles museum proceed to the section called Beit Hashoah (Hebrew for "the house of the Holocaust"). This section resembles the main installation of the Washington museum in that it, too, relates a chronological overview of the Holocaust as a unified and discrete historical event. Yet while similar events—*Kristallnacht,* the Wansee Conference, and the Warsaw Ghetto uprising, among others—are invoked to articulate the Holocaust's master narrative, the differences between the visitor's encounters with this narrative in the Washington and Los Angeles museums are striking. A visit to Beit Hashoah constitutes an even stronger simulation of walking through a documentary film. Here, there are no text panels or item labels; instead, the pace at which museum-goers proceed through the installation is controlled by a running audio narration and coordinated lighting system, which illuminates and dims successive dioramas within this section of the museum, thereby compelling groups of visitors to move through the exhibition at a predetermined, uniform pace.

In Beit Hashoah's installation, the implicitly single, authoritative voice of the text panel is replaced by a trio of voices, who are introduced at the beginning of the Beit Hashoah tour. They are anonymous museum personnel — a designer, a researcher, and a historian — represented by stylized white plastic figures. Periodically these figures appear throughout this section of the museum to explain to visitors something of the decision-making process involved in creating the installation, also providing information on the source materials (photographs, documents, etc.) drawn upon for the creation of the displays. The use of these figures resembles the reflexivity of some documentaries and news reports, in which the filmmakers or journalists call viewers' attention to the process by which the final work is realized and incorporate this awareness of process into the product.

The sense that the visitor has entered the virtual world of a documentary is enhanced by the creation of dioramas, such as a café in Berlin circa 1932, that are painted in various shades of gray, thereby placing visitors in the black-and-white world of the Holocaust. Other sections of the exhibition, however, make powerful use of color, such as a wraparound screen that presents footage from *Triumph of the Will* and then surrounds museumgoers with red, black, and white Nazi flags. In contrast to the Washington museum — where the aesthetic recalls the muted sobriety of the *World at War* series — Beit Hashoah resembles the more emotionally sensational and visually adventuresome *Genocide,* the Wiesenthal Center's 1982 Academy Award-winning documentary film on the Holocaust.[65]

Unlike the Washington museum's main installation, Beit Hashoah does not incorporate material relics of the Holocaust — letters, works of art, utensils, articles of clothing, weapons, religious articles, and so on — in its historical narrative display. Insted, these items are exhibited in a separate section of the Los Angeles museum. Named "They Will Always Be Heard: Artifacts and Documents of the Holocaust," this room displays its contents in glass cases with label captions, and — in an ironic twist, given the section's name — a complete absence of recorded sound as well as any display of moving images. The isolation of these materials indicates the vestigial status accorded to "original" artifacts in a museum whose sensibility is driven by the media. The separate display of these items in what amounts to a reliquary chamber also testifies to the problematic status of artifacts related to the Holocaust in particular, which, besides providing "evidence of the unspeakable," can become the objects of what some consider a "morbid fascination with this century's most absolute evil."[66]

Other Holocaust displays employ different strategies for presenting original artifacts. The Washington museum incorporates relics into its main installation according to a variety of approaches, ranging from massed displays—a heap of books banned by the Third Reich, a cluster of concentration camp uniforms, a floor strewn with thousands of shoes confiscated from prisoners in Majdanek—to individual items, such as one of the milk cans buried by historian Emmanuel Ringelblum to preserve documentation of life and death in the Warsaw Ghetto—displayed as though they were artworks, isolated on pedestals or in separate vitrines. In contrast, the section devoted to the Holocaust in New York's Museum of Jewish Heritage, which opened in 1997, contextualizes original artifacts within its presentation of the Holocaust master narrative by displaying them with videotapes of testimony by survivors, who in some instances discuss these artifacts and their personal attachment to them.[67]

Video displays of vintage images do appear throughout Beit Hashoah, usually as rear projections onto screens that are integrated into the dioramas. Here their distinction as video presentations is less conspicuous than in the Tolerancenter, where the television screen figures as an iconic presence. A remarkable exception is in the Hall of Testimony, one of the final sections of Beit Hashoah. Made of rough concrete, the space evokes the interior of a gas chamber. In the Hall of Testimony visitors listen to the "first-person testimonies of victims, perpetrators and witnesses" as a "series of video-photo montages" appears on television monitors installed along the walls. Designed to address the "difficult[y] for those of us who did not experience the Holocaust personally to imagine the atrocities perpetrated by the Nazis," the Hall of Testimony is described by the museum as "perhaps" its "most moving section."[68]

The Hall of Testimony strives to address the disparity between eyewitnesses to the Holocaust and all other people by fusing a simulation of entering what many have considered the quintessential and most inaccessible locus within the landscape of the Holocaust—the gas chamber—with what has become the most pervasive and accessible point of entry to this chapter of history—the television set. Placed at an angle above museumgoers' heads, the screens call to mind the monitors hooked up to surveillance cameras in stores and banks. But rather than projecting back to the visitors their own image, the screens offer museum-goers encounters with witnesses to Nazism. Thus, the Hall of Testimony exemplifies the length and breadth of television as a cultural force in contemporary American life. The installation draws on the significance of the medium in two contrasting ways: as a ubiquitous presence among people who are constantly observing and being observed through monitors and cameras as a part of their daily routines, and as a vehicle for facilitating otherworldly journeys, à la *The Twilight Zone,* in an effort to create meaningful access to the Holocaust.

The Hall of Testimony, the final installation in Beit Hashoah/Museum of Tolerance in Los Angeles. Photographer: Frédéric Brenner. (© Frédéric Brenner. Reprinted with permission.)

Living-room Holocaust

A report on *ABC News Nightline* late in 1993 pronounced it to be "the year of the Holocaust," citing the recent inauguration of the Los Angeles and Washington Holocaust museums and the opening of the feature film *Schindler's List.*[69] The report examines the motives and consequences of "Americans' desire to acquire knowledge about this horror-filled time in history" and asks whether this will "affect the way we look at our role in the world today." As the images on-screen cut back and forth between footage from recent television newscasts and vintage images of World War II, the correspondent notes that some observers explain the renewed interest in the Holocaust as a response to current events: the rise of "extreme nationalism" in Russia and of neo-Nazi movements in Germany, as well as "the ethnic cleansing in Bosnia." Here the montage makes an especially powerful connection in a cross-fade between images — first in black and white, then in color — of emaciated prisoners standing behind barbed wire and cyclone fences. While the former scene was filmed by a Signal Corps cameraman in a Nazi concentration camp liberated in 1945, the latter was videotaped in Bosnia only one year before the telecast.

Of the various paradigmatic uses of the Holocaust in recent years, perhaps none has been more compelling than the comparison of the Nazi persecution of European Jews with interethnic warfare in the Balkans during the 1990s. By virtue of its European setting, as well as the nature of the images and discourse it has generated, no other event during the past half century has inspired such intense identification as "another Holocaust" or had such extensive implications. In the United States the analogy of the Serbian assault on Bosnian Muslims in the 1990s with the Nazi persecution of European Jewry at midcentury has figured prominently in shaping both public opinion and national policy. This analogy has also generated an extensive discussion on the power and problematics of the Holocaust as a paradigm. Again, television has played an essential role in formulating and disseminating the analogy. Engendered by televised news reports showing the effects of "ethnic cleansing," which resonated with concomitant telecasts marking the fiftieth anniversary of Nazi persecutions, the Balkan conflict took shape in American public culture, in journalist Daniel Schorr's words, as a "living-room Holocaust."[70]

Interethnic strife in the Balkans became a subject of increasing international concern following the death in 1980 of Josef Broz Tito, Yugoslavia's leader since the end of World War II, and this concern intensified with the nation's disintegration following the end of Communist rule in 1990. Serbian forces invaded Croatia in September 1991, shortly after Croatia declared itself an independent nation. In the spring of 1992, following

Bosnia-Herzegovina's declaration of independence, Serbia initiated an aggressive campaign to appropriate Bosnian territory, expelling hundreds of thousands of Croats and Muslims from their homes in the process. Bosnians and Croats were quickly drawn into a complex and violent clash of ethnic, national, and religious loyalties, resulting in extensive human suffering, loss of life, and destruction of property. The official map of the Balkans dissolved into a shifting patchwork of disputed borders, occupied territories, pockets of resistance, and besieged or displaced communities.

All the while, West European nations, Russia, and the United States remained divided over what would constitute an effective and politically viable response to this situation, which followed a release from decades of containment under Communist rule and was understood to be rooted in centuries of ethnic and religious animosity. For several years, a series of sanctions, embargoes, cease-fire agreements, peace negotiations, and the occasional intervention of NATO forces had limited success in stabilizing the Balkans. Following the Dayton agreement of 1995 and the deployment of United Nations peacekeeping units, an uneasy peace has prevailed in the region. While elections of new leaders have been held in partitioned Bosnia and trials of accused Serbian war criminals have been convened before an international tribunal at the World Court, they have not proved to be harbingers of a lasting resolution of the region's interethnic hostility.

Throughout the early 1990s, news reports on American television showing the results of interethnic warfare in the Balkans prompted outcries for the United States government to respond. In May 1992, reports about a "breadline massacre" in Bosnia forced President George Bush's administration to urge the United Nations to issue economic sanctions against Serbia. On 2 August of that year, *New York Newsday* published reports by Roy Gutman on Serbian "ethnic cleansing" operations in Bosnia, which included the mass arrest, rape, torture, and murder of civilians.[71] These reports, which the U.S. State Department first confirmed, then claimed had yet to be substantiated, were corroborated several days later by video footage of the Bosnian civilian victims of Serbian persecution, recorded by Britain's Independent Television Network and broadcast internationally.[72] Of the various images evincing acts committed in the name of "ethnic cleansing," those that received the greatest public attention were not pictures of the murdered and brutalized, including women and children. Rather, they were shots of a group of adult men standing outdoors behind barbed wire; some of them were naked to the waist, revealing emaciated torsos. These men were, the British journalists explained, Muslim prisoners in a Serbian detention camp in the Bosnian town of Trnopolje.

In the United States, stills taken from the video footage of the camp in Trnopolje appeared on the front pages of national newpapers and were fea-

This shot of Muslim prisoners in the Serbian detention camp at Trnopolje, Bosnia, appeared on American television news reports and was widely reproduced on the front pages of newspapers and in newsmagazines during early August 1992. (Independent Television News.)

tured prominently in popular newsmagazines.[73] Journalists promptly identified the televising of these "shocking images" as "a defining event" that "finally . . . succeeded in rousing moral outrage." In the United States, *Time* magazine argued, "the curious alchemy of press coverage, public opinion and a presidential campaign" would have a galvanizing effect on the general public and could influence the Bush administration's policy regarding America's role, if any, in the Balkans. *Time* began its cover story on the "barbarism in Bosnia" by discussing "the shock of recognition" provoked by images of "skeletal figures behind barbed wire," one of which appeared on the magazine's cover that week, and by such terms as "ethnic cleansing" and "detention camps, maybe even concentration camps." These images and stories not only conjured up "Hitler's heyday" as well as the "Dark Ages" and the "Thirty Years' War," but also provoked disturbing thoughts: Hadn't Europeans "learned from the last terrible war on their soil not to murder their neighbors"? Was the rest of the world "sitting by, eager for peace at any price," as it had during Nazi Germany's annexation of Austria and occupation of the Sudetenland?[74]

Watching these images of the detention camp in Trnopolje on television provoked widespread associations of the events in Bosnia with those of the Holocaust. In some instances, individuals described how these televised news reports triggered memories of seeing newsreel or Signal Corps footage of liberated Nazi concentration camps, such as in the following letter to the editor of *New York Newsday,* whose author was prompted to recall a telecast of *Judgment at Nuremberg*:

> Toward the end of the trial, the prosecuting attorney . . . shows pictures from the Nazi concentration camps. At first I couldn't believe what I was seeing: the gaunt, haunted faces of human skeletons staring hopelessly out from behind the barbed wire, the huge piles of emaciated dead bodies. I felt sick and shaken in a way that changed my life forever. It was not until that moment that I realized the degradation and misery that one human being can inflict upon another. . . .
>
> Those images have haunted me my entire life. And now I see those faces before me again, only this time they are not staring out from some scratchy old newsreel. This time they are not the images of long dead ghosts drawn in black and white. No, this time they are in bright vivid colors, staring at me on the evening news about Bosnia-Herzegovina. This time they are alive, and we can do something to end their misery. . . . This time we can't say we did not know.[75]

This letter does more than testify to the continuing role that mediated images have played as Americans' primary encounter with the Holocaust. The letter also demonstrates how analogizing these images with those recorded in Bosnia facilitated the use of the Holocaust as a master paradigm for making sense of the situation in the Balkans. The notion of watching footage of liberated Nazi concentration camps as a morally transformative act of witnessing, first established in the newsreels of May 1945 and sustained through repeated invocations in films and television broadcasts, was extended to watching the video images from Bosnia in 1992. In both cases, filmed images are regarded as constituting unprecedented and irrefutable proof of atrocity, and their initial viewing is characterized as shocking. Indeed, watching the footage from Bosnia was understood by some as the equivalent of a colorized rerun of the Holocaust. Moreover, conceptualizing Bosnia in the 1990s as a repeat performance of the Holocaust enabled viewers of the video footage to formulate a response to the present atrocities that would, in effect, right the previous wrong. Whereas the black-and-white footage signified a call to remember, the color videotape, seen in juxtaposition with the vintage images, constituted a call to action.

Shortly after the images of "ethnic cleansing" in Bosnia were first broadcast on American television, Robert Jay Lifton published an essay in the *New York Times* reflecting on the psychological response to watching these scenes. Lifton, who has written on "the genocidal mentality" with regard to the Holocaust and other atrocities, argued that television "can make us survivors by proxy." Viewers of images of atrocities adopt "a self-imposed responsibility to bear witness to what they have seen and felt as a way of insisting that the world stop the killing and prevent its recurrence" that is analogous to the response of actual witnesses to such atrocities.

The fact that this encounter is televised, Lifton claimed, is "an integral part of the process." What he described as "indelible images" not only "transport us directly to Bosnia" but also "bring about a symbolic reactivization of Holocaust images" that are among those which have "become general public property in representing the pathos accompanying 20th-century evil." The psychological response extends to temporary identification with the victims depicted. This empathy, if shared by a sufficiently large number of people, can lead to actions that "can change the world." Indeed, Lifton called for a reassessment of the potential of television—a medium that generally inspires low expectations and which "we imperfectly understand"—as an instrument that "contribut[es] to our humanity."[76]

These psychological responses to the images of Serbian "ethnic cleansing" operations, which Lifton characterized as being universal, were articulated elsewhere at the time within a specifically Jewish context. A report aired on National Public Radio's *Weekend Edition* on 16 August 1992 focused on American Jewish reactions to the "reports of torture and mass executions in Serbia's detention camps." Jews were among the first to express outrage at these atrocities, reported Tovia Smith: "The images of gaunt and undernourished prisoners kept behind barbed wires of detention camps are painful reminders of their own past." Smith interviewed Israel Arbeiter, a member of the American Association of Jewish Holocaust Survivors (AAJHS), who described seeing the reports from Bosnia on television: "In my mind, I was in the camp and I see that man skinny and—and hungry. I've seen myself there. . . . If the world didn't know then what was happening to us, there is no doubt about it that the world knows what's happening today if we see it on television." Arbeiter explained that while the AAJHS is not a political organization, its members nonetheless "felt compelled to issue a statement" calling on the United States and the United Nations to intervene in Bosnia.

American Jews who are not Holocaust survivors also analogized Bosnian victims of Serbian "ethnic cleansing operations" with Jewish victims of Nazism. They, too, Smith reported, were responding to the interethnic strife in the Balkans as an opportunity to rectify earlier wrongs or to validate choices made in the past. Smith also interviewed Andrew Fisher, an attorney associated with the American Jewish Congress, which was preparing lawyers "to handle the requests for asylum that may come from the war-torn

Bosnia." Fisher stated, "Just as all of our parents . . . or grandparents . . . came here to escape troubled times . . . , the same is true for all these people today, and we owe it to our forefathers . . . to make sure the doors stay open." Sheila Dechter, executive director of the American Jewish Congress, explained why her organization also called for "a check on atrocities" taking place within Serbian-run detention camps. She recalled the unrealized pleas, addressed by members of the American Jewish community to the Roosevelt administration during World War II, that Auschwitz be bombed; then she commented, "As we look at this current situation . . . it's very hard to hear these responses that military action . . . absolutely cannot be considered."[77]

The question of America's response to the situation in the Balkans emerged as a key foreign policy question, especially for candidates in the 1992 presidential elections. The Bosnia/Holocaust analogy was reiterated in various public venues and was often articulated by invoking the similarities between recent videotape recordings of the Serbian-run detention camp and the 1945 footage of liberated Nazi concentration camps. A public service announcement aired during October 1992 (discussed in the first chapter of this volume) urged young adults to exercise their right to vote in the upcoming elections by using images from liberation footage, evocative of the images from Trnopolje, to compel viewers to vote "for all the people who didn't make it" to the United States. In an interview on the 8 December 1992 installment of the *MacNeil/Lehrer NewsHour,* former secretary of state George Shultz called for "western military action in Bosnia" and told anchor Robert MacNeil, "The next time you do a program on Bosnia, I would suggest that you start by showing some films of Bergen-Belsen or Auschwitz, because the message is the same."[78]

Television also facilitated public events inspired by the Holocaust/Bosnia analogy. Among the more elaborate examples was Elie Wiesel's much-publicized trip to Bosnia in late November 1992 to enact, before television cameras, his role as a morally charged witness. This four-day visit to the Balkans was featured on "Elie Wiesel: A Search for Peace," an edition of *ABC News Nightline* aired on 2 December.[79] In the broadcast's opening segment, journalist Dave Marash implicitly invokes the meaning of the term *holocaust* as fiery sacrifice by describing Wiesel as "offer[ing] his body to the burning Balkans, as if it could smother the flames, as if his eyes could make the world see the waste of humanity there." The broadcast's title graphic features Wiesel's portrait next to the image of a half-naked, emaciated prisoner in the camp at Trnopolje (the same image that was featured on the 17 August 1992 cover of *Time*).

Yet for the most part Marash's report documents the frustrations that Wiesel encountered while in Bosnia. Marash describes Wiesel as a "hostage" to diplomats, caught up in a series of time-consuming official visits to various leaders and obligatory stops at memorials dedicated to victims of atrocities during World War II. The report also chronicles Serbian refusals to take Wiesel and his entourage to the detainment camp at Trnopolje and other sites that he wished to inspect. Marash reflects on the impact of the "mobs of media people" accompanying Wiesel as he tries to meet with a group of inmates at another detention camp. At the "inevitable valedictory news conference" concluding his visit, a beleaguered Wiesel informs reporters, "I came with questions, and I leave with more questions."

One answer that Wiesel does provide during the course of this broadcast is that, in his opinion, the situation in former Yugoslavia is not a case of genocide. That term, Marash explains, "has a special meaning. Even . . . serial mass murder is not genocide." Yet Wiesel's very presence — he is introduced at the top of the broadcast by anchor Ted Koppel as "Holocaust survivor, Nobel Peace Prize winner, a voice of conscience" — invokes the Holocaust as a paradigm for conceptualizing a moral response to the interethnic warfare in the Balkans. Wiesel himself alludes to the Holocaust in explaining what compels him to undertake the visit by making references to his Jewishness, which he has presented elsewhere as a sign of his ethical engagement. Citing the Bible in Hebrew, he explains that his life principle is a response to the commandment "Thou shalt not stand idly by." Wiesel's visit with Jewish Bosnian refugees on Saturday, which necessitated his violating traditional prohibitions against traveling on the Sabbath, was justified, Marash explains, because "lives are at stake."

Wiesel was not alone in expressing concern over the implications of analogizing the Holocaust and contemporary interethnic strife in the Balkans. This proved to be as provocative an association as it was a compelling one, raising challenging questions about history and ideology. Philip Cohen wrote in *Midstream* that Serbs had "misappropriated" the history of the Holocaust in order to "portray themselves as victims in the Second World War" and to "conceal the systematic genocide that Serbs had committed against several peoples, including the Jews," during the war. By "usurp[ing]" as propaganda the Holocaust that occurred in neighboring Croatia and Bosnia," Cohen argued, Serbia sought "Jewish support for a war in which both the ideology and methodology . . . tragically echo nazism," thereby "exploiting the powerful symbolism of the Holocaust."[80]

In his *Washington Post* column Richard Cohen characterized the analogy of the Holocaust and the ethnic strife in Bosnia as largely a response by American Jews, intellectuals, and liberals; this was, he claimed, "based on a misreading of events, a headlong rush from certain particulars (brutal detention camps) to an unwarranted generalization (genocide)." Although he wondered whether the distinctions he drew between the Holocaust and interethnic warfare in Bosnia amounted to "quibbling," the columnist, like

Wiesel, asserted that "for all the horror of Bosnia, no Holocaust is taking place." Equating Bosnian Muslims with Jews in Nazi-occupied Europe, or present-day Serbs with Hitler's regime and its supporters, diminishes the magnitude of the Holocaust and "obscures suffering elsewhere." All the world's conflicts, Richard Cohen argued, "are horrible in their own right" without "making historical comparisons freighted with the language of the Holocaust. . . . History has moved on, and if it indeed does repeat itself, there's more reason to think that in Bosnia it will come back not as the Holocaust, but as Vietnam."[81]

These considerations notwithstanding, the Holocaust/Bosnia analogy continued to attract advocates. The official dedication of the United States Holocaust Memorial Museum in Washington, D.C., on 22 April 1993 provided an occasion for reiterating the comparison within the context of a major public ritual of state. Helen Fagin, a member of the museum's council, appeared on ABC's national evening news report on the eve of the museum's formal dedication, where she articulated the connection between the museum's mission and current events in Bosnia: "It is our business to get involved. . . . It is our business to interfere with ethnic cleansing and to say to the world, 'A human being's value is the same, no matter what religion, what nationality, what ethnicity, and what race.'"[82]

The dedication ceremony, which coincided with the fiftieth anniversary of the beginning of the Warsaw Ghetto uprising (as reckoned according to the Jewish calendar), involved an extensive gathering of American government officials, led by President Clinton, Vice President Gore, and Speaker of the House of Representatives Thomas Foley. Also in attendance were the leaders of twelve other countries, including Poland's Lech Walesa and Israel's Chaim Herzog, as well as prominent members of the American Jewish community and others connected with the Holocaust and its remembrance. Among the invited heads of state who attracted the most public attention were the leaders of Slovenia and Croatia. The announcement at the ceremony of the presence of Croatian president Franjo Tudjman—author of a history of World War II considered by many to be anti-Semitic—elicited some jeers from the crowd. The organizers of the ceremony had decided to invite him because he was, like the others asked to attend, the democratically elected leader of his nation. In contrast, Serbia's Slobodan Milosevic was the only European head of state not invited.[83]

The dedication ceremony, which was hosted by Ted Koppel, attracted extensive media coverage—broadcast live on C-SPAN and featured on the national networks' evening news broadcasts—the likes of which are seldom accorded to the opening of a museum or other similar cultural institution.[84] Moreover, the opening itself incorporated its own self-reflexive mediation, which linked vintage images of the Holocaust and the contemporary act of witnessing them. Suspended above the crowd attending the ceremonies, "a huge video screen showed pictures from the Holocaust—corpses, people with their hands in the air. Then," noted the *Washington Post* reporter covering the event, "in a display that has become standard at public events in America, it showed color shots of the crowd watching itself." The official agenda of the museum's dedication ceremony validated its mission of promoting Holocaust remembrance as a vital force in the American moral conscience, worthy of a prominent place in the landscape of the nation's capital. Harvey Meyerhoff, one of the museum's major donors and fund-raisers, remarked, "This is an American museum for the American people. It may prove to be more, but it must never be anything less."[85]

In fact, the occasion of the museum's opening had already been seized as an opportunity for making use of the Holocaust as an exemplar, albeit unofficially, for another morally charged issue. On the day before the museum opened its doors to the public, the Washington Mall was the site of the largest public demonstration for gay and lesbian rights in the nation's history, involving hundreds of thousands of participants. Many of the groups and individuals attending the 25 April demonstration displayed examples of the gay rights movement's ongoing use of Holocaust imagery. Chief among these is the adoption of the pink triangle badge, with which Nazis stigmatized homosexual men incarcerated in concentration camps, as an emblem of gay identity that is displayed on signs, buttons, flags, articles of clothing, and the like.[86] In addition, several speakers who addressed the rally on the Mall alluded to the Holocaust, the anniversary of the Warsaw Ghetto uprising, or the opening of the Holocaust museum in their speeches. At one point, a speaker led the crowd in chanting repeatedly, "Never again!"—the watchword of Holocaust memory culture. During the weekend before the rally, a candlelight vigil for gay and lesbian victims of the Holocaust was held in front of the Holocaust museum, with museum staff members participating.[87]

In contrast to the analogies between the Holocaust and the struggle for gay and lesbian rights communities, which were articulated outside the official time and place of the museum's dedication, parallels between the Holocaust and the ongoing "ethnic cleansing" operations in Bosnia were evoked repeatedly at the opening ceremony, giving the Holocaust/Bosnia analogy an implicit state seal of authority. Prominent among those who spoke at the dedication was Elie Wiesel, who was chair of the council, originally established by President Carter in 1979, that made the initial recommendation to establish the museum and oversaw its realization. Wiesel reminded the audience that, during World War II, government officials in the United States and around the world knew about the Final Solution and were largely silent in response. Then—in a gesture somewhat reminiscent of his appeal, eight

years earlier, to President Reagan regarding the Bitburg controversy—
Wiesel addressed President Clinton: "Mr. President, I must tell you something. I have been in the former Yugoslavia last fall. I cannot sleep since
what I have seen. As a Jew I am saying that. We must do something to stop
the bloodshed in that country. . . . Something, anything, must be done."[88]

Clinton, too, referred to the events in Bosnia in his remarks at the ceremony but, instead of responding directly to Wiesel's appeal, "spoke of brutality around the globe": "We learn again and again that the world has yet
to run its course of animosity and violence. . . . Ethnic cleansing in the former Yugoslavia is but the most brutal and blatant and ever-present manifestation of what we see also with the oppression of the Kurds in Iraq, the
abusive treatment of the Baha'i in Iran, the endless race-based violence in
South Africa. . . . We are reminded again and again how fragile are the safe-
guards of civilization." Later, Clinton responded to Wiesel's charge in
remarks to the press: "I think it is a challenge to all of us, to the United
States and to the East and to the West, to take further initiatives in Bosnia.
I accept it."[89]

The opening of the Holocaust museum in Washington prompted renewed
consideration of the Holocaust/Bosnia analogy, with the museum and the
media serving as morally charged referents. The day before the dedication
took place, John Darnton asked, in the "Week in Review" section of the
New York Times, whether "the world still recognized a Holocaust":

> Not for half a century has the world witnessed events in Europe that have
> stirred such an agonizing echo of past horrors. The television footage of
> houses reduced to rubble, the bombed-out churches and mosques, the lined-
> up bodies and mass graves—they all evoke the flickering black and white
> newsreels of World War II. The words "genocide," "massacre," "Holocaust,"
> "civilian bombing" and "ethnic cleansing" haunt everyday speech and stir up
> guilt-ridden memories like smoke rising from a crematorium.

Another troubling specter of World War II invoked by the situation in
Bosnia, Darton wrote, was the fear of responding to an aggressive regime
with gestures of appeasement that would later prove to have been fatally
misguided: "With reports of atrocities continuing and nightly footage on
international television of wounded and orphaned children, the pressure
for some form of action to stop the slaughter is building. Once again, diplomats are contemplating the lesson of Chamberlain's umbrella." Later that
summer Hobart Rowen wrote in the *Washington Post* that "if we in the
West do not figure out a way to stop the extermination of the Bosnian
Muslims, there will be another Holocaust Museum project 50 years from
now. What the world needs is more contemporaneous courage and fewer
after-the-fact Holocaust Museums."[90]

In the ensuing months many observers were frustrated by the disparity between the ability to record and televise an ongoing series of images of warfare in the Balkans and the inability of these images to galvanize world leaders and bring about an effective response to the violence. Contrary to Elie Wiesel's suggestion nearly a decade earlier that if there had been television during World War II, "millions of lives might have been saved," the presence of the medium seemed to have had limited and inconsistent impact on the progress of international response to the interethnic violence in the former Yugoslavia.[91]

When international action was eventually initiated in the Balkans, journalists covering the story and other commentators often credited television news reportage with having motivating the response. In February 1994 video footage of the shelling of a marketplace in Sarajevo, in which sixty-eight civilians died and dozens of others were wounded, prompted NATO to issue an ultimatum to Serbian forces to remove their artillery from the declared safe zone surrounding the city or face air strikes.[92] "It was the chance presence of TV cameras at the very moment of the massacre . . . that led American and European governments to do 'something' at last, to stop the slaughter," noted Albert Wohlstetter. In his *New York Times* op-ed essay entitled "Genocide by Mediation," Wohlstetter critiqued NATO's failure to pursue a feasible strategy that would resolve "our political, moral and strategic quagmire."[93]

Indeed, it was the "fear of quagmire" that haunted the United States government in its pursuit of an appropriate policy on Bosnia, according to *While America Watched: The Bosnia Tragedy,* a one-hour special presentation produced by ABC News and anchored by Peter Jennings, which was aired on 17 March 1994.[94] The report focused on the critical role played by images of the violence in the Balkans, which had appeared on American television news reports since 1992, in shaping both public opinion and governmental policy. Jennings begins the broadcast by commenting that "we have seen the United States stand by and watch the slaughter in the former Yugoslavia. As the war grew in ferocity, as the images on our television screens grew more horrible, they began to remind us of the last war to ravage Europe." The images of news footage from the Balkans accompanying Jennings's narration cross-fade from color shots of men in the Trnopolje detention camp during the summer of 1992 to a similar black-and-white photograph of half-naked, skeletal men, taken in a Nazi concentration camp. Until sixty-eight people were killed in a Sarajevo marketplace in February 1994 "within easy range of television cameras," Jennings notes, "the United States had not felt compelled to act. How did America's leaders decide to stand by for so long while scenes of mass murder and genocide were once again enacted on European soil?"

Following a commercial break, Jennings appears on camera, standing in the Tower of Faces, part of the main installation of the Holocaust museum in Washington. The Tower displays hundreds of photographs of Jews who lived in the town of Ejszyszki (now part of Lithuania) before World War II, almost all of whom were shot in 1941 by members of a German mobile killing squad and buried in mass graves.[95] Jennings explains that the Jews of Ejszyszki were killed simply because of "who they were," making for "a singular kind of crime . . . genocide." While the Holocaust is "by far the most notorious" example of this crime, Jennings observes that to meet the criteria of the United Nations Genocide Convention "you need only killers and victims—and those who stand by and let it happen."

The broadcast traces the Balkan conflict from the spring of 1992 to February 1994—when, after "a few minutes of videotape . . . everything changes, or seems to"—focusing on the reportage of "ethnic cleansing" atrocities in the American media and the responses that they engendered. John Fox, a former State Department official, describes his frustration over the Bush administration's inaction in response to televised reports: "The images . . . never stopped. And that's what got to people." *While America Watched* also traces the promise of action from the Clinton administration. During the presidential campaign, vice presidential candidate Gore is shown saying, "The world stood by in silence once before when this happened, and . . . the world should have learned a lesson from that." Yet after Clinton took office, the White House maintained the nation's noninterventionist response to the fighting in Bosnia.

References to the Holocaust, both direct and implicit, run throughout *While America Watched*. Clinton's speech at the dedication of the Washington Holocaust museum is excerpted, followed by footage of a tour of the museum's main exhibition by Bosnian prime minister Haris Salajdzic. Looking at monitors displaying footage of liberated concentration camps, he comments, "That is in Bosnia now—we have concentration camps. That should be museum history once and for all. But the world is not listening. So the question is, do we learn from history or do we pretend to learn from history?"

But *While America Watched* indicates that there are competing histories—with their attendant mediations, generating their respective iconic images—on which Americans draw and which have shaped their response to the interethnic warfare in the Balkans. Lawrence Eagleburger, secretary of state under President Bush when the reports of "ethnic cleansing" first reached the United States, defends his administration's decision not to intervene in Bosnia by citing both the shifting strategic interests of the United States in the post-cold-war era and the precedent of earlier interventions, explaining that "Vietnam never goes away."

252 A Household Word

Indeed, Jennings concludes the broadcast while standing before the Vietnam Veterans Memorial, located on the Washington Mall not far from the Holocaust museum. He mentions the distance between these two memorial sites and the historical events that they commemorate as symbolic of American policy on the Balkans, noting that "the fear of appeasement has given way to the fear of quagmire." Criticizing the current and previous administrations for ignoring "the risks of doing nothing, while America watched hundreds of thousands of people die in a particularly evil kind of war," Jennings invokes the onus of witnessing images of atrocities. In his final words, he implies that the moral burden is borne not only by the nation's leaders, but by its citizens as well: "The Bosnians paid a very high price — but so did those who stood by."

Media critics distinguished *While America Watched* for taking "a stand . . . on U.S. inaction" in Bosnia and for demonstrating "television's ability to get across one side of the argument."[96] Yet the ABC report also evinced, albeit less directly, the limited impact that television reporting and watching has on current events. While the plight of Bosnian civilians caught up in the Balkan war was at the visible center of the ABC report, its ultimate concern was for "those who stood by," who watched these images on American television and were left with an unresolved moral burden. In this respect, *While America Watched* exemplifies a more general uneasiness about the act of witnessing and its relationship to remembering the Holocaust, a discomfort that intensified as Holocaust memory culture approached yet another threshold in its history.

"The Real Trial of the Century": Court TV's The Nuremberg Trial

The fiftieth anniversary of the end of World War II in Europe marked the culmination of several years of televised commemorations of events in the Holocaust narrative, beginning with observances of the date of *Kristallnacht* in 1988 (e.g., the documentary *More than Broken Glass: Memories of Kristallnacht*) and ending with numerous documentaries and news reports on commemorations of the liberations of concentration camps.[97] At the same time, much of American Holocaust television that year was more responsive to issues of the present than those of the past, as developments in the Balkans changed the nature of the Bosnia/Holocaust analogy. The most elaborate of these telecasts was a five-day, fifteen-hour presentation on the first Nuremberg war crimes trial, which was aired 13–17 November 1995 on the Court TV channel.[98] Besides marking the fiftieth anniversary of the trial, the broadcasts were offered as a prologue to Court TV's impending broadcasts of the trials, to be convened in the World Court, of Serbians who had been accused of war crimes in Bosnia. (Advertisements

on buses in New York City promoted Court TV's coverage of these proceedings as the first such trials since Nuremberg.) With these broadcasts,
American Holocaust remembrance shifted from marking fiftieth anniversaries of the war years to commemorations of the first efforts to respond to
the Holocaust. Court TV's broadcasts of the Nuremberg trial not only
revisited these historic proceedings against the leaders of the Third Reich,
but also examined the means by which the war crimes were first made public and the consequences of this presentation over the ensuing decades.

In this respect, Court TV's *The Nuremberg Trial* offered a revealing measure of the dynamics of Holocaust remembrance from the formative period
of the immediate postwar years to its current status as a master moral paradigm. This development is epitomized by the opening of the telecast, which
is introduced by Steven Spielberg. Since the release of *Schindler's List* in
1993, the filmmaker has emerged as the most prominent public figure in
America associated with Holocaust memory, his familiarity rivaling and perhaps even eclipsing that of Elie Wiesel. This is a telling development, evincing a larger shift in Holocaust remembrance from its focus on survivors to a
newer center of attention: the creators of Holocaust mediations.

In his remarks Spielberg briefly recounts the historical context of the
first Nuremberg trial and comments that it was convened not only to pros-
ecute Nazi war criminals, but to establish that "from that point on, the
world would hold those who committed such acts accountable." In reponse
to recent news reports of interethnic violence in Bosnia and elsewhere, "we
can't help but hope that the lesson of Nuremberg has not been forgotten."[99] The title sequence for *The Nuremberg Trial* that follows features a
compilation of vintage footage and photographs that situate the Nuremberg trial in the master narrative of the Holocaust—a framework that was
as unfamiliar in the immediate postwar period as it is now so easily signaled and recognized.

Court TV's handling of the trial evinces signal changes in approaches to
mediating the Holocaust from the 1940s to the 1990s. This vintage material
posed daunting technical challenges to the telecast's producers. The international military tribunal did not intend that the film record of the trial serve
as its primary, most comprehensive documentation. Made for use by commercial newsreel companies, the film was recorded without sound by a single camera in ten-minute increments. Court TV producers synchronized the
film with separately recorded audiotapes of the proceedings; where there are
gaps in the footage (as reels of film stock were changed), stills were taken
from the footage to accompany the sound recording. To compensate for the
limited camera work, which was shot from a remote vantage point in the
rear of the courtroom, producers of Court TV's broadcast employ a variety
of devices to "animate" the trial's austere visual record: In addition to pan-
ning or slowly zooming in on or out of still images, subtitles, arrows, haloes,

254 A Household Word

and other graphics were added in order to highlight individual participants in the proceedings. At the same time, Court TV presents the footage as a historical artifact, and its provenance and handling are clearly explained to viewers.[100] This contrasts with the original use of the footage by the producers of commercial newsreels, who added narration and musical accompaniment as they integrated short clips from the trial with other footage to create a synthetic, emotionally engaging presentation.

Similar to its coverage of contemporary trials, Court TV's *The Nuremberg Trial* frames extended sequences from the trial with a wide array of commentary. There are prerecorded interviews with veterans of the trial's prosecution and defense teams, as well as with journalist Walter Cronkite, who reported on the trial for United Press International. In addition, hosts of the broadcast are joined in Court TV's studio by a series of discussants, including prominent law professors and attorneys as well as additional veterans of the U.S. prosecution team at Nuremberg. The prerecorded commentators reminisce and contextualize the trial, while the discussants comment on sequences of the proceedings as they are shown and explore the trial's wider implications.

In this respect, Court TV's *The Nuremberg Trial* recalled the televised coverage of the Eichmann trial in 1961. The television presentation of both trials offered a complex layering of past, present, and future. Much of the discussion on Court TV looks back at the war years and the course of the proceedings in Nuremberg, as well as forward, considering the consequences of the trial in the postwar era and how the Nuremberg proceedings might serve as a precedent in upcoming cases against accused Serbian war criminals. *The Nuremberg Trial* offers a complicated interplay of "history" and "news"; hosts of the Court TV broadcast encourage viewers to stay tuned through commercial breaks with descriptions of "coming attractions" that are, in fact, fifty years old. As was also the case during the coverage of the Eichmann proceedings, discussants consider the performative aspects of the Nuremberg trial, beginning with the question of whether it was a "legal" trial or a "show" trial. The discussants pay considerable attention to the affective presence of the trial's participants, especially the defendants, as was the case in coverage of the Eichmann trial and previous media presentations of the first Nuremberg trial. At the same time, commentators on the Court TV telecast laud the prosecution's primary reliance on documentary evidence rather than eyewitness testimony as more befitting an event of such historical importance.

During the first two days of *The Nuremberg Trial* Court TV presented *Nazi Concentration Camps,* the compilation of liberation footage filmed by the Allies that prosecutors presented as evidence during the Nuremberg trial. Excerpts from this documentary are shown at the point in the original proceedings when the film was offered as evidence. As has been the case since the first public presentations of these images, television viewers are repeatedly warned about the graphic nature of *Nazi Concentration Camps* and some of the other footage screened during the trial.[101] Discussants note the unprecedented use of documentary film in a courtroom and address the problems it poses as evidence.

Court TV's *The Nuremberg Trial* embodies a central dilemma posed by Holocaust memory, as the telecast moves back and forth between presenting the Holocaust as a historical epoch without precedent and offering it as an enduring paradigm for human justice. The broadcasts revisit the challenges that Allied prosecutors initially faced both in creating the legal foundation of their cases against the Nazi defendants and in legitimating the trial itself. Commentators explore these issues further by considering the value of the Nuremberg trial as a precedent for the planned trials of Serbians charged with committing war crimes in Bosnia. The dilemma posed by the question of the Holocaust's paradigmatic value is also reflected in the nature of the telecast. On the one hand, the scope and format of Court TV's presentation of the trial situate it as unique. (Coming shortly after the conclusion of the network's extensive coverage of O. J. Simpson's trial for the murder of Nicole Brown Simpson and Ron Goldman, Court TV advertised the Nuremberg broadcasts as "The Real Trial of the Century.")[102] On the other hand, the Nuremberg trial is positioned within the ongoing pursuit of justice by virtue of being integrated into the flow of broadcasts of this network, which is devoted to "real trials—real people—different television."

The fiftieth anniversary of the end of World War II also marked a half century of learning about and striving to make sense of the events that have come to be known as the Holocaust. During this period the Holocaust emerged as a concept of moral, cultural, and political consciousness as well as a chapter of history, and its iconic stature has risen steadily and grown increasingly complex with the years. But as its symbolic value has increased, so too have the consequences of Holocaust remembrance. The Bosnia/Holocaust analogy epitomizes what is at stake, in that it touches on several limits that Holocaust memory culture must confront.

First, the Bosnia/Holocaust analogy coincided with a generational limit. Like most jubilees, the fiftieth anniversary of the end of World War II was also an implicit reminder that those who were coming of age at the time are now elders, and the youngest of those with any memory of fifty-year-old events are approaching old age as well. Holocaust memory is nearing the point of passing out of the hands of its eyewitnesses—survivors, liberators, perpetrators, bystanders—and soon will rest with other authorities, including the mediations that the generation who lived through the war has helped to create.

Second, there is a historical limit. As Peter Novick has observed of the dynamics of American Holocaust memory culture, "We are finally leaving the postwar/cold-war era, with all that it implies for a reorientation of consciousness." At the same time, the "ethnic cleansing" operations in Bosnia presented an unprecedented semblance of the history of World War II "repeating itself"—that is, the return of what is arguably a case of genocide as a result of the policy of an expansionist European power. This notion alarmed those who had demanded that the Holocaust be remembered so that it will never happen again. In his study of Washington's Holocaust museum, Edward Linenthal noted that the "failure of Holocaust memory" to influence American foreign policy in Bosnia struck "at the heart of one of the museum's reasons for being": the morally transformative power of memory.[103] At the same time, the Bosnia/Holocaust analogy also threatened those determined to conceptualize the Holocaust as an event both without precedent and without subsequent equal in human history.[104]

Finally, the Bosnia/Holocaust analogy revealed the limits of media in facilitating Holocaust remembrance as a public moral touchstone. As had been the case with the war in Vietnam during the 1960s and 1970s, and also with Iraq's persecution of its Kurdish population during the 1980s, millions of Americans watching nightly news reports of interethnic warfare in the Balkans during the 1990s confronted the frustrating disparity between the ability to record and disseminate galvanizing images of the atrocities of war and the inability to realize an effective response to the events to which the images testify. And, as the Rodney King case demonstrated in the early 1990s, the increased ability of media to be "at the scene of the crime" can in no way ensure that the video documentation of events will be uniformly and effectively understood as evidence, whether in the context of legal proceedings or in the public forum of television. Regardless of well-meaning sentiments to the contrary, the presence of television in modern culture cannot prevent another Holocaust from happening. Indeed, its extensive, multifaceted presence at times seems to make confronting the challenge of Holocaust remembrance only that much more complicated and frustrating.

Despite these limitations, television has emerged over the course of the second half of the twentieth century as the most pervasive and diverse source of Holocaust mediations in America. Americans would not be as widely familiar with the Holocaust, and in as complex, emotionally charged, and morally engaged a manner as they are, without television's many presentations of the subject and the responses that they have engendered. Because mediations have figured more fundamentally and extensively as the basis of Holocaust remembrance here than they have elsewhere, much of what can be learned from examining the first half century of American Holocaust television may shed light on the future of Holocaust memory culture here and abroad as this historical epoch passes beyond the memories of its witnesses.

Conclusion

I've been in a place for six incredible years where winning meant a crust of bread and to live another day. Since the blessed day of my liberation I have asked the question "Why am I here? I am no better." In my mind's eye, I see those years and faces, and those who never lived to see the magic of a boring evening at home. On their behalf I wish to thank you for honoring their memory.

—Holocaust survivor Gerda Klein, who appears in the documentary *One Survivor Remembers*, at the 1995 Academy Awards ceremony

More than fifty years after the Holocaust took place, it continues to appear on American television—sometimes prominently, often predictably. Still, it occasionally comes as a surprise, such as when Holocaust survivor Gerda Klein made these brief, moving—and unscheduled—remarks when *One Survivor Remembers* received the 1995 Academy Award for Best Short Documentary. And the appearances of the Holocaust on television continue to be the subject of discussion, popular as well as scholarly.

This discussion is part of an increased attention to all manner of representations of the Holocaust and is responsive not only to the compelling nature of the subject, but also to the highly public profile that the Holocaust has been accorded in the final decades of the twentieth century. Initiated largely by members of the Jewish community, the commitment to public remembrance of the Holocaust has been taken up by many other people, including those—especially in the United States—with no direct connection to this chapter of history. The impressive quantity, variety, and scale of Holocaust representations, as well as the number of people and amounts of time and money devoted to their realization, have become defining characteristics of Holocaust memory culture. As a result, approaching the Holocaust—now widely regarded as a public moral imperative—is inextricably bound up with making sense of its many representations.

Generally, approaches to evaluating Holocaust memory culture have sought to distinguish those examples that are "responsible" or "do justice" to the Holocaust from those that "abuse," "distort," or "trivialize" it. This moral connoisseurship of Holocaust remembrance, like many of the works of memory culture that it surveys, seems to grow out of a larger desire to transform one of the most terribly amoral episodes of human history, to find in presentations of the Holocaust some redemptive message, some inspirational — or, at the very least, cautionary — lesson.

In large part because of its commitment to the public sphere, this conceptualization of the Holocaust and its representation does not merely strive to ameliorate grief over the loss of particular individuals, communities, and cultures; it also aspires to relieve the human conscience. It seeks to provide assurance that even if our species (and perhaps only some of us, and only under the most extreme circumstances) is capable of committing such atrocities, people nevertheless can, with "proper" exposure to "appropriate" presentations of the Holocaust, become beings "never again" capable of such a vile breach of the human social contract.

Such assumptions — which are fundamental to so many Holocaust dramas, monuments, museums, tours, literary works, public ceremonies, documentary films, popular histories, and educational programs — rest on a humanistic commitment to moral edification through education, especially in publicly prominent and accessible venues. While this is the most visible mode of response to the Holocaust, it is important to bear in mind that it is by no means the only one. The past half century has been witness to other, quite different approaches to Holocaust remembrance, both among other parts of the Jewish community — especially among ultraorthodox Jews — and among others involved in this chapter of history.[1] The response of Gypsy communities to what some of them refer to as the *porraimos* (Romany for "devouring") is a particularly instructive case in point. Isabel Fonseca has examined how the Roma recall persecutions of the Nazi era within an internal, localized, and mutable oral tradition. While Jews have responded to the Holocaust with "a monumental industry of remembrance," she has noted that Gypsies, in contrast, "have made an art of forgetting."[2]

The commitment to public commemoration of the Holocaust is also tied to a worldview of the generations who lived through the Holocaust, whether as adults or as children, in the midst of its horrors or at some remove. The Holocaust and the world war during which it took place mark a rift in their personal histories and are also fundamental to the political, cultural, intellectual, social, and economic worlds in which they have lived. For so many of this age, the Holocaust towers over all previous or subsequent events; it serves as the measure of all other human phenomena, even if they always, inevitably, come up short.

Perhaps this is why many people committed to representing the Holocaust as an unparalleled phenomenon find televised presentations of the Holocaust to be particularly problematic. The medium, which by its very nature pulls everything that it presents into its ongoing flow, violates the notion of the Holocaust as a singular event that altered world history, human consciousness, and even the normal flow of time and remains situated on a separate ontological plateau. Moreover, television is so widely and easily disdained as a trivializing or corrupting cultural force that it is seen as a vehicle that cannot help but produce unsatisfactory representations of the Holocaust. With such assumptions, any further discussion of Holocaust television would seem to be moot, save to demonstrate just how a "low" medium can violate the integrity of an elevated subject.

This study has presented alternative approaches to understanding Holocaust television, in the hope that they will offer greater insight into the genre and its value as a distinctive form of memory culture. Besides fostering a more nuanced understanding of Holocaust television, I hope that this study has also made a case for appreciating, rather than denouncing or ignoring, its discomforting nature. Gerda Klein's remarks, heard by the vast audience that watches the annual Academy Awards on television, hint at the ultimate challenge that television poses to Holocaust remembrance — that is, to consider the implications of an encounter with the Holocaust that is facilitated by a medium fundamentally situated within the context of "a boring evening at home."

Holocaust television must always somehow deal, even if only tacitly and obliquely, with the dissonance of presenting the enormity of its subject in this ubiquitous, routine, intimate context. Part of one's "proper" response — if it is useful to think of such a thing — to Holocaust television should include an engagement with this disquietude. This means not simply taking comfort in the broadcasts' ameliorative messages of redemption or in messages of what can be an equally comforting indignation or cynicism, but it also means not simply dismissing the broadcasts outright. Responses to Holocaust television will, of course, vary from one viewer to another and will change from one encounter to the next, but they will not be "proper" if they do not engage with this discomfort and consider its larger implications for Holocaust remembrance. Indeed, the importance of acknowledging and grappling with discomfort, which Holocaust television so readily demonstrates, should be extended to considering other forms of Holocaust memory culture as well.

Public memory is conventionally thought of as being best served by phenomena with purportive powers of endurance, such as stone monuments, official public celebrations, or texts that are widely circulated and regularly read. Television, inherently ephemeral and elusive, might well seem inimical to remembrance. In her study of collective memory, sociologist Iwona Irwin-Zarecka has cast a cautious eye at the implications of television's ability to fabricate what she has termed "instant memory."[3] Indeed, the medium epitomizes historian Pierre Nora's vision of the devolution of traditional collective memory, the replacement of "real environments" of remembrance with the *lieux de mémoire* of modernity—denatured, industrialized, corporate, ritualized, self-conscious "sites of memory."[4]

But there is an alternative to Nora's "declinist approach" to understanding memory culture. "Even so-called 'modern society,'" anthropologist Yael Zerubavel has argued, "continues to nurture shared memories of the past through multiple commemorations of selected historical events." In fact, the modern era has provided greater numbers and variety of people— "poets and writers, journalists and teachers" (and, one might add, the creators of television programming)—with opportunities to play "more decisive roles . . . in shaping popular images of the past." Zerubavel posits a "constant need to mediate between the past and the present that ultimately accounts for the continuing vitality of collective memory."[5]

Television, then, seems especially appropriate to this vision of memory culture, given the medium's polyvalence, its recombinant sensibility and bricolage aesthetic, its endless self-referentiality, and the facility with which it ingests other media and with which it inspires personal responses to its broadcasts. Indeed, these qualities of television as a cultural force resemble those that current research attributes to the human brain in how it creates and uses memory. Far from being a fixed, mechanical process, memory is a "fragile power," according to neuroscientist Daniel Schacter—subjective, selective, and mutable, yet also a "pervasive influence" that "forms the foundation for our most strongly held beliefs about ourselves."[6]

The mutable virtual geography of television—a "center of meaning" and "social context" that constitute "a place without a location"—also has an affinity with notions of "the past as a foreign country."[7] The distance inherent in the medium is better understood not as problematic, but as a defining interest of Holocaust television. The same can be said for the cultural and experiential disparity between Americans and the Holocaust. The mediations that have always constituted Americans' primary encounter with the Holocaust—whether on television or by other means—do not simply erase this distance, creating a "placeless culture," nor do they merely call attention to the disparity.[8] Rather, these mediations and their primacy inform the meaning of the Holocaust in the American context. In particular, they have facilitated an openness of approach to the subject that other contexts have not provided.

Of course, the context of American television is by no means a blank canvas. Its presentations of the Holocaust have been shaped by a complex of limiting forces—the cold war, the dynamic of American attitudes toward the State of Israel or toward Jews in the post–World War II era, the commercial nature of American television broadcasting, and the medium's demand for affect, among others. At the same time, American television's presentations of the Holocaust have been enabled by the innovative impulses of the nation's ecumenism and the moral drive of its civil religion, as well as by the intimacy, dramatic idiom, and even the enduring "newness" of television. Above all, the primacy of television and other mediations in this nation's Holocaust memory culture has situated Americans in the distinctive posture of *watching*—emotionally, ideologically, and intellectually engaged, yet at a physical, political, and cultural remove.

The ties between the Holocaust and television, unlikely and even uncomfortable as they might often seem, continue to develop. Remembrance of the Holocaust is passing from those who witnessed it to those who inherit the challenge of maintaining the memory of events they did not experience. Television is now becoming linked to the much anticipated "information superhighway" of the twenty-first century, which offers the potential of unprecedented access and exchange of materials and ideas. What will the medium's impact be on the dynamics of Holocaust memory culture, both in the United States and abroad, as mediations become ever more prominent in our efforts to approach this chapter of history? How might this relationship serve as a model for other forms of public remembrance, as television becomes a more extensive cultural resource? Stay tuned.

Notes

Most of the television programs cited in this study are not available in published form (i.e., on commercially distributed videocassette or other format) and are available for viewing only in media archives. They have been referenced in the notes as archival documents. When known, the original date and venue (i.e., network, local station, cable channel) of broadcast are given either in the text or in a citation. The existence of some programs can only be documented by listings in media catalogues or other print sources (e.g., published reviews or listings in television broadcast schedules). In such an instance, the print source is given in the citation, along with available information regarding the date and venue of broadcast.

The following abbreviations are used in the notes for archival sources of television programs. Archival inventory numbers for programs are listed where applicable (not all archives use inventory numbers to locate programs):

HJVC = Harvard Jewish Video Collection, Harvard College Library, Cambridge, Massachusetts. See Charles Berlin, comp., *Guide to Judaica Videotapes in the Harvard College Library* (Cambridge: Harvard-Littauer Judaica Endowment, 1989).

LC= Library of Congress, Motion Picture, Broadcasting and Recorded Sound Division, Washington, D.C. See Sarah Rouse and Katharine Loughney, comps., *Three Decades of Television: A Catalog of Television Programs Acquired by the Library of Congress 1949–1979* (Washington: Library of Congress, 1988).

MTR = Museum of Television and Radio, New York City. On-site computer database. Parallel holdings can be found in the museum's Los Angeles branch.

NCJF = National Center for Jewish Film, Brandeis University, Waltham, Massachusetts. No item numbers.

NJAB = National Jewish Archive of Broadcasting, The Jewish Museum, New York. See *National Jewish Archive of Broadcasting: Catalog of Holdings,* 2nd ed. (New York: The Jewish Museum, 1995).

UCLA = University of California Los Angeles Film and Television Archive (Powell Library). On-line computer database. No item numbers.

A number of programs whose existence is otherwise undocumented are listed in Stuart Fox, comp., *Jewish Films in the United States: A Comprehensive Survey and Descriptive Filmography* (Boston: G. K. Hall, 1976); programs cited from this guide are listed as "Fox," followed by their inventory numbers. Some of the programs described in this study can be found in Israeli archives as well; see Sheba F. Skirball, *Films of the Holocaust: An Annotated Filmography of Collections in Israel* (New York: Garland, 1990).

Most direct citations from television programs have been transcribed by the author of this study from viewing copies housed in one of the aforementioned archives, from commercially or privately distributed videotapes, or from videotapes recorded directly from a television broadcast. In some instances, citations are made from printed transcripts of broadcasts or from published scripts; these are referenced in the same way as other print sources.

Introduction

1. CBS News, *60 Minutes*, 2 April 1995 (vol. 27, no. 30); transcript (Livingston, New Jersey: Burrelle's Information Services), p. 3.

2. "Bosnia Commercial/MPAC"; videotape provided by Muslim Public Affairs Council, Los Angeles. The spot was aired on CNN on 27 July 1995 at 7:59 P.M.

3. *ABC News Nightline*, 28 September 1995 (no. 3744); transcript (Denver, Colorado: Journal Graphics), pp. 1, 3.

4. Michael Janofsky, "Increasingly, Political War of Words Is Fought With Nazi Imagery," *New York Times*, 23 October 1995, p. A12.

5. Michael Berenbaum, *The World Must Know: The History of the Holocaust as Told in the United States Holocaust Memorial Museum* (Boston: Little, Brown, 1993), p. 2.

6. Alvin H. Rosenfeld, "Americanization of the Holocaust," *Commentary* 99, no. 6 (June 1995): p. 36.

7. Susan Hicks, "List of Holocaust Museums," *Jewish Studies Judaica eJournal* (jewstudies@israel.nysernet.org) 3.007 (May 1995); "October 1943: The Rescue of the Danish Jews from Annihilation" [brochure], Holocaust Memorial Center, West Bloomfield, Michigan, [1993].

8. "Holocaust Museum Has Too Many Visitors," *New York Times*, 19 November 1993, p. C3.

9. Michael Berenbaum, "The Uniqueness and Universality of the Holocaust," in *After Tragedy and Triumph: Essays in Modern Jewish Thought and the American Experience* (Cambridge: Cambridge University Press, 1990), p. 20.

10. Edward T. Linenthal, *Preserving Memory: The Struggle to Create America's Holocaust Museum* (New York: Viking, 1995), pp. 269–272, passim.

11. Scott Sherman, "Preserving Black History," *The Progressive* 55, no. 12 (December 1991): p. 15.

12. Sighted by Henry Sapoznik and reported to me in October 1993.

13. As cited in Saul S. Friedman, "In Defense of 'Holocaust: The Story of the Family Weiss,'" *Jewish Frontier* 45, no. 7 (August–September 1978): p. 9.

14. Ilan Avisar, *Screening the Holocaust: Cinema's Images of the Unimaginable* (Bloomington: Indiana University Press, 1988), p. 129.

15. Saul Friedlander, ed., *Probing the Limits of Representation: Nazism and the "Final Solution"* (Cambridge: Harvard University Press, 1992), p. 3.

Part One: Creating the Viewer

1. Hans Kellner, "'Never Again' Is Now," *History and Theory: Studies in the Philosophy of History* 33, no. 2 (1994): p. 140.
2. Stephen J. Whitfield, "The Holocaust and the American Jewish Intellectual," *Judaism* 28, no. 4 (1979): p. 393; Leon A. Jick, "The Holocaust: Its Use and Abuse Within the American Public," *Yad Vashem Studies* 14 (1981): p. 306; Deborah E. Lipstadt, "America and the Memory of the Holocaust, 1950–1956," *Modern Judaism* 16 (1995): p. 195.
3. Judith E. Doneson, *The Holocaust in American Film* (Philadelphia: Jewish Publication Society, 1987), p. 61; Lawrence E. Langer, "The Americanization of the Holocaust on Stage and Screen," in *From Hester Street to Hollywood: The Jewish-American Stage and Screen,* ed. Sarah Blacher Cohen (Bloomington: Indiana University Press, 1983), pp. 214–215.

Chapter 1 The Image as Witness

1. Robert H. Abzug, *Inside the Vicious Heart: Americans and the Liberation of Nazi Concentration Camps* (New York: Oxford University Press, 1985), pp. ix–xi, passim.
2. See Sybil Milton, "Confronting Atrocities," in *Liberation 1945,* ed. Susan D. Bachrach (Washington, D.C.: United States Holocaust Memorial Museum, 1995), pp. 57–58. An excerpt from Eisenhower's words is engraved on one of the outer walls of the United States Holocaust Memorial Museum in Washington.
3. Dwight D. Eisenhower, *Crusade in Europe* (New York: Doubleday, 1977[1948]), pp. 408–409.
4. Barbie Zelizer, "The Image, the Word, and the Holocaust: Photojournalism and the Shape of Memory," seminar paper presented at the PARSS Cultural Studies Seminar, University of Pennsylvania, Philadelphia, February 1994, p. 16.
5. Walter Benjamin, "The Work of Art in the Age of Mechanical Reproduction," in *Illuminations,* ed. Hannah Arendt (New York: Schocken, 1968), pp. 236–237. See also Susan Buck-Morss, *The Dialectics of Seeing: Walter Benjamin and the Arcades Project* (Cambridge, Massachusetts: MIT Press, 1990), pp. 267–268.
6. Michael Taussig, *Mimesis and Alterity: A Particular History of the Senses* (New York: Routledge, 1993), pp. 20, 40.
7. Luc Sante, *Evidence* (New York: Farrar, Straus and Giroux, 1992), p. 63.
8. Alfred Kazin, *Starting Out in the Thirties* (Boston: Little, Brown, 1965), p. 166. Kazin described footage filmed by the British at Bergen-Belsen.
9. Susan Sontag, *On Photography* (New York: Doubleday, 1973), pp. 19–20.
10. Ibid., p. 17. More recently, Michael Ignatieff has made similar claims about television: "Television images cannot assert anything: they can only instantiate something. Images of human suffering do not assert their own meaning: they can only instantiate a moral claim if those who watch understand themselves to be potentially under obligation to those they see" (*The Warrior's Honor: Ethnic War and the Modern Conscience* [New York: Metropolitan Books, 1997], pp. 11–12).

11. "In Newsreels," *Motion Picture Herald* 159, no. 5 (5 May 1945): p. 42. During the previous week, Paramount News no. 69 presented a sequence entitled "Nazi Horrors Shock the World," and Universal Newsreel no. 392 included images of liberated camps in the sequence "The Wake of War in Germany"; see "In Newsreels," *Motion Picture Herald* 159, no. 4 (28 April 1945): p. 50.

12. Raymond Fielding, *The American Newsreel 1911–1967* (Norman: University of Oklahoma Press, 1972), p. 220.

13. John Grierson, *Grierson on Documentary* (New York: Harcourt, Brace, 1947), p. 162.

14. See Leo Handel, *Hollywood Looks at Its Audience* (Urbana: University of Illinois Press, 1950), p. 170.

15. On American newsreels during World War II, see Fielding, *The American Newsreel,* pp. 288–303, passim; K.R.M. Short, "American Newsreels and the Collapse of Nazi Germany," in *Hitler's Fall: The Newsreel Witness,* eds. K.R.M. Short and Stephan Dolezel (London: Croom Helm, 1988), pp. 1–27. On the Signal Corps, see Peter Maslowski, *Armed with Cameras: The American Military Photographers of World War II* (New York: Free Press, 1993).

16. "Nazi Prison Cruelty Film to Be Shown Tomorrow," *New York Times,* 25 April 1945, p. 3; "Atrocity Pix Breaking Newsreel House Records," *The Film Daily* (New York) 87, no. 86 (3 May 1945): p. 6; "Congress Irate at Atrocity Reels," *Variety,* 2 May 1945, p. 2; "Nazi Atrocity Films Real Shockers but U.S. Audiences Take It; Some Cuts," *Variety,* 9 May 1945, pp. 6, 18.

17. Universal Newsreel circular, "Advance Information for Newspaper Publicity and Exploitation," vol. 18–393 [26 April 1945], National Archives and Records Administration, Washington, D.C., RG 200.

18. Universal Newsreel 18–393 [ca. 1 May 1945]; all citations transcribed from a copy of this film in the National Archives and Records Administration, Washington, D.C., RG 200.

19. Paramount News 4–70 (2 May 1945); all citations transcribed from a copy of this film in the National Archives and Records Administration, Washington, D.C., RG 200.

20. As cited in "Horror Pictures," *Motion Picture Herald* 159, no. 5 (5 May 1945): p. 8.

21. Paramount News 4–69 (28 April 1945); all citations transcribed from a copy of this film in the National Archives and Records Administration, Washington, D.C., RG 200.

22. "Liberated U.S. Troops Want Atrocity Pix Shown," *Variety,* 9 May 1945, p. 18; "Troops Make Britons See Newsreels of Atrocities," *New York Times,* 21 April 1945, p. 5.

23. A complete transcript of the report appears in Edward Bliss Jr., ed., *In Search of Light: The Broadcasts of Edward R. Murrow, 1938–1961* (New York: Knopf, 1967), pp. 91–95.

24. *WWII Resources from the National Archives and its National Audiovisual Center,* mail-order catalogue [Washington, D.C., 1992], p. 28.

25. Universal Newsreel circular, "Advance Information for Newspaper Publicity and Exploitation," vol. 18–393.

26. See Nöel Carroll, *The Philosophy of Horror, or Paradoxes of the Heart* (New York: Routledge, 1991). Carroll characterizes the repulsion and attraction described above as the "paradox of horror," a distinctive feature of this literary and cinematic genre.

27. "In Newsreels," *Motion Picture Herald* 159, no. 5 (5 May 1945): p. 42.

28. Paramount News 6–52 (26 February 1947); National Archives and Records Administration, Washington, D.C. , RG 200.

29. Terry Ramsaye, "Horror and Newsreels," *Motion Picture Herald* 159, no. 6 (12 May 1945): p. 7; Terry Ramsaye, "Blood and Guts," Motion Picture Herald 159, no. 8 (26 May 1945): p. 7; Ramsaye's reaction recalls the response of pioneer American filmmaker Siegmund Lubin to documentary footage of World War I, recorded for his film company in 1914, which he refused to release: "Such pictures would be anything but neutral in their effect on an audience. . . . There is nothing elevating about the sight of a man being killed. " As cited in Joseph P. Eckhardt and Linda Kowall, *Peddler of Dreams: Siegmund Lubin and the Creation of the Motion Picture Industry 1896–1916* (Philadelphia: National Museum of American Jewish History, 1984), p. 15.

30. James Agee, "Films," *The Nation* 160, no. 12 (24 March 1945): p. 342.

31. James Agee, "Films," *The Nation* 160, no. 20 (9 May 1945): p. 579.

32. Universal Newsreel 18–393; Paramount News 4–70.

33. The length of newsreel segments reporting on the liberation of camps ranged from 400 feet (MGM News of the Day) to 700 feet (Paramount News); see "Nazi Sadism Footage Dominates the Newsreels," *The Film Daily* (New York) 87, no. 83 (30 April 1945): pp. 1, 3.

34. Charles Lawrence Gellert, comp., *The Holocaust, Israel, and the Jews: Motion Pictures in the National Archives* (Washington, D.C. : National Archives and Records Administration, 1989), pp. 38–41. Some of these images, or similar ones from other camps liberated by American armed forces, do appear in some early television documentary and public service programming—for example, *Placing the Displaced* and *Victory at Sea,* discussed below.

35. According to Gellert, *The Holocaust, Israel and the Jews,* there are 176 films currently inventoried in the United States National Archives and Records Administration under the heading "Holocaust. "

36. Jay Leyda, *Films Beget Films* (New York: Hill and Wang, 1964).

37. Ibid., pp. 73–96.

38. Color footage of liberated camps was also recorded; excerpts can be seen on display in the United States Holocaust Memorial Museum in Washington, D.C. , and in the 1985 documentary *Robert Clary A5714: A Memory of Liberation* (HJVC: item no. JV591).

39. According to Commander James Donovan, a member of the U.S. prosecutorial staff, as cited in Telford Taylor, *The Anatomy of the Nuremberg Trials* (New York: Knopf, 1992), p. 186.

40. These and all following citations from *Nazi Concentration Camps* were transcribed from a copy of the film housed in the National Archives and Records Administration, Washington, D.C. , RG 238 (National Archives Collection of World War II War Crimes Records), inventory no. 238. 2.

41. Abzug, *Inside the Vicious Heart,* pp. 127–128.

42. Sante, *Evidence,* pp. 60–62.

43. Lawrence Douglas, "Film as Witness: Screening *Nazi Concentration Camps* Before the Nuremberg Tribunal," *Yale Law Journal* 105, no. 2 (November 1995): pp. 452–453.

44. Taylor, *The Anatomy of the Nuremberg Trials,* pp. 186–187.

45. Court TV aired its fifteen-hour presentation of *The Nuremberg Trial,* including vintage footage of the trial as well as excerpts from *Nazi Concentration Camps,* during the evenings of 13–17 November 1995, with a summary broadcast on 20 November. Floyd Abrams appeared on 13 November; Ben Ferencz appeared on 14 November. Citations are transcribed from a videorecording of the telecast. For further discussion of the Court TV broadcasts of *The Nuremberg Trial,* see Chapter 8, pp. 252–255.

46. See Lucy S. Dawidowicz, *The War Against the Jews, 1933–1945* (New York: Holt, Rinehart and Winston, 1975).

47. *Crusade in Europe:* Episode 22 (MTR: item no. T80:0465); *Victory at Sea: Design for Peace* (MTR: item no. T79:0033).

48. *The Twisted Cross* (NJAB: item no. T75); *Trial at Nuremberg* (NJAB: item no. T207). Two other *Project Twenty* documentaries make passing reference to the Nazi persecution of German Jewry: *Three, Two, One, Zero* (1954), which traces the development of nuclear power (here Nazi anti-Semitism is mentioned in the context of discussing refugee scientists who came to the United States in the 1930s), and *Life in the Thirties* (1959), which offers an overview of life in the United States during this decade.

49. NJAB: item no. T316.

50. Chaim Potok, *The Chosen* (New York: Fawcett Crest, 1968); the film version, directed by Jeremy Paul Kagan, was released by Twentieth Century-Fox. The *Kojak* broadcast, aired 16 February 1985, was based in part on actual incidents described in John Loftus's *The Belarus Secret* (New York: Knopf, 1982).

51. "No Excuse Not to Vote: Reminder," Korey Kay and Partners for Members Only, 1992. The PSA campaign, titled "No Excuse Not To Vote," was sponsored by Members Only, a manufacturer of clothing for the teenage and young-adult market.

Chapter 2. "This Is Your Life"

1. MTR: item no. T82:0443, broadcast 22 September 1953.

2. For recordings of broadcasts of *Reunion,* the WNYC series *Music by New Americans* and *The Golden Door,* and episodes of *The Eternal Light* dealing with DPs, see the Max and Frieda Weinstein Archive for Recorded Sound, YIVO Institute for Jewish Research, New York, RG 130 (Radio Programs).

3. On *Hunger Takes No Holiday,* see "Television Review: 'The World We Live In,'" *Variety,* 15 August 1945, p. 26; *Placing the Displaced* was aired on WCBS-TV on 14 June 1948. See Roberta Newman, "D. P. Docudrama: Institutional Propaganda and Post–World War II Jewish Refugees," *Jewish Folklore and Ethnology*

Review 16, no. 1 (1994): pp. 52–56; "Bill of Rights Day" aired on 15 December 1951. See YIVO Archives, USNA Papers, RG 246, box 66, folder 2600, USNA memo 13 December 1951; "Should we allow 400,000 DPs into the United States?" was debated on *The Court of Current Issues,* presented on New York Station WABD, on 27 April 1948. See "The Court of Current Issues," *Rescue* (HIAS) 5, no. 4 (May 1948): pp. 8–9, 11; an episode of NBC's *The American Forum,* titled "Shall the United States Admit More DPs?" aired 1 April 1950 (Fox: item no. 03181); on WPIX telecasts, see the inventory of "Telepix" Television Newsreels at the National Archives and Records Administration, Washington, D.C. (RG 200); the *Lamp Unto My Feet* episode was presented on 28 November 1948. See Report to the Board of Overseers: The Eternal Light, December 1948; hectograph, pp. 4–6, JTS Archives, RG 11C, box 26, folder 38.

4. NJAB: item no. T965.

5. On the series' approach to life history, see Jeffrey Shandler, "'This Is Your Life': Telling a Holocaust Survivor's Life Story on Early American Television," *Journal of Narrative and Life History* 4, nos. 1–2 (1994), pp. 41–68.

6. See Dean Jennings, "It Makes Him Happy to See You Cry," *Saturday Evening Post* 228, no. 38 (4 February 1956): pp. 19, 52.

7. Ibid. , p. 57.

8. See John Hersey, *Hiroshima,* rev. ed. (New York: Vintage, 1989[1985]), pp. 144–147. Hersey's description of the Reverend Tanimoto broadcast—including a commercial for Hazel Bishop nail polish, a "reunion" with one of the pilots of the *Enola Gay,* and the surprise appearance of Tanimoto's wife and children at the conclusion of the half hour—makes for an interesting comparison with the Hanna Kohner episode.

9. Stuart Elliott, "Ford Will Travel High Road with Adless 'Schindler's List,'" *New York Times,* 21 February 1997, pp. D1, D4.

10. This was not the first time that the UJA had used television for fund-raising purposes. During the 1948–1949 season, "all four networks offered their national facilities to the United Jewish Appeal during its national fund-raising campaign for the production of dramatizations featuring such popular motion picture personalities as Al Jolson and John Garfield." See Irma Kopp, "Radio and Television," *American Jewish Year Book* 51 (New York: American Jewish Committee; Philadelphia: Jewish Publication Society, 1950), p. 239.

11. Newman, "D. P. Docudrama," p. 55.

12. The Rosenbergs, who had been convicted on charges of conspiracy to commit espionage, were electrocuted on 19 June 1953; the progress of their case received extensive publicity, including frequent coverage on local television news programs broadcast in New York. (See, e.g. , the inventory of "Telepix" Television Newsreels at the National Archives and Records Administration, Washington, D.C. [RG 200].)

13. As cited in Jennings, "It Makes Him Happy to See You Cry," p. 52.

14. See Lynn Spigel, *Make Room for TV: Television and the Family Ideal in Postwar America* (Chicago: University of Chicago Press, 1992), pp. 118–119.

15. Murray Hausknecht, "The Mike in the Bosom," in *Mass Culture: The Popular Arts in America,* eds. Bernard Rosenberg and David Manning White (New York: Free Press, 1957), pp. 375–376.

16. Gerald Green, *The Last Angry Man* (New York: Scribner's, 1956).

17. Benny Hoffman, who appeared on *This Is Your Life* on 29 January 1961, was liberated from Buchenwald by American armed forces. Cantors Gregor Shelkin and Bela Herskovitz, who were honored by the series on 17 February 1954 and 8 February 1956, respectively, were also survivors of Nazi persecutions. The series also paid tribute to Jewish refugees Ilse Intrator Stanley (on 2 November 1955), who was credited with saving 412 people from Nazi concentration camps, and Dr. Max Nussbaum (on 22 April 1959), a rabbi and community leader in prewar Germany. Count Felix von Luckner, a World War I hero who appeared on *This Is Your Life* on 4 November 1959, was honored for having "refused high office from the Nazis and sav[ing] at least one Jewess. " As listed in Fox: item nos. 04103 (Hoffman), 04104 (Herskovitz), 04105 (Shelkin), 04107 (von Luckner), 04109 (Nussbaum), 04114 (Stanley).

18. Hanna Kohner, Walter Kohner, and Frederick Kohner, *Hanna and Walter: A Love Story* (New York: Random House, 1984). The presentation of Hanna's life story on *This Is Your Life* is mentioned in the book's epilogue (p. 209).

Chapter 3. The Theater of Our Century

1. Raymond Williams, "Drama in a Dramatised Society," in *Raymond Williams on Television: Selected Writings,* ed. Alan O'Connor (London: Routledge, 1989), pp. 4–5.

2. Gilbert Seldes, *Writing for Television* (New York: Doubleday, 1952), pp. 151, 152.

3. Christopher H. Sterling and John M. Kittross, *Stay Tuned: A Concise History of American Broadcasting,* 2nd ed. (Belmont, California: Wadsworth, 1990), p. 99.

4. Fred Coe, "Television Drama's Declaration of Independence," *Theatre Arts,* June 1954, as cited in Frank Sturcken, *Live Television: The Golden Age of 1946–1958 in New York* (Jefferson, N.C. : McFarland, 1990), p. 40.

5. See, e.g. , David Marc and Robert J. Thompson, *Prime Time, Prime Movers* (Syracuse: Syracuse University Press, 1995), pp. 117–131.

6. Federal Communications Commission, Office of Network Study, *Second Interim Report: Television Program Procurement, Part II* (Washington, D.C. : U.S. Government Printing Office, 1965), p. 626, as cited in William Boddy, *Fifties Television: The Industry and Its Critics* (Urbana: University of Illinois Press, 1990), p. 89.

7. Erik Barnouw, *Tube of Plenty: The Evolution of American Television,* 2nd rev. ed. (New York: Oxford University Press, 1990), p. 160.

8. Erik Barnouw, *The Television Writer* (New York: Hill and Wang, 1962), p. 5; Paddy Chayefsky, "Good Theatre in Television," as cited in Boddy, *Fifties Television,* p. 83; Paddy Chayefsky, *Television Plays* (New York: Touchstone, 1971 [1955]), p. 132.

9. Chayefsky, *Television Plays,* p. 130; John Brady, *The Craft of the Screenwriter: Interviews with Six Celebrated Screenwriters* (New York: Touchstone, 1981), pp. 54–55.

10. Barnouw, *Tube of Plenty*, p. 163.

11. See Boddy, *Fifties Television*, pp. 80–92.

12. Irving Howe, *World of Our Fathers: The Journey of the East European Jews to America and the Life They Found and Made* (New York: Harcourt Brace Jovanovich, 1976), p. 626.

13. See, e.g., Leon A. Jick, "The Holocaust: Its Use and Abuse Within the American Public," *Yad Vashem Studies* 14 (1981): pp. 303–318; Peter Novick, "Holocaust Memory in America," in *The Art of Memory: Holocaust Memorials*, ed. James E. Young (New York: The Jewish Museum; Munich: Prestel, 1994), pp. 159–165; Edward S. Shapiro, *A Time for Healing: American Jewry Since World War II* (Baltimore: Johns Hopkins University Press, 1992), pp. 213–215; Stephen J. Whitfield, "The Holocaust and the American Jewish Intellectual," *Judaism* 28, no. 4 (1979): pp. 391–401.

14. For an early overview of Holocaust literature and scholarship, see, e.g., Philip Friedman, "Research and Literature on the Recent Jewish Tragedy," *Jewish Social Studies* 12, no. 1 (January 1950): pp. 17–26; on communal memoirs, see Jack Kugelmass and Jonathan Boyarin, eds., *From a Ruined Garden: The Memorial Books of Polish Jewry* (New York: Schocken, 1983), pp. 1–19; on memorials, see James E. Young, *The Texture of Memory: Holocaust Memorials and Meaning* (New Haven: Yale University Press, 1993), pp. 287–294.

15. Stuart Svonkin, "The Return to Parochialism: American Jewish Communal Life in the 1960s," conference paper presented at the Second Annual Scholars' Conference on American Jewish History, June 1996, p. 1. See his *Jews Against Prejudice: American Jews and the Intergroup Relations Movement from World War to Cold War* (New York: Columbia University Press, 1997).

16. Judd Teller, *Strangers and Natives: The Evolution of the American Jew from 1921 to the Present* (New York: Dell, 1968), pp. 259, 261.

17. MTR: item no. T87:0491; Sturcken, *Live Television*, p. 48.

18. Chayefsky, *Television Plays*, p. 8.

19. Ibid. , p. 36.

20. Paul Deutschman, "It Happened on the Brooklyn Subway," *Reader's Digest* 54, no. 325 (May 1949): p. 45; Jon Kampner, *The Man in the Shadows: Fred Coe and the Golden Age of Television* (New Brunswick: Rutgers University Press, 1997), pp. 62–63; Chayefsky, *Television Plays*, p. 37.

21. Lawrence L. Langer, "The Americanization of the Holocaust on Stage and Screen" in *From Hester Street to Hollywood: The Jewish-American Stage and Screen*, ed. Sarah Blacher Cohen (Bloomington: Indiana University Press, 1983), p. 214.

22. Fox: items nos. 03937 (*The Refugee*), 03936 (*The Ransom of Sigmund Freud*), 04667 (*Homeward Borne*).

23. *Produced by . . . Herbert Brodkin: A Signature of Conviction and Integrity* (New York: Museum of Broadcasting, 1985), pp. 38–39.

24. UCLA: *Walk Down the Hill*.

25. Donald Bevan and Edmund Trczinski, *Stalag 17: A Comedy Melodrama in Three Acts* (New York: Dramatists Play Service, 1951). The film version was

directed by Billy Wilder for Paramount Pictures; screenplay by Edwin Blum and Wilder, based on the Broadway play.

26. See Mitchell G. Bard, *Forgotten Victims: The Abandonment of Americans in Hitler's Camps* (Boulder, Colorado: Westview, 1994), especially pp. 71–76. Among the informants whom Bard interviewed was Ernest Kinoy (pp. 89, 111). Bard says he first became aware of the special treatment of American Jewish GIs taken prisoner by Nazis "while watching the 1987 TV documentary 'POW—Americans in Enemy Hands'"; see Douglas Century, "Forgotten Prisoners," *Forward* [English-language edition], 8 July 1994, p. 10.

27. Laura Z. Hobson, *Gentleman's Agreement* (New York: Simon and Schuster, 1947). The film version, directed by Elia Kazan, was produced by Twentieth Century-Fox.

28. Melville J. Herskovits, "When Is a Jew a Jew?" *Modern Quarterly* 4, no. 2 (June–September 1927): pp. 109, 117, emphasis in original; Melville J. Herskovits, "Who Are the Jews?" in *The Jews: Their History, Culture and Religion,* ed. Louis Finkelstein (Philadelphia: Jewish Publication Society, 1949), p. 1168.

29. NJAB: item no. T336; Michel del Castillo, *Child of Our Time,* trans. Peter Green (New York: Knopf, 1958).

30. NJAB: item no. T339–340.

31. A remake of *In the Presence of Mine Enemies,* aired on the Showtime cable channel in April 1997, transformed the production of the teleplay from a live studio broadcast to a prerecorded film. Exterior scenes were filmed in Montreal.

32. "Ani ma'amin" (I believe) is an avowal of belief based on the Thirteen Articles of Faith formulated by medieval Jewish philosopher Maimonides. A version of the hymn has figured frequently in Holocaust memorial programs and rituals.

33. Joel Engel, *Rod Serling: The Dreams and Nightmares of Life in the Twilight Zone* (Chicago: Contemporary Books, 1989), pp. 195, 199.

34. Jack O'Brian, "Should It Have Been Televised?" *New York Journal-American,* 19 May 1960, p. 26; Gordon F. Sander, *Serling: The Rise and Twilight of Television's Last Angry Man* (New York: Dutton, 1992), p. 156.

35. Engel, *Rod Serling,* pp. 200–201.

36. See Patricia Erens, *The Jew in American Cinema* (Bloomington: Indiana University Press, 1984), pp. 12–13, 63–64.

37. Engel, *Rod Serling,* p. 23.

38. Alex Ward, "A Producer of the Provocative," *New York Times,* 15 November 1981, sec. 2, p. 39; *Produced by . . . Herbert Brodkin,* pp. 5–6, 15.

39. See *Les Brown's Encyclopedia of Television,* 3rd ed. (Detroit: Gale Research, 1992), p. 223.

40. See Jeffrey Shandler and Elihu Katz, "Broadcasting American Judaism: The Radio and Television Department of the Jewish Theological Seminary," in *Tradition Renewed: A History of the Jewish Theological Seminary,* ed. Jack Wertheimer (New York: Jewish Theological Seminary, 1997), pp. 363–401.

41. Morton Wishengrad, *The Eternal Light* (New York: Crown, 1947), p. viii.

42. Morton Wishengrad, *Anne Frank: The Diary of a Young Girl,* Jewish Theological Seminary Archives, RG 11C, box 32, folder 36; mimeograph, p. 1.

43. See Lawrence Graver, *An Obsession with Anne Frank: Meyer Levin and the Diary* (Berkeley: University of California Press, 1995), as well as Levin's own account of the subsequent controversy surrounding his adaptation of the diary, *Obsession* (New York: Simon and Schuster, 1973). A version of Levin's script was broadcast on the radio series *The Eternal Light* on 14 December 1952 (*Anne Frank: Diary of a Young Girl,* program no. 366).

44. Wishengrad, *Anne Frank,* p. 9.

45. Ibid. , pp. 25–26.

46. *The Diary of Anne Frank: The Critical Edition,* ed. David Barnouw and Gerrold van der Stroom, trans. Arnold J. Pomerans and B. M. Mooyaart-Doubleday (New York: Doubleday, 1989), p. 600.

47. Wishengrad, *Anne Frank,* p. 33.

48. NJAB: item no. T1004.

49. This and all following citations from the drama, except where noted, are from Reginald Rose, *The Final Ingredient* (New York: Jewish Theological Seminary of America, 1959). The script (identified as "Telecast: Chapter T-72"), one of a series of separate booklets issued by the Seminary, has a copyright date of 1958.

50. This last line is spoken in the telecast of *The Final Ingredient* but does not appear in the published script.

51. This is how the broadcast of *The Final Ingredient* ends. The description of the concluding moments in Rose's published script includes a final image not seen in the telecast, and the stage directions make explicit the impact that the inmates' celebration has on the guards: "Camera pans the faces now as the others join in. The song swells and grows in power. Louder and louder it becomes, lustier and lustier, and soon it is a tremendous, booming sound, slow, but shocking in its strength. The squad of soldiers reaches them and halts, stands facing them, and makes no move. We see the shocked faces of the soldiers and their lieutenant. Still no move is made. These soldiers, for now, are gripped in the defiant power of the song. . . . Medium shot from inside tower. The corporal crouches over his gun. The light sweeps across the area, and catches the group. They turn into the light, and a final burst of strength lifts their song to the heavens. Camera moves in close on the corporal's hands. They rest on top of his gun, and they tremble, as we fade out" (Rose, *The Final Ingredient,* p. 24).

52. Mordekhai Eliav, *Ani Ma'amin* (Jerusalem: Mosad Harav Kook, 1965), p. 186, as cited in Irving J. Rosenbaum, *The Holocaust and Halakhah* ([New York]: KTAV, 1976), p. 99. For a discussion of the issues of rabbinical law concerning the observance of Passover during the Holocaust, the response of various rabbinical authorities and accounts of actual observance (or nonobservance), see Rosenbaum, *The Holocaust and Halakhah,* pp. 97–108. According to David Amram, who composed an opera for television based on *The Final Ingredient* (see note 57 for this chapter), the original drama "is based on memories of events shared by survivors of the Holocaust. . . . These extraordinary stories, recounted by survivors, were the foundation of Reginald Rose's moving play" (*The Final Ingredient: An Opera of the Holocaust in One Act* [booklet accompanying compact disc recording; New York: Premier Recordings #PRCD 1056, 1996], p. 1).

53. Jose, "The Final Ingredient," *Variety,* 22 April 1959, p. 50.

54. On connections between the Holocaust and Passover observance, see, e.g., Anita Schwartz, "The Secular Seder: Continuity and Change among Left-Wing Jews," in *Between Two Worlds: Ethnographic Essays on American Jewry,* ed. Jack Kugelmass (Ithaca: Cornell University Press, 1988), pp. 105–127; Jenna Weissman Joselit, " 'A Set Table': Jewish Domestic Culture in the New World, 1880–1950," in *Getting Comfortable in New York: The American Jewish Home, 1880–1950,* Susan L. Braunstein and Jenna Weissman Joselit, eds. (New York: The Jewish Museum, 1990), p. 53.

55. According to Fox (item no. 03528), *In the Beginning* is based on the short story "The Last Dance" by Hillel Seidman; Wallenberg's efforts to rescue Hungarian Jews from Nazi persecution were dramatized on *Eternal Light* in 1957 (*One Man;* Fox: item no. 03412); Danish resistance to the Nazi persecution of Jews was dramatized on *Look Up and Live* (*An Act of Faith,* 1961; NJAB: item no. T143–144) and *The Eternal Light* (*The Bookseller,* 1962; Fox: item no. 13352); Korczak's story is dramatized in *A Field of Buttercups* (*Eternal Light,* 1969; NJAB: item no. T780); the artwork of children confined to Terezín was the subject of episodes of *The Eternal Light* (1966; NJAB: item no. T784) and *Look Up and Live* (1967; Fox: item no. 03864), both titled *I Never Saw Another Butterfly.*

56. ABC's broadcast of *The Diary of Anne Frank,* with Diane Davila as Anne, was presented on 26 November 1967 (MTR: item no. T79:0304–0306). Another production of the Hackett and Goodrich script was presented by *NBC Monday Night at the Movies* on 17 November 1980, with Melissa Gilbert as Anne (MTR: item no. T82:0072–0073).

57. The operatic version of *The Final Ingredient* was first broadcast on 11 April 1965 (MTR: item no. T81:0161 [black-and-white copy of color telecast]). According to Fox (item no. 03279), the opera was rebroadcast on 23 April 1967, 7 April 1968, and 30 March 1969. A sound recording of the original telecast of the opera is available (see note 52 for this chapter). On the television production, see Walter Carlson, "Add a Touch of Bitters," *New York Times,* 11 April 1965, sec. 2, p. 21.

58. Emil Fackenheim, "Holocaust," in *Contemporary Jewish Religious Thought: Original Essays on Critical Concepts, Movements, and Beliefs,* eds. Arthur A. Cohen and Paul Mendes-Flohr (New York: Scribner's, 1987), p. 401.

59. MTR: item no. T77:0169–0170; The *Playhouse 90* production of *Judgment at Nuremberg* was directed by George Roy Hill. The cinematic version of *Judgment at Nuremberg,* with an expanded screenplay by Abby Mann, was released by United Artists in 1961. Directed by Stanley Kramer, it starred Spencer Tracy, Maximilian Schell (reprising his role in the television production), Richard Widmark, Burt Lancaster, Judy Garland, Montgomery Clift, and Marlene Dietrich.

60. See Jack C. Ellis, *The Documentary Idea: A Critical History of English-Language Documentary Film and Video* (Englewood Cliffs, New Jersey: Prentice Hall, 1989), pp. 153–164; Raymond Williams, *Television: Technology and Cultural Form* (Hanover, New Hampshire: University Press of New England and Wesleyan University Press: 1992), pp. 67, 66.

61. Jay Leyda, *Films Beget Films* (New York: Hill and Wang, 1964), p. 73. See discussion of this concept above in Chapter 1, p. 19.

62. Telford Taylor, *Final Report to the Secretary of the Army on the Nuremberg War Crimes Trials Under Control Council Law No. 10* (Washington, D.C. : U.S. Government Printing Office, 1949), p. 168.

63. On Taylor's refusal to serve as consultant for the 1961 film version of *Judgment at Nuremberg,* see Judith E. Doneson, *The Holocaust in American Film* (Philadelphia: Jewish Publication Society, 1987), pp. 103–104.

64. This footage also appeared in *The Nazi Plan,* a compilation film prepared in 1945 by the U.S. Counsel for the Prosecution of Axis Criminality and shown at the first Nuremberg war crimes trial. See Telford Taylor, *The Anatomy of the Nuremberg Trials* (New York: Knopf, 1992), pp. 200–201.

65. In the first dissolve sequence, the dialogue clearly indicates that the images are to be read as Byers's recollection of Nuremberg in the early 1930s. The second sequence, in which Haywood looks up at the sculpted eagle that frames the dissolve, suggests that this vision of the past is the judge's. Because Byers describes the rallies as the dissolve to the footage from *Triumph of the Will* begins and this footage echoes his mention of horns and drums, the sequence might be read as Haywood conjuring up in his mind's eye a vision of Byers's account (although it is unclear from the dialogue whether the young Byers saw the Nazi Party rally or knows of it only indirectly).

66. American telecasts featuring footage of Nazi Germany in the 1930s include the 1956 NBC documentary *The Twisted Cross,* a history of the rise and fall of Nazi Germany (see Chapter 1), and *Hitler Invades Poland,* a 1956 episode of the CBS series *You Are There* (LC: item no. FCA 0590).

67. This statistic is not mentioned in the U.S. Government film *Nazi Concentration Camps.* Its inclusion in *Judgment at Nuremberg,* along with other references in the script to Jews, points to the emerging conceptualization of the Holocaust as a distinct, Jewish-centered phenomenon.

68. This act of metawitnessing plays on what anthropologist Michael Taussig has described as the "cathartic, even curative function" of mimesis, as well as its ability to "give one power over that which is portrayed. " See his *Mimesis and Alterity: A Particular History of the Senses* (New York: Routledge, 1993), pp. 30, 13.

69. "Tele Follow-up Comment: *Playhouse 90,*" *Variety,* 22 April 1959, p. 46.

70. As cited in Ward, "A Producer of the Provocative," sec. 2, p. 39. A comical reenactment of this off-camera conflict between sponsor and network appears in the 1976 feature film *The Front* (Columbia Pictures, directed by Martin Ritt), which dramatizes the impact of anti-Communist blacklisting on the television industry in New York during the 1950s.

71. See, e.g. , Boddy, *Fifties Television,* pp. 197–198.

72. Annette Insdorf, *Indelible Shadows: Film and the Holocaust* 2nd ed. (Cambridge: Cambridge University Press, 1989), p. 3.

73. A copy of the kinescope of *Judgment at Nuremberg* available for screening at the Museum of Radio and Television in New York (see note 59 for this chapter)

includes these "blanked out" references to gas, which occur during the screening of *Nazi Concentration Camps* as well as in dialogue.

74. "Tele Follow-up Comment: *Playhouse 90*," p. 46.

75. The voice-over narration of the commercial, accompanying scenes of a family vacation at a lake in the countryside (boating, making a campfire) runs, in part, as follows: "Adventure ahead—only seconds to take this wonderful picture. But that's time enough for Mom and her new Ansco Cadet—the 'A-plus' snapshot camera from Ansco that's always ready when you are. Hasn't this happened to you? You see a great picture like this—but it's gone before you can focus your camera. But not with the Cadet. . . . You've got it—just as you saw it. "

76. As cited in New York Graphic Society, *Life: The First Decade: 1936–1945* (Boston: Little, Brown, 1979), p. 171.

Part Two: Into the Limelight

1. Leon A. Jick, "The Holocast: Its Use and Abuse Within the American Public," *Yad Vashem Studies* 14 (1981): pp. 312–313.

2. As cited from the *New York Times* in International Center for Holocaust Studies, Anti-Defamation League of B'nai B'rith, *The Holocaust in Books and Films: A Selected, Annotated List,* 3rd ed. (New York: Hippocrene, 1986 [1978]), p. 7.

Chapter 4. The Man in the Glass Box

1. The word *Holocaust* is used during the proceedings to translate the Hebrew term *sho'ah,* which can be heard in prosecutor Gideon Hausner's summation, for example, in the documentary *Verdict for Tomorrow* (see note 59 for this chapter).

2. For an English-language record of the Eichmann trial proceedings, see *In the District Court of Jerusalem, Criminal Case No. 40/61. The Attorney-General of the Government of Israel v. Adolf, the Son of Adolf Karl Eichmann: Minutes of Sessions* (Jerusalem, 1961); *The Trial of Adolf Eichmann: Record of Proceedings in the District Court of Jerusalem* (Jerusalem: The Ministry, 1992).

3. Robert Hariman, ed., *Popular Trials: Rhetoric, Mass Media, and the Law* (Tuscaloosa: University of Alabama Press, 1990), p. 1.

4. For a bibliography of works on Eichmann's life and Nazi career, see Randolph L. Braham, *The Eichmann Case: A Source Book* (New York: World Federation of Hungarian Jews, 1969), items nos. 12–69.

5. Gideon Hausner, *Justice in Jerusalem* (New York: Harper and Row, 1966), pp. 270, 272.

6. Tom Segev, *The Seventh Million: The Israelis and the Holocaust,* trans. Haim Watzman (New York: Hill and Wang, 1993), p. 324.

7. For sources on the pursuit and capture of Eichmann, see Braham, *The Eichmann Case,* items nos. 70–99. See also Peter Z. Malkin and Harry Stein, *Eichmann in My Hands* (New York: Warner, 1990). *The Man Who Captured Eichmann,* a

television drama based on Malkin's memoir and starring Robert Duvall as Eichmann, was aired on TNT on 10 November 1996.

8. For the complete text of the fifteen-count indictment, see *American Jewish Year Book 1962* (New York: American Jewish Committee; Philadelphia: Jewish Publication Society, 1962), pp. 120–131. For a narrative summary of the course of the trial, see Léon Poliakov, "The Eichmann Trial: The Proceedings," *American Jewish Year Book 1962,* pp. 54–84.

9. For sources on preparations for the Eichmann trial, see Braham, *The Eichmann Case,* items nos. 211–228. See also Jochen von Lang and Claus Sibyll, eds., *Eichmann Interrogated: Transcripts From the Archives of the Israeli Police,* trans. Ralph Manheim (New York: Farrar, Straus and Giroux, 1983).

10. Ephraim Bendor, "As Seen in Israel," *Congress Bi-Weekly* 27, no. 10 (20 June 1960): pp. 8–9. The film version of Leon Uris's *Exodus* (Garden City, New York: Doubleday, 1958), directed by Otto Preminger, was released by Metro-Goldwyn-Mayer in 1960. Both novel and film figure as seminal resources for conceptualizing the relationship between the Holocaust and the establishment of the State of Israel in the American popular consciousness. See Deborah Dash Moore, *To the Golden Cities: Pursuing the American Jewish Dream in Miami and Los Angeles* (New York: Free Press, 1994), pp. 243–260.

11. Hariman, *Popular Trials,* pp. 21, 3.

12. The United Nations adjudicated Argentina's complaint that Israel violated its laws by abducting Eichmann from Buenos Aires in Security Council meetings nos. 865–868 (22–23 June 1960).

13. Hausner, *Justice in Jerusalem,* p. 288.

14. Segev, *The Seventh Million,* pp. 329–330.

15. As cited in George Salomon, "The Eichmann Trial: America's Response," *American Jewish Year Book 1962* (New York: American Jewish Committee; Philadelphia: Jewish Publication Society, 1962), p. 88.

16. "Thoughts on Eichmann," *National Review* 10, no. 15 (22 April 1961): pp. 238–239.

17. "The Eichmann Case as Seen by Ben-Gurion," *New York Times,* 18 December 1960, sec. 6, pp. 7, 62. On Ben-Gurion's political motives with regard to the Eichmann trial, see Segev, *The Seventh Million,* pp. 328–331.

18. Hausner, *Justice in Jerusalem,* pp. 4, 291, 296.

19. Segev, *The Seventh Million,* p. 353.

20. See "Court Approves Filming of Trial," *New York Times,* 11 March 1961, p. 4; Hausner, *Justice in Jerusalem,* p. 307.

21. As cited in Horace Sutton, "Eichmann Goes on Trial: The Charged Air," *Saturday Review* 44, no. 14 (8 April 1961): p. 49.

22. "The Big Story," *Newsweek* 57, no. 15 (10 April 1961): p. 60.

23. "The Rush of History," *Time* 77, no. 17 (21 April 1961): p. 45; Lawrence Fellows, "Eichmann Goes to Trial," *New York Times,* 9 April 1961, sec. 4, p. 5; Samuel Caplan, "At the Eichmann Trial: Six Million Prosecutors," *Congress Bi-Weekly* 28, no. 9 (1 May 1961): p. 5.

24. Hausner, *Justice in Jerusalem,* p. 307.

25. Lawrence Fellows, "TV Makes Its Israeli Debut with a Tragedy," *New York Times*, 2 July 1961, sec. 2, p. 9.

26. Hausner, *Justice in Jerusalem*, p. 307.

27. Peter Kihss, "Eichmann Trial to Be Seen on TV," *New York Times*, 14 November 1960, p. 13; Richard F. Shepard, "U.S. TV Networks Irked at Coverage of Eichmann Trial," *New York Times*, 25 February 1961, p. 45; "Eichmann on TV," *Newsweek* 57, no. 9 (27 February 1961): p. 54; "Court Approves Filming of Trial," *New York Times*, 11 March 1961, p. 4; Val Adams, "News of TV and Radio—Eichmann," *New York Times*, 9 April 1961, sec. 2, p. 15; E. Z. Dimitman, "How Television Is Watching the Eichmann Trial," *TV Guide* 9, no. 18 (6–12 May 1961): p. A3.

28. "Newsfront: The Eichmann Trial," *Television Age* 9, no. 1 (7 August 1961): p. 27; Jack Gould, "TV: The Eichmann Trial," *New York Times*, 10 April 1961, p. 55. Major congressional investigations had been televised during the 1950s, notably the Senate Crime Committee hearings, conducted by Estes Kefauver in 1951, and the Army-McCarthy hearings in 1954. In addition, American television had previously offered regional telecasts of local trials, despite a 1952 ruling by the American Bar Association against the broadcasting of court proceedings. According to Paul Thaler, *The Watchful Eye: American Justice in the Age of the Television Trial* (Westport, Connecticut: Praeger, 1994), television cameras were briefly allowed into Oklahoma courts in 1953, and the first live television broadcast of a trial in America was a murder case in Texas, broadcast by KWTX-TV in Waco, beginning on 6 December 1955 (pp. 25–26).

29. Fellows, "TV Makes Its Israeli Debut with a Tragedy," p. 9.

30. "Newsfront: The Eichmann Trial," pp. 25–27. Emphasis in original.

31. "Eichmann Goes to Trial," *New York Times*, 9 April 1961, sec. 4, p. 5; Dimitman, "How Television Is Watching the Eichmann Trial," p. A3.

32. Fellows, "TV Makes Its Israeli Debut with a Tragedy," p. 9. Fellows noted that the knowledge of the live, albeit unseen, audience in Ratisbonne Hall helped the television crew to remain "alert in its work. "

33. Copies of extant tapes of the Eichmann trial repose in the National Jewish Archive of Broadcasting, the Jewish Museum, New York, and in the Steven Spielberg Film Archive at the Hebrew University, Jerusalem. According to Alan Rosenthal, who was an assistant producer and director of Capital Cities's videotaping of the trial, some tapes were erased: "Videotaping was still in its primitive infancy. In fact, tape was so expensive and Capital Cities so poor, that tapes of the trial were reused and lost forever" (as cited in Jeffrey Gaster, "TV Professionals Who Covered the Eichmann Trial Form Panel," *Connecticut Jewish Ledger*, 23 April 1986, p. 7).

34. Dimitman, "How Television Is Watching the Eichmann Trial," p. A3.

35. "TV Trial Films Delayed," *New York Times*, 12 April 1961, p. 16.

36. Telstar I inaugurated satellite relays of television programs in July 1962, shortly followed by the enactment of the Communications Satellite Act. COMSAT (the Communications Satellite Corporation) was established in 1962. The Early Bird (Intelsat I), which enabled synchronous transmission, was the first commercial communications satellite; it was launched in 1965.

37. On 15 December 1961, the Jerusalem District Court sentenced Eichmann to be hanged. His appeal to the Israeli Supreme Court, which rejected the plea, was convened on 22 March 1962. After his final appeal, to the president of Israel, was denied on 29 May, Eichmann was hanged on 31 May.

38. Daniel Dayan and Elihu Katz, *Media Events: The Live Broadcasting of History* (Cambridge: Harvard University Press, 1995), pp. 1–9.

39. "Eichmann Trial: Daily Videotapes, WNTA-TV" [advertisement], *New York Times,* 12 April 1961, p. 53; "Eichmann, Gagarin: 'Instant TV,'" *Variety,* 19 April 1961, p. 43.

40. See Salomon, "The Eichmann Trial: America's Response," p. 96; "TV Guide Close-up: Eichmann Trial," *TV Guide* 9, no. 14 (8–14 April 1961): p. A8; Bert Burns, "Another Nazi in Spotlight," *New York World-Telegram and Sun,* 11 April 1961, p. 30.

41. Marie Totre, "Survived 8 Nazi Camps, Tells of Revisit There," *New York Herald Tribune,* 11 April 1961, p. 35.

42. Bert Burns, "Eichmann Case Stymies Comics," *New York World-Telegram and Sun,* 13 April 1961, p. 32.

43. Gould, "TV: The Eichmann Trial," p. 55.

44. Jack Gould, "TV: Live Court Drama," *New York Times,* 13 April 1961, p. 71.

45. On coverage of the Eichmann case in the American press, see American Jewish Committee, *The Eichmann Case in the American Press* (New York: Institute of Human Relations, 1962); George Salomon, "The Eichmann Trial: America's Response," pp. 85–103; George Salomon, "The End of Eichmann: America's Response," *American Jewish Year Book 1963,* eds. Morris Fine and Milton Himmelfarb (New York: American Jewish Committee; Philadelphia: Jewish Publication Society, 1963): pp. 247–259.

46. Quoted from the television documentary *Verdict for Tomorrow* (Capital Cities Broadcasting Company, 1961); see note 59 for this chapter.

47. "Timely Topics: Reliving the Past," *Congress Bi-Weekly* 28, no. 9 (1 May 1961): p. 3. Emphasis in the original.

48. "Eichmann, Gagarin: 'Instant TV,'" p. 43.

49. Mary Ann Watson, *The Expanding Vista: American Television in the Kennedy Years* (New York: Oxford University Press, 1990), p. 4.

50. Erik Barnouw, *Tube of Plenty: The Evolution of American Television,* 2nd rev. ed. (New York: Oxford University Press, 1990), pp. 281, 284, 282; Barbie Zelizer, *Covering the Body: The Kennedy Assassination, the Media, and the Shaping of Collective Memory* (Chicago: University of Chicago Press, 1992), pp. 28, 29.

51. NJAB: item no. T309. On the other reports in this series, see Fox, items nos. 04140, 04142.

52. There were other ways that journalists covering the Eichmann trial used their presence in situ as a means of demonstrating their authority. *Time* magazine notes that many journalists en route to Jerusalem "stopped off first at the gas chambers of Dachau, Buchenwald and Auschwitz to refresh readers' memories" ("In the Dock," *Time* 77, no. 16 [14 April 1961]: p. 34).

53. NJAB: item no. T403.

54. There are no commercials included on the NJAB copy of this broadcast. According to Hannah Arendt, *Eichmann in Jerusalem: A Report on the Banality of Evil*, rev. ed. (New York: Viking Penguin, 1964), the program was sponsored by the Glickman Corporation, a real estate business (p. 5).

55. For a bibliography of works dealing with Eichmann's experiences in Hungary, see Braham, *The Eichmann Case*, items nos. 138–161.

56. Gould, "TV: Live Court Drama," p. 71; Jay Michael, "For the Record," *TV Guide* 9, no. 16 (22–28 April 1961): p. A1; Howard Thompson, "Screen: Stalking a Nazi," *New York Times*, 4 May 1961, p. 40 (*Operation Eichmann*, with screenplay by Lewis Coppley, was an Allied Artists presentation, starring Werner Klemperer as Eichmann); Art, "The Eichmann Trial," *Variety*, 26 April 1961, pp. 176, 190.

57. Mimi White, "Television: A Narrative—a History," *Cultural Studies* 3, no. 3 (October 1989): pp. 282–284.

58. Hausner, *Justice in Jerusalem*, p. 308.

59. NJAB: item no. T382.

60. Hausner, *Justice in Jerusalem*, p. 300.

61. Historian Stuart Svonkin notes that the American Jewish Committee and the Jewish Anti-Defamation League embarked on a media campaign, in print and on radio, to promote a distinctive reading of the trial, which "emphasized that there was no doubt that Jews were the chief victims of the Nazis' systematic campaign of extermination." "The Return to Parochialism: American Jewish Communal Life in the 1960s," conference paper presented at the Second Annual Scholars' Conference on American Jewish History, 12–14 June 1996, p. 8.

62. "The Judgment of Eichmann: WABC-TV" [advertisement], *New York Times*, 12 April 1961, p. 82. Other local newspapers carried the same advertisement, e.g., *New York World-Telegram and Sun*, 12 April 1961, p. 51; *New York Herald Tribune*, 12 April 1961, p. 29; *New York Post*, 12 April 1961, p. 90.

63. Watching Eichmann on the videotape record of the trial has continued to hold the interest of viewers. For example, a visitor to an exhibition of the trial footage and related broadcasts, which was presented at the Jewish Museum in New York in 1986, commented that "it was fascinating to see him—it was like watching those films of Hitler kissing his dog. . . . He [i.e., Eichmann] looked so normal" (as cited in Peter Kerr, "Eichmann Trial Recalled in Exhibit," *New York Times*, 31 March 1986, p. B5).

64. Lawrence Fellows, "Eichmann Is Neat in New Gray Suit," *New York Times*, 12 April 1961, p. 16.

65. Eliezer Veyzel [Elie Wiesel], "Der ershter tog" (The first day), *Jewish Daily Forward*, 12 April 1961, p. 1. My translation from the Yiddish; emphasis in original.

66. Matthews, "The Meaning of the Eichmann Trial," *Saturday Evening Post* 234, no. 23 (10 June 1961): p. 75; "Servatius Wins Respect in Trial," *New York Times*, 3 July 1961, p. 3; Lawrence Fellows, "Eichmann the Witness," *New York Times*, 25 June 1961, sec. 4, p. 4; Leyb Rakhman, "Zitsndik in gerikht baym Aykhman-protses" (Sitting in judgment at the Eichmann trial), *Jewish Daily Forward*, 14 April 1961, p. 2, my translation from the Yiddish; C. L. Sulzburger, "Foreign Affairs: Kafka Nightmare Come to Court," *New York Times*, 2 August 1961,

p. 28. According to the *New York Times,* the men selected to guard Eichmann were all "non-European Jews" who had not "suffered under the Nazis and presumably would not take revenge" against the defendant (Fellows, "Eichmann Is Neat in New Gray Suit," p. 16).

67. Segev, *The Seventh Million,* p. 345.

68. Special legal provisions were made to allow Eichmann to remain in the glass-enclosed defendant's dock when he was called as a witness. See, e.g., "Heavy Security Protects Nazi from Himself and from Others," *New York Times,* 11 April 1961, p. 14; Homer Bigart, "Eichmann to Stay in Glass Cage if He Testifies at Israeli Trial," *New York Times,* 5 June 1961, p. 5.

69. Martha Gellhorn, "Eichmann and the Private Conscience," *Atlantic Monthly* 29, no. 2 (February 1962): p. 52.

70. Horace Sutton, "Eichmann Goes on Trial," p. 49.

71. Leyb Rakhman, "Vi Aykhman firt zikh oyf in gerikht" (How Eichmann behaves during the trial), *Jewish Daily Forward,* 19 April 1961, p. 2.

72. Patrick O'Donovan, "Reflections on the Eichmann Trial," *New Republic* 144, no. 20 (15 May 1961): p. 7; Matthews, "The Meaning of the Eichmann Trial," p. 75.

73. Hausner, *Justice in Jerusalem,* pp. 347–348.

74. Homer Bigart, "Eichmann to See Preview of Death-Camp Films," *New York Times,* 28 May 1961, p. 8.

75. Homer Bigart, "Eichmannn Is Unmoved in Court as Judges Pale at Death Films," *New York Times,* 9 June 1961, p. 16.

76. "The Inferno," *Newsweek* 57, no. 25 (19 June 1961): p. 43.

77. "Jews for Trucks," *Time* 77, no. 24 (9 June 1961): p. 20.

78. "U.S. Psychologist Says He Outstared Eichmann," *New York Times,* 30 May 1961, p. 2.

79. Homer Bigart, "Defense Attorney Challenges Legality of the Trial as Eichmann's Case Begins," *New York Times,* 12 April 1961, p. 16.

80. The producers of the recent documentary *The Trial of Adolf Eichmann* (PBS, aired 30 April 1997) replaced the sequential translation by courtroom translators in the original footage with overlapping English-language translations performed by professional actors. The result, along with the editing out of footage in which people "wait" for the translation process, is a much tighter, more dramatic exchange than that which actually took place in the courtroom.

81. Matthews, "The Meaning of the Eichmann Trial," p. 75; Hariman, *Popular Trials,* p. 25.

82. Benjamin Harshav, *The Meaning of Yiddish* (Berkeley: University of California Press, 1990), p. 3.

83. Alvin Rosenfeld, "Israel Prints Glossary of Nazi Terms," *New York Herald Tribune,* 11 April 1961, p. 2.

84. Fellows, "Eichmann the Witness," sec. 4, p. 4.

85. Gellhorn, "Eichmann and the Private Conscience," p. 58.

86. M[ordkhe] Tsanin, "Vegn di yidishe buletins fun dem Aykhman-protses" (About the Yiddish bulletins of the Eichmann trial), *Jewish Daily Forward,* 16 April 1961, sec. 1, pp. 1, 10. My translation from the Yiddish.

87. Anita Norich, "Yiddish Literary Studies," *Modern Judaism* 10, no. 3 (October 1990), p. 298.

88. Gellhorn, "Eichmann and the Private Conscience," p. 53.

89. Herbert Freeden, "The Case Against the Prosecution," *Congress Bi-Weekly* 28, no. 12 (26 June 1961): p. 9.

90. Homer Bigart, "Servatius Wins Respect in Trial," *New York Times,* 3 July 1961, p. 3.

91. "Eichmann Paints a Robot Portrait," *New York Times,* 26 June 1961, p. 8.

92. Wilcke, "Eichmann Image Repels Germans," sec. 1, p. 27.

93. One possible indication of the declining interest in watching the Eichmann trial is the suspension of daily reports showing footage of the proceedings by WNTA New York (Channel 13) in mid-May.

94. In addition to frequent references in the press to Eichmann as the man in the "glass box" (or "booth" or "cage"), the image was selected as the title of Robert Shaw's play *The Man in the Glass Booth* (New York: Grove Press, 1968), which is based somewhat on Eichmann's capture and trial.

95. For a bibliography of reactions to the Eichmann case, see Braham, *The Eichmann Case,* items nos. 211–916. There is also an appendix offering a selective overview of reactions to the trial (which are generally supportive) published in the international press in Hausner, *Justice in Jerusalem,* pp. 455–472.

96. American Jewish Committee, *The Eichmann Case in the American Press,* p. 18.

97. Arendt's views were first published as a series of articles entitled "Eichmann in Jerusalem" in the *New Yorker* during February and March 1963. An expanded version of these articles was first published in book form as *Eichmann in Jerusalem: A Report on the Banality of Evil* (New York: Viking, 1963); a revised and enlarged paperback edition was published the following year. For a bibliography of critiques, reviews, and comments on Arendt's work, see Braham, *The Eichmann Case,* items nos. 926–1172.

98. Irving Howe, "The Range of the New York Intellectual," in *Creators and Disturbers: Reminiscences by Jewish Intellectuals of New York,* eds. Bernard Rosenberg and Ernest Goldstein (New York: Columbia University Press, 1982), pp. 285–286.

99. Arendt, *Eichmann in Jerusalem,* rev. ed., pp. 4–8, passim.

100. Jacob Robinson, *And the Crooked Shall Be Made Straight: The Eichmann Trial, the Jewish Catastrophe, and Hannah Arendt's Narrative* (New York: Macmillan, 1965), pp. 108, 109, 135, 113.

101. Harold Rosenberg, "The Trial and Eichmann," *Commentary* 32, no. 5 (November 1961): pp. 369–389, passim.

102. Susan Sontag, "Reflections on *The Deputy,*" *Against Interpretation and Other Essays* (New York: Delta, 1966 [1964]), pp. 125–127.

103. As cited in Gaster, "TV Professionals Who Covered the Eichmann Trial Form Panel," p. 7.

104. John Ciardi, "Manner of Speaking: Six Million and One," *Saturday Review* 45, no. 27 (7 July 1962): p. 14.

105. Michel Foucault, "The Dangerous Individual," in Michel Foucault, *Politics, Philosophy, Culture: Interviews and Other Writings, 1977–1984,* ed. Lawrence D. Kritzman (New York and London: Routledge, 1988), pp. 126–128.

106. NJAB: item no. T383. An interesting private screening of *Engineer of Death* at Purdue University in 1961 is described in Gerard Engel, "Campus Reactions to Eichmann," *Congress Bi-Weekly* 28, no. 11 (29 May 1961): pp. 7–8, 13. For a discussion of this screening, see Jeffrey Shandler, "The Holocaust on Television: A New American Jewish 'Rite of Spring,'" in *Freedom and Responsibility: Exploring the Challenges of Jewish Continuity,* eds. Rela Mintz Geffen and Marsha Bryan Edelman (Hoboken: KTAV, 1998), pp. 263–271.

107. NJAB: item no. T380.

108. Joel Engel, *Rod Serling: The Dreams and Nightmare of Life in the Twilight Zone* (Chicago: Contemporary Books, 1989), p. 189.

109. On proposals for Eichmann's punishment, see, e.g., Homer Bigart, "Eichmann to Stay in Glass Cage if He Testifies at Israeli Trial," *New York Times,* 5 June 1961, p. 5.

110. Sidra DeKoven Ezrahi, *By Words Alone: The Holocaust in Literature* (Chicago: University of Chicago Press, 1980), p. 205; see Salomon, "The End of Eichmann," pp. 257–258.

111. The results of the Gallup poll are analyzed in Irving Crespi, "Public Reaction to the Eichmann Trial," *Public Opinion Quarterly* 28, no. 1 (spring 1964): pp. 91–103. See also the American Jewish Committee, *The Eichmann Case in the American Press.* The University of California study was published as Charles Y. Glock, Gertrude J. Selznick, and Joe L. Spaeth, *The Apathetic Majority: A Study Based on Public Responses to the Eichmann Trial* (New York: Harper and Row, 1966).

112. Glock et al., *The Apathetic Majority,* pp. 192, 209.

113. Ibid. , pp. 48–50.

114. Ezrahi, *By Words Alone,* pp. 205–206.

115. For titles of specific broadcasts, see Salomon, "The End of Eichmann," pp. 256–257.

116. See, e.g., Barnouw, *Tube of Plenty;* Bliss, *Now the News;* Christopher H. Sterling and John M. Kittross, *Stay Tuned: A Concise History of American Broadcasting,* 2nd ed. (Belmont, California: Wadsworth, 1990); Michael Winship, *Television* (New York: Random House, 1988).

117. On Holocaust travel, see, e.g., Jack Kugelmass, "The Rites of the Tribe: The Meaning of Poland for American Jewish Tourists," *YIVO Annual* 21 (1992): pp. 395–453, and Oren Baruch Stier, "Lunch at Majdanek: The March of the Living as a Contemporary Pilgrimage of Memory," *Jewish Folklore and Ethnology Review* 14, nos. 1–2 (1995): pp. 57–66; on Yad Vashem, see James E. Young, *The Texture of Memory: Holocaust Memorials and Meaning* (New Haven: Yale University Press, 1993), pp. 243–261; on American Yom Ha-Sho'ah commemorations, see Lucia Ruedenberg, " 'Remember 6,000,000': Civic Comemmoration of the Holocaust Among Jewish Survivors in New York City" (Ph.D. diss., New York University, 1994).

118. Ethan Katsh, *The Electronic Media and the Transformation of the Law* (New York: Oxford University Press, 1989), p. 12.

119. Lance Bennett and Martha S. Feldman, *Reconstructing Reality in the Courtroom: Justice and Judgment in American Culture* (New Brunswick, New Jersey: Rutgers University Press, 1981), pp. 3, 4.

120. See, e.g., Segev, *The Seventh Million,* pp. 353–354; Arendt, *Eichmann in Jerusalem,* rev. ed., p. 225.

121. Arendt, *Eichmann in Jerusalem,* rev. ed., p. 224. This scene is prominent in the footage shown annually on Israeli television on Yom ha-Sho'ah. See Segev, *The Seventh Million,* p. 8.

122. "The Eichmann Trial," *Television Age,* p. 25.

123. Lawrence Fellows, "Eichmann Goes to Trial," *New York Times,* 9 April 1961, sec. 4, p. 5.

124. James Wolcott, "Prime-time Justice," *The New Yorker* 68, no. 41 (30 November 1992): p. 159.

Chapter 5. A Guest in the Wasteland

1. Mary Ann Watson, *The Expanding Vista: American Television in the Kennedy Years* (New York: Oxford University Press, 1990); James L. Baughman, *The Republic of Mass Culture: Journalism, Filmmaking, and Broadcasting in America Since 1941* (Baltimore: Johns Hopkins University Press, 1992). Baughman notes that "by 1965, 92.6 percent of all [American] households had at least one TV set; 22 percent had more than one" (p. 91).

2. William Boddy, *Fifties Television: The Industry and Its Critics* (Urbana: University of Illinois Press, 1990), p. 226. For the text of Minow's "vast wasteland" speech (delivered at a meeting of the National Association of Broadcasters on 9 May 1961), see his *Equal Time* (New York: Atheneum, 1964), pp. 45–69.

3. Christopher H. Sterling and John M. Kittross, *Stay Tuned: A Concise History of American Broadcasting,* 2nd ed. (Belmont, California: Wadsworth, 1990), p. 396.

4. Erik Barnouw, *Tube of Plenty: The Evolution of American Television,* 2nd rev. ed. (New York: Oxford University Press, 1990), p. 314.

5. *The Last Chapter* (NCJF), *Trial at Nuremberg* (LC: item no. FDA 3703), *Who Killed Anne Frank?* (NJAB: item no. T319), and *Change My Name to Life* (NJAB: item no. T129).

6. Wiesel's earliest appearances on American television, shortly after he settled in the United States in the mid-1960s, include *Elie Wiesel,* a 1967 episode of *Directions* (Fox: item no. 03304) and *The Jews of Silence,* a 1969 episode of *Eternal Light* (Fox: item no 03390). In 1974 *Directions* also presented *Simon Wiesenthal: A Conscience for Our Time* (NJAB: item no. T609).

7. J. Fred MacDonald, *Blacks and White TV: Afro-Americans in Television Since 1948* (Chicago: Nelson-Hall, 1983), p. 102.

8. See George Lipsitz, "The Meaning of Memory: Family, Class, and Ethnicity in Early Network Television Programs," *Camera Obscura* 16 (January 1988), esp. p. 111.

9. MacDonald, *Blacks and White TV,* p. 103.

10. Michael Elkin, "Jews Behind the Camera Change Portrayal of Jews on TV Screen," *Long Island Jewish World,* 30 August–6 September, 1985, p. 16; Alex Grobman, "Hollywood on the Holocaust," *Shoah: A Journal of Resources on the Holocaust* 4, no. 1–2 (fall–winter 1983–1984): p. 10.

11. MTR: item no. T80:0751.

12. See *Produced by . . . Herbert Brodkin: A Signature of Conviction and Integrity* (New York: Museum of Broadcasting, 1985), p. 35.

13. *Season of Vengeance* (Fox: item no. 04095); *The Indelible Silence* aired on 29 September 1962; citation from caption accompanying CBS press photo for the telecast, Photofest, New York; *QB VII* (MTR: item no. T87:0410–0413).

14. Former Nazis and neo-Nazis figure in the plots of episodes of several police and detective shows produced during this period, according to the listings in David Martindale, *Television Detective Shows of the 1970s: Credits, Storylines and Episode Guides for 109 Series* (Jefferson, North Carolina: McFarland, 1991): "The Big Explosion," a 1967 episode of NBC's *Dragnet* ("pseudo-Nazi hate mongers"; p. 134); "The Butcher," a 1968 episode of ABC's *The FBI* ("a dangerous Nazi-style paramilitary organization"; p. 163); "The Man Who Couldn't Forget," a 1974 episode of CBS's *Cannon* ("a war criminal accused of World War II concentration camp atrocities"; p. 75); "Now You See Him," a 1976 episode of NBC's *Columbo* ("a Nazi war criminal . . . kills a blackmailer"; p. 117).

15. NJAB: item no. T1411.

16. NJAB: item no. T1174.

17. NJAB: item no. T172.

18. Collin came to national attention in the spring of 1977, when he and the NSPA planned to stage a public demonstration in Skokie, Illinois (see Chapter 7). News of Collin's Jewish parentage was "first divulged by Chicago columnist Mike Royko" (Donald Alexander Downs, *Nazis in Skokie: Freedom, Community, and the First Amendment* [Notre Dame, Indiana: University of Notre Dame Press, 1985], p. 25). The Skokie incident may have inspired this episode of *Lou Grant,* which was first aired on 18 October 1977.

19. Jean-Paul Sartre, *Anti-Semite and Jew,* trans. George J. Becker (New York: Schocken, 1948), p. 69; see Raul Hilberg, *The Destruction of the European Jews* (Chicago: Quadrangle Books, 1961); Hannah Arendt, *Eichmann in Jerusalem: A Report on the Banality of Evil* (New York: Viking, 1963); Ben Hecht, *Perfidy* (New York: Messner, 1961); Robert Shaw, *The Man in the Glass Booth* [novel] (New York: Harcourt, Brace and World, 1967); Robert Shaw, *The Man in the Glass Booth* [play] (New York: Grove Press, 1968).

20. See Clayton R. Koppes and Gregory D. Black, *Hollywood Goes to War: How Politics, Profits and Propaganda Shaped World War II Movies* (Berkeley: University of California Press, 1990).

21. Arthur D. Morse, *While Six Million Died: A Chronicle of American Apathy* (New York: Hart, 1967). Morse's appearance on television in conjunction with the subject of his book includes *The Sins I Have Sinned, Part I,* an episode of *Lamp Unto My Feet* aired on 14 July 1968 (Fox: item no. 03793).

22. One possible explanation for retroactively identifying *Hogan's Heroes* as an example of Holocaust television might be found in a 1985 documentary, produced by Kent State University, entitled *Robert Clary A5714: A Memory of Liberation* (HJVC: item no. JV 591). In this program, actor Clary—who played Corporal Louis LeBeau, one of the prisoners of war regularly featured on the situation comedy—relates the story of his childhood in the Jewish quarter of Paris, his family's fate during World War II, including his own internment at Buchenwald and other camps, and his postwar experiences as a survivor of the Holocaust. Clary has also told his story as part of fund-raising efforts on behalf of the Simon Wiesenthal Center (see, e.g., Simon Wiesenthal Center, *Beit Hashoah / Museum of Tolerance* [Santa Barbara, California: Albion Publishing Group, 1993], p. 9). Some television viewers who are familiar with Clary's wartime experiences may have conflated actor and character and have come to think of LeBeau as a concentration camp inmate and *Hogan's Heroes* as a situation comedy about the Holocaust.

23. See Brenda Scott Royce, *Hogan's Heroes: A Comprehensive Reference to the 1965–1971 Television Comedy Series* (Jefferson, North Carolina: McFarland and Co., 1993), pp. 1–3. In the mid-1990s the series has become popular among young audiences in Germany, where it is aired with revised dialogue dubbed in German. See, e.g., "Hogan! Germans Need You," *New York Times,* 20 March 1997, sec. 4, p. 3.

24. Jack Davis (artist) and Larry Siegel (writer), "Hokum's Heroes," *MAD* 108 (January 1967), pp. 4–8.

25. Stuart Svokin has noted that in the early 1960s there was a rash of acts of anti-Semitic vandalism in the United States involving the defacing of buildings and other sites with swastikas. This "swastika epidemic" engendered increased attention to combating anti-Jewish sentiments and acts in America on the part of the Jewish Anti-Defamation League and the American Jewish Committee. See Stuart Svonkin, *Jews Against Prejudice: American Jews and the Intergroup Relations Movement from World War to Cold War* (New York: Columbia University Press, 1997), pp. 183–185.

26. See Marc Scott Zicree, *The Twilight Zone Companion* (New York: Bantam, 1982), p. 322.

27. For a discussion of the role of soundtracks in Jewish film in general, and the identification therein of Jews and Jewishness with stringed instruments, especially the violin, see Mark Slobin, "The Music of Jewish Film: A Research Report," *Jewish Folklore and Ethnology Review* 16, no. 1 (1994): p. 45. Slobin discusses associations of Jews with the minor mode, and thus with sadness, in his *Tenement Songs: The Popular Music of the Jewish Immigrants* (Urbana: University of Illinois Press, 1982), pp. 182–197.

28. The silent display of a number tattooed on a forearm has become a convention of identifying a character as a Holocaust survivor and of invoking the Holocaust as a plot element in film and television dramas. At one point late in the black comedy *Harold and Maude* (1971), for example, the madcap septuagenarian Maude (played by Ruth Gordon) "displays a number on her arm and speaks of her past. . . . Conceivably, her attitude [toward life] stems from her experience in the camps when her fate was in the hands of the Nazis" (Judith E. Doneson, *The Holo-*

caust in American Film [Philadelphia: Jewish Publication Society, 1987], p. 120).
See also the example of *Homefront* discussed below in Chapter 7, p. 201.

29. NJAB: item no. T1309.

30. This device is not a science-fiction invention but resembles a historical phenomenon. The Nazi regime produced television broadcasts for large screens in public places, rather than for private, domestic viewing, during the 1930s. On the subject of television in Nazi Germany, see Anthony Smith, "Television as a Public Service Medium," in his *Television: An International History* (Oxford: Oxford University Press, 1995), pp. 76–80.

31. For a discussion of how Spock is variously read as an archetypal "other," see Jeffrey Shandler, "Is There a Jewish Way to Watch Television?: Notes from a Tuned-in Ethnographer," *Jewish Folklore and Ethnology Review* 16, no. 1 (1994): pp. 19–22.

32. When Spock comments to Kirk that he makes a convincing Nazi, this joke, too, has an extra level of significance for the viewer who is aware that Shatner also is a Jew.

33. Alasdair Spark, "Vietnam: The War in Science Fiction," in *Science Fiction, Social Conflict and War*, Philip John Davies, ed. (Manchester [England]: Manchester University Press, 1990), p. 124; John Hellmann, *American Myth and the Legacy of Vietnam* (New York: Columbia University Press, 1986), p. 220.

34. Barnouw, *Tube of Plenty*, p. 399. The first American telecast of *The Investigation*, a British production (Granada TV), took place in March 1967 (Otta., "The Investigation," *Variety*, 22 March 1967, p. 46); the second, on NBC on 14 April, featured the cast of the play's Broadway production (Les., "The Investigation," *Variety*, 26 April 1967, p. 173).

35. See John J. O'Connor, "TV: Nuremberg's Relevance to the Vietnam War," *New York Times*, 7 June 1971, p. 67.

36. The phrase originally appears in George Santayana, *The Life Of Reason*, vol. 1: *Reason in Common Sense* (New York: C. Scribner's Sons, 1905–1906). Santayana's words are often cited in Holocaust memory culture, for example, in promotional material for the Simon Wiesenthal Center, Los Angeles.

37. NJAB: item no. T725, first aired 24 February 1973.

38. This disguise of the militant Jewish Defense League (JDL), founded by Rabbi Meir Kahane in Brooklyn, New York, in 1968, is so transparent that the first mention of the HDA elicits chuckles from the studio audience present at the taping of the episode.

39. MTR: item no. T81:0434.

40. NJAB: item no. T320.

41. NJAB: item no. T217. Host Amos Elon was the author of *The Israelis: Founders and Sons* (New York: Holt, Rinehart and Winston, 1971).

42. *The Israelis* was aired on 19 October 1973, thirteen days after the Yom Kippur War had begun and eight days before the final cease-fire went into effect.

43. Leon A. Jick, "The Holocaust: Its Use and Abuse Within the American Public," *Yad Vashem Studies* 14 (1981): pp. 312–313.

44. Baughman, *The Republic of Mass Culture*, p. 92.

45. David Marc, *Comic Visions* (Boston: Unwin Hyman, 1989), p. 125.

Chapter 6. The Big Event

1. "NBC-TV Says 'Holocaust' Drew 120 Million," *New York Times*, 21 April 1978, p. B4. The audience for the Tuesday night episode of the *Holocaust* miniseries received a Nielsen national rating of 30.3 and a 49 share, indicating that almost half of those watching television that night were tuned to NBC, and that this audience included about one third of all homes in America equipped with television sets.

2. Peter Novick, "Holocaust Memory in America," in *The Art of Memory: Holocaust Memorials in History*, ed. James E. Young (New York: The Jewish Museum; Munich: Prestel, 1994), p. 162.

3. See Jeffrey Shandler, "Schindler's Discourse: America Discusses the Holocaust and Its Mediation, from NBC's Miniseries to Spielberg's Film," in *Spielberg's Holocaust: Critical Perspectives on "Schindler's List,"* ed. Yosefa Loshitzky (Bloomington: Indiana University Press, 1997), pp. 153–168.

4. Harry R. Moody, "Reminiscence and the Recovery of the Public World," in *The Uses of Reminiscence: New Ways of Working with Older Adults*, ed. Marc Kaminsky (New York: Haworth, 1984), pp. 160–161.

5. Jonathan S. Woocher, *Sacred Survival: The Civil Religion of American Jews* (Bloomington: Indiana University Press, 1986), p. 132; Elie Wiesel, *The Jews of Silence: A Personal Report on Soviet Jewry*, trans. Neal Kozodoy (New York: Holt, Rinehart and Winston, 1966); on the relationship between Holocaust memory and support for Israel, see, e.g., Edward S. Shapiro, *A Time For Healing: American Jewry Since World War II* (Baltimore: Johns Hopkins University Press, 1992), pp. 212–217.

6. See Sidra DeKoven Ezrahi, *By Words Alone: The Holocaust in Literature* (Chicago: University of Chicago Press, 1980), pp. 214–216. On Plath, see James E. Young, *Writing and Rewriting the Holocaust: Narrative and the Consequences of Interpretation* (Bloomington: Indiana University Press, 1988), pp. 117–133.

7. David R. Blumenthal, "On Teaching the Holocaust," *Reconstructionist* 16, no. 2 (April 1980): p. 13. See also Ellen K. Coughlin, "On University Campuses, Interest in the Holocaust Started Long Ago," *Chronicle of Higher Education* 16, no. 10 (1 May 1978): pp. 1, 8; Douglas E. Kneeland, "Interest in Holocaust Study Rising," *New York Times*, 22 April 1978, p. A44.

8. Alice and Roy Eckardt, "Studying the Holocaust's Impact Today: Some Dilemmas of Language and Method," *Judaism* 27, no. 2 (spring 1978): p. 229. See, e.g., Leon A. Jick, "The Holocaust: Its Use and Abuse Within the American Public," *Yad Vashem Studies* 14 (1981): pp. 303–318; Robert Alter, "Deformations of the Holocaust," *Commentary* 71, no. 2 (February 1981): pp. 48–54; David Mirsky, "Abuse of the Holocaust in Literature," *Jewish Book Annual* 37 (1979–1980): pp. 39–48.

9. Stephen J. Whitfield, "The Holocaust and the American Jewish Intellectual," *Judaism* 28, no. 4 (1979): pp. 391, 392, 398–399.

10. Erik Barnouw, *Tube of Plenty: The Evolution of American Television*, 2nd rev. ed. (New York: Oxford University Press, 1990).

11. Ibid., p. 466.

12. The museum was renamed the Museum of Television and Radio in 1991; a branch of the museum was opened in Los Angeles in 1996.

13. Barnouw, *Tube of Plenty,* p. 467.

14. See Christopher H. Sterling and John M. Kittross, *Stay Tuned: A Concise History of American Broadcasting,* 2nd ed. (Belmont, California: Wadsworth, 1990), p. 511; Barnouw, *Tube of Plenty,* p. 468.

15. Doug Hill and Jeff Weingrad, *Saturday Night: A Backstage History of Saturday Night Live* (New York: Vintage, 1987), pp. 20–21.

16. Nicholas Johnson, *How to Talk Back to Your Television Set* (Boston: Little, Brown, 1970); Anne Rawley Saldich, *Electronic Democracy: Television's Impact on the American Political Process* (New York: Praeger, 1979); Jerry Mander, *Four Arguments for the Elimination of Television* (New York: Morrow, 1978); on guerilla television and underground humorists, see Hill and Weingrad, *Saturday Night,* pp. 26–29.

17. Horace Newcomb, "Toward a Television Aesthetic," in *Television: The Critical View,* 4th ed. (New York and Oxford: Oxford University Press, 1987), p. 613, citing Robert Lewis Shayon, *Open to Criticism* (Boston: Beacon, 1971), pp. 48–49 (Newcomb's essay originally appeared in his *TV: The Most Popular Art* [Garden City, New York: Doubleday, 1974]); Tania Modleski, ed., *Studies in Entertainment: Critical Approaches to Mass Culture* (Bloomington: Indiana University Press, 1986), p. x.

18. For background on the production of the miniseries, see Judith E. Doneson, *The Holocaust in American Film* (Philadelphia: Jewish Publication Society, 1987), pp. 141–196.

19. See Alex MacNeil, *Total Television* (New York: Penguin, 1991), p. 87.

20. Ray Walters, "Paperback Talk," *New York Times,* 16 April 1978, sec. 7, p. 44.

21. On the notion of *Holocaust* as a Jewish analogue to *Roots,* see, e.g., Letty Cottin Pogrebin, *Deborah, Golda and Me: Being Female and Jewish in America* (New York: Crown, 1991), pp. 302–305, and Jacob Neusner, *Stranger at Home: "The Holocaust," Zionism and American Judaism* (Chicago: University of Chicago Press, 1981), pp. 89–91.

22. See "Holocaust Study Aids and Spinoffs," *New York Times,* 14 April 1978, p. C26; Sander A. Diamond, "'Holocaust' Film's Impact on Americans," *Patterns of Prejudice* 12, no. 4 (July–August 1978): pp. 1–9, 17; Ray Walters, "Paperback Talk," pp. 44–45; Doneson, *The Holocaust in American Film,* p. 188.

23. "Watching Holocaust," *Moment* 3, no. 5 (April 1978): p. 34.

24. See Jeffrey Shandler, "The Holocaust on Television: A New American Jewish 'Rite of Spring,'" in *Freedom and Responsibility: Exploring the Challenges of Jewish Continuity,* eds. Rela Mintz Geffen and Marsha Bryan Edelman (Hoboken: KTAV, 1998), pp. 263–271.

25. Ruth R. Wisse, "The Anxious American Jew," *Commentary* 66, no. 3 (September 1978): p. 48.

26. John J. O'Connor, "TV Weekend" (14 April 1978, p. C26); John J. O'Connor, "TV: NBC, 'Holocaust,' Art versus Mammon" (20 April 1978, p. C22); Elie Wiesel, "Trivializing the Holocaust: Semi-Fact and Semi-Fiction" (16 April 1978, sec. 2, pp. 1, 29); "TV's Story of Nazi Terror Brings High Ratings and Varied Opinions" (18 April 1978, p. 78); Israel Shenker, "Holocaust: Systematic Slaughter of

Six Million of Europe's Jews" (18 April 1978, p. 78); Douglas E. Kneeland, "Interest in Holocaust Study Rising" (22 April 1978, p. A44); Kenneth Briggs, "Christians and Jews Seeking New Understanding" (17 April 1978, pp. A1, B8); Israel Shenker, "Holocaust Survivors Remember" (20 April 1978, p. C24); John Vinocur, "Germans Buy TV 'Holocaust'" (28 April 1978, p. C26).

27. George Hoover letters (28 April 1978, p. A26; 30 April 1978, sec. 2, p. 30); Gerald Green, "In Defense of Holocaust" (23 April 1978, sec. 2, pp. 1, 30); Elie Wiesel, "Wiesel Answers Green" (30 April 1978, sec. 2, p. 29); "TV Mailbag: The 'Holocaust' Controversy Continues" (30 April 1978, sec. 2, pp. 29–30); William Proxmire letter (25 April 1978, p. 36); William Safire, "Silence is Guilt," (24 April 1978, p. A23).

28. For a bibliographic overview of American English-language media response to the premiere of *Holocaust,* see Diamond, "'Holocaust' Film's Impact on Americans. " (N. B. : Diamond incorrectly lists the *Daily World* article as appearing in the *Daily Worker.*) For a list of articles appearing in the *Jewish Daily Forward,* see Jeffrey Shandler, "While America Watches: Television and the Holocaust in the United States, from 1945 to the Present," Ph.D dissertation, Columbia University, 1995, p. 419, n. 55.

29. John Vinocur, "Germans Buy TV 'Holocaust,'" *New York Times,* 28 April 1978, p. C26; Don Kowet, "The 'Holocaust' Breakthrough: Despite Resistance, the Miniseries Took Europe by Storm," *TV Guide* 27, no. 17 (28 April–4 May 1979): pp. 2–6; Hazel Guild, "Germany and the TV 'Holocaust,'" *Variety,* 23 May 1979, pp. 1, 108; "German Reaction to 'Holocaust,'" *Society* 17, no. 1 (November–December 1979): p. 2; "'Holocaust' at Home," *Newsweek* 93, no. 6 (5 February 1979): p. 62.

30. Studies on the impact of *Holocaust* include American Jewish Committee, *Americans Confront the Holocaust: A Study of Reactions to NBC–TV's Four-part Drama on the Nazi Era* (New York: Institute of Human Relations, 1978); "Impact: Four Days in April Saw Greater Awareness of the Holocaust, and Its Significance, than in Three Decades Preceding," *Anti-Defamation League Bulletin* 35 (June 1978); *International Journal of Political Education* 4, nos. 1–2 (May 1981), a special issue of the journal devoted to this topic. For works in German on Germans' response to the miniseries, see, e.g., Günther Anders, *Besuch im Hades* (Munich: Beck, 1979); Friedrich Knilli and Siegfried Zielinski, eds. , *Holocaust zur Unterhaltung: Anatomie eines internationalen Bestsellers: Fakten, Fotos, Forschungsreportagen* (Berlin: Verlag für Ausbildung und Studium, 1982); Peter Märthesheimer and Ivo Frenzel, eds. , *Im Kreuzfeuer: Der Fernsehfilm "Holocaust"—eine Nation ist betroffen* (Frankfurt am Main: Fischer, 1979). For works in English on German responses, see, e.g., essays by Jean-Paul Bier, Jeffrey Herf, Andreas Huyssen, Andrei S. Markovits, Rebecca S. Hayden, and Moishe Postone, in *New German Critique* 19 (winter 1980); some of these articles were reprinted in Anson Rabinbach and Jack Zipes, eds. , *Germans and Jews Since the Holocaust: The Changing Situation in West Germany* (New York: Holmes and Meier, 1986). Major studies of Holocaust film that discuss the miniseries include Ilan Avisar, *Screening the Holocaust: Cinema's Images of the Unimaginable* (Bloomington: Indiana University Press,

1988); Doneson, *The Holocaust in American Film;* and Annette Insdorf, *Indelible Shadows: Film and the Holocaust* (New York: Vintage, 1983). See also Alvin H. Rosenfeld, "The Holocaust as Entertainment," *Midstream* 25, no. 8 (October 1979): pp. 55–58, and "The Holocaust in American Popular Culture," *Midstream* 29, no. 6 (June–July 1983): pp. 53–59; Drew Middleton, "Why TV Is Fascinated With The Hitler Era," *New York Times,* 16 November 1980, sec. 2, pp. 1, 31; Michiko Kakutani, "40 Years After, Artists Still Struggle with the Holocaust," *New York Times,* 5 December 1982, sec. 2, pp. 1, 16.

31. Family Cable Network aired *Holocaust* on 10–14 April 1994, and the History Channel's broadcast was on 7–10 September 1997; "Holocaust" [advertisement], *TV Guide* 42, no. 15 (9–15 April 1994): p. 98; "Hollywood Holocaust Film Revived in Germany," Reuters [wire service], 2 March 1993.

32. John Brady, *The Craft of the Screenwriter: Interviews with Six Celebrated Screenwriters* (New York: Simon and Schuster, 1981), p. 65.

33. Frank Rich, "Reliving the Nazi Nightmare," *Time* 111, no. 16 (17 April 1978): p. 58.

34. Wiesel, "Trivializing the Holocaust," sec. 2, p. 1; see also Bernard Martin, "NBC's Holocaust: The Trivialization of the Tragic," *Journal of Reform Judaism* 25, no. 3 (1978): pp. 43–46; "'Holocaust' for Profit" [editorial], *Reconstructionist* 44 (May 1978): pp. 4–5; Paddy Chayefsky in Brady, *The Craft of the Screenwriter,* pp. 64–65; James Lardner, "Making History," *New Republic* 178, no. 19 (13 May 1978): p. 28; Novick, "Holocaust Memory in America," p. 162.

35. Dennis Potter, "The Final Insult," *Encounter* 51, no. 6 (December 1978): p. 17. Potter's comments originally appeared in *The Sunday Times* (London).

36. Menachem Z. Rosensaft, "Distorting the Holocaust," *Midstream* 24, no. 6 (June–July 1978): p. 55.

37. Demp., "Television Reviews: Holocaust—Part One," *Variety,* 19 April 1978, p. 48; Lance Morrow, "Television and the Holocaust," *Time* 111, no. 18 (1 May 1987): p. 53.

38. Wiesel, "Trivializing the Holocaust," pp. 1, 29; O'Connor, "TV: NBC 'Holocaust,' Art Versus Mammon," p. C22; Molly Haskell, "A Failure to Connect," *New York* 11, no. 20 (15 May 1978): p. 79, emphasis in original.

39. Haskell, "A Failure to Connect," p. 79; Paul Chedoff, quoted in Middleton, "Why TV Is Fascinated with the Hitler Era," sec. 2, p. 31; Rosensaft, "Distorting the Holocaust," p. 54.

40. Andreas Huyssen, *After the Great Divide: Modernism, Mass Culture, Postmodernism* (Bloomington: Indiana University Press, 1986), pp. 113, 95. This chapter originally appeared in *New German Critique* 19; see note 30 for this chapter.

41. Milton Shulman, "Forty Years On," *Encounter* 51, no. 6 (December 1978): p. 13.

42. Peter Sourian, "Television," *The Nation* 226, no. 24 (24 June 1978): p. 773, emphasis in original.

43. Saul S. Friedman, "In Defense of 'Holocaust: The Story of the Family Weiss,'" *Jewish Frontier* 45, no. 7 (August–September 1978): p. 9; emphasis in original.

44. Claude Lanzmann, "From the Holocaust to 'Holocaust,'" *Dissent* 28, no. 2 (spring 1981): p. 193; Helen Yglesias, "Genocide for Everyone," *New York Times,*

16 April 1978, sec. 7, p. 15; James Wolcott, "Slouching Toward Buchenwald," *Village Voice,* 24 April 1978, p. 53.

45. Diamond, "'Holocaust' Film's Impact on Americans," p. 5.

46. O'Connor, "TV: NBC 'Holocaust,' Art Versus Mammon," p. C22.

47. Henry Feingold, "Four Days in April: A Review of NBC's Dramatization of The Holocaust," *Shoah: A Journal of Resources on the Holocaust* 1, no. 1 (1978): pp. 15–16.

48. Martin, "NBC's Holocaust: Trivializing the Tragic," p. 45; Brady, *The Craft of the Screenwriter,* pp. 64–65; Friedman, "In Defense of 'Holocaust,'" p. 8.

49. O'Connor, "TV: NBC 'Holocaust,' Art Versus Mammon," p. C22; Martin, "NBC's Holocaust: Trivializing the Tragic," p. 45.

50. O'Connor, "TV: NBC 'Holocaust,' Art Versus Mammon," p. C22.

51. Wiesel, "Trivializing the Holocaust," sec. 2, p. 1; Rachleff, "Assessing *Holocaust,*" pp. 50–51, passim.

52. Wisse, "The Anxious American Jew," p. 47; emphasis in original.

53. Lanzmann, "From the Holocaust to 'Holocaust,'" p. 190; Jean Baudrillard, *The Evil Demon of Images* (Sydney [Australia]: Power Institute Publications, University of Sydney, 1987), pp. 22–23.

54. See Max Horkheimer and Theodor W. Adorno, *Dialectic of Enlightenment,* trans. John Cumming (New York: Continuum, 1972).

55. Judith Miller, *One, by One, by One: The Landmark Exploration of the Holocaust and the Uses of Memory* (New York: Simon and Schuster, 1990), p. 300, n. 7.

56. NJAB: T410. For another reflection on the impact of the miniseries, see "The Museum of Broadcasting Seminar Series: Produced by . . . Herbert Brodkin, Seminar 1: Producing 'Holocaust,'" (MTR: item nos. T86:0213–T86:0214). This videotape of a public program convened at the Museum of Broadcasting, New York (now Museum of Television and Radio), on 15 March 1985, features miniseries executive producer Brodkin, producer Robert Berger, author Gerald Green, and actor Fritz Weaver, and was moderated by Robert M. Batscha. Responding to questions from the audience, the panelists reflect on the making of the miniseries, its impact on viewers in the United States and abroad, and on its limitations and merits.

57. Paula E. Hyman, "New Debate on the Holocaust," *New York Times Magazine,* 14 September 1980, pp. 65, 67, 78.

58. See Anton Kaes, "History and Film: Public Memory in the Age of Electronic Dissemination," *History and Memory* 2, no. 1 (fall 1990): p. 116; Doneson, *The Holocaust in American Film,* p. 208.

59. "The Fortunoff Video Archive for Holocaust Testimonies," brochure (New Haven: Yale University, [1990?]), unpaginated.

60. Miller, *One, by One, By One,* p. 273.

61. Geoffrey H. Hartman, "Preserving the Personal Story: The Role of Video Documentation," *Dimensions: A Journal of Holocaust Studies* 1, no. 1 (spring 1985): p. 14.

62. Miller, *One, by One, by One,* pp. 266–275, passim.

Part Three: A Household Word

1. Owen S. Rachleff, "Assessing *Holocaust,*" *Midstream* 24, no. 6 (June–July 1978): p. 51.

2. Christopher H. Sterling and John M. Kittross, *Stay Tuned: A Concise History of American Broadcasting,* 2nd ed. (Belmont, California: Wadsworth, 1990), p. 511.

3. John Thornton Caldwell, *Televisuality: Style, Crisis, and Authority in American Television* (New Brunswick, New Jersey: Rutgers University Press, 1995), pp. ix, 3, 4.

4. See Jeffrey Shandler, "The Holocaust on Television: A New American Jewish 'Rite of Spring,'" in *Freedom and Responsibility: Exploring the Dilemmas of Jewish Continuity,* eds. Rela Mintz Geffen and Marsha Bryan Edelman (Hoboken, New Jersey: KTAV, 1998), pp. 263–271.

5. Eric A. Goldman, "Film as Haggadah for the Holocaust," *Shoah* 4, no. 1–2 (fall–winter 1983–1984): p. 4; James E. Young, *Writing and Rewriting the Holocaust: Narrative and the Consequences of Interpretation* (Bloomington: Indiana University Press, 1990), p. 157.

6. See, e.g., James Carroll, *Shoah in the News: Patterns and Meanings of News Coverage of the Holocaust* (Cambridge, Massachusetts: The Joan Shornstein Center on the Press, Politics and Public Policy, John F. Kennedy School of Government, Harvard University, 1997). Although this report deals only with newspaper coverage, it has noteworthy implications for the dynamics of news reportage related to the Holocaust in other media as well.

Chapter 7. The Rise of the Survivor

1. Movietone News (Twentieth Century-Fox) 43–28, 1960. National Archives and Records Administration, Washington, D.C., RG 200.

2. See, e. g. , "The Avenger," a 1962 episode of *The Defenders,* discussed in Chapter 5, pp. 136–137. A notable film example is the 1965 feature *The Pawnbroker,* directed by Sidney Lumet and produced by Ely Landau, based on the eponymous novel by Edward Lewis Wallant (New York: Macfadden-Bartell Corp., 1961).

3. Terrence des Pres, *The Survivor: An Anatomy of Life in the Death Camps* (New York: Oxford University Press, 1976); Dorothy Rabinowitz, *New Lives: Survivors of the Holocaust Living in America* (New York: Knopf, 1976).

4. For competing analyses of the legal issues raised in the Skokie incident, see David Hamlin, *The Nazi/Skokie Conflict: A Civil Liberties Battle* (Boston: Beacon, 1980); Donald Alexander Downs, *Nazis in Skokie: Freedom, Community, and the First Amendment* (Notre Dame, Indiana: University of Notre Dame Press, 1985).

5. Milton Ellerin, "Intergroup Relations," in *American Jewish Year Book* 79, eds. Morris Fine and Milton Himmelfarb (New York: American Jewish Committee; Philadelphia: Jewish Publication Society, 1979), p. 117.

6. According to the Television News Index and Abstracts of Vanderbilt University, the Skokie incident was featured on national evening news broadcasts on the following dates in 1977: 4 July (CBS); 12 August (CBS); and in 1978: 27 January (CBS, NBC); 30 January (ABC); 17 February (NBC); 23 February (ABC, CBS, NBC); 16 April (CBS); 19 April (ABC); 12 June (ABC, CBS, NBC); 20 June (ABC, CBS, NBC); 21 June (ABC); 16 October (CBS, NBC).

7. *Donahue* (NJAB: item no. T915); *Skokie* (NJAB: item no. T699–701).

8. Todd Gitlin, *Inside Prime Time* (New York: Pantheon, 1983), pp. 165–166.

9. *Skokie* shows nothing of Collin's background or personal life, nor does it explore the internal dynamics of the neo-Nazis as a community. Kinoy's script also does not deal with revelations that Collin was "not only half Jewish, but also the son of a survivor of . . . Dachau" or that he was "arrested and convicted of sexually molesting and abusing young boys" (Downs, *Nazis in Skokie,* pp. 25, 26).

10. Kenneth Turan, "Making 'Skokie': The Passions Came Flooding Back," *TV Guide* 29, no. 41 (10–16 October 1981): p. 36; John J. O'Connor, "TV: 'Skokie,' Nazis March in Illinois," *New York Times,* 17 November 1981, p. C19.

11. "Carl Reiner, Serious Actor, Returns to His Beginnings," CBS Television Network Press Information, 11 September 1981, National Jewish Archive of Broadcasting, The Jewish Museum, New York; "Eli Wallach: 'I Would Have Played Any Role in This Script,'" CBS Television Network Press Information, 22 September 1981, National Jewish Archive of Broadcasting, The Jewish Museum, New York; "Danny Kaye, John Rubinstein, Carl Reiner, Kim Hunter and Eli Wallach Star in 'Skokie' Drama Special . . . ," CBS Television Network Press Information, 18 September 1981, National Jewish Archive of Broadcasting, The Jewish Museum, New York.

12. NJAB: item no. T1432.

13. According to the Television News Index and Abstracts of Vanderbilt University, the major commercial networks presented reports on the World Gathering during national evening newscasts on the following dates: 14 June (ABC, NBC), 15 June (ABC, CBS, NBC), and 18 June (ABC, NBC). ABC's *Directions* offered a discussion of the World Gathering with author Sylvia Rothschild on 14 June 1981. WNET/New York (Channel 13) presented four forty-minute broadcasts, entitled *Holocaust: The Survivors Gather,* on 15–18 June, beginning at 11:30 P.M. *Holocaust—The Survivors Gather: A Look Back* (NJAB: item no. T713).

14. Jacob Neusner, *Stranger at Home: "The Holocaust," Zionism and American Judaism* (Chicago: Unversity of Chicago Press, 1981), p. 1.

15. Jonathan S. Woocher, *Sacred Survival: The Civil Religion of American Jews* (Bloomington: Indiana University Press, 1986), p. 12.

16. *In Dark Places,* videocassette: Mastervision (New York) Humanities Series, no. 913; *A Generation Apart* (HJVC: item no. JV391); *Breaking the Silence* (HJVC: item no. JV871).

17. *Forever Yesterday* (MTR: item no. B:20575); *Holocaust: The Children* (MTR: item no. T81:0706). This format has been employed repeatedly in more recent documentaries, e.g., *Survivors of the Holocaust* (aired on TBS on 8 January 1996), which uses interviews made for the Shoah Visual History Project.

18. Hans Kellner, "'Never Again' Is Now," *History and Theory: Studies in the Philosophy of History* 33, no. 2 (1994): p. 132.

19. See Kitty Hart, *Return to Auschwitz* (New York: Atheneum, 1982), p. 23. In this volume Hart not only recalls her wartime experiences but also describes her return visit to Auschwitz and its filming (pp. 163–173). Hart also wrote another memoir, *I Am Alive* (London and New York: Abelard-Schuman, 1962). After the PBS broadcast on 4 February 1981, an edited version of the documentary was shown on an *ABC News Closeup* on 24 July 1981 (MTR: item no. T84:0179); videocassette (full-length version): Films Incorporated (Chicago).

20. NJAB: item no. T695.

21. Linked to this sense of the disparity between images and memories are examples throughout the film of alternative readings of various icons. These include Marzynski and his friend mocking the May Day celebrations shown on Polish television and Lech Walesa's wearing a portrait of the Black Madonna of Czestochowa on his lapel as a sign of resistance to the Communist regime. These images, in turn, resonate with Marzynski's alternative existence as a Jew who passed for a non-Jew during the war, as well as his ambivalent relationship with the Polish Catholic church.

22. Claude Lanzmann, *Shoah: An Oral History of the Holocaust* (New York: Pantheon, 1985), p. 117. The documentary is available on videocassette from Paramount Home Video.

23. Nora Levin, "Some Reservations about Lanzmann's Shoah," *Sh'ma* 16, no. 312 (18 April 1986): pp. 91–93.

24. Kellner, "'Never Again' Is Now," p. 129.

25. Paul Connerton, *How Societies Remember* (New York: Cambridge University Press, 1984), p. 73.

26. On the protocols of interviewing survivors, see, e.g., Toby Blum-Dobkin, "Videotaping Holocaust Interviews: Questions and Answers from an Interviewer," *Jewish Folklore and Ethnology Review* 16, no. 1 (1994): pp. 46–50; Young, *Writing and Rewriting the Holocaust,* p. 163.

27. NJAB: item no. T1111 (labeled "English version"); videocassette: Ergo Media (Teaneck, New Jersey), no. 625.

28. The photograph in question is the thirteenth in the sequence of images that comprise the *Bildgericht* section of the Stroop Report. Its original caption is *"Mit Gewalt aus Bunkern herausgeholt"* (Pulled out of the bunkers by force). See Jurgen Stroop, *The Stroop Report: The Jewish Quarter Is No More!*, trans. Sybil Milton (New York: Pantheon, 1979).

29. Lucy S. Dawidowicz, *The War Against the Jews, 1933–1945* (New York: Holt, Rinehart and Winston, 1975), pp. 166; Yala H. Korwin, "The Little Boy with His Hands Up," *To Tell the Story: Poems of the Holocaust* (New York: Holocaust Library, 1987), pp. 75–76; Susan Sontag, *"Persona*: The Film in Depth," in S. Kaminsky, ed., *Ingmar Bergman: Essays in Criticism* (New York: Oxford University Press, 1975), p. 266.

30. *The Cafeteria* (NJAB: item no. T81), based on Isaac Bashevis Singer, "The Cafeteria," trans. Isaac Bashevis Singer and Dorothea Straus, in *The Collected Stories* (New York: Farrar Straus Giroux: 1982), pp. 287–300; *The Ghost Writer* (MTR: item no. T21345), based on Philip Roth, *The Ghost Writer* (New York: Fawcett Crest, 1979); *The Quarrel* (MTR: item no. B:30509–30510), based on Chaim Grade, "My Quarrel with Hersh Rasseyner," trans. Milton Himelfarb, in *A*

Treasury of Yiddish Stories, ed. Irving Howe and Eliezer Greenberg (New York: Viking, 1954), pp. 579–606; *Miss Rose White* (MTR: item no. T:30159), based on Barbara Lebow, *A Shayna Maidel* (New York: New American Library, 1988 [1985]).

31. "Hit Play 'A Shayna Maidel' Becomes Hallmark Hall of Fame Presentation, 'Miss Rose White,'" press release (Hallmark Hall of Fame, [1992]), unpaginated (2 pp.).

32. Roth, *The Ghost Writer,* pp. 186, 180.

33. The *American Playhouse* adaptation, largely faithful to Roth's text, begins very differently from the novella, which opens with Zuckerman's visit to the home of a famous writer, where he encounters Amy Bellette. There is no mention of Anne Frank in Roth's novella until halfway through the text. The televised version of *The Ghost Writer,* however, starts with a montage of familiar images—photographs of Anne, the text of her diary, and a shot of the interior of the *Achterhuis* (i.e., the "secret annex") where she and her family hid in Amsterdam—which, by virtue of the ease with which they can be readily identified, demonstrate for viewers Frank's iconic status.

34. The series premiere of *Homefront* aired 24 September 1991.

35. This episode of *Homefront* aired 13 April 1993.

36. Robert McAfee Brown, *Elie Wiesel: Messenger to All Humanity* (Notre Dame, Indiana: University of Notre Dame Press, 1978); Ellen Norman Stern, *Elie Wiesel: Witness for Life* (New York: KTAV, 1982).

37. Peter Novick, "Holocaust Memory in America," in *The Art of Memory: Holocaust Memorials in History,* ed. James E. Young (New York: The Jewish Museum; Munich: Prestel, 1994), p. 162.

38. On Wiesel's early appearances on television, see Chapter 5, n. 6; televised biographies include NBC's 1972 *The Itinerary of Elie Wiesel: From Sighet to Jerusalem* (NJAB: item no. T119) and PBS's 1988 *In the Shadow of Flames: A Portrait of Elie Wiesel* (NJAB: item no. T1219).

39. Wiesel received the Medal of Liberty, along with eight other honorees, in New York on 3 July 1986, in conjunction with celebrations marking the centennial of the Statue of Liberty; the ceremony was televised on ABC. The Nobel Committee announced that Wiesel was the recipient of their Peace Prize on 13 October 1986.

40. Wiesel's 1987 appearance on the syndicated series *Open Mind* is excerpted in *The Promise of Television,* part 8 of the 1988 PBS documentary series *Television* (MTR: item no. T88:0249); his appearance on *Beyond Hate* aired on PBS on 13 May 1991 (MTR: item no. T:29609); his appearance on *The Oprah Winfrey Show* (syndicated) aired on WNBC, New York, on 15 July 1993.

41. MTR: item no. T84:0245–0246.

42. Loft., "The Day After," *Variety,* 23 November 1983, p. 102. In an unusual move, CBS's *60 Minutes* presented "The Week Before 'The Day After,'" a segment devoted to the extensive controversy surrounding the impending broadcast of the ABC movie, on 13 November 1983.

43. "Messenger of Peace," *MacNeil/Lehrer NewsHour,* aired on 14 October 1986 (MTR: item no. T:29313).

44. Geoffrey H. Hartman, ed., *Bitburg in Moral and Political Perspective* (Bloomington: Indiana University Press, 1986), p. xiv. For a chronology of events surrounding the Bitburg visit, see pp. xiii–xvi.

45. According to the Television News Index and Abstracts of Vanderbilt University, Wiesel was mentioned or appeared on national evening newscasts on 12 April (on ABC), 16 April (ABC, CBS, NBC), and 18 April (ABC, CBS, NBC).

46. Weinraub, "Wiesel Confronts Reagan on Trip; President to Visit Bergen-Belsen," *New York Times,* 20 April 1985, p. A4.

47. Hartman, *Bitburg in Moral and Political Perspective,* pp. 241, 243. The complete text of Wiesel's speech appears on pp. 241–244.

48. Bernard Weinraub, "Wiesel Confronts Reagan on Trip," pp. A1, A4; Rudy Abramson, "Reagan's Trip to Include Visit at Death Camp: Emotional Appeal to Cancel Visit to Cemetery Rejected," *Los Angeles Times,* 20 April 1985, pp. A1, A23. Under the headline "Honoring Wiesel, Reagan Confronts the Holocaust," the *Washington Post* ran two stories on 20 April 1985: Lou Cannon, "Reagan Team Falters on Damage Control," pp. A1, A8; David Hoffman, "Bergen-Belsen Put on Trip Itinerary," pp. A1, A8.

49. According to the Television News Index and Abstracts of Vanderbilt University, Wiesel was mentioned or appeared on national evening newscasts on 21 April (on ABC, NBC), 25 April (NBC), 26 April (ABC, CBS, NBC), and 3 May (ABC); coverage of Castillo's confrontation with Reagan appeared on national news telecasts on 26 April (ABC, NBC).

50. Hedrick Smith, "Delicate Reagan Path," *New York Times,* 6 May 1985, p. A10; "TV Plans to Present Visit to Bitburg Live," *New York Times,* 3 May 1985, p. A10.

51. NJAB: T707. CBS's *Face the Nation* offered a discussion of the Bitburg visit with Holocaust activist Simon Wiesenthal and secretary of state Shultz. Guests on ABC's *This Week with David Brinkley* included former West German chancellor Helmut Schmidt, Hyman Bookbinder of the American Jewish Committee, and Wiesel. See "Late Television Listings," *New York Times,* 5 May 1985, sec. 1, p. 45.

52. Television News Index and Abstracts of Vanderbilt University, 5 May 1985.

53. Thomas Elsaesser, "Between Bitburg and Bergen Belsen," *On Film* (Santa Barbara, California) 14 (spring 1985): p. 40.

54. Laurence Jarvik, "Bitburg as Media Event," *On Film* (Santa Barbara, California) 14 (spring 1985): p. 38. Ronald Reagan was host of the CBS drama anthology series *General Electric Theater* from 1954 to 1962.

55. John Weisman, "If Only We'd Had TV During Hitler's Time," *TV Guide* 36, no. 53 (31 December 1988–6 January 1989): pp. 6–8, passim.

Chapter 8. The Master Paradigm

1. Leon A. Jick, "The Holocaust: Its Use and Abuse Within the American Public," *Yad Vashem Studies* 14 (1981): p. 303.

2. Larry Kramer, *Reports from the Holocaust: The Making of an AIDS Activist* (New York: St. Martins, 1988), pp. 265, 233 (for Kramer's discussion of the paral-

lels between the Holocaust and the AIDS crisis in the gay male community—which relies extensively on Hannah Arendt's analysis of the former in her reflections on the Eichmann trial—see pp. 217–281, passim); Peter Novick, "Holocaust Memory in America," in *The Art of Memory: Holocaust Memorials in History,* ed. James E. Young (New York: The Jewish Museum; Munich: Prestel, 1994), p. 159.

3. On comparing the Holocaust and the massacre of Native American tribes, see, e.g., David E. Stannard, *American Holocaust: Columbus and the Conquest of the New World* (New York: Oxford University Press, 1992). An early example of the now quite common analogy between the Holocaust and African-American slavery is Stanley M. Elkins, *Slavery: A Problem in American Institutional and Intellectual Life* (Chicago: University of Chicago Press, 1959). In a 1963 edition of the book (New York: Grosset and Dunlap), Elkins writes that "my use of the German concentration camp as an analogy to illuminate certain aspects of Negro slavery encountered more comment than did anything else in the book. That portion of the comment which was hostile took fairly direct form; I was simply told that the analogy, being both repellent and misleading, did not fit" (p. 225). I am grateful to Kirsten Fermaglich for bringing Elkins's work to my attention.

4. Susan Sontag, *AIDS and Its Metaphors* (New York: Farrar Straus Giroux, 1989), p. 5; Philip Lopate, "A Distance from the Holocaust: Resistance to the Holocaust," *Tikkun* 4, no. 3 (May–June 1989): p. 56.

5. See, e.g., Lucy Dawidowicz, "Smut and Anti-Semitism," in *The Jewish Presence: Essays on Identity and History* (New York: Harcourt Brace Jovanovich, 1978), pp. 216–224; Saul Friedländer, *Reflections of Nazism: An Essay on Kitsch and Death* (New York: Harper and Row, 1984); Deborah Lipstadt, *Denying the Holocaust: The Growing Assault on Truth and Memory* (New York: Free Press, 1993); Pierre Vidal-Naquet, *Assassinations of Memory: Essays on the Denial of the Holocaust* (New York: Columbia University Press, 1993).

6. Yehuda Bauer, "Whose Holocaust?" *Midstream* 26, no. 9 (November 1980): p. 42.

7. Edward Alexander, "Stealing the Holocaust," *Midstream* 26, no. 9 (November 1980): p. 48.

8. Edward Alexander, *The Holocaust and the War of Ideas* (New Brunswick, New Jersey: Transaction, 1994), pp. 181, 206.

9. See Carol Rittner and John K. Roth, eds., *Memory Offended: The Auschwitz Convent Controversy* (New York: Praeger, 1991); Edward T. Linenthal, *Preserving Memory: The Struggle to Create America's Holocaust Museum* (New York: Viking Penguin, 1995), pp. 228–248.

10. *Playing for Time* (MTR: item nos. T81:0667–T81:0669); *Liberators* (NJAB: item no. T1677).

11. Fania Fénelon, with Marcelle Routier, *Playing for Time,* trans. Judith Landry (New York: Atheneum, 1977). "The Music of Auschwitz" first aired on 16 April 1978.

12. Tony Schwartz, "Names of Redgrave Film's Sponsors Guarded by CBS-TV and Ad Agencies," *New York Times,* 25 September 1980, p. C26.

13. Val Adams, "CBS Unskeds That Redgrave Epic," *New York Daily News,* 20 March 1980, p. 131; Schwartz, "Names of Redgrave Film's Sponsors Guarded,"

p. C26; Frank Coffey, *60 Minutes: 25 Years of Television's Finest Hour* (Santa Monica, California: General Publishing Group, 1993), p. 257.

14. Tony Schwartz, "CBS Plans Auschwitz Film For Sept. 30 Amid Protest," *New York Times,* 30 August 1980, p. 43; Schwartz, "Names of Redgrave Film's Sponsors Guarded," p. C26; "12 Actresses Back Vanessa Redgrave's TV Appearance," *New York Times,* 19 September 1980, p. A17. See also the discussion of the sponsorship of *Playing for Time* in Todd Gitlin, *Inside Prime Time* (New York: Pantheon, 1985), pp. 187–190.

15. "'Playing for Time' Draws Large Audience," *New York Times,* 2 October 1980, p. C24 (according to the article, the drama was seen by "41 percent of the viewing audience in New York, 35 in Los Angeles and 36 in Chicago," based on Nielsen ratings); John J. O'Connor, "TV: Vanessa Redgrave, Inmate," *New York Times,* 30 September 1980, p. C9; Kay Gardella, "Protested 'Playing for Time' Drama Is Worth the Viewing," *New York Daily News,* 17 September 1980, sec. 3, p. 17; Arthur Unger, "Moving—and Controversial—New Arthur Miller Drama," *Christian Science Monitor,* 3 September 1980, p. 19.

16. Gardella, "Protested 'Playing for Time' Drama Is Worth the Viewing," sec. 3, p. 17; O'Connor, "TV: Vanessa Redgrave, Inmate," p. C9; Richard Corliss, "Soloist in a Choir of Martyrs," *Time* 116, no. 30 (29 September 1980): p. 83; Jack Kroll, Katrine Ames, and Martin Kasindorf, "The Activist Actress," *Newsweek* 96, no. 13 (29 September 1980): p. 52.

17. Gardella, "Protested 'Playing for Time' Drama Is Worth the Viewing," sec. 3, p. 17; Corliss, "Soloist in a Choir of Martyrs," p. 83; Unger, "Moving—and Controversial—New Arthur Miller Drama," p. 19; O'Connor, "TV: Vanessa Redgrave, Inmate," p. C9.

18. "The Redgrave Controversy," *Near East Report* 24, no. 40 (3 October 1980): p. 183; I. L. Kenen, "Media Monitor: Ecstacy . . . Agony . . . Irony," *Near East Report* 24, no. 41 (10 October 1980): p. 190.

19. Neil Kressel, "Correspondence: 'Playing for Time,'" *Reconstructionist* 46, no. 7 (November 1980): pp. 29, 30; Joseph Hochstein, as cited in Kenen, "Media Monitor: Ecstacy . . . Agony . . . Irony," p. 190.

20. "The Redgrave Controversy," p. 183; Hannah Grad Goodman, "Television: Redgrave at Auschwitz," *Hadassah* 62, no. 3 (November 1980): p. 26.

21. Arthur Miller, *Playing for Time: A Full-length Stage Play Adapted from the Television Film . . .* (Chicago: Dramatic Publishing Company, 1985), p. 49. On analogies between anti-Communist blacklisting and the Holocaust during the 1950s, see Victor S. Navasky, *Naming Names* (New York: Penguin, 1991), pp. 407–416.

22. Richard Dyer, *Stars* (London: British Film Institute, 1979).

23. This and all following citations from *Liberators: Fighting on Two Fronts in World War II* were transcribed from a videotape recording of its broadcast on WNET/New York (Channel 13), on 19 December 1992.

24. The program, which I attended, was cosponsored by The Studio Museum in Harlem and was convened at the New-York Historical Society, where "Bridges and Boundaries" was on display. On the exhibition, see Jack Salzman, ed., *Bridges and*

Boundaries: African Americans and American Jews (New York: George Braziller and The Jewish Museum, 1992).

25. See "TV Ticker: Jabbar Is Now a Hollywood Player," *New York Post,* 5 May 1992, p. 76.

26. See Jerome R. Mintz, *Hasidic People: A Place in the New World* (Cambridge: Harvard University Press, 1992), pp. 328–347. A chronology of events concerning the Crown Heights incident appears in Anna Deavere Smith, *Fires in the Mirror* (New York: Doubleday, 1993), pp. xlviii–liii. This drama about the Crown Heights incident (televised on PBS's *American Playhouse* series on 28 April 1993) includes a monologue in which an African-American minister compares slavery to the Holocaust; see pp. 54–55.

27. "Dinkins on 'Liberators,'" *Forward* [English-language edition], 13 November 1992, p. 6.

28. Martin Zimmerman, "'Liberators' Captures Slice of History," *Los Angeles Times,* 11 November 1992, p. F12; John J. O'Connor, "America's Black Army and a Dual War Front," *New York Times,* 11 November 1993, p. C24; Dorothy Rabinowitz, "Leisure and Arts: Liberators," *Wall Street Journal,* 5 November 1992, p. A15.

29. "Neighbor to Neighbor: New York Communities Coming Together" [souvenir program], New York, 17 December 1992, unpaginated; "African Americans and Jews Come Together for 'Neighbor-to-Neighbor' Effort at Harlem's Apollo Theatre," press release, The Liberators Commemoration Committee, New York, 17 December 1992, pp. 1–2.

30. This and the following citations from the Apollo Theater public progam, except where indicated, were transcribed by the author of this essay from a videotape of the 17 December 1992 broadcast. See note 23 for this chapter.

31. Ari L. Goldman, "Blacks and Jews Join Hands for a Brighter Future," *New York Times,* 18 December 1992, p. B1.

32. Alessandra Stanley, "After a Night of Unity at the Apollo, Optimism Wavers," *New York Times,* 19 December 1992, p. 25.

33. Goldman, "Blacks and Jews Join Hands for a Brighter Future," p. B3.

34. Stanley, "After a Night of Unity at the Apollo, Optimism Wavers," pp. 25–26.

35. The association of *Liberators* with the Crown Heights incident offers a lesson in the complex consequences of identity politics. While *Liberators* concerns African-Americans and addresses issues of general interest to American Jews, the Crown Heights incident involved a clash between two distinctive communities, neither of which typifies blacks or Jews in America. Crown Heights's black community is mostly of Caribbean heritage, and most of its Jewish community are members of the Lubavitcher sect of Hasidim. The blacks and Jews in the audience that gathered at the Apollo Theater for the 17 December screening came from different neighborhoods throughout New York, where they do not necessarily face the particular challenges of coexistence that the residents of Crown Heights confront.

36. See "Fib-erators," *Village Voice,* 19 January 1993, p. 9; Richard Bernstein, "Doubts Mar PBS Film of Black Army Unit," *New York Times,* 1 March 1993, pp. B1, B3.

37. Jeffrey Goldberg, "'Liberators' Controversy Fueled by New Charges," *Forward* [English-language edition], 5 February 1993, p. 5; see Lou Potter, William Miles, and Nina Rosenblum, *Liberators: Fighting on Two Fronts in World War II* (New York: Harcourt Brace Jovanovich, 1992).

38. Jeffrey Goldberg, "The Exaggerators," *New Republic* 208, no. 6 (8 February 1993): pp. 13–14, passim.

39. Joseph B. Treaster, "Film Halted on Blacks Freeing Jews," *New York Times,* 12 February 1993, p. B3; Bernstein, "Doubts Mar PBS Film of Black Army Unit," pp. B1, B3.

40. John Carmody, "The TV Column: Report on a Controversy," *Washington Post,* 8 September 1993, p. D6; Joseph B. Treaster, "WNET Inquiry Finds No Proof Black Unit Freed 2 Nazi Camps," *New York Times,* 8 September 1993, p. B1.

41. Treaster, "WNET Inquiry Finds No Proof Black Unit Freed 2 Nazi Camps," p. B1; Carmody, "The TV Column: Report on a Controversy," p. D6.

42. Alan Rosenthal, ed., *New Challenges for Documentary* (Berkeley: University of California Press, 1988), pp. 5–7.

43. Richard Cohen, "'Liberators'—It's Not Only About the Holocaust," *Washington Post,* 30 March 1993, p. A21; Joel Lewis, "Fighting Together?" *Forward* [English-language edition], 13 November 1992, p. 9.

44. Cohen, "'Liberators'—It's Not Only About the Holocaust," p. A21; Goldberg, "'Liberators' Controversy Fueled by New Charges," p. 5; Bernstein, "Doubts Mar PBS Film of Black Army Unit," p. B3.

45. Goldberg, "'Liberators' Controversy Fueled by New Charges," p. 5.

46. See Potter et al., *Liberators,* pp. 218, 232–236. At approximately the same time, questions arose regarding the fallibility of Holocaust survivors' testimony at the war crimes trial of John Demjanjuk in Jerusalem. While several survivors gave evidence that the defendant was the notorious guard at Treblinka known as Ivan the Terrible, documentary evidence was produced to the contrary.

47. Horace M. Newcomb and Paul Hirsch, "Television as a Cultural Forum: Implications for Research," *Quarterly Review of Film Studies* 8, no. 3 (summer 1983): pp. 45–56; Paul C. Adams, "Television as Gathering Place," *Annals of the Association of American Geographers* 82, no. 1 (1992): pp. 117–135; Cecelia Tichi, *Electronic Hearth: Creating an American Television Culture* (New York: Oxford University Press, 1991); James W. Carey, *Communication as Culture: Essays on Media and Society* (Boston: Unwin Hyman, 1988); John Fiske and John Hartley, *Reading Television* (London: Methuen, 1978); Lynn Spigel, "Introduction," in Raymond Williams, *Television: Technology and Cultural Form* (Hanover, New Hampshire: University Press of New England and Wesleyan University Press: 1992 [1974]), p. x.

48. On the plan to build a shopping mall near Auschwitz, see, e.g., "Plans for Market Near Auschwitz Dropped," *New York Times,* 26 March 1996, p. A3; Jack Kugelmass, "The Rites of the Tribe: The Meaning of Poland for American Jewish Tourists," *YIVO Annual* 21 (1993), p. 421 (Kugelmass discusses Jewish singles tours to Poland on p. 404).

49. On the Washington museum, see Linenthal, *Preserving Memory.* On the Los Angeles museum, see Judith Miller, *One, by One, by One: The Landmark Explo-*

ration of the Holocaust and the Uses of Memory (New York: Simon and Schuster, 1990), pp. 220–275, passim; see also James E. Young, *The Texture of Memory: Holocaust Memorials and Meaning* (New Haven: Yale University Press, 1993), pp. 335–349.

50. Sheli Teitelbaum, "The Holocaust Goes High-Tech," *Jerusalem Report* 3, no. 21 (25 February 1993): p. 31; Miller, *One, by One, by One*, p. 237.

51. See., e.g., Christopher John Nash, "Interactive Media in Museums: Looking Backwards, Forwards and Sideways," *Museum Management and Curatorship* 11, no. 2 (1992): pp. 171–184; Branislav Jakovljevic, "Picturing the Screen: The American Museum of the Moving Image," *Museum Management and Curatorship* 15, no. 4 (1996), pp. 351–369.

52. Edward Norden, "Yes and No to the Holocaust Museums," *Commentary* 96, no. 2 (August 1993): p. 27. On the political and ideological issues raised by the museum's exterior design, see Linenthal, *Preserving Memory*, pp. 57–108.

53. Curt Schleier, "Steven Spielberg's New Direction," *Jewish Monthly* 108, no. 4 (January–February 1994): 12. For further discussion of this issue, see Jeffrey Shandler, "Schindler's Discourse: America Discusses the Holocaust and Its Mediation, from NBC's Miniseries to Spielberg's Film," in *Spielberg's Holocaust: Critical Persectives on "Schindler's List,"* ed. Yosefa Loshitzky (Bloomington: Indiana University Press, 1997), pp. 153–170.

54. Michael Berenbaum, *The World Must Know: The History of the Holocaust as Told in the United States Holocaust Memorial Museum* (Boston: Little, Brown, 1993), p. xiv.

55. Hans Kellner, "'Never Again' Is Now," *History and Theory: Studies in the Philosophy of History* 33, no. 2 (1994): pp. 130–131.

56. The *World at War* series addresses the Holocaust in episode no. 20, entitled "Genocide." For a discussion of the series, see Alan Rosenthal, *The Documentary Conscience: A Casebook in Film Making* (Berkeley: University of California Press, 1980), especially an interview with Raye Farr that appears on pp. 76–88.

57. In the fall of 1993 the museum reported problems resulting from "too many visitors," including "bottlenecks form[ing] daily in front of the exhibits" ("Holocaust Museum Has Too Many Visitors," *New York Times,* 19 November 1993, p. C3).

58. Miller, *One, by One, by One*, p. 243.

59. Simon Wiesenthal Center, *Beit Hashoah/Museum of Tolerance* (Santa Barbara, California: Albion Publishing Group, 1993), pp. 13, 7.

60. Ibid., p. 13.

61. Ibid., p. 17.

62. Ibid., pp. 14, 18.

63. See Toni Stoos and Thomas Kellein, eds., *Nam June Paik: Video Time— Video Space* (New York: Harry N. Abrams, 1993).

64. Simon Wiesenthal Center, *Beit Hashoah/Museum of Tolerance*, p. 43.

65. *Genocide,* directed by Arnold Schwartzman, was scripted by Martin Gilbert and Marvin Hier and narrated by Orson Welles and Elizabeth Taylor.

66. James Sturz, "Evil for Sale," *New York Times,* 28 November 1993, sec. 6, pp. 70–72.

67. For a discussion of the relationship of these video testimonies to the presentation of artifacts, see Toby Blum-Dobkin, "Videotaping Holocaust Interviews: Questions and Answers from an Interviewer," *Jewish Folklore and Ethnology Review* 16, no. 1 (1994): pp. 46–50.

68. Simon Wiesenthal Center, *Beit Hashoah/Museum of Tolerance,* p. 40.

69. *ABC News Nightline,* "America Remembers the Holocaust," 28 December 1993; citations transcribed from a videotape of the broadcast.

70. Daniel Schorr, interviewed by Scott Simon, *Weekend Edition,* National Public Radio, 15 July 1995.

71. Roy Gutman, "The Death Camps of Bosnia," *New York Newsday,* 2 August 1992, pp. 1, 4, 13.

72. According to the Television News Index and Abstracts of Vanderbilt University, all three commercial networks' national evening newscasts featured ITN footage of the detention camp in Trnopolje on 6 August 1992; this was the opening story on the ABC and CBS broadcasts. Footage of this and/or other detention camps in the Balkans was shown on 7 August (ABC, CBS, NBC), 8 August (ABC, CBS, NBC), 9 August (ABC, CBS, NBC), 10 August (ABC, NBC).

73. *New York Times* (caption: "A picture of agony emerges from Serbian camps in Bosnia"; 7 August 1992, p. A1), *New York Newsday* (caption: "Muslim prisoners at Serbian-run camp in northern Bosnia-Herzegovina in British TV footage broadcast yesterday"; 7 August 1992, p. 1 [with additional photographs from the telecast on p. 5]), *Los Angeles Times* (caption: "Muslim Slavs stand behind a barbed-wire fence at a Serbian-run camp in northern Bosnia-Herzegovina"; 7 August 1992, p. A1), and the *Washington Post* ("Photo taken from ITN network video shows Muslim prisoners at a Serb camp"; 8 August 1992, p. A15).

74. Russel Watson et al., "Ethnic Cleansing," *Newsweek* 120, no. 7 (17 August 1992): p. 16; J.F.O. McAllister, "Atrocity and Outrage," *Time* 140, no. 7 (17 August 1992): p. 21.

75. John B. Moore, in "Letters: Haunted by Holocaust," *New York Newsday,* 14 August 1992, p. 51.

76. Robert Jay Lifton, *The Genocidal Mentality: Nazi Holocaust and Nuclear Threat* (New York: Basic Books, 1990); Robert Jay Lifton, "Can Images of Bosnia's Victims Change the World?" *New York Times,* 23 August 1992, sec. 2, p. 26.

77. Tovia Smith, reporter, "Jewish Reaction to Bosnia," *Weekend Edition,* National Public Radio, 16 August 1992, unedited transcript.

78. "No Excuse Not To Vote: Reminder," Korey Kay and Partners for Members Only, 1992; see Chapter 1, p. 26; *MacNeil/Lehrer NewsHour,* 8 December 1992 (show no. 4515), transcript, pp. 8, 9.

79. *ABC News Nightline,* "Elie Wiesel: A Search for Peace" [videocassette] (MPI Home Video, [1992]). Copies of the videocassette were available for purchase in the gift shop of the Museum of Tolerance/Beit Hashoah, Los Angeles, in 1994.

80. Philip J. Cohen, "Holocaust History Misappropriated," *Midstream* 38, no. 8 (November 1992): pp. 18, 20.

81. Richard Cohen, "It's Not a Holocaust: Rhetoric and Reality in Bosnia," *Washington Post,* 28 February 1993, pp. C1, C4.

82. *World News Tonight with Peter Jennings,* 21 April 1993, ABC News Transcript no. 3079, p. 5, as cited in Linenthal, *Preserving Memory,* p. 264.

83. See John M. Goshko, "Influx of VPs for Museum Dedication Strains White House Hospitality," *Washington Post,* 21 April 1993, p. A9.

84. According to the Television News Index and Abstracts of Vanderbilt University, all three commercial networks' national evening newscasts featured footage of President Clinton and Elie Wiesel speaking at the museum's opening ceremonies on 22 April 1993. Public television stations also marked the opening with broadcasts of *For the Living,* a documentary on the making of the museum. See, e.g., Patricia Brennan, "'For the Living': The Holocaust Museum," *Washington Post: TV Week,* 25 April 1993, pp. 6–7.

85. Henry Allen, "Holocaust Museum Dedicated with Hope," *Washington Post,* 23 April 1993, p. A14.

86. On the Nazi persecution of homosexuals, see Henry Heger, *The Men with the Pink Triangle,* trans. David Fernbach (Boston: Alyson, 1980); Richard Plant, *The Pink Triangle: The Nazi War against Homosexuals* (New York: Henry Holt, 1986).

87. The 25 April march and rally were televised live on C-SPAN, and a videotape of highlights of the event was produced (*March for Freedom: The 1993 March on Washington Video,* Project 1993 Productions). For a description of the vigil, see Alisa Solomon, "An American Tragedy?: The Holocaust Museum Shapes Shoah for Domestic Consumption," *Village Voice* (New York), 11 May 1993, p. 36. For a discussion of the presentation of Nazi persecution of homosexuals within Washington's Holocaust museum, see Rick Rose, "Museum of Pain," *The Advocate* (Los Angeles), no. 628 (4 May 1993): pp. 40–42.

88. Allen, "Holocaust Museum Dedicated with Hope," p. A14.

89. Diana Jean Schemo, "Holocaust Museum Hailed as Sacred Debt to Dead," *New York Times,* 23 April 1993, p. A24; Laurence McQuillan, "Holocaust Museum Opens to Remembrances, Warnings," Reuters [wire service], 22 April 1993; Allen, "Holocaust Museum Dedicated with Hope," p. A14.

90. John Darnton, "Does the World Still Recognize a Holocaust?" *New York Times,* 25 April 1993, sec. 4, pp. 1, 5; Hobart Rowen, "Holocausts: Past and Present," *Washington Post National Weekly Edition,* 9–15 August 1993, p. 5.

91. Elie Wiesel, as cited by John Weisman, "If Only We'd Had TV During Hitler's Time," *TV Guide* 36, no. 53 (31 December 1988–6 January 1989): p. 8. See Chapter 7, p. 209.

92. According to the Television News Index and Abstracts of Vanderbilt University, all three networks aired footage of the shelling of the Sarajevo marketplace on 5 February 1994.

93. Albert Wohlstetter, "Genocide by Mediation," *New York Times,* 3 March 1994, p. A21.

94. ABC News, *While America Watched: The Bosnia Tragedy* [videocassette] (MPI Home Video, [1994]).

95. The photos were collected over several decades by Dr. Yaffa Eliach, a professor of Jewish Studies at Brooklyn College, who was a four-year-old resident of Ejszyszki when the majority of its Jewish population was murdered; see Beren-

baum, *The World Must Know,* pp. x, 151–153. On the Tower of Faces, see Jeffrey Shandler, "The Tower of Faces in Washington's Holocaust Museum: East European Jewry's 'Vanishing Act,'" *Jewish Folklore and Ethnology Review,* forthcoming.

96. Tom Shales, "Bosnia's War: ABC News Takes a Stand," *Washington Post,* 17 March 1994, p. D1; Walter Goodman, "Advocacy Journalism: A Medium's Strength," *New York Times,* 17 March 1994, p. C20.

97. *More than Broken Glass,* NJAB: item no. T1220; the anniversaries of the liberation of Auschwitz, Buchenwald, Bergen-Belsen, and Dachau were noted on nightly national news reports and were commemorated by a number of documentaries, including *Nightmare's End: The Liberation of the Camps* (Discovery Channel, 23 April) and *One Survivor Remembers* (HBO, 7 May). According to a table compiled by Judith Keilbach, there were over a hundred telecasts, including rebroadcasts of dramas and documentaries, related to the Holocaust or the end of World War II in Europe aired on television in the New York metropolitan area between 21 January and 8 May 1995. See Judith Keilbach, "Der 50. Jahrestag der Befreiung im amerikanischen und deutschen Fernsehen," Magisterprüfung, Ruhr-Universität Bochum, 1996, pp. 117–123.

98. The telecasts of *The Nuremberg Trial* were from 5 to 8 P.M. each evening. Each day's broadcasts was recapitulated on the series *Prime Time Justice* from 8 to 10 P.M. A three-hour summary of the trial presentation was aired at 8 P.M. on Monday 20 November 1995.

99. *The Nuremberg Trial,* Court TV, 13 November 1995; citation transcribed from a videotape of the broadcast.

100. In several places, Court TV integrates other vintage images into the trial footage. For example, U.S. chief prosecutor Robert Jackson's description of the Stroop Report is intercut with images of the report. During footage of former Auschwitz commandant Rudolf Hoess's appearance as a witness for the defense, liberation footage of the camp filmed by Soviet cameramen is used to illustrate his testimony. This constitutes a problematic use of scenes of liberated inmates in the camp to stand in for events that took place during the war; however, it is in keeping with a primary intent of liberation footage as evidence of past crimes.

101. Court TV's *The Nuremberg Trial* also presents *The Nazi Plan,* a compilation produced by U.S. prosecutors of prewar Nazi propaganda and newsreel footage, as well as films of liberated death camps at Majdanek and Auschwitz recorded and presented by the Soviets.

102. Alex Ross, "Watching for a Judgment of Real Evil," *New York Times,* 12 November 1995, sec. 2, p. 37.

103. Novick, "Holocaust Memory in America," p. 165; Linenthal, *Preserving Memory,* p. 262.

104. See, e.g., Steven T. Katz, *The Holocaust in Historical Context* (New York: Oxford University Press); this three-volume work, the first volume of which was published in 1994, is the latest and perhaps most extensive work that argues for understanding the Holocaust as a unique, unprecedented and subsequently unrivaled historical event.

Conclusion

1. On other Jewish responses to the Holocaust, see, e.g., Bernard Rosenberg, ed., *Theological and Halakhic Reflection on the Holocaust* ([New York]: KTAV, 1992); Yaffa Eliach, ed., *Hasidic Tales of the Holocaust* (New York: Oxford University Press, 1982).

2. Isabel Fonseca, *Bury Me Standing: The Gypsies and Their Journey* (New York: Alfred A. Knopf, 1995), p. 276.

3. Iwona Irwin-Zarecka, *Frames of Remembrance: The Dynamics of Collective Memory* (New Brunswick, New Jersey: Transaction, 1994), pp. 161–174.

4. Pierre Nora, "Between Memory and History: *Les Lieux de Mémoire,*" *Representations* 26 (spring 1989): pp. 7–25.

5. Yael Zerubavel, "The Death of Memory and the Memory of Death: Masada and the Holocaust as Historical Metaphors," *Representations* 45 (winter 1944): pp. 73, 92.

6. Daniel L. Schacter, *Searching for Memory: The Brain, the Mind, and the Past* (New York: Basic Books, 1996), p. 7.

7. Paul C. Adams, "Television as Gathering Place," *Annals of the Association of American Geographers* 82, no. 1 (1992): p. 117; David Lowenthal, *The Past Is a Foreign Country* (Cambridge: Cambridge University Press, 1985).

8. Joshua Meyerowitz, *No Sense of Place: The Impact of Electronic Media on Social Behavior* (New York: Oxford University Press, 1986).

Index

Page references in *italics* refer to captions.